Secrets of a Vet Tech II

A Low Cost Pet Care Guide for Pet Parents, Animal Shelters, Rescues, & Homesteaders

Written by JC Farris

Editorial Team:

Haseleah Fraysier-Farris
Nancy Farris
Jessica Carter
Deb Harris
Rhonda Thompson
Ellen Barker
Bob Barker, Pharm.D, (Retired)

All Rights Reserved. 2015

Acknowledgments and Dedications

A special thank you to all my editors and consultants who believed so much in this project, that they gave their skill and time without cost. My thanks to Haseleah Fraysier-Farris, not only for editing, but for utilizing her microbiology degree and research background to consult on the immunology chapters and to help interpret the many studies cited. I would also like to thank Nancy Farris, Deb Harris, and Ellen Barker for their editing skills and input. Thank you to Rhonda Thompson, for her assistance on medical terminology and to Jessica Carter, former shelter director, for her input on animal shelter life. Thank you Bob Barker, a retired pharmacist, whom I consulted with regarding many drug calculations. Thanks also to Drs. Becky and Kitty, our veterinarians, for answering many questions for me and to my readers and Facebook friends for answering my surveys that targeted the subjects important to them.

On a personal note, I would like to give a special thank you to all the animals who have given me the strength and inspiration to write this book and who have shown me unconditional love. With this unconditional love, the animals of T.Paws Rescue and ARFanage, my rescue, have saved my life many times. I owe a debt of deep gratitude to my parents, Earl and Nancy Farris, who instilled the love of nature into me. Finally, to all of my animal friends on Rainbow Bridge. I miss you.

Chloe
1997-2015

Disclaimer:

Any information presented is for general information purposes only. This information is not intended to serve as medical advice. I am not a veterinarian. Please contact your veterinarian and discuss your options for treatment. In addition, none of the companies or their products have compensated me in any way for mentioning them. This book is not specifically endorsed by any veterinarian or veterinarian hospital. This book should serve as a starting point in research you conduct for your own pet family or rescue. Instead of footnotes or end notes, I provide the online link or book reference in the body of the paragraph.

Table of Contents

Introduction to the New Edition   11
- A Note on Research and Evidence in Conventional vs Holistic Medicine   17

Section I: A Short Autobiography and The Struggle of the Pet Parent   22
- **Chapter 1**: Poverty and Pet Parenting   23
  - Financial Ruin & the Resurrection of Self-Sufficiency   24
- **Chapter 2**: Motivation   27

Section II: Proactive Pet Parenting   32
- **Chapter 3**: Defining Proactive Pet Parenting & Tips for Finding a Quality Veterinarian   33
- **Chapter 4:** The Number One Way to Save Money as a Pet Parent   38
  - Approaches to Spay and Neuter   39
  - Extending the Life of Your Pet and Wallet   40
  - Spaying or Neutering Non-Traditional Pets   42
  - The Early Spay/Neuter Controversy   42
- **Chapter 5**: The Realities and Solutions to Re-homing Pets   46
  - The Difficulty of Successfully Re-homing a Pet   46
  - Reasons Given for Re-homing and Possible Prevention Methods   47
    - Moving   47
    - We're Having a Baby   49
    - Pet Training Issues   50

- Additional Reasons Given for Surrendering Pets **51**
- Tips for Safer Re-homing **52**
- Things to Consider Before Getting a Pet **53**

Section III: Our Evolving Ethics and the Science of Emotion, Intellect, and Awareness of Animals 57

- **Chapter 6:** The Effects of Religion and Philosophy on the Treatment of Animals **58**
  - The Slippery Slope: From Animal Cruelty to Human Cruelty **59**
  - We Are More Alike Than Different **60**
  - Pain and Morality **62**
- **Chapter 7:** Modern Controversial Practices **64**
  - Selective Breeding **64**
  - Declawing **65**
  - Ear Cropping and Tail Docking **68**
  - Anesthesia-Free Dental Cleanings **69**

Section IV: The Immune System, Vaccines, Nutrition, and Parasite Control 71

- **Chapter 8**: Understanding the Immune System **72**
- **Chapter 9:** A New Vaccine Protocol **74**
  - The Research on Vaccine Duration **74**
  - Why Veterinarians Don't Reveal the Research **75**
  - Canine Viruses **76**
    - Distemper **76**
    - Parvovirus **77**
    - Adenovirus **77**
    - Coronavirus **78**
    - Leptosporosis **78**
    - Bordetella **78**
    - Rabies **79**
  - The "New" Canine Flu **79**
  - Vaccine Cost **81**
  - Feline Viruses **82**
    - Feline Panleukopenia **82**
    - Feline Viral Rhinotracheitis **82**

- - - Feline Calicivirus **82**
    - Feline Leukemia **82**
    - Feline Immunodeficiency Virus **82**
  - The Vaccine Debate: Are We Making our Pets Ill? **83**
  - The Conundrum of Vaccinating Puppies in Animal Shelters **85**
  - My Vaccine Protocol for Dogs and Cats **88**
- **Chapter 10**: Simplifying The Confusing World of Pet Food **89**
  - The Evolutionary Basis of Pet Nutrition **90**
  - The Safety of Our Pet Food **91**
  - The Grain-Free Hoax and Beyond **95**
  - Homemade Pet Foods and the BARF Diet: Are They Safe and Nutritionally Complete? **98**
  - Nutritional Needs of Dogs **104**
  - Nutritional Needs of Cats **106**
  - Common Sense Pet Nutrition **107**
  - Special Dietary Considerations for Cats **111**
  - Comparison of Pet Food Ingredients **113**
- **Chapter 11**: Fleas and Other Ectoparasites **116**
  - The Flea Life Cycle **116**
  - Choosing a Safer Flea Preventative **117**
  - Topical Tricks of the Trade **120**
  - Other Commercial Flea Preventatives **122**
  - Food Grade Diatomaceous Earth **124**
  - Beneficial Nematodes **125**
  - Borax Powder **125**
  - Other Natural Alternatives **126**
  - Other Ectoparasites **127**
- **Chapter 12:** Heartworm Prevention **129**
  - Heartworms and Transmission **129**
  - Preventing Heartworms **130**
  - Drug Sensitivity Gene and Heartworm Prevention **133**
  - Ivomectin for Heartworms **134**
  - Possible Evidence of Resistance to Heartworm Preventatives **137**

- ○ Long Term Affects of Monthly Heartworm Preventatives **141**
- ○ Conventional vs "Natural" Heartworm Prevention: Defining Toxicity **142**
- ○ Cats and Heartworms **145**
- ○ Testing for Heartworms **147**
- ○ A Final Note on Heartworm Prevention **148**
- **Chapter 13**: Intestinal Parasites and Protozoas **149**
  - ○ Types of Intestinal Parasites and Protozoas **149**
    - Roundworms/Ascaris **150**
    - Hookworms **150**
    - Whipworms **151**
    - Tapeworms **151**
    - Pinworms **151**
  - ○ Protozoans **152**
    - Coccidia **152**
    - Giardia **152**
    - Toxoplasmosis **152**
    - Cryptosporidium **153**
    - Amoebas **153**
    - Trichomoniasis **153**
  - ○ Types of Dewormers and Protozoa Treatments **155**
    - Pyrantel Pamoete **155**
    - Fenbendazole **156**
    - Praziquantel **157**
    - Sulfadimethoxine **158**
    - Toltrazuril **158**
    - Ponazuril **159**
    - Metronidazole **159**

Section V: Home Physicals and Lab Tests 160
- **Chapter 14**: The Home Physical Exam: Learning to Be a Good Pet Health Detective **161**
  - ○ The Pet Exam Train (PET) **162**
  - ○ Mouth and Dentition **163**
  - ○ Muzzle/Nostrils/Eyes **165**

- Outer and Inner Ear **168**
- Trunk: Withers, Back, Abdomen, Rump **169**
- Skin and Fur **170**
- Extremities **171**
- Vital Signs: Temperature, Heart Rate, Respiratory Rate and Body Weight **172**
- How to Make Grooming a Part of the Physical Examination **173**
  - Shaving **174**
  - Nail Trims **175**
  - Ear Cleaning **176**
  - Anal Gland Expression **178**
- **Chapter 15**: In-Home or In-Rescue Lab Tests **180**
  - Fecal Tests **180**
  - Heartworm Tests by Direct Smear & SNAP Tests **181**
  - Learning the Skill of Venipuncture (Blood Draw) **182**
  - Performing a Heartworm Test and Reading the Results **182**
  - FeLV/FIV Tests **183**
  - Parvo Test **183**
  - Skin Scrape for Sarcoptic or Demodex Mange **184**
  - Blood Glucose Test **184**
  - Urine Test Strips **184**
  - Ear Mite Test **186**
- **Chapter 16:** Essential Tests Only your Veterinarian Can Perform **187**
  - Complete Blood Count (CBC) **187**
  - Chemistry Profiles **188**
  - Thyroid Test **188**
  - Radiographs (X-Rays) **189**

Section VI: Emergencies and Common Illnesses **191**

- **Chapter 17**: Emergencies **192**
  - Acute Allergic Reactions **192**
  - Burns **193**
  - Choking **194**
  - Dehydration **197**

- Dizziness or Vertigo **200**
- Heat Stroke **201**
- High Fever **201**
- Hypoglycemia/Low Blood Sugar **202**
- Intestinal Blockage, Bloat and Gastric Torsion **203**
- Minor Wounds **204**
- Orphaned Animals **205**
- Pain **209**
- Pancreatitis **211**
- Poisoning **213**
- Seizures, Seizure-Like Activity and Collapse **217**
- Saddle Thrombosis **218**
- Shock and CPR **219**
- Strains and Sprains **221**
- Vomiting and/or Diarrhea **223**

- **Chapter 18:** The Most Common Illnesses of the Dog and Cat **227**
  - Abscesses **227**
  - Arthritis **228**
  - Asthma and Bronchitis **230**
  - Cancer **232**
  - Cognitive Dysfunction **236**
  - Diabetes (Hyperglycemia) **238**
  - Ear Problems **239**
  - Eye Disorders **243**
  - Hepatic Lipidosis (Fatty Liver Syndrome) **245**
  - Heart Disease **246**
  - Hypothyroidism and Hyperthroidism **248**
  - Hypoadrenocorticism (Addison's) and Hyperadrenocorticism (Cushings) **252**
  - Obesity **255**
  - Pregnancy and Its Complications **257**
  - Skin Disorders and Conditions **260**
  - Upper Respiratory Infections and Kennel Cough **268**
  - Urinary Tract Disorders **269**

Section VII: Understanding Our Pets and Solving Behavioral Issues 275
- **Chapter 19**: Development of the Puppy and Kitten **276**
- **Chapter 20**: Introduction to Miscommunication **279**
- **Chapter 21**: Perception: Seeing the World Through Their Eyes **281**
- **Chapter 22**: Canine Body Communication **284**
- **Chapter 23**: Starting Out on the Right Paw: Mistakes We Make from the Beginning **286**
- **Chapter 24**: Canine Behavior Problems **289**
  - Excessive Barking **289**
  - Potty Training **292**
  - Excessive and Inappropriate Digging **295**
  - Separation Anxiety **297**
  - Noise Anxiety: Thunderstorms and Fireworks **300**
  - Aggression **301**
- **Chapter 25**: Cat Behavior and Human Relationships **312**
- **Chapter 26**: Cat Communication **313**
- **Chapter 27**: Feline Behavioral Problems **315**
  - Potty Training and Inappropriate Urination **315**
  - Unusual or Inappropriate Vocalization **318**
  - Inappropriate/Inconvenient Sleep Cycle **319**
  - Scratching Furniture **320**
  - Feline Aggression **321**
  - Anxiety in Cats **324**

Section VIII: Practical Considerations 327
- **Chapter 28**: Keeping the Peace in Multi-Pet Households **328**
- **Chapter 29**: Bedding and Housing **332**

Section: IX: Exotic and Non-Traditional Pets 334
- **Chapter 30**: Exotic Pet Introduction **335**
- **Chapter 31**: Pocket Pets **339**
- **Chapter 32**: Guinea Pigs and Rabbits **344**
- **Chapter 33**: Rats and Ferrets **350**
- **Chapter 34:** Birds **355**

- Chapter 35: Herps (Amphibians and Reptiles) **360**
- Chapter 36: Aquatic Fish **364**
- Chapter 37: Farm Animals as Pets: The Plight of the Pot-Bellied Pig **368**

Section X: Frugal and Efficient Financing Of Pet Care 372
- **Chapter 38**: Making the Unaffordable, Affordable: A Whole-Life Approach **373**
- **Chapter 39:** Cost Saving Tips for Dogs and Cats **377**
- **Chapter 40**: Cost Saving Tips for Exotics **380**
- **Chapter 41:** The Keys to Low Cost At-Home Pet Care and Tips for Financing Vet Care **386**

Section XI: Senior Pets and Letting Go 393
- **Chapter 42:** Living with a Senior Pet **394**
- **Chapter 43:** Making the Final and Humane Decision **396**
- **Chapter 44:** Euthanasia Defined **399**
- **Chapter 45:** Euthanasia Policy and Procedures **401**

Section XII: Pet Medication Overview 403
- **Chapter 46:** The Pet Care Kit **404**
- **Chapter 47:** Over-the-Counter Supplies **406**
- **Chapter 48:** Antibiotics and their Responsible Use **411**
  - How Veterinarians Determine Dosage **412**
  - Common Antibiotics, Antimicrobials, and Antifungals **416**
- **Chapter 49**: Anti-Parasitic Drugs **420**
- **Chapter 50:** Additional Supplies to Consider **425**
- **Chapter 51:** Homemade Treatments and Shampoos **427**
- **Chapter 52:** Tips for Administering Medication **430**
- **Chapter 52**: In Conclusion **433**

Appendix and Links for Further Study 434
Books for Recommended Reading 435

Introduction to the New Edition

Since **Secrets of a Vet Tech** was first published, so much has happened. I received a lot of feedback on how to make a better book including topics readers would like included in this edition. Thanks to one suggestion, I have created a very thorough table of contents.

I am very appreciative for all the feedback I received. You will see some great improvements in this edition. Most feedback was positive and readers sent me some of their cost saving tips. A few readers believed I revealed too much information. Not surprisingly, one veterinarian called my book a "ticking time bomb".

I understand their concerns. I am grateful for their input. I am not critical of quality veterinarians, but I am also a realist who would prefer an animal get some treatment rather than none.

I live in an area of the country that experiences a lot of poverty. Remote Area Medical (RAM) vans set up yearly to offer free health services to the *human* population. People wait in line for hours for the only medical care they receive all year. I'm sure many people would be surprised to read that the services the US offers to third world countries is needed right here in Appalachia. When people living in poverty have to stand in line for free medical help themselves, how much veterinary care do you think their pets receive?

In a time, when I had lost my enthusiasm for writing this edition, and after nearly two years of intensive research, writing, and rewriting, I received this message from a reader:

"You are a GOD -send, [you] helped me save a litter of kittens I rescued, had ear mites, and bacterial infection. I don't have a job right now, but I borrowed the money to purchase your book."

This message reminded me just how many animal lovers are in the same position and why I began writing this book in the first place.

After being an animal cruelty investigator in Appalachia, I found that most poor families *wanted* to provide the best for their pet, but they couldn't always do that. The families needed and pleaded for help. Thousands, if not hundreds of thousands of people could improve the lives of animals and save lives of animals, if they had access to the information they needed.

In the first edition, I provided links to organizations that could help individuals in need, afford proper vet care. In researching for this second edition, many of those organizations have been so overwhelmed with requests, they had to stop taking applications.

So I have to honestly say, if it means a few poor reviews to stop the suffering of a pet and the heartbreak of a pet parent, I will gladly accept it.

I have received good responses from local shelters and rescues who were looking for ways to save money. So many of them are busy saving animals that they don't have time to do the research I provide in this book. Local shelters and rescues beg for assistance from veterinarians and vet techs who could help them save more animals by saving money on the needs of each individual animal.

This edition focuses less on the autobiography and serves more as an encyclopedia of my knowledge and my vast research done over many years. The book also encompasses the latest research on health topics, behavior problems, animal intelligence and the emotional lives of animals.

The book encourages the pet parent to take responsibility for the care of their pets with education and preparation. **Secrets of a Vet Tech II** also encourages working with a veterinarian as part of their pet's health care team.

I realized after the first edition was published, that the key to being able to afford my pets was proactive pet parenting. In other words, preventing disease rather than treating it; thinking ahead instead of thinking on the spot. While I cannot tell anyone how to treat a disease, I can tell you some of the options to explore with your veterinarian and what I have done to help my own pets. I can also train others how to examine their pet, and understand the basics of veterinary medicine as I was taught.

Thus began the idea for this book with a different perspective in pet care. Too many times, in the Appalachian region, we do nothing until our pet is sick. While I understand the financial issues that many pet parents face, when made affordable, preventative care can become the norm rather than the exception. Preventative care goes beyond vaccines, and that is one thing I hope to add here.

I was blessed in finally finding a veterinary hospital in my area that I trust and that understands my financial situation. Both veterinarians on staff have helped me determine who among my pets need care that only the veterinarian can provide. Once these decisions are made, we prioritize that care. I use **Care Credit ®** to finance my pets' vet care as it allows me to pay with zero interest when I pay in full within the allotted time.

So the spring following the publication of **Secrets of a Vet Tech,** all of my dogs went to the veterinarian during rabies month, to get their discounted rabies vaccine. The doctors examined them, gave me their suggestions, discussed possible alternatives, and helped me come up with a plan. One dog needed a dental, while another dog needed blood work. One dog appeared to be a candidate for hernia repair surgery. The vet offered a discount in doing all three at once.

During that time, I had lab work performed on many of the oldest pets in the group. The pets tested included dogs over 10 years old and my [then] 17 year old cat, Chloe. As I said in the previous edition, a complete blood count and full chemistry panel tells you things your pet can't. The results were all good and the doctor was impressed with the condition of their teeth at their age. So for my critics, I ask that you take those results into consideration.

A few months later, with lots of tightening of the financial belt, I was able to pay that bill in full. I then addressed some additional issues. My two oldest chihuahuas, Blue and Tinker, and my oldest cat, Chloe, developed common senior health issues including heart and thyroid disease. My wife Haseleah and her dog Abigail, and cat, Jerry, joined the family. Abigail's medication, along with the medication for Blue, Tinker, and Chloe added up to over $100 per month.

This is the ultimate example of forming a health care team for your pet. First, finding a doctor who will work with the resources you have. Secondly, the pet parent learning to take the ultimate responsibility for the health care of his or her pet.

I am thankful that I now have the support of two compassionate and experienced veterinarians who do, indeed go by their first names, Dr. Becky and Dr. Kitty. I have learned ways of financing my pet's care when needed, while still utilizing the things that I *can* do at home. For example, by doing my own vaccinations and utilizing the heart worm prevention protocol I outlined in the first edition, I can use those savings to pay for the medication they need.

Throughout this new edition, I hope to teach you the following:

- How to be proactive in your pet's care to improve his/her health and avoid costly health conditions
- How to examine your pet monthly to detect any possible health issues
- Secrets to financing for quality food, care, and preventative medicine
- How to recognize and react to emergencies without panic
- What items to stock in your pet medical kit and where to get it
- How to get financial assistance if needed
- How to work together with your veterinarian to give your pet a quality life as long as possible.

This book is not about how to replace your veterinarian, but how to work in conjunction with your vet as part of the health care team. If you are not happy with the doctor you have now, keep searching until you have a veterinarian you can trust. There are so many approaches to pet care from the veterinarian point of view. One approach will suit your style and your budget.

Don't assume that you have to settle for the cheapest vet clinic and never assume the most expensive clinic is the best. Look for a veterinarian willing to listen to you, take into consideration your financial situation, and appreciate that you know your pet better than anyone.

I have had so many people approach me with the frustration that I mentioned in **Secrets of a Vet Tech.** Those forgotten and judged pet parents who love their pets as much as anybody, but are criticized for not being able to provide certain things because of financial constraints. I am angry when knowledge is held back from them that would allow them to take care of their pets because it might cost the animal care industry money. It saddens me when animals are not vaccinated because we have convinced the world that the only proper vaccination is that one that is given by the hands of a veterinarian. How many cases of parvo, for instance, could have been prevented, if the pet parent was able to afford to vaccinate the entire litter? How many litters of puppies and kittens could we have stopped if we shared with their family that their pet could be altered (spayed/neutered) for less than $75?

Unfortunately, sometimes, instead of understanding that finances are tight, some clinic staff make the pet parents feel guilty for not paying for optional (and for the parent, unaffordable) pre-surgical lab testing prior to a spay or neuter. As a result, the parents walk away humiliated and embarrassed, leaving their pet unaltered. Thankfully, few veterinarian clinics are like this.

Rescue organizations and shelters could save so many more animals if they could find a way to reduce veterinary costs of each animal. Many rely on veterinarians who may help them at a reduced cost, but if they could vaccinate, deworm, and test for heartworm, parvo, and feline leukemia themselves, their costs could be significantly reduced. A $35 vaccine could cost $5 or less. Deworming could be done for pennies. Heartworm, parvo, and feline leukemia tests could be purchased in bulk. An employee, who, most likely already serves as a euthanasia technician, can perform venepuncture. Instead of having to inject a euthanasia drug into the vein, simply pull the blood for testing. Not only would this allow the shelters to save money and save pets, it would help with the compassion fatigue so many euthanasia technicians must endure.

Just as shelter employees are demonized when they can't save every animal, so too are veterinarians when they can't work for free. It is time to stop criticizing and figure out what we as pet parents and animal lovers can do to help.

Many people do not realize that, unlike human doctors who specialize, veterinarians have to be general practitioners, dentists, radiologists, gastroenterologists and more. Instead of studying one species like human physicians do, they often must know several species including the canine, feline, numerous small animals, birds, and reptiles. Their field of study is incredibly difficult and they are expected to practice as doctors with much less pay than the average human physician.

There are many, many good, compassionate and qualified veterinarians. There are also some unethical ones who would allow a pet to die instead of offering less expensive options. I have had the misfortune of working for a few. Thankfully however, the good doctors most certainly outweighed the bad.

On the other hand, too many times the staff are made to feel guilty by clients because they can't perform miracles for nothing. Keep in mind that the equipment, staff, and resources cost the hospital money too, and they have to be able to cover those costs to stay open. Just as you wish to be respected as a pet parents, show them respect as well.

Not all pet parents have lots of discretionary funds to use toward pet care, but when you adopted or purchased your pet, you became 100 % responsible for their care. I will help you learn how to do that on a budget and tell you what options and resources are available.

My purpose is to make sure no one ever has to use the excuse "I would get Fluffy vet care if only the prices were reasonable." While you may not be able to afford perfect "best practice" medicine, you can take care of your pet properly.

So what is "best practice" in veterinary medicine? In a perfect world, every pet undergoing anesthesia would have pre-surgical lab work. Every pet would get yearly checkups, yearly lab work. Each one would be on heart worm preventative, flea preventative, and the best food money can buy. Every client would be willing and able to do as the vet suggests. Each sick pet would get needed x-rays, lab testing, ultrasounds. They could quickly be hooked up on IV fluids, medication on board, all without concern for price. **But it is not a perfect world. It just isn't.**

Think of how many pets, during this latest economic crisis in America, were surrendered to local shelters because the pet parents believed they couldn't take care of them. The standard for "care" has been so greatly expanded over my lifetime, that few of us could live up to it. I certainly believe our pets deserve every wonderful thing we can give them. However, convincing ourselves (or being convinced) that we are offering such substandard care that we unnecessarily turn our animals in to shelters is uncalled for. There are far too many people giving the response "I can't afford to take care of him anymore" as a reason for surrender.

We can be good pet parents. We can afford care if we know what to do. We just have to learn to think outside the box, and when we are lucky enough to find a vet who understands, we become the best team possible for our pets health and well being. That is what I offer in this book.

In this revised edition, the background story remains the same. I included it for those who did not read the first edition of the book. It is important to know that I am coming from a place of understanding. I know first hand the struggles that come in being a pet parent in a financially tough world. For those of who who have read the first edition, feel free to skip on to other chapters.

Throughout most of the book, I use the term "pet parent". I do this because "owner" insinuates that animals are "things" rather than individuals. It is just another way we convince ourselves that our pets are "less than" and not worthy of love and proper care. I also use the pronouns "he" and "she" interchangeably when referring to animals. I will never use the term "it" to refer to a pet.

This book is written from my own personal perspective and experience, and is a combination of both conventional and natural medicine.

Although it may not have been proper form to put the research links within the text instead of creating end notes, I wanted to make it as easy as possible for all of my readers to find the links necessary to do further study. The photos throughout the book are not professional photos, but photos of the pets here at T.Paws Rescue.

The prices and price ranges I quote reflect average prices found online, including 1-800-Pet Meds, Ebay, and Amazon. Some may be regional costs in the East Tennessee area, so in your area, the prices may vary. The prices are current as of this writing.

Another thing to keep in mind: Although this is primarily a reference book, do not just look at the charts, but read the information surrounding them. There could be very important information or warnings you need to know.

I have included in the discussion more information regarding small animals (rats, rabbits, guinea pigs, ferrets), pocket pets (mice, gerbils, hamsters), birds (finches to parrots) and herps (amphibians & reptiles). There is no way to cover them all, so you will find a general discussion of their needs, environmental requirements, and common illnesses, as well as a chapter discussing money saving tips for exotics.

Some of the medication used for dogs and cats can be used with exotics, but it is important to never assume that because a medication is safe for one species, it is safe for another. Always do your research.

I do answer questions of clarification about my book *for those who have purchased it* by contacting me through my website www.jcfarris.com or at jcfarris.com@gmail.com. **I do not offer advice for treatment.**

A Note on Research and Evidence in Conventional vs Holistic Medicine

Conventional (or traditional) medicine is what you will find at most veterinary hospitals. Conventional vets determine the illness and treat for that specific illness. **Holistic (or natural) medicine** is practiced by veterinarians who specialize in one or more disciplines of homeopathy, acupuncture, acupressure, chiropractic, herbal therapy, and aromatherapy. They believe in a "whole health" approach and work to increase the potential of the immune system so that it may fight the disease itself. One may recommend using a heartworm and intestinal parasite all-in-one preventative year around while the other may recommend heartworm nosodes and other homeopathic treatments while focusing on maintaining a high immune system.

These approaches often disagree with one another. Holistic practitioners and their clients often see conventional medicine as too focused on the illness rather than the patient. Doctors of conventional medicine, on the other hand, sometimes see holistic medicine as being unscientific and unproven. I see both as having merit, and included both when I could, however, both disciplines had to be weighed against actual scientific research. It would be in the pet parents best interest to have as many options as possible for treating their pets.

The research for this book was often difficult. Many studies were taken out of context to "prove" many things that the studies did not support. Facts and figures were misconstrued, something no one would have noticed if he or she did not read the original studies. Other studies were funded by groups with special interests creating a situation that was biased. Scientists were hired to "prove" something that was not supported by good research. Other studies that were too small were improperly cited as absolute evidence of a hypothesis.

I found it necessary to find and read each study as I was writing this book. There were times when I could only find the abstract, which is an abbreviated version of the final report. However if I could obtain the entire study, I did so. When one vital study wasn't available on the internet or in any medical journals I could find, I contacted the researcher directly and he was kind enough to send a copy to me.

I discussed the studies at length with my wife, Haseleah, who has a degree in microbiology, experience writing technical papers, and special training in reading and interpreting scientific studies. Together with my educational background in experimental methodology and statistics, Haseleah and I searched for studies that were reproducible by other scientists, available for peer review, and published in professional scientific and/or medical journals. These are some of the necessities of a well done study. We also took into account the sponsors of the studies who could influence the study outcome.

There is a great difference in anecdotal proof (testimonials, etc) and hard scientific fact based upon unbiased, well prepared and executed research . Proponents of homeopathy, one of many forms of holistic medicine, have plenty of anecdotal evidence, yet in the hundreds of years of its existence (since 1796) there are almost no well done, unbiased, scientific studies to prove that it works. I found this disappointing.

While some homeopaths claim that there are 299 studies published in 114 journals *"in evidence of homeopathy to produce significant to substantial health benefits in a wide array of health conditions,"* https://drnancymalik.wordpress.com/article/scientific-research-in-homeopathy/ a review of these studies have shown the "evidence" and research method is seriously lacking. It was noted, that not one study was published in a respected medical or veterinary journal.

In 2010, a large study was conducted on the best evidence homeopathy had to offer. The evidence and studies were provided by the Cochrane Central Register. The studies included some of those 299 mentioned above. The study conclusion said that *"[t]he findings of currently available Cochrane reviews of studies of homeopathy do not show that homeopathic medicines have effects beyond placebo."*
https://www.mja.com.au/journal/2010/192/8/homeopathy-what-does-best-evidence-tell-us

There are few studies that attempt to support the efficacy of nosodes in veterinary medicine. However, there are studies showing that *"giving animals placebos can play active roles in influencing pet owners to believe in the effectiveness of the treatment when none exists."*
http://veterinaryrecord.bmj.com/content/157/8/224

The FDA and both British and Australian veterinary associations do not support homeopathy, and the Australians have gone so far to include it on the their list of ineffective therapies.

Haseleah and I read and discussed some of the studies claiming to prove the validity of homeopathic nosodes. We wanted to rule out any possible influence by large pharmaceutical companies to find homeopathy ineffective.

Nosodes are homeopathic substances that are created by diluting the secretions of a diseased person or animal with alcohol or distilled water until no molecules of the original substance remains. This substance is then put to the test in "provings" or homeopathic pathogenetic trials (HPTs).

We had difficulty finding a veterinary-related study, so we read several others. One of those HTP's was "The Proving of the AIDS Nosode". In this study, the blood of an individual who died of the AIDS virus was diluted into a homeopathic remedy.

The paragraph on the following page was part of the report:

"We followed Jeremy Sherr's general proving methodology in this proving, however, individuals, timings and codes are not given. Additionally we recorded our experiences some minutes after beginning the proving. This is given at the beginning of the proving report. We got images (such as billowing clouds, popping seed pods, orange flowers, and responses to these images such as associated feelings, sensations or thoughts); feelings (such as joy, sadness, and their responses such as smiling or closing off); sensations (such as floating, burning, itching, and their responses such as restlessness or scratching); thoughts and concepts which in turn may evoke images, feelings and sensations. This then is our primary data. It would be in accordance with tradition to say that proving responses are headed up by an image at the top of a natural hierarchy which proceeds down the levels, through thoughts to feelings to sensations. But some provers vary here, for instance, by having a preponderance of sensation experiences, or feeling responses. This depends upon their innate personality structure, as would be described elementally as preponderances of Fire, Air, Water, Earth."

This is just one example of the homeopath research method.

We weren't surprised to learn that the World Health Organization (WHO) warns against using homeopathy to treat serious illnesses http://www.bmj.com/content/339/bmj.b3447 , or that the Australian National Health and Medical Research Council (NHMRC), Swiss and British government, all found no proof that homeopathic medicine was effective.
http://theconversation.com/no-evidence-homeopathy-is-effective-nhmrc-review-25368
Unlike conventional medicines which undergo a long, rigorous, and expensive process before being released, herbal "remedies" are considered nutritional supplements, and not subjected to the same process. Neither efficacy or safety have to be proven before the "remedy" is sold.

Nutraceuticals, commonly sold as nutritional products, are derived from food sources and are said to have extra health benefits in addition to basic nutrition. These products can be sold, but must not make any claim suggesting they are a medication or offer a cure.

This rule is often ignored, or the product description written in such a way that it is very close to crossing the line.

In 2014, the Food and Drug Administration (FDA), sent a warning letter to one nutraceautical company, Amber Technologies. The letter stated that:

"We have determined that several of your products marketed as "nutraceuticals for pets" are intended for use in the mitigation, treatment, or prevention of disease in animals, which makes them drugs under section 201(g)(1)(B) of the Federal Food, Drug, and Cosmetic Act (the FD&C Act) [21 U.S.C. § 321(g)(1)(B)]. Further, under the FD&C Act, drugs intended for use in animals require an approved new animal drug application unless they are generally recognized as safe and effective. As discussed below, we have determined that your drugs are not generally

recognized as safe and effective and therefore your marketing of them without an approved new animal drug application violates the law."
http://www.fda.gov/ICECI/EnforcementActions/WarningLetters/ucm384594.htm

Further investigation revealed that the products were created by those with no medical training.
http://ambertech.com/about-us/

In 2005, the company published an e-book, **Puppies and Parvo: A Self-Help Guide.**
http://www.animalsnaturallyonline.com/files/1861275/uploaded/Parvo_Information_Self_Help_Guide.pdf

In the book, the company claims that while not all cases will be successful, 85% of the animals treated with their products would be cured.

On one of their websites, they also claim that their products prevent parvo in puppies 90% of the time, http://www.parvopuppy.com/index.htm and is said to work on both viral and bacterial infections (page 25).

In the book, "hydrating enemas" are given as a viable option to IV fluids. The author claims that the large intestine will absorb the fluid and that a series of enemas should be given to prevent dehydration. The author misses the key component of the parvovirus....it destroys the lining of the intestines making it difficult, if not impossible, to absorb any fluids.
Pet parents are misguided when the author refers to their product as an antibiotic (page 14). On the same page, the writer shows a lack of understanding of the immune system by explaining that veterinarians give antibiotics "due to the lack of white blood cells the body is producing." While the white blood cell count does drop, antibiotics do not encourage the white blood cells to multiply. Antibiotics fight possible opportunistic bacterial infections. Parvo is a virus. No anti-viral exists at this time that will fight this virus. The claim is also made that by using their products Vibactra Plus and Parvaid (now called Paxxin), the puppy will eat within two days compared to four days without their products (page 55).

The author addresses the "research" done on their products with a "Parvo Study Sheet" (page 69). This "research" is referred to as "case studies". The health of the puppies are described as "preaty good" (their spelling) , "wonderful" "short-tempered", "fine", and "great".

The two primary "nutraceuticals" mentioned in the book cost between $71-204 depending on the size purchased.

Since the FDA warning, the company now states that their products *may* help certain conditions, but have not removed the e-book from the web.

Interestingly, even though the company owners admit that they have no medical training, they still offer "parvo consultations" http://www.parvopuppy.com/holistic_consult.htm.

This highlights the need for better regulation and standards for "natural remedies."

While I believe some herbal remedies may be helpful, most have not met the burden of proof beyond antidotes. They have also not been tested well enough to assure their safety. We tend to believe that because something is "natural", it is safe, and this simply is not true.

Our concern needs to remain on what is best for our pets. If pure scientific research has been done that supports the efficacy of a treatment, it should be used whether its a nutraceautical or pharmaceutical. But, for the safely and best interest of our pets, these standards need to be met.

A SHORT AUTOBIOGRAPHY AND THE STRUGGLES OF THE PET PARENT

"Until one has loved an animal, a part of one's soul remains unawakened." ~ Anatole France

1

Poverty and Pet Parenting

We have all fallen on hard times during our lives. We often wonder if we can make it until the next paycheck or if we will ever find a job. This situation is not something anyone looks forward to but, unfortunately it happens.

It becomes difficult enough to feed ourselves and get medical care. What about our pets? Should we find them a new home? Take them to the shelter? Have them put to sleep?

At present **46 million** Americans are living in poverty.
http://www.reuters.com/article/2013/09/17/us-usa-economy-poverty-idUSBRE98G0PN20130917

Many say that those people shouldn't have pets. *"If you can't afford them, don't get them,"* is a statement I have heard more than once.

Here's a reality check. **Five (5) million animals** entered animal shelters in 2012. Of that number **3.5 million** were euthanized. http://www.statisticbrain.com/animal-shelter-statistics/

The fact of the matter is, we need as many people as possible adopting and the same (or more) number spaying and neutering. I searched for statistics showing the income level of those who adopt from shelters, but so far, that information is not available. However, having worked in shelters over the years, I think I can fairly say that the majority of families that adopt from animal shelters are low to middle income families. This is not to say that wealthier people do not adopt from the shelter, or to demean the upper class. What I am saying is, before judging the poor for having pets, it is important to realize that often, *they are the ones saving shelter animals from certain death.* **They need each other.**

Many of our poor are the disabled, widows/widowers, and children. Having a companion to love not only has emotional benefits, but health benefits as well.

"University of Wisconsin-Madison pediatrician James E. Gern has conducted a number of studies that demonstrate having a pet in the home can actually lower a child's likelihood of developing related allergies by as much as 33 percent. In fact, his research -- as published in the Journal of Allergy and Clinical Immunology -- shows that children exposed early on to animals tend to develop stronger immune systems overall."
http://animal.discovery.com/pets/benefits-of-pets.htm

In addition, *"The Centers for Disease Control and Prevention (CDC) and the National Institute of Health (NIH) have both conducted heart-related studies on people who have pets. The findings showed that pet owners exhibit decreased blood pressure, cholesterol and triglyceride levels -- all of which can ultimately minimize their risk for having a heart attack down the road."*

In a country in which health coverage is one of the biggest debates of the decade, anything that will increase immunity, increase overall health, and result in few doctor visits, is an asset.

So it behooves us to pull together as a nation and appreciate the hardships we all face and work together to not only help each other, but be more responsible about our pets as well.

We can decrease the number in the shelter by spaying and neutering and adopting. But we can also decrease that number by finding ways to keep our own pets when finances get tight. This is in many ways what my story is about.

Many are faced with the decision that I was faced with. Not everyone needed to supply food, medical care, and basic necessities to as many pets as I did, but the same rules apply.

I combined necessity, self sufficiency, and years of professional pet care experience to support T.Paws Rescue & ARFanage. I shared my story in the first edition of **Secrets of a Vet Tech.** The purpose of this new edition is to empower pet parents with a practical reference for pet care, and to offer animal shelters and rescues ideas to help provide the best care for the most animals possible.

Financial Ruin and the Resurrection of Self-Sufficiency

Growing up in Appalachia in my generation, there were wonderful examples of self sufficiency. My parents built our home by hand, and our extended family tended our own water supply. My grandfather and his sons built a family reservoir that was fed by a stream that caressed down Walker Mountain. If things broke, it was most often fixed without calling a repairman. Even a family church was built to tend to the spiritual side of life. This was the way of living on Walkers Creek.

As I grew up, I tried not to forget the things I learned. Although I moved away, the spirit of the creek continued to run through me. Relocating to the other side of the country was a huge step, but as often occurs, one finds a reason to return close to home.

When America's financial crisis finally found my backyard and threatened the care of my pets, I found my reason to go home. I lost my business, my home, everything. When I found my heart was much bigger than my wallet, I realized that I had to do something.

I had always wanted to have my own animal rescue, and my dream came true in a small way while running my business, Gentle Hands Animal Care and Pet Sitting, throughout the Inland Empire area of California. I had developed a wonderful network of people, rescues, vet offices, and friends who helped me place unwanted animals. I tended to take in animals with behavioral and physical problems, and, to be honest, many were not adoptable. I couldn't turn them away. The ones who could be placed in a new home, were adopted. However, those who could not be adopted, stayed with me.

Then the bottom dropped out. Gas prices went to nearly $4.00 per gallon and, in my business, that meant a gasoline bill that could exceed $600 per month. A pet sitting client disappeared for over a month, and I cared for his farm full of animals at my own expense, never to see the money again or be paid for the job. Next, after working months without a day off, I became ill and couldn't drive. It was the perfect storm: an the end to life as I knew it.

Financially, the "easy" thing to do would have been to take the pets I had to the local shelter. But I knew what would happen to them. Several were terrified of people and would have bitten the employees and potential adopters. Others had physical issues that would have meant they would be put to sleep. I couldn't abandon them. **I wouldn't abandon them.**

It was the call of home. It was time to move from Southern California back to the Appalachian Mountains of Southwest Virginia and Northeast Tennessee. There, the cost of living would be much cheaper, and sweet tea could be enjoyed by the gallon!

Getting twenty-five animals across the United States was indeed a chore. The trip took planning, hard work, and lots of luck. The weather was perfect: cool, but not too cool. In total, it took five days to get all the dogs, cats, birds, and a guinea pig home to Tennessee. It was April when we arrived.

Returning home, thankfully, pushed me to remember the principles I learned growing up and to embrace my roots as a child of Appalachia. I was humbled as I left a brand new home in Southern California, for an old farm house in East Tennessee.

The 1947 remodeled farm house was on an acre of land. I named the farmhouse "Whisper Creek." Having my parents were close by was a blessing.

Once we were settled, we were able to dedicate additional areas for the dogs and cats. It was a slow evolution that was made possible thanks to my father who did all of the carpentry. In addition to insulating an old outbuilding and putting up a fence, we enclosed and insulating an attached patio just off of our dining area. We added heat and air and a large custom-made doggie bunk bed. We also converted an unattached open patio area to an insulated and heated cat building and added a separate outdoor run on the other northern side of the house. The dogs were divided into two groups based upon many factors. One, we refer to as "the patio dogs" as they preferred living on the cozy enclosed patio. The second we call "the chihuahuas", even though it includes one schnauzer mix.

While still working for a veterinarian in California, I had purchased as much heartworm preventative, flea prevention, and various medications as I could afford. Unfortunately, those supplies only lasted for a short time. When that supply was exhausted, I had to get creative to find a way to supply their needs.

I have worked in the animal care world since the mid 1990's. I've been an animal cruelty investigator, a veterinary technician, a pet sitter, a rescuer, and a certified euthanasia technician. I've worked in up- scale veterinary clinics, and in humane societies which provided limited vet care to the poor. I've assisted small country veterinarians and specialty veterinarians. I took all this experience and began to research in depth. I studied labels. I watched what was being used by the doctors I assisted. I looked at ingredients and even took continuing veterinary technician courses. I utilized every secret, every nugget of knowledge, everything I had learned behind the scenes. This is my story and the results of all that effort.

While to some, it may seem foolish and unwise to go to the lengths I have gone to keep this rescue together; I see it as keeping my family together. We are a band of misfits, outcasts, and the perfectly imperfect. Many in this family have social anxieties, damage from past abuse, health problems, and/or advanced age. So we do all we can to maintain a loving, forever home.

Necessity lead me to return to my roots of Appalachian ingenuity, self-sufficiency, and resourcefulness.

Now, in 2015, I bring you **Secrets of a Vet Tech II**. The information in this edition not only exceeds that in the first, but is supported by confirmed research and by well done studies, all which can be found throughout the book.

2

Motivation

Growing up in Southwest Virginia, I had loved animals for as long as I could remember and they were always my best friends. This was during a time when few thought about taking their pets to the vet except in an emergency. Spaying and neutering was rarely considered. In fact, I grew up afraid of the vet as the one in our town did not have a good reputation.

Then one day I witnessed my dear sweet puppy, Pepper, a little Pekingese mix, choke to death on a small piece of candy she had found in my room. My parents tried everything to save her. They rushed her to the vet as they tried to get the candy out. But Pepper died. I thought her death was my fault. The candy was in my room. It was my piece of candy.

I was a tiny, impressionable child. Life wasn't the same after that.

I went on to have other pets, but would often have nightmares of their deaths. My best buddy, Cuddles, who came along after Pepper, was my best friend and companion from about 10 years old until I was in college. I had many other animals, but he was very special to me. I recall sitting on the patio with him doing homework. Other times I recall crying and asking him what was wrong with me? I didn't seem to fit in anywhere, and I felt sad so often. Cuddles helped me survive my teen years.

He came with me to live at college after I was married and living in student housing at age 19. He knew no fear. One day, when an emergency helicopter landed in the field behind our house, Cuddles took off and ran the length of a football field and tried to jump in. The co-pilot caught him and gave him back to me with a strange look on his face. Cuddles was brave and full of spunk.

Cuddles' body inevitably aged so much over the years and his heart finally started to weaken. Cuddles was diagnosed with congestive heart failure. Our veterinarian at the time1, Dr. Lee Pilkington, was such a wonderful man. He wasn't scary, and I learned veterinarians could be kind. He allowed me to volunteer at his clinic, when I had the time between work and classes, to see what I thought of veterinary medicine. I loved it.

Cuddles' health continued to worsen. He was so swollen from the fluid and no matter how much medication he took, things wouldn't improve. The week I knew his end was close, I begged and pleaded with God to take him on, and not make me decide to put him to sleep. But it was not to be.

The day I took him was one of the worst days of my life. Cuddles was ready. When Dr. Pilkington came in to give him the injection, Cuddles handed him his paw. The kindness of that man continued to be evident as he cried with me. I never in my wildest dreams imaged a doctor who would allow himself to feel the sadness of his clients. Even after Cuddles took his last breath, Dr. Pilkington, who knew I had no place to bury Cuddles, told me of a cremation service. Giving me that option made a big difference in my grieving. I wouldn't have to leave Cuddles behind when I left college. So Cuddles was cremated and I still have his ashes.

For someone who couldn't seem to let people close, losing Cuddles was incredibly difficult. I didn't handle it well, but it showed me how important animals were to me and what I was supposed to be doing. My degree in human psychology was put to the side, and a new adventure began.

Dr. Pilkington had encouraged me to go back to school to be a veterinarian using the many college credits I already had. Life got in the way, however, I began working instead, as a receptionist and veterinarian assistant in clinics in New Orleans, Louisiana and later in Johnson City, Tennessee.

Over the next several years, the depression and panic I had suffered as a child intensified to the degree that I was unable to maintain my job or my marriage. I was diagnosed with severe depression, social agoraphobia with severe panic attacks, and PTSD (Post Traumatic Stress Disorder). I was often unable to leave the safety of my home, a challenge that I continue to confront more than twenty years later.

Going out of the house was a terrifying experience. I would dissociate easily, meaning my world would look to me as if a dream. I would lose hours, days, and even weeks of time. It was very disconcerting and frightening. Dissociating made driving dangerous and the freedom driving brought was taken away for a time.

My saving grace was the opportunity to serve as an animal cruelty investigator with a local humane society. When someone said an animal needed me, I was focused on helping the animal and overcame the panic that came with leave the house. For a while my mother had to drive me to the locations I was to investigate. Not only did being an investigator begin my road to recovery, it fueled the fire I had always had for animal rescue.

Over the years as I was recovering I investigated over a hundred cases a year. I educated those who needed it, and those who were simply cruel, had them arrested, prepared the cases and presented them to the judge. I had a 100% conviction rate.
I also developed my own little rescue that focused on small pets like hamsters, ferrets, and guinea pigs. I had witnessed so many of these tiny animals brought to the shelter and not finding a home. Once I moved to California, I continued to rescue and still do. Once animal rescue is in your blood, it remains a passion and deep calling.

I have come to realize that saving the animals is the only way of saving myself. As I have continued to battle with my issues, it is the animals who have kept me going. Ms. Ruby, who is my closest companion now, has been with me through so many difficult times: ending relationships, losing loved ones, a cancer diagnosis and the terrible menopause that came with getting the necessary hysterectomy. Ruby is the reason I am able to leave the house. She has become my PTSD companion dog and goes many places with me.

T.Paws Rescue and ARFranage began as a foster home for adoptable animals. In two years, we were able to partner with a local humane society to foster and adopt more than thirty animals. The number of unadoptable pets began adding up and the California rescues that returned to Tennessee with me, grew older, increasing the cost of care.

Our specialty at T.Paws has always been special needs pets who have had their spirits broken by abuse or neglect. Those animals who are unadoptable will live out their lives at T.Paws.

The special needs animals we take in need to learn to trust us and realize not all humans are evil. The power of pack love has brought peace to many terrified dogs. Members of our established pack teach these broken little ones how to play, something they had never learned. They also reassure them that they are safe. It is an amazing transformation to watch. At this time, there are 13 members of that pack, 7 of them 10 years old or older. You will see their photos throughout this book.

In 2014, my new wife, Haseleah, and her dog, Abigail, and cat, Jerry, joined our pack.

We joke that our rescue has transitioned from a foster home to an assisted-living facility. Many are on medication and prescription food. It takes both Haseleah and I to manage the pack and attend to their increasing needs.

We fund most of their care ourselves. However, when money is particularly tight, we raise money through an online fund raising website called "GoFundMe". We have had benefit sales which has helped raise needed funds, and all the royalties from all of the books I have written go directly to T.Paws as well. Haseleah contributes financially by making and selling all natural home and body care products, dog soaps, pet comfort pillows, and hand crocheted sweaters for dogs, among many other things.

Since the last edition, there have been some additional changes at T.Paws. My precious six-year old guinea pig passed away as did my beloved bearded dragon and two elderly rats. My basset, Buster, developed an aprocrine gland tumor of the anal sac. It was a terribly hard mass that made him very uncomfortable. The high calcium that was a result of the tumor changed his disposition and he attacked one of my other dogs, Teddy, and nearly killed him. It was then that I had to make a very difficult decision. Teddy was saved thanks to my veterinarians, Drs. Becky and Kitty, however, because the Buster's condition would only continue to worsen and possibly result in more violence, I made the decision to put him to sleep. He was 11 years old. I still miss him.

Not long after Buster died, a kitten crossed my path. She was a tiny little thing running under moving cars on Main Street. No one stopped to help her, but me. She couldn't have been more than 4 weeks old and she was absolutely terrified. So, as much as I tried not to add additional pets, Willow is sleeping nearby even as I write. As a kitten, she had a tiny mouse named Maple as her companion. When Maple passed away, a new companion mouse, Butters, became her friend.

During the writing of this edition, our 18 year old cat, Chloe, who will be mentioned throughout the book, passed away. In our sorrow, I told Haseleah, when one steps out of our lives, another who needs us, steps in. Several weeks later, a tiny, undernourished, underfed, unneutered chihuahua was brought to us. We named him Brody. He didn't seem to know how to eat, how to enjoy a treat, or even how to play. It took some time and lots of pack love, but Brody has learned all those things.

My pets saved me yet again from the terrible depression and self destruction that has plagued me and has been made worse by menopause. The hormones that could ease the symptoms could also cause the cancer to return, so it has been difficult to find medications to help me. As a result, the depression became so dark, suicide seemed my only escape.

When these dark moments have befallen me, Ms Ruby has put one paw on my hand that held the knife, and another on my heart. The dogs have gathered in puppy piles, surrounding me on the bed, while I shivered in terror from another panic attack. They have fought so hard to keep me alive, so I fight to provide a good life for them with the little that I have. How I do that is outlined in this book.

Haseleah came into our lives. The pack needed her as much as I did, and our hearts feel joy and contentment in her presence. She is not only my wife, but a true partner in the rescue.

Over the years I have learned that jobs come and go. Friendships come and go. Success comes and goes. But in the end, it is your dog, your cat, your furry, feathered, or scaled companion, that remains. They open your heart in ways no one else can. They have saved me over and over by giving me a reason to live. So for them, and those who also need a companion to survive, I dedicate this book.

PROACTIVE PET PARENTING

"The greatness of a nation and its moral progress can be judged by the way its animals are treated." ~Mohandas Gandhi

3

Defining Proactive Pet Parenting and Tips for Finding a Quality Veterinarian

According to the English Dictionary, the term proactive means *"acting in advance to deal with an expected difficulty"* or *"tending to initiate change rather than reacting to events"*. In other words, planning ahead and doing everything to encourage good health, prevent illness, and avoid emergencies.

This is the meaning of, **"proactive pet parenting"**. Pet parents can learn to think ahead and plan for the unexpected. Careful observation allows one to know what is normal behavior or body condition for the pet, so the abnormal is recognized immediately.

The approach helps ease the panic of a midnight emergency. When one has limited knowledge about something, it is frightening. What may look like a non- emergency to a trained eye can have the untrained eye already planning the funeral. So, by learning proactive pet parenting, one can apply that knowledge and feel more in control.

So what factors are included in Proactive Pet Parenting?

- Educating yourself on the species and/or breed of your pet. Behavior normal to one species may be abnormal in another species. This is true also of body language.
- Learning how to perform regular physical exams and recording the information. The intent is to learn what is normal for your pet in order to quickly recognize when something is abnormal.
- Learning how to ask the right questions so that you can gather the information needed.
- Making smart decisions based upon the information gathered.
- Developing a good relationship with a local veterinarian and creating a pet care team.

An example of the benefits of knowing the normal behavior of your species, is coprophagia, or the unappetizing habit of eating feces. While unappetizing to us, coprophagia is common among guinea pigs, bunnies, and other herbivores. For them, the practice is a necessary digestive process that requires that food be digested twice in order to maximize nutrition. For these herbivores, it is not a habit that should be discouraged. Dogs, on the other hand, often like to raid the litter box. It is not done out of any known nutritional necessity, and is a habit that can, and should be discouraged.

While there are certain "norms" for most species, each animal is an individual. "A cat is a cat" is as true as saying "a human is a human". The same goes for any group. What is normal for one individual, may not be normal for others. This is true in behavior as in health. While one dog is happy eating one meal a day, another may prefer two smaller meals a day. One cat may enjoy canned food, while another cat wouldn't even consider it. One dog, if given the chance, will consume an entire bag of dog food, while another could be trusted with leaving the bag of dog food sitting by his bowl. You have to know your individual pet.

This is also true with lab work and is why it is recommended to get baseline lab work every few years when your pet is healthy. Know what is normal for your pet in all aspects so there is no question when something is abnormal.

In people and animals, baselines can vary slightly. Although a normal human temperature is 98.6°F, some people run a little under or over. The same goes for pets although baseline temps run higher in dogs and cats than in humans.

Pets obviously cannot communicate in the same way we do. When your child is sick, he or she can say, "Mommy, I don't feel well. My tummy hurts". Pets cannot do that. It is important to keep in mind that a pet's natural instinct tell her to hide illness and pain. To reveal either would be a weakness and make her vulnerable to predators. Although it doesn't seem this instinct is as strong in the canine who has been domesticated much longer, it is still very strong in the feline species. Cats are extremely reluctant to show vulnerability. Too often, it is when the cat does something inconvenient to the pet parent that illness is noticed. An example is a cat urinating outside the litter box. A trip to the vet reveals that this "inconvenience" was, in fact, a urinary tract infection.

While animals cannot communicate vocally for the most part, they are expressive with their body language. A tail tucked between the legs may be fear for some, but pain for another. There are many clues to watch for when observing your pet including facial expression, body posture, and others that may come up in a physical exam. That's why learning to perform a basic physical and gather as much data as possible is essential when you are trying to understand what your pet is trying to tell you.

When you do realize your pet is not feeling well, there are certain questions you must ask. This is when you have to become a detective. You have to know the questions to ask, how to find the answer, and what the answer could indicate. Only then can you make a good educated decision as to what to do next.

One of the goals of this book is to teach the pet parent the skills needed to be proactive and become a pet care detective. In a later chapter, you will learn how to perform an exam using, what I call, the **"Physical Exam Train" (PET).** This process will guide you to examine every inch of your pet and know what you should be looking for. You can record your findings to share with your vet. Recording your findings may allow you to see changes, you may not have seen otherwise. When you live with a pet everyday, you may not notice gradual changes such as weight loss, but if you have the weight of the pet recorded over a series of months, you will discover a possible symptom that may need to be addressed by your veterinarian.

Developing a good relationship with your veterinarian is important. You, your family, and your veterinarian make up your pet's **"Pet Care Team"**. If you have a groomer, or use a pet sitter, those people can also be part of the team.

Mutual respect between you and your vet can help ensure that the vet listens to your observations and that you listen to the veterinarian's recommendations. We have been able to develop the type of relationship with Dr. Kitty and Dr. Becky, that we trust them not to recommend tests or procedures that our pets do not need. If they recommend it, we do it. They help us get the most out of our vet dollars. In turn, we purchase the needed prescription medications from their clinic, instead of asking for a prescription and shopping around. We tell our friends and family about them and send business their way. It is a comforting relationship to have whether you have one pet or a rescue full of animals.

Not everyone is as lucky as we are.

Veterinarians and veterinary clinics vary widely in their approach. There is not a one-size-fits-all animal practice. Some practices may take walk-ins, while others prefer to schedule appointments. One clinic may be very formal, while another is informal. In some practices, the vet is able and eager to have more one-on-one time with his or her client and patient, while in other practices, the technician, not the vet, gets to know both well. Some clinics attempt to see as many patients in a day as possible, while others prefer to see fewer patients per day but spend more time with each one. One may employ several veterinarians including board certified surgeons, while another is a single, doctor owned practice. Before searching for a veterinarian, determine what qualities are important to you.

Personal preferences are important, but finding a good quality clinic, that treats pets humanely and the pet parent with respect, is important as well. Good references from family and friends as well as online reviews, can help point you in the right direction. Ask your local animal shelter what vet clinic they use. If you have a particular clinic in mind, mention the clinic to a local animal cruelty officer or animal control officer. While he or she may not be able to reveal specifics, the officer's initial reaction upon hearing the name of a clinic may reveal a lot. Hesitation often indicates that the officer associates negative information with the clinic.

Low income families tend to look for the least expensive clinic in the area, which is understandable. However, most low cost vet practices make up the difference in high volume. This may mean long waiting periods, crowded lobbies, little one-on-one veterinarian attention, and a very stressful environment for your pet.

When looking for a new veterinarian, call to ask for an appointment to speak to the veterinarian and to get a tour of the facility. You may choose to go without your pet, or take your pet to see how the staff reacts to her and how she reacts to the staff. Good clinics should welcome this request. If they don't, consider looking elsewhere. Use the opportunity to get a feel for the staff, ask questions, and look around. If you feel positive about your experience, but didn't bring your pet for the initial visit, ask for the paperwork to complete so the receptionist can have your chart prepared for the next time.

Signs that you have found a good veterinary clinic:

- The lobby is clean and free of strong odors.
- The reception staff is welcoming and their area is well organized. Whether they are on the phone, or talking among themselves, the staff are respectful of both the pet parents and the pets.
- The pace is prompt, but the staff is not hurried or frustrated.
- The other pet parents waiting to be seen tell you positive things about the clinic staff.
- The reception staff has your pet's chart out before you arrive and greet you and your pet upon your arrival.
- The technician who calls you into the exam room is friendly and approaches your pet in a non-threatening manner.
- The exam rooms are disinfected between patients and are well stocked and organized.
- The veterinarian is friendly and knowledgeable. He or she is comfortable approaching your pet and is willing to listen to your concerns and answer your questions.
- When or if your pet is taken to the treatment area for a procedure, he is not excessively fearful upon return.
- The veterinarian and staff listen to your concerns about finances. When you assure the staff that you will do everything you can afford to do, the staff works within the confines of your budget as much as possible.
- You leave after the exam feeling that your pet was in a safe and humane environment. Your pet does not seem traumatized after the experience, although some fear is normal.

Tips to Being a Good Client:

- Make an appointment and ask what records the staff would like you to obtain from your previous veterinarian (if applicable) and bring them with you to the appointment. If you can, stop by before the appointment time and fill out the necessary paperwork. It will save time and save you the difficulty of trying to do paperwork and calm your pet at the same time.

- Have your dog leashed or your cat in a carrier. Never assume that your pet will behave. It will make the staff and the other clients more comfortable.
- Come prepared with all your questions written down.
- If you have your records from doing exams at home, bring them with you. The records will provide the veterinarian with important information. It is not necessary to make copies for your pet's chart unless asked to do so.
- Sometimes veterinarians do not see the symptoms the pet parent does, because the pet is afraid. That fear can mask some symptoms. If you have a smart phone, you can take a video at home when the pet is relaxed and demonstrating the symptom. Bring the video with you to show the veterinarian. Anything you think the veterinarian needs to know that you have difficulty describing or believe the pet will not show, take photographs and/or videos.
- Assume your veterinarian has you and your pet's best interest at heart unless proven otherwise.
- Be as polite to the staff as you would want them to be polite to you.
- If your clinic provides an estimate of services, ask that each itemized item be explained. It is important to understand the necessity of each service. If the bill is more than you can afford, be honest with the veterinarian and ask there are any options to make it less expensive.
- Never assume you know more about veterinary medicine than the veterinarian, but understand that you know more about your pet and your pet's habits than anyone. Be you pet's health care advocate.

4

The Number One Way to Save Money as a Pet Parent

Believe it or not there is a very simple secret. Hundreds, even thousands, of dollars can be saved by doing one thing.....spaying or neutering your dog or cat. Too often, pet parents feel that they can't afford to spay or neuter their pet. The truth is, in order to prevent disease, prolong life and save money, you can't afford *not* to.

As I said, I spay and neuter all my animals. One reason I spay and neuter, is because about **2.7 MILLION dogs and cats are euthanized every year because of pet overpopulation. 70 % of pets will end up in a shelter during their lifetime. This statistic means that for 10 cute puppies and kittens allowed to be born, 7 of them will not find forever homes and have a huge chance of being euthanized.** http://www.aspca.org/about-us/faq/pet-statistics

If that weren't incentive enough, saving hundreds of dollars over the lifetime of the pet, should be.

For instance, at some point in the life of an intact (unspayed) female dog, she will most likely be rushed to the vet clinic, terribly ill. Often she is running a fever and lab results will reveal an increased white blood cell count, indicating a heavy infection. Pyometra will be her diagnosis, an infection of the uterus. The cure? Spaying her. Only this time it won't be cheap.

Instead of a normal uterus and surrounding tissues, the veterinarian will find these tissues swollen, often, to the size of full term pregnancy. Instead of puppies, the uterus will be full of infection. If not very carefully removed, the vet can puncture the tissue sending infection throughout her body. Even if the uterus is successfully removed, the dog will have to be on IV fluids and strong antibiotics. The incision will probably be much bigger than it would have if her organs had been a normal size.

The cost of a pyometra surgery ? Depending on the clinic and the severity of the infection, $350-$2500. The cost to have spayed her in the beginning ? $60-$250.

Approaches to Spay and Neuter

There are different approaches to spaying and neutering that will determine its cost. I have worked in spay/neuter clinics where the cost of a cat neuter was $21. I've also worked in a nationally known pet hospital where the cost of a cat neuter was $199.

So what is the difference that makes one much more expensive than the other?

In a spay/neuter clinic where a cat neuter cost $21, the veterinarian's focus is only on spay and neuter surgeries. He or she may never see patients for any other procedure, and becomes an expert spay and neuter- focused veterinarian. A good veterinarian can neuter a cat in about five minutes.

The process of surgery in a spay and neuter clinic is an assembly line of sorts. One technician may be assigned to give a pre-surgical sedative. Once the pet is unconscious, another technician will intubate and prepare the surgical site. The fur will be shaved and the surgical area scrubbed with Betadine ® or Nolvasan ®. The pet will be transferred to the surgical table, and may be hooked up to an inhalation anesthesia. Most doctors will not intubate for a cat neuter since it can be performed so quickly. All female dogs and cats, as well as male dogs, are intubated.

The technician will then open the surgery pack, ensuring it remains sterile. The veterinarian will then perform the surgery while the technician monitors the pets vital signs. Once finished, another technician will move the pet to his recovery cage and monitor him until he wakes up. The process is repeated over and over. It is not unusual to perform 30-40 of these procedures in a day.

Contrast that cat neuter approach to the one performed for $199. Blood is taken for in-house, pre-surgical lab work. The results are available in about 25 minutes. The veterinarian checks the lab work, and declares the pet healthy for surgery. Any anomalies found are noted. The pet is weighed, and the technician calculates the amount of sedative to be used and the amount of of emergency medication needed should that pet have problems under sedation. Next, an IV catheter is placed in the foreleg. The catheter not only provides a ready vein for sedation, it is also available for any emergency that may occur during surgery. The vet reviews all calculations, and a pre-sedative is administered. Once the pet is groggy, he is then given the short-acting IV anesthesia, Propofol ® and intubated. The pet is moved to the surgical table, hooked up to an inhalant anesthesia to maintain complete sedation. The surgical site is prepared using sterile procedures, and the instrument pack opened. Using a pulse oximeter, blood pressure cuff, and ECG machine, the technician monitors the vital signs and records them on the pet's chart. Once the surgery is complete, the pet is monitored in his recovery cage, and the intubation tube removed. This surgical approach may take an hour or longer, although the actual surgical time may last five to ten minutes.

While the second option may be consider "best practices", it is out of reach for many pet parents. Although ideal, many of the procedures performed in this option are excessive, particularly for a cat neuter. Not only does the cat have to endure the pain of an IV catheter, he must remain under anesthesia longer, putting him at risk.

In a time when 2.7 million pets a year die because their parents were not spayed/neutered it seems imperative to offer a less expensive option. That is what a spay and neuter clinic does.

Some pet parents may prefer the comfort of knowing an IV is going into their pet for a surgery that takes five minutes. For them, that option is available.

So examine your options when you decide to spay or neuter. Call your local humane society which can point you in the right direction. In our area, as I write this, our local clinic, **The Margaret B. Mitchell Spay and Neuter Clinic,** in Bristol, Virginia alters all dogs for $60, female cats for $55, and male cats for only $40. http://www.mbmspayneuterclinic.org/

Many clinics may offer financial assistance and may also provide vaccines, heartworm tests, or feline leukemia tests at time of surgery.

Extending the Life of your Pet and Wallet

Research from the University of Georgia which examined 40,139 death records from the Veterinary Medical Database from 1984–2004 found that **unsterilized dogs lived only an average of 7.9 years vs. 9.4 years for sterilized dogs.**

http://journals.plos.org/plosone/article?id=10.1371/journal.pone.0061082

So in addition to saving money, by spaying or neutering, you are saving lives and extending life as well.

The chance of many potential health problems are eliminated by spaying and neutering.

For the females, the risk of uterine and ovarian cancer, as well as pyometra is eliminated. If spayed before the first heat cycle, her chances of breast cancer are drastically reduced. Spaying also eliminates the chances of venereal tumors.

Compare that to the cost of the surgeries, medications, and chemotherapy needed to treat those conditions and you are talking about thousands of dollars. Not to mention that by spaying her, her lifespan and quality of life is much improved.

At least eight diseases or conditions are either eliminated or the chances greatly reduced by neutering your male dog. Those include testicular cancer and torsion (twisting of the testicles), rectal cancer, prostate abscess, cancer, and/or enlargement, hernias, benign perineal tumors, orchitis (infection of the testicles, and venereal tumors (dogs can and do have venereal diseases).

Imagine the money needed to treat any one of those diseases.
This doesn't even include the practical side of the issue. Intact dogs and cats have as strong of a desire to mate as the average human male teenager. (Scary, I know). The male of the species (canine and feline) can detect a female in heat from over a mile away. That's why **80% of the pets hit by car are intact (unneutered) males.** They have one thing on their mind and watching for traffic is not it.

The females often try to escape and in the case of the female cat, drive the pet parent insane. Years ago, the spay surgery for my (then) kitten, Chloe, had to be delayed for a more pressing medical issue. At the time, I had lots of small little rescues including a ferret and even a fighting rooster whom I had rescued from an abusive situation. Chloe begged everyone, including Chatty, the rooster, to do something. Anything! Nature was telling her she needed to breed! She didn't care with whom or what! Needless to say, the moment the doctor said she was ready for her spay surgery, I had her at the clinic to the relief of the animals at home.

Never underestimate your pet's need to breed. Instinct makes them driven to procreate. They will jump fences or dig under them. They will dart out the door when you least expect it. However, when overpopulation is a serious problem, that drive doesn't conveniently go away. The drive simply results in more animals than the human population can sustain. Thus we have millions of homeless pets euthanized.

Female dogs, unlike cats, bleed during their heat cycle. That means blood on the carpet, the furniture, the bed, or on you. Dealing with her mood swings can be unpleasant and can lead to aggressive behavior.

Unaltered males tend to fight more and urine mark more often. They pee on everything, including your furniture. The cost of having your own dog or cat repaired after a fight is one thing. Having an aggressive pet may mean paying to have the neighbor's pet (or child) medically treated. Unaltered male cats tend to pick up deadly diseases and get bite abscesses more often.

Contrary to popular belief, an unneutered male dog is NOT a better protection dog than a neutered dog. A neutered dog is more focused on the task at hand.

For many men, the idea of neutering hits too close to home. They feel as if they are doing a disservice to their dog or cat. In fact, the opposite is true. The pet dad is helping his animal companion live a longer, happier life.

I ask pet parents who do not wish to neuter, one thing. "If you could give your dog or cat many more years with you, would you do it?" The answer is inevitably "yes".

Pet dads can't let their egos get in the way of doing what is right for the pet. The dog or cat will not miss out on "the joy of sex". He will, however, have a greater chance of missing out on the joy of being hit by a car. Isn't that more important?

Spaying and Neutering Non-Traditional Pets

Not everyone thinks about spaying and neutering small, non-traditional pets such as bunnies or guinea pigs. Non-traditional pets are pets other than dogs or cats. Many pet parents do not realize the health benefits of spaying and neutering, and it can be difficult to find a veterinarian who is comfortable with the procedure.

The advantages of spaying or neutering are many. Just like with dogs and cats, **altered bunnies and guinea pigs live longer.** The risk of ovarian, uterine, mammary, and (in males) testicular cancers are eliminated. Both species prefer to be with others of their kind and in not spaying and neutering, the pet parent runs the risk of fighting among each other leading to injuries.

As pets, both species are more tame-able and loving once altered. They are easier to train and enjoy as a pet. Rabbits can be trained to a litter box.

Both species can breed, well, like rabbits. Guinea pigs can go into heat by two months old and continue to do so every two to three weeks until bred. Rabbits do not have a heat cycle, so they can reproduce at any time.

If you do chose to spay or neuter your guinea pig or rabbit, be sure your veterinarian has adequate experience and is experienced in surgery on these non-traditional pets.

The Early Spay/ Neuter Controversy

A topic of late is the controversy surrounding early spay and neuter. A spay or neuter is considered early by most if done before six months of age. The goal has been to alter the pet before sexual reproduction is possible.

The reason for this is simple...to lower the number of unwanted pets. It is common, for instance, to spay or neuter a pet prior to allowing him or her to be adopted from an animal shelter or rescue. Sometimes this is done as young as twelve weeks old.

While there are some responsible people who will spay or neuter their puppy or kitten at a later date, experience has shown rescuers that too many will not have their pet altered and will, in fact, add to the problem of overpopulation.

 Dr. Brenda Griffin, an adjunct associate professor of shelter medicine at the University of Florida, believes that this early spay/neuter policy has made a huge difference in population control. Griffin said that *"in the 1980s, an estimated 17 million cats and dogs were killed annually in shelters in the United States. Now, between 4 million and 6 million enter shelters*

annually, and of these, approximately 3 million are euthanized."
http://news.vin.com/VINNews.aspx?articleId=27205

Haseleah and I spent hours reading and discussing every study we could find that pertained to any negative health risks for spayed and neutered pets.

We looked for a few things in the studies: the sponsor of the study, the size of the study group, length of time of the study, who was reporting the study (if the study itself was not available), and if all other factors were ruled out before the conclusion was drawn. We avoided studies sponsored by anyone who would benefit from the results of the study. This included breeding groups and a nationwide pet hospital network. We began our search on the website "VIN: Veterinary Information Network."

In general, the longer the study and the more subjects involved, the more credible and accurate the results. While this does not completely dismiss smaller studies, it is something to keep in mind.

An important thing to remember is that a correlation is not a causation. While "A" is related to "B", "A" does not always cause "B". The most vivid example given to me in one particular college course was the correlation between ice cream consumed in the United States and the incidences of rape. As the rate of ice cream consumption increased, so did rape. There was a solid correlation between ice cream and rape, but did eating ice cream cause rape? Obviously not. However, there is one thing both ice cream and rape have in common. Warm weather. More people eat ice cream in warm weather and people are more likely to be outdoors later at night when most rape occurs. This is a vivid example of the correlation-causation conundrum that one must avoid when reading studies or considering statistics.

A factor that we found particularly disconcerting was the presentation of the results by certain websites. "Spaying: The One Procedure That Could Reduce Your Pet's Lifespan by Over 30%" was one of the most irresponsible article titles we came across. It would be easy for a person to read the title and immediately assume that spaying would be an early death sentence for their pet without reading the actual study.

The following were three major studies that we found.

- The University of Georgia study with more than 40,000 subjects in the study over a 20 year period. http://journals.plos.org/plosone/article?id=10.1371/journal.pone.0061082

- The UC Davis study with 759 Golden Retriever subjects over an unknown period http://www.vin.com/apputil/image/handler.ashx?docid=5800949

- The Rottweiler Study with 186 subjects over an unknown period http://www.vin.com/apputil/image/handler.ashx?docid=5808186

As already reported, research from the University of Georgia which examined 40,139 death records from the Veterinary Medical Database from 1984–2004 found that unsterilized (not spayed/neutered) dogs lived only an average of 7.9 years vs. 9.4 years for sterilized dogs. The information for this study was collected over a twenty year period and included the largest number of subjects. The study included sampling of many breeds (including mixed breeds), from many different regions of the United States, living with families of various socioeconomic statuses.

One of the studies that proposed the risk of a early neuter (in this case "early" being before one year of age), was conducted at UC Davis College of Veterinary Medicine. The researchers, studying golden retrievers only, found a greater occurrence of hip dysplasia, cranial cruciate ligament tears and two types of cancer in sterilized golden retrievers compared with their intact counterparts. The research found the health risks generally were greater for dogs that were younger than one year when sterilized.

Unlike the University of Georgia study which had a sample size of more than 40,000 pets, the UC Davis study had only 759 golden retrievers. In addition, the researchers did not consider other factors such as poor breeding (genetics), environments factors, or even over vaccination.

Another study that did seem to consider more factors was conducted in 2009 by The Center of Exceptional Longevity. The study (which actually sought to apply the study results to human females) found that *"intact female Rottweilers were more likely to achieve...exceptional longevity"* than their male counterparts — just as women have a greater chance of living to age 100 than men. But Rottweilers whose ovaries were removed before age 4 lost that female survival advantage. *"Though the biological mechanism remains unknown, this study indicated a significant relationship between retaining ovaries and longer life spans."*

The results of the last two studies do need to be taken into consideration. Since studies conducted on only two breeds, I believe more studies need to be conducted, but the information not ignored.

However we have to ask ourselves what we know for sure. Regarding females, we know that spaying completely eliminates the risk of uterine, ovarian cancer, and pyometra. We also know that the chances of venereal tumors are reduced. If spayed before her first heat cycle, her chance of breast cancer is significantly reduced. In males, we know of at least eight diseases or conditions are either eliminated or the chances greatly reduced by neutering. Those conditions include testicular cancer and torsion (twisting of the testicles), rectal cancer, prostate abscess, cancer, and/or enlargement, hernias, benign perineal tumors, orchitis, and venereal tumors.

We also know that the female that isn't spayed can, with the help of an unneutered male, produce two litters of 6-10 puppies per year. That female and her offspring can produce 67,000 puppies in 6 years. One unspayed female cat and one unneutered male cat and their offspring can produce 420,000 kittens in 7 years. An estimated 80 percent of those offspring will be euthanized in animal shelters.

Considering the overpopulation problem in the United States and the high euthanasia rates, I believe a strong emphasis needs to remain on spaying and neutering because it is a lifesaver. You cannot work in an animal shelter and not see the importance of spay/neuter programs. There are simply too many irresponsible people who, either intentionally or unintentionally, contribute to the problem. My concern is that these studies will only add to the excuses not to spay or neuter.

Having access to this information is important for responsible pet parents to make the best decision for their pets.

5

The Realities and Solutions of Re-homing Pets

The Difficulty of Successfully Re-homing a Pet

So you've bred your pet intentionally or by accident. Maybe you have decided you'd let her have just one litter, then get her spayed. Doing so would allow your children to see the "miracle of life" and your pet is the "cutest pet ever." The world would certainly miss out if it didn't have another like her.

Your options are to try to sell the puppies, kittens, or bunnies on nationwide and local classifieds, sell them at the flea market, or, (one of the new popular options) offer them on Facebook.

You just know you will get him/her a good home. You know lots of pet lovers.

Statistics, however, offer a sober perspective to this attitude. **The percentage of people who acquire animals that end up giving them away, abandoning them, or taking them to the shelter is 70%.**

Those friends who will make a great pet parent, will, in the future, probably face the decision of giving up the pet. Whether they are moving, having a baby, or a family member is allergic, **there is only a 30% chance that your puppy, kitten, or other pet will remain in that home.**

If you are unaware, there is a nation wide outcry to stop allowing pets to be made available in online classifieds. This is with good reason. Many pets adopted or sold online end up as bait dogs for training other dogs to fight. Guinea pigs and kittens may become snake supper. Bunnies may become a human dinner. Dogs and cats may be sold for scientific experimentation. We have even seen several instances of individual claiming the many "free" pets online and using them for sick abusive playthings.

In other instances, which occur with frequency in my area, people posing as wonderful "forever homes" adopt the free or low cost pet and sell him or her to the top bidder for a profit.

This is nothing new. When I was young, a local "animal lover" was caught up in a scandal of acquiring animals to sell for experimentation. Only then the acquiring was done by stealing family pets and grabbing every stray pet he could find. Now, thanks to "free to good home" ads, sadly, this process is much easier.

Charging a re-homing fee helps to ward off unscrupulous individuals, but **the chances of your pet finding a loving forever home remains the same. Only 30%.**

http://www.oxfordpets.com/index.php?option=com_content&view=article&id=61

Purebred dogs are not immune. According to the same source listed above and statistics from across the country **25-30% of pets surrendered to shelters are purebreds.**

This information offers a strong reality check. **If you love animals, spay and neuter.**

Reasons Given for Re-homing and Possible Prevention Methods

One of the purposes of this book is to stop the inflow of surrendered family pets to animal shelters because of financial concerns. However, there are a lot of reasons given for surrendering, and several options to prevent it.

Moving

"I have to move and can't take my dog/cat/iguana with me"

This is a sentence uttered quite often at local shelters. Almost everyone has been hit hard by the economy over the last few years. Many are losing their homes or apartments as they lose their jobs. It's a fact of life.

At the same time, sometimes there are ways to avoid losing the pet when moving, and most certainly, a better way to transition the pet if surrender is necessary.

Before moving, check http://www.petfinder.com/dogs/living-with-your-dog/pet-friendly-apartments-online/ to help you locate pet friendly apartments. It would also behoove your local shelter and humane society to keep a list of local apartments that rent to pet owners.

The US government, realizing that many people would rather be living in substandard conditions rather than give up their pets, passed a law that many people are unaware of:

"Tenants in federally assisted housing for the elderly or handicapped are allowed by law to own pets. (Housing and Urban-Rural Recovery Act of 1983, 12 U.S.C. section 1701r-1.) This rule applies even if the federal government does not own the rental housing—it's enough that a federal agency (the U.S. Department of Housing and Urban Development, for example) subsidizes it. Owners and managers may place reasonable regulations on pets, after consulting with tenants. Contact a local HUD office or your county Housing Authority to find out if a particular rental is covered."

This also applies to disabled individuals, particularly if the pet is an emotional support pet as designated by your doctor. For more information about this law, please reference this site: http://www.nolo.com/legal-encyclopedia/free-books/dog-book/chapter4-3.html

Next, talk to the landlord of the potential place you will be renting and ask for specifics about the "no pet" rule. You may find that he/she is referring to dogs/cats only, and your iguana or bearded dragon is no problem. Also inquire as to whether a little extra rent per month or labor to improve the home or apartment would persuade the landlord to reconsider. In one house I rented many years ago, I agreed that in exchange for allowing pets, I would improve the property over time. I painted the entire house, inside and out which helped the landlord rent the home for more money when it was time for me to move out. I made sure no damage was caused by my pets, and if it was, I repaired it at my cost. If I ever needed a good reference for further renting, I proved my worth as a tenant and was more likely to be trusted with pets down the road.

If your situation is temporary, perhaps a friend would be willing to care of your pet for a few months.

Once you have done everything you could, what is the best way to go about finding a new home?

If you know the move is coming in a month or two, contact a local rescue group and see if they would be willing to do a **courtesy listing** for you on www.Petfinder.com .

Having your pet adopted out through a rescue organization should ensure that the applicant has been carefully considered by the rescue and his or her references checked. Instead of dumping your pet at the rescue, "foster" your pet at your home until a good match is found.

If your dog is a particular breed, look for **breed rescues**. Some rescues specialize in German Shepherds for instance, and may even consider a mix breed that is "close enough". Be willing to look not only in your immediate area, but in neighboring states. Thanks to the power of the internet and social networking sites, there is a great network of animal rescuers who will drive and even fly a pet to another rescue to save his/her life. Be willing to be the driver, or help pay for gas. A local humane society in Gate City, VA, for instance, recently arranged transport of nearly a dozen chihuahuas to a huge and fabulous rescue called Popcorn Park in New Jersey. The power of Facebook networking and the willingness to ask makes a world of difference.

It is natural to want to look for "no kill" rescues. However, not all "no kill" rescues are alike, so research the rescue first. Keep in mind, if an animal can't find a home in a no kill facility, that sometimes means a lifetime in a cage. Not all "no kill" shelters have a good group of volunteers willing to foster. Utilize the internet to research the rescue, and ask fellow animal lovers or humane society volunteers what they have heard about the rescue.

"Kill shelters" are often given a bad reputation. The term itself assumes that the shelter employees and volunteers are evil entities. In fact, they are usually the good guys who are willing to work in an environment where they know they will love an animal, only to have to euthanize her. I've noticed over the years having volunteered and worked in "kill shelters" that the same people who condemn the shelter are the same ones who allow their pets to breed or who say they love animals "too much" to work in a place "like that". They refuse to volunteer at weekend adoption events or even buy kitty litter for the shelter. One thing I can tell you, although no two shelters are the same, most have good people who love animals enough to allow themselves to hurt when they can't save them all.

With that said, save a "kill" shelter for last. Not only for your pet, but for the people who work there. If you do take your pet there, offer something that will be a great incentive for adoption. For instance, if he/she is not already altered, offer to pay for the spay or neuter. Get the pet fully vaccinated at least two weeks before entering the shelter. The vaccines will protect the pet and also give her an extra boost for adoption. Write down everything you know about him. Is he good with kids? Does he get along with other animals? Is she house broken? Did she go to obedience school? Does he love to cuddle? Is he a great lap dog? Is she particularly gentle? Consider it like writing a resume for a job, but never lie. If your dog hates kids, make sure the rescue knows that. If he is owner protective, or food aggressive, be honest about it. It may not disqualify him for adoption, but it will help the shelter place him in a situation to suit his needs.

We're Having a Baby

The young couple desperately in love adopt a pet, not even considering that they will probably have a baby during the lifetime of that pet. The baby is born, replaces the dog or cat and no one understands why the pet gets upset. Then the pet is considered "too dangerous" to be around the child and off to the shelter he goes.

It is tempting when you start a new relationship and a new family to want a pet. However, consider the fact that dogs, cats, and other common pets can live twenty years. Instead, **consider getting a pet with a shorter lifespan.** Buy an aquarium and stock it with colorful fish. Get a rat or a guinea pig both who make excellent pets. Both of these pets can be held and cuddled when raised from young ones, yet their life expectancy is 4-6 years.

Canine pet parents can prepare for the inevitable introduction to the new baby, by participating in a **dog training course**. The training course gives the dog the discipline needed to learn to sit and stay while the parents take care of baby needs. It will also build a good relationship between the pet parent and dog that will give the confidence needed to know that she will obey. A well behaved pet can be involved in activities with the baby. For instance, baby can ride in the stroller while the dog gets some great exercise walking on a local path.

Feline pet parents are some times convinced by their doctor of the dangers of having a cat living in the same home as the infant. While it is possible for the pregnant mother to contract **toxoplasmosis**, a disease that can be fatal to the unborn child, common sense precautions can be implemented to avoid potential problems. Assign someone besides the potential mother to clean the litter box. If that is not possible, the expectant mother can wear gloves and a mask when cleaning the litter box. This is an inexpensive solution that keeps mom and baby safe, and the cat in the home.

An additional concern often cited is the potential that the cat will smother the baby. This concern also has a simple solution: don't leave the cat and infant alone. To a cat, a person, baby or adult, is a heating pad. The cat is not an evil creature with a diabolical plan to kill the baby. He just wants to be warm and cozy. Consider buying the cat a heating pad and sprinkle a little catnip on it.

Zoonoses are diseases that can be passed from animal to human or human to animal, and many pet parents worry about these diseases. To minimize or eliminate this worry, all pets should be well vaccinated and dewormed. Pet parents should practice good sanitation, including washing hands after cleaning up after the pet or infant. The litter box should be placed out of the reach of the growing child.

While having a new baby in the house can be very overwhelming, we, as pet parents, should take our commitment to our pets seriously. If, however, the solution to the situation is putting an inside pet outside with little family interaction, then, yes, find a another home for him or her. There is nothing sadder than a single pet once part of the family, abandoned outside where he can only watch life go by. A multiple pet home, such as one with two large dogs, can at least entertain one another outside.

Pet Training Issues

Not all pets are easy to train. Some are difficult to potty train, while others are so full of energy, getting her to sit still is a challenge. Other pets may chew up new shoes, rip up the sofa, or potty on the bed. Sadly, this is another reason pets are surrendered to shelters. The pet parent simply didn't know how to properly train their pet.

Paying for training may seem difficult, but it should be seriously considered and included in the pet care budget. Nationwide pet store offer training for around $100 for a 6 week course. Training can make dramatic changes in your dog.

Larry, a weimaraner who belonged to a childhood friend of mine, came into the vet hospital where I was employed. Larry was out of control. I felt like he would rip my arm off because he pulled on the leash so hard. My friend Renea asked what she could do.

I recommended that he first be neutered and then participate in a puppy training course.

Photo courtesy Renea Stoots Neeley

Renea convinced her husband to do both, and Larry is a well behaved dog now. Larry was a handful during the first few training sessions, but he graduated with flying colors.

If you cannot afford a training course, the ASPCA website is full of free information on training. They even have a **"Virtual Pet Behaviorist"**. http://www.aspca.org/Pet-care/virtual-pet-behaviorist

Additional Reasons Given for Surrendering Pets

I recently asked some of my rescue friends to list reasons pet parents have given for surrendering a pet. Some of those are as follows with their reaction or solution included:

- **The pet is too old:** *"A senior purebred German Shepard was turned into [our] shelter this past week and the director said 'you know I am not going to be able to adopt this dog out' and they said that was fine. They didn't want to take the responsibility for making that decision [to euthanize] so they passed it on to someone else. It's not fair."* -Angie E

- **The pet is too big or not as expected:** I had an experience with this one. The woman was giving up a Great Dane because he was too large. A Great Dane!! She wanted to trade him for a chihuahua. The moral of this story: Research your breed and don't make snap decisions because the puppy is cute.

- **Pet parent has passed away:** *"Plan ahead in case something happens to you. Don't assume your family will take care of your pets after you're gone. Have a plan of action."* -Angie E

- **Someone in family is allergic to pet:** *"Regular grooming of the dog can help (not by you but by someone else). Always brush the pet outside to keep the dander to a minimum. Take allergy medicine. If your child is allergic, sometimes being around pets can actually help them develop an immunity to it. The first couple months could be horrible but it does generally get better. Keep the pets out of the bedrooms. Use air purifiers. Vacuum often. It doesn't work for everyone but try it before getting rid of a pet. Keep in mind, no matter what claims are made, there are no dog or cat breeds that are 100 percent guaranteed never to trigger an allergy. You have to decide before adopting, if someone in my family is allergic, am I willing to do what it takes to keep the pet? If the answer is no, consider getting a fish tank instead. "* -Jessica C.

Animal shelter director, Jessica C. put it very well when she said, **"In my experience, most reasons given can be solved with time, patience and research. Unfortunately there seems to be a trend to not even try sometimes."**

Tips for a Safer Re-homing

If, after exploring all options, the pet parent has no choice but to re-home the family pet, utilize some of the methods used by animal rescue groups to find the best home possible.

- **NEVER adopt on a first come-first serve basis**. Advertisements including "must go today" can easily attract those with ill intentions. This may work for yard sale items, but not living and breathing creatures.

- **NEVER offer the pets for free.** "Free to good home" ads also attract poor quality homes. These ads can result to the pet being used as bait to train fighting dogs, resold to the highest bidder, or turned into a free lunch for reptiles. The picture to the right was found on a social media "yard sale" page. Its difficult to look at, but makes the point very real. Insist on a re-homing fee.

- **NEVER guilt someone into adopting.** Most of the time, these placements never work out.

- **Have the potential adopter fill out an application** for the pet prior to the meeting, that also serves as a contract. Include in the contract that the pet will not be sold for profit, baiting, or experimentation. Also include that you, the former pet parent, will be contacted if the pet is no longer wanted. Include questions that ascertain the home environment. Will he be an inside or outdoor pet? Does the adopter have a fenced in yard, or will the pet be kept on a chain or in a kennel? Are there any other pets in the house? How long has the other pets lived with the family? Are there children in the family?

- **Get vital information** including name, address, phone, and drivers license number. Refusing to give this information can be one indication that the adopter may not have the best of intentions.

- **Ask for references.** Vet references are preferred. Inquiring on the care of other pets can help the pet parent determine if the potential home is a responsible one. Ask if the pets are up to date on vaccines and if she or he is neutered and spayed. If the information indicates that the family has a history of giving away their pets, or breeding. Pet parents should also ask the potential adopter for the name of their landlord and make sure they are allowed pets. Although some good people sneak animals into homes or apartments, if the landlord finds out, the pet will have to be re-homed again.

- **Insist on a home visit:** It is important to see the environment in which your beloved pet will live. How are the other pets treated? How clean is the home? How do the children and family members interact with your pet? Was the adopter honest in the application? Are the other pets kept outdoors on chains when the adopter indicated otherwise? Pet parents that find that they are uncomfortable with the situation, should not leave their pet behind.

- **Give an honest impression of your pet.** If the pet is not potty trained for instance, tell the potential pet parents. One of the main reasons pets are surrendered to shelters is the lack of potty training. Never adopt a pet who does not get alone well with other pets or children into a home that has either. Your pet will be the first out the door when it doesn't go well.

- **Offer the re-homing fee back once the pet is spayed or neutered.** Pet parents looking to re-home unaltered pets can give the incentive of returning the re-homing fee once proof of spay or neuter is provided. Often, those who refuse to spay or neuter are looking for a breeding dog There are often local groups or clinics that will spay, neuter, vaccinate, and more at a reduced price. The pet parent can also have the pet spayed or neutered before offering the pet for adoption as good rescue groups do.

- **Consider keeping the microchip information in your name.** If the pet is micro-chipped, some recommend keeping the information in your name so you are contacted if the pet is surrendered to the shelter or if he/she runs away from a bad situation.

- **Vaccinate prior to surrender.** Pets, particularly young pets, going to the shelter or rescue group should be vaccinated 1-2 weeks before being surrendered. Unvaccinated pets have a greater chance of getting sick in a crowded environment, and less chance of being adopted.

Things to Consider Before Getting a Pet

While there are important steps to take when surrendering a pet, there are also vital considerations when adopting a pet. The cost, not only of adopting a pet, but of continuous care of the pet should be added to the family budget. Potential pet parents should consider how much time and talent they have to spend training the pet to exhibit good behavior as well as potty training. The family should discuss the type of pet they wish to adopt. Would a playful, active dog fit into the family lifestyle, or would a quiet, independent cat be more comfortable in your family? Is the home large enough to accommodate a large breed dog or would it be better to consider a smaller breed?

These are just some of the common sense questions one should ask. There are, however a few things rarely discussed when determining what kind of pet to adopt.

- **Natural weaning:** The transition from the mother's milk to solid food begins around four weeks of age and is usually complete by six weeks. This process is essential to providing proper immunity to the puppy or kitten. Pets weaned too early do not have the proper innate immunity that protects them during the first eight weeks of life. At six weeks old, the puppy or kitten should begin vaccinations to ensure a good immune transition from mother's innate immunity to the acquired immunity provided by the vaccination. Adopting a pet that has not been properly weaned, increases the risk that you may be buying a pet that will become very ill. If offered a puppy or kitten that requires bottle-feeding, consider that a feeding every 2-4 hours is required, even at night. These pets should be isolated from other pets until immunity is acquired.

- **Potty Training:** Probably one of the top reasons for giving up a pet is the owner's inability to potty train (not the pet's inability to be trained). Never expect a puppy or adult dog to come into your home fully potty trained. At the very least, the pet may mark the territory to make it a more familiar environment. Until potty training is complete, the pet should be limited to the room where he can be monitored. The best method for puppy training is the crate method. For instructions on crate training, see Chapter 24.

- **No-shed guarantee**: No matter what any breeder says, there is no guarantee that a certain breed of dog or cat will not shed. Shedding is a natural process. If the shedding issue is so vital that the dog or cat will be given away if he or she sheds, consider adopting another pet, such as a reptile, lizard, or tank full of beautiful fish.

- **Tiny breeds destined for struggle:** Tiny tea cup puppies are adorable, but nature never meant for dogs to be so small. This has lead to serious health concerns. Tea cup breeds such as the Yorkie, Maltese and Chihuahua, are very popular. If they make it through weaning, they are likely to be faced with many challenges. An open fontanel, often called a soft spot, is a condition in which the plates of the skull do not close properly to protect the brain. It is an area where brain damage can easy occur. Open fontanels can also be accompanied by hydrocephalus. Excess fluid surrounding the brain can retard development of brain tissue. Tea cup puppies must eat several small meals a day to avoid hypoglycemia, or low blood sugar. Tea cup puppies should not be left alone for long periods for this very reason. Hypoglycemia, if not treated quickly can lead to coma and death. Breeders will instruct pet parents to keep honey, syrup, or some other form of glucose (sugar) ready for this purpose.

- **The heavy price of being adorable:** One of the most widely recognized and loved dogs is the English Bulldog. With the big body, no neck, and a pushed-in face only a mother could love, they are one of the most expensive dogs to own. Not only do they usually cost in the thousands to buy, they are riddled with health problems. In fact, if you look at the makeup of the dog, they were bred to have health problems. They are very heat intolerant, have many skin issues and ear problems, and find it very difficult to breed. Potential pet parents must be prepared for large vet bills throughout the life of the pet. Many English bulldogs and similar breeds may need to have one or more surgeries to make it easier to breathe. They are also prone to yeast infections in the folds of the skin around the tail, nostrils, and even in the ears.

- **Puppy Mills:** By now, most people are aware that most dogs sold in pet stores are from puppy mills. Puppy mills are horrid places where the breeding pets spend most of their lives in small, filthy cages. Rather than being treated like a loving pet, the dogs are treated like a breeding machine. Raids on puppy mills produce terrible images of neglect, feces covered cages, and worse. Yet by the time the puppies get to the store to sell, they have been cleaned up and made to look beautiful. Often they have underlying diseases. While people purchase the puppies, the parents are left behind in a life of misery. Puppy mills are now finding that pet stores will not buy their pets anymore, so they are resorting to the classifieds. A clue you are dealing with a puppy mill is that they advertise several different breeds for sale. **Just because a dog comes with AKC (American Kennel Club) papers or a pedigree, this does NOT mean the puppy is healthy, comes from well cared parents, or a responsible breeder.** The AKC will register any puppy coming from a registered litter and whose parents and grandparents have been registered. The puppy (or his parents) do not have to meet any qualification of health or temperament. AKC does not require the breeders to treat the breeding dogs or cats with care. If a visit to a breeder does not include access to the home and kennel areas and meeting the parents of the puppy or kitten, then, most likely, it is not a good and healthy situation from which to adopt to a pet.

- **Backyard Breeders:** A backyard breeder is described as someone with all or some of the following characteristics. (1) Excessive breeding of a female to the detriment of her health. (2) Poor veterinary care. (3) Tail docking at home instead of under veterinary care. (4) Lack of or improper vaccination and deworming schedule for the pets. (5) Selling the pet before proper weaning. (6) Selling the pets on a first come, first serve basis, instead of concern for the pet's future. (7) Lack of knowledge of selective breeding goals. (8) Breeding for fighting, or as bait animals. (9) Allowing breeding without the concern of finding good quality homes. (10) The breeders inability to spell the name of the breed they are selling. ("chiwawa" instead of chihuahua).

- **Designer Dogs:** A recent fad in puppy breeding is "designer dogs". Goldendoodles, Pekapoos, and Morkies are just a few examples. Designer dogs are mixed breed dogs intentionally crossbred, that people pay hundreds of dollars for. No matter how you phrase it, mix a chihuahua with a dachshund and you get a mixed breed dog, sometimes called a mongrel, or mutt. The creator of the first "designer dog", the labradoodle, regrets his part in the creation of designer breeds. Wally Conron, former breeding manager for the Royal Guide Dog Association of Australia said, " *"I opened a Pandora's box, that's what I did. I released a Frankenstein. So many people are just breeding for the money. So many of these dogs have physical problems, and a lot of them are just crazy......Today I am internationally credited as the first person to breed the Labradoodle. People ask me 'Aren't you proud of yourself?' I tell them 'No! Not in the slightest.' I've done so much harm to pure breeding and made so many charlatans quite rich. I wonder, in my retirement, whether we bred a designer dog—or a disaster!"* https://www.psychologytoday.com/blog/canine-corner/201404/designer-dog-maker-regrets-his-creation . You know the best place to get a great "designer dog?". The animal shelter. There are millions of them just waiting for a good home.

With all this being said, there are good breeders out there. It is the pet parent's responsibility to do the research necessary to adopt a happy, healthy pet from an ethical source. This is a commitment of years, not months. Pets are not leased vehicles that you turn back in when you get tired of them. Be sure of your decision before purchasing or adopting a pet.

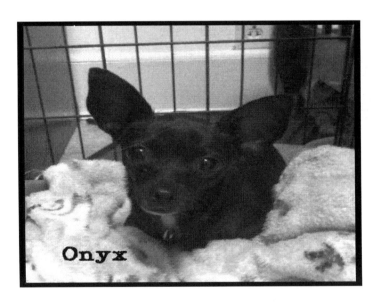

OUR EVOLVING ETHICS AND THE SCIENCE OF EMOTION, INTELLECT, AND AWARENESS OF ANIMALS

"The animals of the world exist for their own reasons. They were not made for humans any more than black people were made for white, or women created for men." ~Alice Walker

6

The Effects of Religion and Philosophy on the Treatment of Animals

Perhaps my biggest pet peeve is hearing the phrase "its *just* a dog," " its *just* a cat," "its *just* a (fill in the blank here)".

Since I was a child, when I saw an animal mistreated or even spoken poorly of, I always asked the question *"How would you feel if it was you?"* To me it was the natural question.

I was taught in the church to *"Do unto others as you have them do unto you,"* yet when I applied that concept, I found it came with an exception...it was conditional and selective. The concept only applied to humans (not non-human animals) and sometimes, humans were excluded because of their race, religion, gender, or sexual orientation.

I didn't buy that philosophy then, and I don't buy it now.

We have long tried to ignore that animals possess intelligence, sentience, and emotions because its easier on us to assume they don't. If we admitted it, we'd have to acknowledge the intense suffering animals have endured at the hand of man.

The denial that animals could feel and perceive emotions, and thus warrant concern, has been ingrained in Western thought for centuries. Aristotle, believed that animals could experience hunger, pain, and anger, but doubted that they could think rationally. Zeno, the founder of the Stoic school of philosophy in the 3rd century BC, completely discounted the idea that any non-human could feel. Early Christian church thinkers embraced Zeno's idea and took it a step further teaching that it was only humans who were created in the image of God and thus, possessed a soul. Both Christianity and Islam taught that humans must have dominion over animals, which allowed for great cruelty.

The 17th century philosopher Rene Descartes, proposed that we, as humans, have a duality. We have our physical body, which he called a "material body," and our mind and soul, he termed the "immaterial body." The immaterial body linked us to God, and since animals did not have souls, they were, by birth, lesser beings.

We even convinced ourselves that animals feel no pain. In the 17th and 18th centuries, animals were dissected alive to understand how the body works. Voltaire, upon witnessing this cried out,

"There are barbarians who seize this dog, who so greatly surpasses man in fidelity and friendship, and nail him down to a table and dissect him alive, to show you the Mesaraic veins! You discover in him all the same organs of feeling as in yourself. Answer me, Mechanist, has Nature arranged all the springs of feeling in this animal to the end that he might not feel? Has he nerves that he may be incapable of suffering? Do not suppose that impertinent contradiction in Nature."

The Slippery Slope: from Animal Cruelty to Human Cruelty

Once the lesser status of animals was firmly established, determining that a race of humans were "only" animals, gave permission to subject them to the cruelties endured by animals. Philosophies such as this proposed the idea that certain races were evolutionary inferior and did not warrant the same protections that the white, European man did.

While some used religious texts to support this view, others turned to science and polygenism, which held that human "races" were of different lineages and suggested a hierarchy outlined in the "Chain of Being" that positioned Africans between man and lower primates."
http://www.understandingrace.org/history/science/one_race.html

In his book **Eternal Treblinka: Our Treatment of Animals and the Holocaust,** Charles Patterson reminded us that by giving our enemies and even entire races the status of animals, we rationalized the mistreatment and killing.

During the Nazi regime Jews were commonly called "swine", "dogs", "vermin", "rats" and "parasites" in an effort to set the Jewish people below the Aryan race. Native Americans were described by colonists as 'wild animals' and "savages" that needed to be" civilized" and 'tamed like sheep'.

During wartime, the Japanese were called "yellow monkeys" or "mad dogs", while the Vietnamese were described as 'termites' that "infested the land".

Today, we know that most all serial killers were first, animal killers. This is why I find the term "its just an animal" dangerous. https://www.animallaw.info/article/link-cruelty-animals-and-violence-towards-people

It seems Theodor W. Adorno agreed with my premise when he said:

"Auschwitz begins wherever someone looks at a slaughterhouse and thinks: they're only animals."

We are More Alike Than Different

Some years later, as we start the very long climb out of the pits of deep racism, science is revealing that we were wrong from the beginning.
Not only has science shown through DNA that all humans share a singular lineage, we find that animals are more alike us than different.

Humans, who all share the same genes, (though in a different sequence to make us all unique) also share 98 percent of our DNA with chimpanzees. According to Ewen F. Kirkness of the Institute for Genomic Research in Rockville, MD, of the 24,000 identified human genes, at least 18,000 are shared with the dog. In other words, dog and man share 75% of their DNA.
http://www.cabi.org/agbiotechnet/news/3177

Science has also shown that we are created from the same basic elements including (but not limited to) oxygen, carbon, hydrogen, nitrogen, calcium, and phosphorus. In fact, every living thing around us is carbon based. Carl Sagan, on his show "Cosmos" put it best when he said:

"The nitrogen in our DNA, the calcium in our teeth, the iron in our blood, the carbon in our apple pies were made in the interiors of collapsing stars. We are made of star stuff."

We are more alike than different.

This is important because our history has shown that the more we distance ourselves from other beings, determines how we treat them. The more alike we are, the less likely we are to inflict harm.

Those who believe that animals are more than instinctual robots are often accused by scientists and laymen, of anthropomorphism. **Anthropomorphism** is defined as the applying of human traits to something non-human.

Humans engage in anthropomorphism or personification in order to explain our world. We have given the perceived higher power many names, including God, Allah, Jesus and Zeus. The English language is so vast, yet we are still limited to using personification to describe everything from the animal world to God. When applied to God it is acceptable. When we apply it to animals, however, anthropomorphism becomes a dirty word.

We are at the genesis of research as to what animals think, feel, and experience, but even with what we know now, we can say now that animals are capable of independent thought, of emotional joy and sadness, and most certainly pain. Voltaire was right.

We have found that *"we share common neurochemicals (such as serotonin and testosterone) and brain structures (such as the hypothalamus) that are important in the expression and feeling of anger, aggression, and revenge,"* says professor emeritus of biology and ethologist, Marc Bekoff in his book **The Emotional Lives of Animals.** He goes on to say *"the latest science argues for the existence of love in many different species. The brain machinery for love- the neuroanatomy and neurochemistry that allow us to feel love-is similar or identical to that of numerous other animals."*

"[H]as Nature arranged all the springs of feeling in this animal to the end that he might not feel? "

Indeed.

Becoff is not alone in his discoveries. Gregory Berns, author of **How Dogs Love Us: A Neuroscientist and His Adopted Dog Decode the Canine Brain,** reported in his research that utilized MRI scans that found that dogs respond emotionally in very similar ways as humans.

Science has also proven that rodents and chickens display empathy. Science has proven that chickens and pigs, whom we raise in factory farms in a most inhumane way, are highly intelligent. Elephants can learn to paint and they mourn for their dead. Crows can understand that by putting pebbles in a glass of water, they can raise the level so they can get their treat floating on the top. Rats and dogs can laugh. Baboons show stress and release the hormone glucocorticoids, just like humans do.

http://www.psychologytoday.com/blog/animal-emotions/201103/empathic-chickens-and-cooperative-elephants-emotional-intelligence-expan

http://www.psychologytoday.com/blog/animal-emotions/201112/empathic-rats-and-ravishing-ravens

Dr. John Pilley, in his book **Chaser:Unlocking the Genius of a Dog Who Knows A Thousand Words**, describes his experience with training his dog to recognize the names of over one thousand stuffed animals in addition to other names. Chaser knows more words than any non-human animal.

Alex, an African gray parrot, was the subject of a thirty year study by animal psychologist, Irene Pepperberg. Dr. Pepperburg was able to show that instead of simply mimicking behavior, Alex was able to understand the meaning of words. Before his untimely death in 2007, Alex was said to possess the intelligence of a five year old human. Alex's story was chronicled by Dr. Pepperburg's book, **Alex & Me: How a Scientist and a Parrot Discovered a Hidden World of Animal Intelligence--and Formed a Deep Bond in the Process**

Dogs and cats can benefit from anti-depressants and anti-anxiety medications. Fluoxetine

(Prozac ® Reconcile ®) for example, can treat some forms of aggression, compulsive behaviors, and certain phobias. http://www.veterinarypracticenews.com/April-2013/Fluoxetine-Treats-A-Number-Of-Behavioral-Issues-In-Animals/

Abigail, our dog, has been treated effectively with fluoxetine for her obsessive-compulsive behaviors. If the chemistry of the brain of both human and animal can be similarly affected, doesn't that suggest that our body's chemistry is more alike than many care to admit?

Pain and Morality

According to research gathered by science writer and author, Virginia Morell in the book **Animal Wise: The Thoughts and Emotions of Our Fellow Creatures**, even fish, who have the smallest brains relative to body size of all vertebrates, are capable of intelligent behaviors that indicate more than simply a dependence on lower brain functions and instinct. They can learn and have long term memories. They can work cooperatively to hunt with other species as groupers do with moray eels. We have also seen reason to believe that fish can make friends. With no physical reward, fish and dogs have developed friendships. The only reward was companionship.

Animals can also feel pain. Nociceptors, the nerve cells that give us the ability to detect pain is found in birds, mammals, amphibians, and even invertebrates. The question is do they process the pain cognitively and suffer mentally?

By studying rainbow trout, Victoria Brauthwaite, a fish biologist at the Pennsylvania State University, found that, indeed, they do. By detecting the nociceptors on the face, lips, and head of the fish, she was able to follow the pain receptors from these areas to the brain, proving that **fish do have the necessary biology to detect and process pain.**

Neuroscientists gathered recently in Cambridge to discuss the research regarding this issue. They left with **"The Cambridge Declaration of Consciousness"** which states that:
"Convergent evidence indicates that non-human animals have the neuroanatomical, neurochemical, and neurophysiological substrates of conscious states along with the capacity to exhibit intentional behaviors. Consequently, the weight of evidence indicates that humans are not unique in possessing the neurological substrates that generate consciousness. Non-human animals, including all mammals and birds, and many other creatures, including octopuses, also possess these neurological substrates." http://www.psychologytoday.com/blog/animal-emotions/201208/scientists-finally-conclude-nonhuman-animals-are-conscious-beings

It seems, also, that the one thing that man has always claimed is exclusively his own – morality – is also found in non-human animals. While many believe morality to be dependent on religion, morality has also been shown to have an evolutionary advantage.

The community that cooperates, survives. The ones that fight among themselves do not. While an individual may succeed in being the best competitor, the most cunning, or the fastest, that individual can be rejected by the whole. Bullies win the match, but it is the one who can adapt and work well with others, that wins the game.

There is also evidence that altruistic behavior may be a natural tendency in both human and in animal. In studies conducted by Felix Warneken and Michael Tomasello, and reported in **The Emotional Lives of Animals** by Marc Bekoff, children as young as 18 months will help those in need. Young chimpanzees will do the same.

In the world of dogs, play between one another, is a large part of their social lives. Play only takes place if both parties participate, and it has strict standards. If those rules are broken, play immediately stops. Yet forgiveness, which in itself has a biological component, is possible, if the offending dog, bows (the signal for play) and returns to the standards of canine play. It is in play, that we learn social skills, the importance of fairness, and the necessity of boundaries, that are required as adults to survive in a social system.

We must realize that when judging the intellectual, moral, and emotional capacity of animals and humans, the words attributed to Albert Einstein, ring true. *"Everybody is a genius. But if you judge a fish by its ability to climb a tree, it will live its whole life believing that it is stupid."*

If we compare our ability to gather information by scent, to that of a dog, we will come up lacking. Compare our ability to fly without the ability of a machine to the skills of a bird, and we hang our heads in shame. Compare our compulsion for violence and cruelty, to that of most any non-human animal, and we are Satan himself.

The science of animal emotion and intelligence is still in its infancy. However, even if we never conducted experiments, studied animals in their natural habitat, and never proved that animals are sentient beings, we can never erase our responsibility in caring for them without cruelty.

As Jeremy Bentham said in his book, **The Principles of Morals and Legislation**:

"The question is not, "Can they reason?" nor, "Can they talk?" but "Can they suffer?"

We know without a doubt, that the answer to that is yes.

7

Modern Controversial Practices

As far as we have come as a society in our treatment of non-human animals, we still engage in some questionable practices. As science has ventured into the world of emotion, intellect, and awareness in animals, we must stop denying that our actions have little impact. In domesticating the dog, cat, and other species, we have taken over responsibility for their welfare. We need to take that responsibility very seriously.

Selective Breeding

In order to create some of the most appealing dog and cat breeds, humans have bred animals to have traits that are not in the best interest of the animal. To put it bluntly, we are breeding defects into the pet. As I mentioned in a previous chapter, tea cup and brachycephlic breeds are two examples.

" Teacup dog breeds often have malformed skulls with permanent soft-spots, and the structural deficits don't stop there. Many teacup dogs have poor bone density, making their bones brittle throughout life. Dogs who stay small may be eternally cute and precious, but at what cost to their quality of life?

Regardless of breed, teacup dogs suffer more frequently from major organ malfunctions. Enlarged hearts and heart murmurs occur more often in undersized dogs than in their normal-sized brethren. Liver shunts, conditions in which blood fails to reach or be cleaned in the liver, are more common in teacup dogs. Teacup dog breeds are at higher risk for developing, or being born with, serious problems in their digestive and respiratory systems. Because he is so small, a teacup puppy is also subjected to constant stress, which not only causes its own digestive issues, like diarrhea and constipation, but also puts added pressure on lungs and hearts, which may already be underdeveloped." http://www.dogster.com/lifestyle/teacup-dogs-small-dog-breeds-health-ethics-puppies-pictures-photos

Breeds that have been bred in teacup sizes include the Yorkie, Pomeranian, Maltese, Chihuahua, Pug, Boston Terrier, French Bulldog, and Papiillon. Now designer dogs have been added to the mix as breeds such as the Malti-poo (Maltese/Poodle cross) have been bred and sold for high profits.

Inbreeding is often required to produce a teacup breed. Other breeders will often breed the runts of the litters, hoping to produce similar offspring. Some dogs sold as teacups breeds can be the runt, premature puppy, or malnourished puppy pulled from the mother too soon. These unhealthy puppies can bring huge financial gain if marked as teacups, even if they are not.

Teacup dog breeds often die while giving birth, especially if bred to a larger dog. Many must have cesarean sections to deliver.

Brachycephalic breeds are those who, through selective breeding, have developed a flat and wide skull shape. Pugs, English Bulldogs, French Bulldogs, Pekingese, Boston Terriers, are some dog breeds with this conformation. Cat breeds include British Shorthair, Himalayan, Persian, and Scottish fold.

"This [Brachycephalic] skull shape gives these dogs the characteristic flattened face and short nose. Although this conformation makes them appear extremely cute; a feature which matches the big personalities of many of these breeds, it also causes some serious health issues. These include skin, eye and breathing problems and a poor ability to tolerate heat.

Health issues related to a dog being brachycephalic are becoming a more significant problem. Genetic pressure has been applied over many years to achieve more extreme versions of this appearance but this has been to the detriment of their general health. This means that we are seeing these breeds earlier in life with more severe manifestations of these health problems. If we compare the skull shape and appearance of the English Bulldog of today with a skull from the same breed from fifty years ago the change is quite dramatic. Fifty years ago the skull was much longer and there was an obvious nose. However, today in most of the breed the nasal bones are extremely short or almost absent altogether." http://www.theveterinaryexpert.com/nose-and-throat/what-is-a-brachycephalic-dog/

Many breeds have been so unnaturally altered, that they cannot breed without assistance. Males are given assisted masturbation by the breeder or veterinarian and the semen collected. The semen is then transferred to the female by artificial insemination. Once the female reaches full term, she must go through a c-section as she cannot give birth naturally. She is then expected to feed the puppies.

This unnatural breeding method is a disgusting practice that only emphasizes the fact that we have gone too far in selective breeding. A clear indication that a breed should not be bred is when natural breeding or birth cannot occur.

When it seems that we have gone far enough, unethical breeders find yet another way to make breeds with even more health concerns. Breeders do this by forcing a brachycephalic breed into a teacup size, thus doubling the chance of genetically abnormalities.

We must stop intentionally breeding defects into pets because we think its adorable. Period.

Declawing

Many people have their cats declawed. This is a controversial procedure as the term itself is misleading. Declawing includes removing not only the nail, but the bone. It would be **similar to having the tips of our fingers cut off down to the last knuckle**. Keep in mind that cats are digitigrade mammals, meaning they walk on their toes.

In many vet practices, declawing is presented as a normal procedure, much like a spay or neuter. In fact, some veterinarians will perform both surgeries at the same time. This would be equivalent to a human female having a hysterectomy at the same time as amputation of of all ten fingertips.

Both areas circled are distal phalanges of the cat (upper image) and human (lower image). Distal phalanges are removed during a cat declaw.

Uninformed pet parents often think of declawing as a quick solution to prevent couch and chair damage. However, declawing is outlawed and considered inhumane in many countries, including most all of Europe, New Zealand, and Brazil. There are many good reasons for this.

Pet parents are often not informed about is the chance of lameness and the increased chance of having a cat that refuses to use the litter box. Carpet and bed linens are often softer than cat litter and feel much better on paws that have had a declaw procedure done.

The temperament of the cat is often changed. They may become fearful, withdrawn, or aggressive. Since their first line of defense (claws) are gone, declawed cats will often resort to biting first and asking questions later.

Removing the nails changes the way a cat walks as well. This can lead to back and paw pain in later years, including arthritis. Imagine wearing ill fitting shoes all the time and the damage it would do to you in the long run. When done improperly, partial nails can grow back and bone spurs can develop.

Another matter of concern is the cat's lack of defense if he or she is to escape outside. Without nails, there is no climbing trees and escaping predators. Phantom pain, like the pain humans experience after an amputation is also possible in cats which goes a long way to understanding an irritated cat.

These are some things that can happen after a declaw. Does that mean it will occur in every cat? Of course not, but informed pet parents make informed decisions.

Kittens over the age of a year have a much harder time with a declaw and many veterinarians will not perform the procedure on an older cat. The recovery time is much longer.

The procedure has evolved to recognize the intense pain that comes from having multiple amputations in one day. In the past, (and still in some vet practices) a typical declawing procedure would proceed as follows:

Prior to anesthetizing the cat, bandages, surgical glue, and tape are prepared, sterile surgical tools opened and at the ready along with a tourniquet. The cat is anesthetized but few vets intubate (use a breathing tube) for this procedure. The paws are sterilized using surgical soap and the hair of the paw pushed back to make the area more readily accessible. With the veterinarian on one side of the table and a technician on the other, the technician slips the tourniquet over the first paw and tightens it tightly. This is to prevent the pet from bleeding. Using guillotine nail clippers, the vet cuts the nail and distal (end) of the bone completely off. He then uses a surgical blade to remove the remaining bone. The empty hole where the digit was is closed with surgical glue. Once this is completed with each paw, a very tight bandage is applied. The tourniquet is removed. This is repeated for all paws unless the pet parent requests only the front paws declawed. Then the cat is put into a cage for recovery and given a pain injection.

Post-surgical recovery often included the cat thrashing about, crying, and even flipping over and over in the cage if allowed. The bandages were left on until the following morning. The next morning, the bandages were removed. By removing the pressure bandages that prevented bleeding, all the blood rushed back in the leg and paw. This was repeated for each declawed paw. Even on pain medication and with the natural instinct to hide their pain, it was obvious that intense pain was being experienced. During the following week or more of recovery time, the cat had no choice but to walk on his painful paws. He didn't have the advantage of a wheelchair to keep pressure off the surgical site, and he must continue to use the litter box.

While it would be nice to say that the procedure has improved tremendously, it really hasn't. Using a nerve block in the paw in addition to pain injections makes for a more gentle transition from anesthetized to being fully awake. Oral medications also help and are generally given every 12 hours. Laser surgery makes it a little less barbaric, but the end results are the same.

With this information in mind, **if your furniture is going to be so important to you that you feel the need to declaw your cat, carefully consider what that kitten will have to go through for your furniture's sake. Your cat will love you. Your furniture will not.**

Get a scratching post. Get two. You can teach your cat not to scratch the furniture. A good resource to get you started in properly training your cat is:
http://www.humanesociety.org/animals/cats/tips/destructive_scratching.html

Ear Cropping and Tail Docking

Ear cropping is defined as trimming (or cropping) the ears so that they stand erect. It is usually performed under general anesthesia between 4-6 months old. Tail docking is simply removing a portion of the tail. This procedure is done without anesthesia within 2-5 days of birth. The amount of tail remaining depends on the standard for that breed.

According to the American Kennel Association (AKC):
"Ear cropping and tail docking are historical procedures...that help some dogs better and more safely perform the functions for which they are originally bred."
http://www.akc.org/pdfs/canine_legislation/Crop-Dock-Debark-Article.pdf

The author goes on to say that tail dockings are performed shortly after birth *"when the puppies nervous system is not fully developed. As a result, the puppy experiences little or no pain..."*

While it is true that the tail is considered "soft" in the first three days following birth, the pups do cry out in pain when the tail is cut.

Both ear cropping and tail docking have a long history and until the last few decades were done without any anesthesia. Today, some cruel, unethical breeders still do the procedure at home. Tails are docked either with scissors, or a rubber band is tightly applied to the tail until the blood circulation is cut off. Eventually, the deadened tail will fall off.

We know that the early Romans performed both of these procedures believing that they prevented rabies. In the middle ages, it was believed that if the tails of the parents were cut off, that the offspring would be born with a shorter tail. Fighting and baiting dogs had their tails and ears cut to give their opponent less skin to grab, increasing their chances of winning the fight. Long-eared or long-tailed hunting dogs were cropped and docked to prevent injury during the hunt. Some livestock guardian dogs were also cropped and docked for similar reason.

Today, the number of dogs used for these purposes have diminished and it is done mostly for cosmetic reasons. Even the AKC acknowledges it is a *"historical procedure."*

The American Veterinary Medical Association (AVMA), in its 1999 policy stated:

"Ear cropping and tail docking in dogs for cosmetic reasons are not medically indicated nor of benefit to the patient. These procedures cause pain and distress, and, as with all surgical procedures are accompanied by inherent risks of anesthesia, blood loss, and infection."

In their updated policy in 2012, the AVMA went a step further when they encouraged that **ear cropping and tail docking be removed from breed standards.**
https://www.avma.org/KB/Resources/Reference/AnimalWelfare/Documents/tail_docking_history.pdf

Ear cropping proponents responded by claim that cropping prevents ear infections, by allowing air flow into the ears. however, according to the Textbook of Small Animal Surgery, 3rd Ed, there is no medical advantage to the procedure at all.

Labradors and Golden Retrievers are both hunting breeds who spend a lot of time in water and develop frequent ear infections, yet ear cropping is never suggested for either breed.

The truth is, this procedure is done because tradition has dictated it. Dog show conformation standards have required it for certain breeds. Others have the procedures done and because they make the breed look much more fierce.

The AKC has said, *"While it is true that some breeds are shown with their ears cropped, there is nothing in AKC rules and in fact nothing in any breed standard that compels an owner to have this procedure performed as a prerequisite to entry at a dog show. Even if it is traditional in a particular breed that the dogs have one of these alterations, it has the same potential to win as any other dog of the breed and will only be judged based on the compliance of that dog to the breed standard."*

Hopefully, things are changing. Pet parents are realizing that these procedures are elective and their pet will be no less of a dog with intact ears and tail. We are also recognizing that if we are going to change the vicious reputation of "bully breeds" particularly, the pit bull, we have to stop making them look the part.

Anesthesia-Free Dental Cleanings

Pet parents are often concerned about having their pet anesthetized for a thorough dental cleaning. Unscrupulous groomers and even some veterinarians have taken advantage of this concern and offer anesthesia-free dental cleanings, referred to as Non-Professional Dental Scaling (NPDS) by the American Veterinary Dental College (AVDC).

A dental cleaning is not the same as brushing the teeth. A dental cleaning is a medical procedure that requires sedation for the comfort and safety of the pet as well as for maximum quality and efficiency.

A very thorough exam can be performed under anesthesia that cannot be performed on a dog or cat that is not sedated. The exam includes examination of all the structures of the jaw, muzzle, and inner oral area. This includes palpation of the lymph nodes and salivary glands, inspection of the tongue, palate, pharynx, tonsils, and the lining of the cheeks and gums.

As soon as the patient is sedated, many veterinarians will use a spring-loaded mouth gag to keep the mouth open during the procedure while others will open the mouth manually as needed.

During a dental cleaning, each tooth is inspected for fractures, cavities, and mobility. Each of these conditions, as well as any receding of the gum line and tooth resorption is recorded. Every tooth is probed with an explorer checking for periodontal pockets. The veterinarian also looks for any exposed pulp that could be causing pain. Once this is addressed, the veterinarian may take dental x-rays. X-rays are not common in most clinics.

A proper dental cleaning not only removes hard dental tartar with an ultrasonic cleaner, but cleans under the gum line, specifically in the gingival pocket (the subgingival space between the gum and the root), where periodontal disease hides.

Each tooth is cleaned on every side as well as under the gum line where periodontal disease hides. If loose or diseased teeth are discovered, they may be pulled during this time. While removal of incisors and premolars is usually relatively easy, canine teeth and molars have very deep roots and removal is difficult. All the teeth are numbered to make identification easier and any tooth removed or repaired is noted in the chart according to that number.

Teeth are lightly polished to remove microscopic etches caused by the ultrasonic cleaner. Too much or too aggressive polishing can cause loss of tooth enamel. Once polishing is completed, fluoride or dental sealants are applied to help prevent future buildup of plaque.

The procedure takes a minimum of thirty minutes if no extractions are necessary.

Now, imagine accomplishing this procedure with a dog or cat that is fully awake. In order for an anesthesia-free "cleaning" to take place, your pet would have to be physically restrained and have his mouth forced open for long periods. If an ultrasonic cleaner is used (as it should be), the vibration caused by the scaling wand would be terrifying for the pet. Each time this instrument touches the gums and tissues, it would cause immediate pain.

After all of the terror and pain induced, you would still take that pet home with active dental disease.

Dr. Tony Woodward, DVM, AVDC, a veterinarian who specializes in animal dentistry, wrote of a case in which a dog who had received regular anesthesia-free dental cleanings for years, was found to have profound periodontal disease. Dental x-rays revealed such massive bone loss that nearly two dozen teeth had to be extracted. Even abscessed molars had been missed during the last cleaning. The dog had been in pain for years and the pet parent had no idea because the pet continued to eat. http://www.wellpets.com/anesthesia-free-vet-dentistry/

Anesthesia is a safe when performed by a professional. If you are worried about your pet's ability to withstand anesthesia, request a thorough exam and lab work prior to the dental cleaning.

Do not allow yourself to be convinced that anesthesia-free dental cleaning is a efficient or humane.

THE IMMUNE SYSTEM, VACCINES, NUTRITION AND PARASITE CONTROL

"We need, in a special way, to work twice as hard to help people understand that the animals are fellow creatures, that we must protect them and love them as we love ourselves." ~ Cesar Chavez

8

Understanding the Immune System

Immunity is everything to humans and animal alike. Immunity is what keeps us healthy. A good working animal immune system comes from proper vaccination, proper deworming, healthy eating, exercise, and avoiding as many environmental toxins as possible. Genes also play a part. No where is this most readily seen than in the dog.

As we bred for a character or trait we liked, humans inadvertently bred certain dogs to be more susceptible to certain diseases. Hip dysplasia is common in German Shepherds. The Lhasa apso breed suffers from dry eye, while lupus erythematosus is often found in Collies.
http://ic.upei.ca/cidd/breeds/overview

Understanding how the immune system works and knowing what specific challenges may lay ahead for your pet, may help you prevent it.

One can be easy overwhelmed by the functioning of the immune system, but it is important in understanding how vaccines work as well as understanding lab work. Most people don't care to know, as long as it works, but when you realize every one, including your pets, have their own personal military inside, its really cool!

The immune system works like this:

Just as the military is broken down into branches like the marines/navy, army, and air force, the body's military is broken down into **physical immunity**, **innate immunity**, and **adaptive immunity**. Physical immunity is like the marines, the first line of defense. The immune system is made up of the skin, the membrane lining the organs, and even secretions like tears and digestive tract juices.

The bad guys are the antigens of germs, viruses, and bacteria. They show up and the physical immunity marines (PIM's) kick into gear. If for some reason, antigens break through the PIM's, innate immunity, also known as nonspecific immunity, takes over. This is the 1st Calvary division of the army. The 1st Calvary is made up of platoons of white blood cells which I will explain more about in a moment.

Part of the security force is adaptive immunity or specific immunity. These are the intelligence officers that help identify the bad guys. While innate immunity has been in the field fighting every enemy, adaptive immunity identifies specific targets. How do they acquire this information? Being exposed to it in the past through past battles or in small skirmishes caused by guess what? Vaccines. The vaccines, in causing a small fight, help the force know exactly what the evil antigens look like, so when they see them in the future, they recognize them sooner. The antigens are marked for death and adaptive immunity is the memory of what those guys look like.

The blood vessels are used as the transportation system for this military response. While the red blood cells (RBC's) are providing oxygen to keep the troops alive, the platelets, which are made by the bone marrow, jump in like medics and create blood clots where any damage is done. It is thanks to the platelets that we don't bleed out.

Meanwhile, the white blood cells (code name leukocytes) are carefully split into platoons with specific jobs. Phagocytes are the special forces that dive into the bloodstream to carry them into the heat of battle. The lymphocytes begin producing the weapons, called antibodies against the antigens, be they infection, virus, cancer cells, etc. These guys are further divided into T cells, that pick up the weapons and begin fighting, and B cells that dive on top of the enemy so that the special forces guys can easily recognize them.

When the phagocytes get to the battleground, they divide into small groups. First are the monocytes that morph into macrophages that consume large foreign particles and the cellular debris left behind. Second are the granulocytes that split up into three groups. The eosinophils and basophils concentrate on any allergic reactions, be it food allergy, bee stings, etc. The neutrophils jump into battle anywhere they detect bacteria and fungi. If there is inflammation, you can bet the neutrophils are there.

The carefully organized immune military is what keeps us, and our pets, alive and healthy. Our immunity is an amazing feature of our shared anatomy that is beautiful when it works. When lab work is taken on a sick animal (or human), the presence of these guys gives us a clue as to what is going on in the body. If white blood cells are abundant, you know a battle of some kind is going on. If there are a high number of eosinophils and basophils, you are more than likely looking at some type of allergic reaction. If neutrophils are present in high numbers, you are looking at some type of infection.

Occasionally, this system stops working correctly. It can no longer recognize the enemy, so it starts killing its own. This is an auto-immune response and it is very bad news. Certain allergies are caused by an auto-immune response. Lupus, rheumotoid arthritis, inflammatory bowel disease, Addison's disease, all are auto-immune disorders.

9

A New Vaccine Protocol

By understanding how immunity works, one can make better decisions regarding vaccines.

In our rescue, we must vaccinate around 20 animals, which is not an inexpensive undertaking.

Across the country, vaccine protocols have evolved with new research. The distemper/parvo vaccine is now given every three years in many practices, and in many states, rabies is required only once every three years. The vaccine itself has not changed. There is no one-year or three-year vaccine. The only thing that has changed is the protocol.

The Research on Vaccine Duration

Contrary to popular belief, the efficacy of most vaccines lasts far longer than one year. Extensive research had shown that immunity can last for years. One study conducted at the University of Wisconsin by Dr. Ronald Schultz and staff found that BOTH rabies and distemper immunity in dogs typically lasts about 7 years. Dr. Schultz has been conducting this research since the seventies.

"From our studies it is apparent, at least to me," said Dr. Schultz, *"that the duration of immunity for the four most important canine vaccines (core vaccines) that the duration of immunity is considerably longer than one year. Furthermore, we have found that annual revaccination, with the vaccines that provide long term immunity, provides no demonstrable benefit and may increase the risk for adverse reactions."*
(http://www.rabieschallengefund.org/education/duration-of-immunity-to-canine-vaccines)

On the following page you will find the minimum duration of immunity for the core and non-core vaccines found in Dr Shultz's experiments:

http://www.rabieschallengefund.org/images/Duration_of_Immunity_Schultz.pdf

Disease	Minimum duration
Canine Distemper Rockborn strain	7-15 years
Canine Distemper Onderstepoort strain	5-9 years
Canine Adenovirus	7-9 years
Canine Parvovirus	7 years
Bordetella	9 months
Canine Coronavirus	Lifetime
Canine Parainfluenza	3 years

A similar study on cats was performed at Cornell University in the late 1990's.

Feline Panleukopenia Virus (FPV), Feline Herpesvirus (FHV), and Feline Calicivirus (FCV) were the subjects of the study. The results of the study did indicate that duration of immunity was about 7 years with FPV having a greater success rate than FHV and FCV. Their recommendation to ensure immunity was to vaccinate every 3 years.
http://www.ncbi.nlm.nih.gov/pubmed/10328440

While this study proved that vaccines *can* provide immunity for the months or years listed, it does not mean that *all* dogs or cats will have immunity for that amount of time. Antibody titers, used in these studies, are the measurement of the protective antibody generated by exposure to the disease either by vaccinations or having a bout of the actual disease.

Some veterinarians, particularly holistic vets, prefer sending a sample of the blood to laboratories to have the antibody titers measured instead of automatic annual vaccinations. Antibody titer testing is often cost-prohibitive to many pet parents.

More veterinarians are vaccinating patients as individuals, considering their lifestyle and environment. Pets potentially exposed to other animals, and by that exposure, to more diseases, are vaccinated differently than the lap dog who only goes outside to potty. Hunting dogs may be vaccinated against Lyme disease, and dogs who love to play in area lakes and beaches may be vaccinated against leptosporosis. Outdoor cats may be vaccinated against feline leukemia, while indoor cats receive only the basic core vaccines and rabies.

Why Veterinarians Don't Reveal the Research

Many veterinarians have been hesitant to let their clients know about this research because they know that it is often only vaccinations that brought a healthy animal into a clinic. Most people will not take their pet to the vet for a yearly physical exam unless the animal needs vaccines.

During a physical exam, many illnesses and/or potential problems are detected before they can do further harm. **A dog or cat who misses a yearly physical is equivalent to a human going for ten years without seeing their doctor. The veterinarians' hesitation is understandable.**

However, there are some concerns that arise by with this approach including:

- The over-vaccination of our pets and its health risks.
- Our tendency to put the focus on vaccines and not the overall health of the pet.
- The money wasted on unnecessary vaccines that could be used on yearly lab work or dental cleanings.

If veterinarians are expected to be forthcoming about the research, however, **pet parents must accept the responsibility of bringing their pets in for yearly physical exams even if vaccines aren't required that year.**

With knowledge, comes responsibility.

Thanks to the efforts of many veterinarians and the availability of information via the internet, pet parents are beginning to understand that just as our own health is not solely dependent on vaccinations, neither is the health of our dogs and cats. The whole-body approach found in holistic medicine is slowly becoming a part of conventional medicine and preventative medicine is becoming the prime focus of it all.

Canine viruses

There are several viruses that our canine companions are susceptible to that we vaccinate against. Early vaccination is essential and should begin at 6-8 weeks of age, repeating every three weeks until 4 months of age. These vaccinations are:

- **Distemper:** Distemper attacks so many different areas including the brain, the mucous membranes (think nose/eyes), the skin, respiratory tract and on to the gastrointestinal tract. It can mimic a cold, allergies, and even parvo. Over a few days, the nasal discharge turns from clear to yellow and thick. The pet may have a dry cough.

    Several years ago, distemper struck a puppy I found along the road. I named the puppy Petra. Even though I had her vaccinated within a day of finding her, she suffered seizures and died from distemper two weeks later. It's a bit unusual for dogs to die as quickly from distemper as Petra did. However, she was in such poor shape when I found her that her immune system couldn't fight the virus. In some cases, puppies may improve temporarily if antibiotics are started to fight off secondary infections.

The second stage can take up to two to three weeks after exposure. At this point that the brain becomes involved. Petra's seizure was the distemper attacking the brain. Sometimes pets will walk in circles, fall over, or appear to be blind. At this stage, an untrained eye would fear rabies, when in fact, it is the distemper causing the damage. The muscles will contract painfully. Often pets with distemper will develop hard pads on the feet and a rough, thorny texture to the nose.

Dogs can survive distemper, although it is not without lasting effects. The pet may not be able to walk normally, and the paw pads become hard. The teeth may not be well protected by enamel. Generally dogs who do survive will do so with some type of lasting brain damage. An infected dog's behavior may be abnormal and the dog may be epileptic. Eventually, the damage will most likely worsen and most will need to be humanely euthanized.

- **Parvovirus:** If you have ever worked in an animal shelter, you are terrified of Canine Parvo Virus (CPV) commonly called simply "parvo". The parvovirus is enemy "number two" of the shelter world, trailing just behind overpopulation.

  Parvo was first recognized as a separate virus in 1978 and spread like wildfire. While proper vaccination is the first step toward eradicating it, too many pets remain unvaccinated. The virus spreads through feces. The infected pet defecates on the ground, the feces decays into the ground where it can live for up to ten years. Another pet visits the same area or a person walks on that infected ground and often, takes the virus with them.

  Parvo has two forms. The most common form is explosive, bloody diarrhea that causes extreme dehydration if not treated. There is no cure for parvo, only medical support. A puppy that has been diagnosed as positive by a parvo test must be hooked up to IV fluids, and all medication given through the IV port, in the fluids, or by injection. Giving medication by mouth to a parvo pup will usually result in vomiting.

  The second form, once considered rare, attacks the heart muscle. I have only seen this form once in my career and it happened to be in a young dog I was fostering. The time from noticeable lethargy to death was a matter of hours. Her sister, and kennel mate, survived and showed no symptoms. This form of parvo seems to be spreading in the United States. It is referred to as Parvovirus 2 and can kill in less than 72 hours. Pet parents should fully vaccinate and avoid taking the puppy to high-risk areas (such as a park or dog park) until the vaccines are completed.

- **Adenovirus:** Two types of this virus exist. Type 1 is called infectious canine hepatitis and affects the liver. The pet may present with fever, depression, a tender abdomen, and sometimes coughing. In young unvaccinated puppies, it may be confused with parvo. When the liver is affected, the mucus membranes may appear yellow. In severe cases, a bleeding disorder can occur and you will see bloody hematomas in the mouth. Type 2 is more upper respiratory related and can present with a dry hacking cough, gagging, phlegm production, and conjunctivitis or swelling and redness around the eyes.

- **Corona virus:** A highly contagious intestinal virus that can be brutal to young puppies but not frequently seen in normal litters (Puppy mills are a different story). In adult dogs, it is usually mild unless the immune system has been otherwise compromised. It may present with a yellow to orange color in the stool, loss of appetite, but usually, no fever. Since it is usually mild, most veterinarians do not vaccinate for it. In fact, the only veterinarian I ever worked for that did vaccinate for corona was located in none other than, Corona, California.

- **Leptosporosis**: There are several strains of lepto. Since the virus is carried by so many different animals, particularly wildlife, it is very present in our environment. Leptosporosis is spread in the urine of infected animals and can be transmitted to humans. Fairly recently, a veterinarian in East Tennessee was infected with lepto and had to be hospitalized. Lepto can be difficult to diagnose, but lepto most typically presents with a very high fever, joint and muscle pain, shivering, excessive drooling, loss of appetite, eye discharge, and sometimes, yellowing of the mucus membranes. Large hunting breeds who are likely to drink out of puddles and are often closest to wild life, tend to be the dogs most at risk. There are obviously exceptions. In smaller dogs, the lepto vaccine is often the culprit in vaccine reactions, so if you feel that your pet needs the vaccine, ask the vet about giving Benadryl ® thirty minutes before the vaccine is given.

- **Bordetella:** Also known as infectious tracheobronchitis, or simply kennel cough, this is a virus that can spread rapidly through a kennel or rescue. **Parainfluenza** is also one of the causes of kennel cough. Bordetella usually presents as a dry, hacking cough. I recently had this come through my rescue, apparently brought in by a new foster. The foster showed no symptoms, but my tiniest chihuahua, Pearl, had to spend three days going back and forth to the vet for treatment. Since it is a virus, antibiotics are not the choice of treatment, but Ms. Pearl, started coughing, and literally, could not stop, unable to catch her breath. It took injections, cough suppressant medication, and antibiotics to battle the opportunistic bacteria, to get her better. My pack had been vaccinated the year before. My fostering was put to an immediate halt. A few of the others got a mild case of it, but nothing as severe as Ms Pearl. My vet recommended vaccinating for bordatella every six months if I began fostering again.

- **Rabies:** Thanks to vaccination, rabies is not a disease that is commonly seen in the United States. Rabies is a virus of mammals and is usually passed from one mammal to another through a bite wound. The virus causes acute inflammation of the brain. Early signs of the virus may include fever and tingling at the site of exposure. As the virus advances, symptoms increase to include violent movements, hyper-excitement, and the inability to move certain areas of the body. Vaccinating your dog or cat with the rabies vaccine according to your state law is imperative. If your unvaccinated pet bites another pet or human, he will be quarantined and possibly euthanized so that the brain can be tested for rabies. Rabies may be given yearly, or in some states, every three years.

The "New" Canine Flu

Recently in the news, we heard of an outbreak of canine influenza. The influenza affected more than one thousand dogs in Illinois and has spread to several states.

There are two strains of this "new" influenza. One strain, called H3N8, originated in horses. Somehow the virus was able to mutate and spread to dogs.

Although the H3N8 strain has been recorded in the horse population for more than 40 years, according to the Centers for Disease Control (CDC) it wasn't until 2004 that it was detected in greyhounds. It adapted over time and became a dog-specific virus.
http://www.cdc.gov/flu/canineflu/keyfacts.htm

"The first recognized outbreak of H3N8 canine influenza occurred in racing greyhounds in January 2004 at a track in Florida. From June to August of 2004, outbreaks of respiratory disease were reported at 14 tracks in 6 states (Florida, Texas, Alabama, Arkansas, West Virginia, and Kansas). Between January and May of 2005, outbreaks occurred at 20 tracks in 11 states (Florida, Texas, Arkansas, Arizona, West Virginia, Kansas, Iowa, Colorado, Rhode Island, and Massachusetts). Since then, the H3N8 canine influenza has been documented in 30 states and Washington, DC. The H3N8 strain of canine influenza virus is endemic in areas of Colorado, Florida, New York, and Pennsylvania."
https://www.avma.org/KB/Resources/Reference/Pages/Canine-Influenza-Backgrounder.aspx

If mere compassion isn't enough to stop greyhound racing, providing a clear and easy path to spreading disease should put an end to this cruel "sport".

A second strain of influenza, H3N2, was detected in dogs in South Korea in 2006. The H3N2 virus spread throughout Asia and Thailand, and somehow arrived in the United States. In April 2015, H3N2 showed its virulence in Chicago when more than 1000 dogs were infected.
http://mediarelations.cornell.edu/2015/04/12/midwest-canine-influenza-outbreak-caused-by-new-strain-of-virus/

The H3N2 virus has since spread to other states.

Canine influenza viruses are easily transmitted. The most common are sneezing (aerosols) and droplets with direct contact to the pet (dogs meeting and sniffing one another, or contact with droplets on the ground) Thankfully, this virus does not survive for long in the environment like the parvovirus.

Symptoms of most canine influenza viruses are similar: coughing, sneezing, clear nasal mucus discharge that becomes yellow and thick, rapid and difficult breathing, lethargy, loss of appetite and fever.

Since influenza is a virus, not a bacteria, treatment is mostly supportive care. Such care may include feeding enticement, IV fluids, actions and medications to reduce fever, and the use of a humidifier to make breathing easier.

Since the immune system is compromised by the virus, secondary bacterial infections can soon set in, leading to pneumonia and death.

One external indication that a bacterial infection may be present, is the change in color of the nasal discharge from clear to yellow. At this point, your veterinarian may put your dog on antibiotics.

A test is available at your veterinarian to confirm this strain of influenza. However, with any respiratory virus, be it canine infectious tracheobronchitis (kennel cough) or canine H3N8 or H3N2, the virus must run its course. It is not surprising for this to take two weeks to one month.

Affected dogs must be quarantined from other dogs to stop the spread of the virus. High canine population areas such as kennels, shelters, and dog parks put your pet at risk for the virus. If there is an outbreak in your area, keep your dog at home if possible.

Shelters, kennels, and veterinary offices need to disinfect food bowls, cages, and bedding with bleach or other approved disinfectants. Employees should wash their hands before and after handling each pets. Dogs with any sign of infection should be isolated immediately.

There are two vaccines available for the H3N8 virus, although neither is guaranteed to prevent the virus, but significantly reduce its duration and severity. No vaccine is presently available for the H3N2 virus.

At this time, the vaccine is not included in core vaccines, but given according to the pet's lifestyle. If the dog is frequently boarded, travels, or plays at the dog park, the vaccine is recommended.

Vaccine Cost

Vaccinating all the animals at T.Paws Rescue can be costly. If we were to have each pet vaccinated at a vet clinic, the cost would be approximately $1000 for the vaccines alone. This would not include exam fees and would only cover rabies, DHPP (for dogs) and FVRCP (for cats). Vaccinating for DHPP and FVRCP at home dropped that expense to about $200.

In Tennessee, the rabies vaccination must be given by a veterinarian. When my veterinarian clinic offered rabies vaccines for $10 compared to the usual $18, I had everyone vaccinated for rabies. The vet also examined each one. I was able to pay for it using Care Credit ® Health Credit card.

While I can vaccinate for rabies, I still vaccinate for other diseases myself. These are called "core vaccines" and vaccinate for the most common diseases. There are generally two kinds of core vaccines for dogs. Often called a 5 in 1 or DHPP, this vaccine covers parvo, distemper, hepatitis/adenovirus type 2, and para influenza. The second vaccine is the 6 in 1 or DHLPP, which vaccinates all the aforementioned, PLUS leptospirosis. In some areas the corona virus is a concern and is added to the core vaccine.

The leptosporosis vaccine has commonly been associated with vaccine reactions. However, in a study reported in the October 2005 edition of the Journal of the American Veterinary Medical Association it was found that there were only 13 reactions to the lepto vaccine for every 10,000 doses of the vaccine given. http://www.veterinarypartner.com/Content.plx?A=527 . Small breed dogs did face a greater risk of reactions.

For dogs who go to a boarding facility, dog park, groomer, or other places where they can be exposed to other dogs, it is wise to give the bordetella vaccine to prevent kennel cough. Internasal bordetella works faster than the injectable form of the vaccine, but should be administered every nine months. If your family is a foster home for an animal shelter or other rescue, it is imperative to keep this vaccination up to date. While the virus is generally mild, it can sometimes cause great discomfort for the dog. Once one dog in the family or kennel is infected, it can quickly spread.

Pet parents that learn to vaccinate their own pets, can put those savings toward lab work, dental care, or in an emergency pet care fund. Vaccines must be kept refrigerated and must be ordered or purchased from a reputable source.

For those who are not comfortable vaccinating on their own, these same rabies clinics often vaccinate for other viruses if requested by the pet parent. Also, spay and neuter clinics in your area may also offer low cost vaccines.

For a guide on how to vaccinate your pet, the website, Drs. Foster and Smith, from whom I order my vaccines, has a great tutorial. http://www.drsfostersmith.com/pic/article.cfm?aid=84

Feline Viruses

- **Feline Panleukopenia:** Known also a feline infectious enteritis, feline distemper, it is most closely related to the parvovirus. Symptoms include lethargy, diarrhea, vomiting, fever, and dehydration.

- **Feline Viral Rhinotracheitis:** FVR is an upper respiratory viral infection that causes sneezing, eye and nasal discharge and coughing. The virus can also cause a loss of appetite because a cat that cannot smell his/her food will often not eat. Failure to eat can lead to hepatic lipidosis, a very serious condition.

- **Feline Calicivirus:** The calicivirus is also an upper respiratory infection but it presents differently. There are often blisters on the tongue, fever, and it can quickly lead to pneumonia.

- **Feline Leukemia Virus:** FeLV can be present for a long time without symptoms. Feline leukemia can also manifest itself in different ways. Testing is the only way to know for sure if it is present. It weakens the immune system, allowing all kinds of medical concerns to present themselves. Overall poor health in a young cat is often the first indication. Poor coat, loss of appetite, energy loss, and repeated infections are common. Feline leukemia can eventually lead to kidney disease as well as lymphosarcoma, a cancer of the lymph nodes. For cats who are tested while still in good health, a positive diagnosis is not an immediate death sentence, but the cat can transmit the disease to other cats.

- **Feline Immunodeficiency Virus:** FIV is similar in that it compromises the immune system. One of the most common indications that it may be present is red, swollen gums (gingivitis) or mouth (stomatitis) in a young cat. Secondary infections can take over the cat and so the patient is treated symptomatically. Again, as with FeLV, FIV can be present without symptoms for a long time and is not always an immediate death sentence.

Although I did not move to Tennessee with the intentions of letting the cats live outdoors, eventually it happened quite by accident. I was always hesitant to have free roaming cats because of the diseases and danger they were exposed to. Then one day the garage door opened at the wrong time and out went the cats.

At first I started to panic, then I simply sat down and watched them. What a wonderful time they were having! No one was running away. No one ran to the road which was quite a distance away. They were the happiest I had ever seen them. I struggled with the decision and decided that in my family right now, happiness was very important, and if that meant the cats were allowed outside, then so be it. Allowing cats outside is not something I recommend for everyone.

Cats that live strictly indoors are typically given one core vaccine known as FVRCP or a 4-in-1 vaccine (panleukopenia, chlamydia, rhinotracheitis, and calicivirus), and rabies. I had added a feline leukemia vaccine every year while I was employed as a technician. I chose not to vaccinate for FIV.

Cats vaccinated for FIV, when tested, can show a false positive in an ELISA FIV test. Cats found to be positive for the virus are often the ones quickly euthanized in many animal shelters in order to protect the other cats. At this time, there is no way to determine without a medical history, if the test is made positive by the virus itself or the vaccine. The ELISA test is an antibodies test that determines whether a cat has been exposed to the virus. The ELISA test does not differentiate how he had been exposed. This often leaves the shelter staff in an uncomfortable position of choosing what is best for the individual cat or the shelter population as a whole.

Pet parents should take all of this into consideration and discuss the individual needs of each pet based upon age, vaccine history, and environment, among other things.

The Vaccination Debate: Are we making our pets ill?

For many years, there has been great debate about the over-vaccination of dogs and cats.

I first read about this debate several years ago from Dr. Jean Dodds DVM. Dr. Dodds has been a proponent for a conservative vaccine protocol for many years.

After I became aware of the notion that vaccines may have unknown side effects, I began to pay attention to pets coming in the veterinary hospitals where I worked. I began to notice that many older, otherwise healthy pets, who came for their yearly vaccinations and exam, returned days to weeks later with serious diseases. Sometimes, the pet may have had minor health concerns that became huge concerns after being vaccinated.

I came to believe that if an animal has an age related illness lurking in the background, the last thing you want to do is to challenge their immunity with a vaccine. However, this was based only on antidotal evidence.

According to the studies mentioned earlier, immunity lasts much longer than previously thought. I asked myself if the elderly pet has longer lasting immunity than previously thought, why vaccinate and take the chance that over-vaccination could trigger or activate diseases?

More research was necessary.

Some research has been done asking the important question *"Are we making our pets ill with vaccines?"*

The Purdue University School of Veterinarian Medicine has conducted two studies to determine if vaccination or over vaccination can cause immune-mediated diseases. Since the study was published many years ago, it has been used to "prove" that vaccinations cause auto-immune disease.

Since a copy of study was not available online, I contacted Purdue University, and professor Harm Hogenesch, one of the leaders of the study, sent me a complete copy of the study.

Professor Hogenesch also added:

"It is important to recognize the limitations of the study: (1) it was a small study with only 5 dogs per group; (2) the dogs were vaccinated with a greater frequency than what is used in practice. Although we found laboratory evidence of autoantibodies (antibodies that react with self proteins) in the vaccinated dogs, none of the dogs became sick or had any clinical evidence of autoimmune disease or allergies. **This small study attests to the safety of normal vaccination procedures.** *"* (emphasis mine)

In the research study, **"Vaccine-associated immune-mediated hemolytic anemia (IMHA) in the dog"** it was hypothesized that vaccines can trigger hemolytic anemia, a form of anemia caused by the abnormal breakdown of red blood cells.
http://onlinelibrary.wiley.com/doi/10.1111/j.1939-1676.1996.tb02064.x/pdf

The researchers found that vaccines did indeed cause vaccine-associated immune-mediated hemolytic anemia in some dogs but concluded the following:

"Effective and safe vaccination is an important part of preventative health care for dogs and people, since the risks of contracting infectious diseases are much higher than those of vaccine-associated problems, including IMHA. However, the currently available vaccines for dogs and cats may be capable of providing long-lasting immunity, and the need for yearly vaccination in healthy adult animals has been recently questioned. Reducing the frequency of vaccination or the number of vaccine components may decrease the incidence of vaccine-induced IMHA in susceptible dogs."

Several other similar studies have been conducted, but a review by the Colorado State University Center for Companion Animal Studies determined that *" manuscripts have failed to associate vaccines with IMHA in dogs."*

Colorado State did go on to say, however, that *"multiple things are considered prior to vaccinating canine patients including infectious disease risk, legal issues (rabies), the immune status of the patient, and the potential for vaccine reactions. In our opinion, the benefits of vaccinating against appropriate infectious disease agents likely outweigh the risks of developing IMHA and IMTP in the majority of the cases. However, larger prospective veterinary studies with appropriate control groups are needed to more thoroughly evaluate this potential relationship."* http://csu-cvmbs.colostate.edu/documents/vaccines-cytopenias-faq-companion-animal-studies.pdf

One thing we do know for sure is that in vaccinated cats *"sarcomas [a malignant tumor of connective or other nonepithelial tissue] occur at vaccination sites at rates ranging from 1case/10,000 cats to 10 cases/10,000 cats and develop primarily after administration of rabies virus and FeLV"* http://avmajournals.avma.org/doi/pdfplus/10.2460/javma.2001.218.697

This, in itself, is enough to suggest that maybe we are doing something wrong.

Veterinarians have a specific protocol for the location they give each vaccine. The purpose for this protocol is to identify which vaccine is causing a reaction or potentially cancerous sarcoma. Rabies and FeLV are given in the rear legs. As a veterinarian once said when I asked why the vaccines weren't given subcutaneously in the withers (between the shoulder blades) he answered "its easier to amputate a leg."

With the exception of feline sarcomas, it doesn't seem that we can say for sure that vaccines do cause other health concerns or trigger underlying health issues to come to the forefront. However, there seems to be a consensus that vaccines are vital to the health of our pets, but over-vaccinating is unnecessary. Veterinarians are slowly moving to a new protocol of vaccinating for many viruses every three years instead of yearly. It will be interesting to see if this change in protocol makes a positive impact on the health of dogs and cats.

The Conundrum of Vaccinating Puppies in Animal Shelters

As an individual who rescues animals and as a vet tech, I have wondered if vaccinating shelter pups (and even young adults) while in the shelter, or immediately upon leaving the shelter, is causing more harm than good.

No matter how diligently shelter staff clean the kennels and cages, animals surrendered to the shelter can still become exposed to viruses and diseases.

Older pets usually have at least some immunity to the parvovirus and distemper. Puppies (up to 12 months old) may have little, and sometimes, no immunity at all.

If a puppy is surrendered to the shelter and exposed to either parvo or distemper, his immune system attempts to fight the virus. So what happens if we add a live vaccine to the body while the immune system is already doing its best to fight? Are we asking too much of the immune system?

Twice I have seen shelter pups die from parvo within a short time of being vaccinated. The puppies were picked up from the shelter, taken directly to the veterinarian, and then to me. Within one or two days the puppies showed signs of parvo.

After those experiences, I asked that the puppies not be vaccinated until they had been quarantined at my home for two weeks. No other puppy I fostered after that came down with parvo or distemper.

While there is no proof that vaccinating an already exposed puppy was the cause of the deaths, it is enough to give pause.

In the mid-1990's when I was on the board of a local humane society who ran the local shelter, we were asking this very question.

Puppies have passive immunity passed down from their mothers that last only about 8 weeks. This is why most vaccines protocols have you begin vaccines at 6-8 weeks. As the mother's passive immunity dissipates, the vaccine begins to build up acquired immunity. If this is not started before heavy exposure to disease, what happens?

The standard parvo vaccine is a modified "live" virus, which means it is a virus that has been chemically or genetically weakened but is nevertheless viable or able to multiply in the host. A modified live vaccine (MLV) is known to be more effective than a "killed" vaccine which is a dead form of the virus plus an adjuvant to stimulate the immune system. The job of both is to elicit a response from the immune system so that when the immune system does "meet" the actual disease in the environment, it has "learned" how to fight it.

The problem occurs when an immunocompromised animal meets a MLV. Veterinarians are aware that there is a "higher potential for vaccine-induced disease" as well as a "possible risk in immunocompromised animals." http://www.dvmvac.org/killvmodified.asp

We already know that stress lowers the immune system.
http://www.apa.org/research/action/immune.aspx

This impact of stress is true in both people and pets. Imagine the stress of puppies in a crowded shelter environment. No matter how well maintained or how loving the staff, because of the horrid overpopulation problem, being in a shelter environment is going to be stressful.
A pet shop will also be stressful with the crowds of people and busy shop keepers. Often, the pet shop puppy is produced in the horrid, filthy environment of a puppy mill, a dog breeding facility that operate more for profit than producing happy, healthy puppies. This is much like the smaller scale "backyard breeder", in that the conditions are generally substandard (to say the least).

The needs of the pets in puppy mills and backyard breeders are often disregarded in order to maintain a low overhead. Even if vaccinated and dewormed, which is often in question, the environment and experience, and often poor breeding, creates an immunocompromised puppy.

So it seems illogical to give a modified-live vaccine to a shelter pup until one is sure that the body isn't already fighting the virus and the immune system already compromised.

It seems the safest and most prudent action should be to vaccinate most puppies with a killed parvo/distemper vaccine.

Dr. Jean Dodds seems to agree. *"I share the view of experts in the field that a properly constituted inactivated "killed" vaccine is always preferable to one of modified-live virus origin. The primary reason for this preference reflects safety to the host and the environment. Killed vaccines do not replicate in the vaccinated animal, they do not carry the risk of residual virulence, and do not shed attenuated viruses into the environment. Furthermore, killed vaccines do not bear the risk of contamination with adventitial viruses present in the tissue culture cells used to grow modified-live virus vaccines. Even if killed vaccines are proven to be somewhat less efficacious (produce lower levels or less sustained protection) than modified-live virus products, they are more safe. All killed vaccines on the market today have passed current efficacy and safety standards in order to be licensed for use by the USDA. In my view, therefore, medical professionals and the public should urge manufacturers to produce an assortment of killed vaccine products for use in companion animals."* http://devinefarm.net/rp/rpvaccin.htm

The problem is, most parvo/distemper vaccines are modified-live vaccines. Killed vaccines have a difficult time breaking through the maternal passive immunity antibody. So in an ideal situation in which the puppy is raised by his mother, in a stress-free environment, and weaned at the proper time, the best vaccine for him is the modified-live vaccine. This begins his journey toward developing his own acquired immunity. http://www.veterinarypartner.com/Content.plx?A=589

Unfortunately, shelter puppies do not always have this advantage. This puts animal shelters and rescues in quiet a conundrum.

Recombinant vaccines are now available. These vaccines are made up of a single purified protein of the virus or bacteria. Since it is just one protein and not the entire virus or bacteria, there is little chance that it will cause a vaccine-induced illness. So, this may be the answer for shelter pups. I urge shelters and rescues to talk to their veterinarian about recombinant vaccines. As a rescuer myself, I have chosen to quarantine all foster puppies with no vaccination history for 14 days before I begin vaccinations particularly if they are near the age of 8-10 weeks old. This is the incubation period of parvo and many other viruses that could challenge the puppy's immune system. If, after 14 days, the puppy has shown no signs of illness, I will then vaccinate.

My vaccine protocol for dogs and cats

As a result of my research and experiences, I created my own minimum vaccine protocol. I have made some changes to the protocol from the previous edition. Small breed dogs and cats tend to live up to 18 years old making 9 years old middle age. At 9 years old, large breed dogs are in their senior years as their life expectancy is 9-12 years old. For this reason, I vaccinate my small breed dogs at 9 years old, but stop vaccinating any large breed dogs at 6 years old. One should consult with their veterinarian on the specific needs of your pet.

Puppy	**Kitten**
DHPP (6/9/12/15 wks) then 1/3/6/9 years old	FVRCP (6/9/12/15 wks) 1/3/6/9 years old
Rabies (15 wks) then as ordered by state	Rabies (15 wks) then as ordered by state
Bordatella (15 wks) then every 6-12 months	FELV (12/15 wks) then 1/3/6 years old
*for smaller breeds consider staggering puppy vaccines	*for both dog & cat, cease vaccines (except rabies and bordatella for dogs)

Brody

10

Simplifying the Confusing World of Pet Food

If there is a political issue in the pet world, it is the food we feed. There is no quicker way to be looked down upon in many circles than to admit that you feed an inexpensive brand of pet food.

We have been taught that the amount we spend on pet food equals the love we have for our pets. I bought into it myself. Years as a vet tech and pet sitter had ingrained in me that pet foods available in the grocery store were not good enough for my pets. In California, I spent an untold amount of money having premium dog and cat food delivered to my house so my animals could have the best in the world.

When I found us in East Tennessee, barely able to buy ANY dog food, I felt terribly guilty buying cheap dog and cat food. I remember one day being in tears over the guilt of not being able to give the best to my pets.

I was being too hard on myself. My animals were the happiest they had ever been. They were outside playing in the temperate climate, with an old shed for shelter, with plenty to eat. I was doing the best I could at the time.

Growing up, I don't even recall buying much dog food. When I was a kid, a beagle/shepherd mix dog adopted me and I named her Bear. My mother let me keep her as long as I used my allowance to have her spayed, which I did. Like other dogs on Walkers Creek, Bear was not confined to our property. She hunted all over the backwoods of Southwest Virginia. When Bear wasn't hunting for rabbits, she went from house to house eating scraps everyone dumped by the creek. She lived a long, happy life, and I never recall her being ill until one day in her teens, she passed away.

Times have changed and so has the world. I must obey leash laws and realize that my pets do better being on a steady diet. The indiscriminate use of table scraps can cause lots of digestive problems in pets and it is not nutritionally complete. Bear lived a life where she could follow her instincts and hunt for what her body needed. The pets of today do not have that option.

While cheap store brand food may not be ideal, demonizing the pet parents that cannot afford more expensive brands, helps nothing. There are ways to improve a pet's diet on a strict budget. First we have to sort through the bad information to get to the truth.

The evolutionary basis of pet nutrition

There is an enormous amount of bad information regarding pet nutrition available to the public. While claims are made that the diets are based on years of research, it is often biased and poorly done research funded by the pet food companies themselves. Much like the Bible, if you pick and choose, you can prove anything.

Other times, companies prey on unsuspecting pet parents, with false information and fear mongering, in order to sell their product.

Getting to the truth about pet food was a long journey.

I started with the evolutionary basis of dog and cat nutrition.

"The Evolutionary Basis for the Feeding Behavior of Domestic Dogs (Canis familiaris) and Cats (Felis catus)" is an in depth study reported in the "Journal of Nutrition" in 2006. In the study, the researcher John W.S. Bradshaw introduced his study by saying: "The dentition, sense of taste, and meal pattering of domestic dogs and cats can be interpreted in terms of their descent from members of the order Carnivora." http://jn.nutrition.org/content/136/7/1927S.long

The consensus was that although both canine and felines originated in the group of carnivores, they were of different branches.

It had always been assumed that dogs descended directly from wolves. A recent genetic study found that dogs and wolves descended a common ancestor, rather than the dog descending from the wolf. http://news.discovery.com/animals/pets/dogs-not-as-close-kin-to-wolves-as-thought-140116.htm

"The common ancestor of dogs and wolves was a large, wolf-like animal that lived between 9,000 and 34,000 years ago," Robert Wayne, co-senior author of the study, told Discovery News. *"Based on DNA evidence, it lived in Europe."*

The canine was domesticated about 100,000 years ago as this ancestor learned the advantage of living and hunting with humans. Over thousands of years, many changes occurred to create the dogs we have today. Those changes include different breeds, size, dentition, and the ability to digest grain.

Cats, were domesticated more recently, and still retain the instinct to hunt.

According to a new genetic analysis by Carlos S. Driscoll et al, modern-day housecats are descended from a population of domesticated wildcats that prowled the Middle East more than 100,000 years ago. http://www.sciencemag.org/content/317/5837/519.full and http://www.nature.com/news/2007/070628/full/news070625-10.html

"The theory [of domestication] is that when hunter-gatherers became farmers, they began to store grain. The grain attracted rodents, which probably attracted wildcats, which gradually ingratiated themselves with their human neighbors." http://www.nature.com/news/2007/070628/full/news070625-10.html

While the beginning of the relationship between human and cat began around 10,000 years ago, it took much longer to evolve to the domestic cat we have today. In fact, it wasn't until this past century that cats began to live indoors and learn dependence on human caretakers. Feral cats are excellent examples of the cats ability to still care for him/herself in the wild.

Unlike dogs, the dietary needs of the cat has changed little. Cats still need a source of animal protein, and require a higher percentage of protein than the dog.

More on dietary requirements later in the chapter.

The Safety of our Pet Food

There are many websites claiming to tell you the "truth about pet food". They tell long interesting tale of conspiracies, backdoor pet food soap operas, and even provide video which "proves" their claims. Some of these claims are based on actual events and research, but highly exaggerated versions of the events, and only bits and pieces of research.

Higher priced pet foods benefit greatly from these websites. This chapter explores some of those accusations and actual facts surrounding them.

To begin, the FDA assures pet parents that pet food is safe. In their Code of Federal Regulations, Title 21, Food and Drugs, Part 500. the FDA says the following:

"There is no requirement that pet foods have pre-market approval by FDA. The Act does require that pet foods, like human foods, be safe to eat, produced under sanitary conditions, contain no harmful substances, and be truthfully labeled "
http://www.accessdata.fda.gov/scripts/cdrh/cfdocs/cfcfr/CFRSearch.cfm?CFRPart=500

While the word of the FDA is far from proof that the food is actually safe, it is a beginning.

There have been serious complaints from animal rights and rescue groups that the FDA regulations are not enough. One very serious allegation alleged that the FDA allowed for the rendered remains of euthanized pets to be used in pet food.

In 2002, the FDA conducted a small sampling of various dog foods brands purchased in the Washington, DC area. The FDA researchers did find traces of the most common euthanasia drug pentobarbitol. However, DNA testing performed by the FDA found no cat DNA, no dog DNA, and no horse DNA.
http://www.fda.gov/AboutFDA/CentersOffices/OfficeofFoods/CVM/CVMFOIAElectronicReadingRoom/ucm129131.htm

The brands of dog food that tested positive for pentobarbitol, included Ol' Roy ®, Trailblazer ® Ken'l Ration ® Gravy Train, Dad's ®, and Heinz ® Kibbles and Bits Lean, among others.
http://www.fda.gov/AboutFDA/CentersOffices/OfficeofFoods/CVM/CVMFOIAElectronicReadingRoom/ucm129135.htm

With no DNA found, the results were said to be inconclusive.

The allegation came up again in 2007. In April of that year, Last Chance of Animals, produced an undercover video taken at D & D Disposal's West Coast Rendering Plant in Vernon, CA.

Rendering is a process that simultaneously dries the material and separates the fat from the bone and protein.

D & D Disposal was accused by Last Chance for Animals of rendering deceased pets for use in pet foods.

At that time, I was working at a pet hospital in Southern California. The deceased pets that were not sent for cremation or burial by the pet parents did, indeed go to D & D. While the process is unsettling and the video was gruesome to watch, it was not illegal and there was no proof that the rendered product went to make pet food. The video proved that the disposal and rendering took place.

In reference to the use of rendered products, the FDA has said:

"No regulatory action will be considered for animal feed ingredients resulting from the ordinary rendering process of industry, including those using animals which have died

otherwise than by slaughter, provided they are not otherwise in violation of the law.

Rendered animal feed ingredients which contain harmful microorganisms, toxins or chemical substances may be considered adulterated under Section 402(a)(1) or (2) of the Act. Where a rendering procedure itself raises a question of disease transmission, the ingredient made may be deemed adulterated under Section 402(a)(4)."
http://www.fda.gov/ICECI/ComplianceManuals/CompliancePolicyGuidanceManual/UCM074717

However, in the same policy, the FDA did admit that diseased animals were used in animal feed prior to the discovery Bovine Spongiform Encephalopathy, more commonly known as Mad Cow Disease :

"Prior to the appearance of BSE [Bovine Spongiform Encephalopathy,] CVM had no evidence of human or animal disease associated with the feeding of properly rendered and handled animal feed ingredients despite the use of tissues from diseased animals or animals that have died otherwise than by slaughter. In addition, the Center for Veterinary Medicine does not believe that Congress intended the Act to preclude application of different standards to human and animal foods under Section 402. Different standards have historically existed for human and animal food concerned with aesthetics. The Center has permitted other aesthetic variables in dealing with animal feed, as for instance the use of properly treated insect or rodent contaminated food for animal feed. "

The FDA states that it will consider, (but not necessarily approve) adulterated human food for animal food use. Adulterated foods are those that are unfit for human consumption.
https://www.law.cornell.edu/uscode/text/21/342

*"The *Center* will consider the requests for diversion of food considered adulterated for human use in all situations where the diverted food will be acceptable for its intended animal food use.*

Such situations may include:

  a. *Pesticide contamination in excess of the permitted tolerance or action level.*
  b. *Pesticide contamination where the pesticide involved is unapproved for use on a food or feed commodity.*
  c. *Contamination by industrial chemicals.*
  d. *Contamination by natural toxicants.*
  e. *Contamination by filth.*
  f. *Microbiological contamination."*

In March 2007, the FDA was alerted of possible food contamination by Menu Foods, the makers of nearly 100 brands of low cost and high end dog and cats foods. Several dogs and cats had died of renal failure, including 9 cats after routine taste trials of the company's own food.

http://www.fda.gov/AnimalVeterinary/SafetyHealth/RecallsWithdrawals/ucm129932.htm

A recall was issued with nearly 5300 brands effected. For some pets, the recall was too late.

Veterinarians across the United States and abroad reported an increase in the number of kidney related illnesses and deaths while many more pet parents attributed the illness or death of their pets to food contamination.

By the end of March, veterinarians had reported 471 cases of pet kidney failure with 104 of those resulting in death. http://www.nytimes.com/2007/03/28/science/28brfs-pet.html?ex=1176264000&en=8ee0fb91fd221e4b&ei=5070&_r=0

Eventually the contaminate was identified as the industrial chemicals melamine, and a related compound, cyanuric acid. These chemicals were found in the wheat gluten and rice protein provided to the pet food manufacturers from Chinese based companies. After a thorough investigation, Chinese authorities closed down two companies linked to the contamination: Xuzhou Anying Biologic Technology Development Company and Binzhou Futian Biology Technology Co. Ltd..

In January 2011, the federal government responded with the **Food Safety Modernization Act (FSMA)**. This Act enhanced the cooperation of local, state, tribal, and territorial partners. The hope was that further contamination could be prevented.
http://www.fda.gov/Food/GuidanceRegulation/FSMA/

However, in 2013, contamination of dog jerky treats resulted in the deaths of approximately 580 dogs. Again the contamination was linked to Chinese companies.
http://www.foodsafetynews.com/2013/10/fda-update-nearly-600-dogs-dead-in-connection-to-chinese-jerky-treats/#.VbUMaPldjNU

In 2014, the FDA instituted the **Animal Feed Regulatory Program Standards (AFRPS).** The FDA intended to initiate uniform regulation and standards for all animal feed.
http://www.fda.gov/downloads/ForFederalStateandLocalOfficials/AnimalFeedRegulatoryProgramStandardsAFRPS/UCM402506.pdf

In 2014, the number of recalls began to drop. Reasons for the recalls included salmonella contamination, metal fragments in food, and vitamin deficiency. As before, both high end and low cost pet foods were included in the recall. Most recalls were preventative measures and no contamination was found.

There is no doubt that pet parents have a reason to be concerned. However, contamination of pet food doesn't appear to be any more of a threat than having our human food contaminated. There is also no proof that high end foods are less likely to be contaminated that economy foods.

The decision as to what to feed your pet should be an informed choice. We do need to do what is the best for our pets, but the reality is, we have to do that within the confines of our personal family budget. No pet parent should be condemned for that.

The Grain-Free Hoax and Beyond

Grains are seeds of grasses cultivated for food. Wheat, rice, corn, oats, barley, millet, quinoa, and oatmeal, are the most common. Grains provide carbohydrates that provide the body with energy. The outer layer, or bran, provides fiber. The endosperm is the inner portion that is a good source of starch. The germ is the reproductive part of the seed that supplies vitamin E, folic acid, magnesium, and phosphorous. Whole grain is the entire grain seed.

Grains are an important part of the diet of most animals who are natural prey animals for dogs and cats. If our pets were able to and had to survive on their own, the animals they would chose to kill and eat would all be dependent on grain as a food source. As the dog or cat ate their prey, they would ingest these grains and be able to digest them.

Following the deaths and country-wide health scare in 2007, pet food companies scrambled to assure their customers that the food they were feeding their pets was safe. Since the containment was found in wheat gluten, companies raced to produce grain-free pet food. Thus, the grain-free diet fad began.

Many animal nutritionists and veterinarians agree that **the grain-free diet was not created by the veterinary world, but by pet food manufacturers.**

"Vilification of food grains as pet food ingredients may be myths started by small pet food companies as a way to compete with larger, established companies, according to four diplomates of the American College of Veterinary Nutrition." interviewed by Veterinary Practice News."

"I honestly don't know where [grain-free] got started. It's not based on any data, and there are excellent diets that contain one or more of those items," said Cailin Heinze, MS, VMD, and a diplomate of the American College of Veterinary Nutrition (ACVN).

"Companies or salespeople often warn against corn, wheat or soy because of pet food marketing and propaganda, and then they develop a mythology about why all these might be harmful," said Jennifer Larsen, DVM, Ph.D., Dipl. ACVN.

"There is no science to back up many claims. Americans love conspiracy theories, but they aren't equally skeptical of all sources," added Larsen, of the nutrition support service at the Pritchard Veterinary Medical Teaching Hospital at the University of California, Davis.

"Corn, [a grain] is not an inherently good or bad food for dogs and cats, and there have been very few corn allergies in dogs and cats in this country," said Lisa Weeth, DVM, Dipl. ACVN, a clinical nutritionist for Red Bank Veterinary Hospital in Tinton Falls, N.J. *"But corn is used frequently as an ingredient in lower-cost pet foods, so in my opinion the boutique pet food companies are looking for ways to distinguish themselves from the bigger, more established competition."* http://www.veterinarypracticenews.com/August-2012/Vet-Nutritionists-Weigh-In-On-Pet-Food-Allergies-Grains/

Research, discussed later in this chapter, show that both dogs and cats are fully capable of digesting grains, and the nutrition is not wasted.

"Carbohydrates [found in grains], aren't inherently bad for cats, "according to Dr. Elizabeth Colleran, President of the American Association of Feline Practitioners (AAFP), "Rather cats are just able to derive more energy from protein and use it more."
http://animal.discovery.com/healthy-pets/cat-health-101/5-human-foods-cats-can-eat.html

A recent Chinese study suggested that, even though cats were more recently domesticated (compared to the dog), cats were already eating grain as early as 5300 years ago:

"This study of cats living 5,300 y ago at the agricultural village of Quanhucun, China provides the earliest known evidence for mutualistic relationships between people and cats. Isotopic data demonstrate that humans, rodents, and the cats ate substantial amounts of millet-based foods, with cats preying on grain-eating animals. One cat was old and one ate less meat and more millet than others, suggesting it scavenged leftovers or was fed. Diverse data demonstrate rodent threats to stored grain, indicating cats were advantageous to farmers, whereas food in villages was attractive to cats. These findings provide evidence for commensal processes of cat domestication." http://www.pnas.org/content/111/1/116.full

A clinical nutritionist at Cornell University, Dr. Joseph Wakshlag states, *" I don't understand is why certain ingredients that are in our diets such as corn, soy and rice have been getting a bad rap. Corn and rice are highly digestible have low fiber content compared to other grains and to my knowledge are associated with allergies only due to the sheer number of products that have these things in them. These carbohydrate sources are essential to the processing and extrusion of kibble. If it's grain free it doesn't mean carbohydrate free. "*http://dinersjournal.blogs.nytimes.com/2011/01/21/q-and-a-with-a-pet-nutritionist/

This does not mean that grain-free diets are in any way harmful.

"Some dogs do benefit from grain-free diets but definitely not to the magnitude the pet food industry would lead you to believe", says Dr. Donna Solomon of The Animal Medical Center of Chicago. *"Some pets have allergies to specific grains and some pets have dietary intolerance to specific grains. There is no breed, sex, or age predilection.*
"http://www.huffingtonpost.com/donna-solomon-dvm/grainfree-pet-food-trend-_b_5429538.html

Surprisingly, grains are not the culprit in most food allergies, but can be in food intolerances. Allergies are a reaction to protein components.

"True incidents of food allergy are about 10 percent of the animal population", according to Rebecca L. Remillard, DVM, Dipl. ACVN, of the North Carolina State University Nutrition Service.

When grains are removed from pet food, they must be replaced with something else. According to Cummings Veterinary Medical Center at Tufts University:

" Many of these [grain-free} diets merely substitute highly refined starches such as those from potatoes or tapioca (cassava) in place of grains. These ingredients often provide fewer nutrients and less fiber that whole grains, while costing more."

http://vet.tufts.edu/nutrition/faq/frequently-asked-questions-about-general-pet-nutrition/

Grain-free diets are more expensive than those that contain grain. Marion Nestle, the Paulette Goddard professor of nutrition, food studies and public health at New York University, and co-author of the book **Feed Your Pet Right: The Authoritative Guide to Feeding Your Dog and Cat** , said in an interview,

"People are willing to spend anything on their pets. The $18-billion-a-year pet food industry is considered to be recession-proof. Although during this economic downturn shelters have been overwhelmed with pets people could not afford to keep, those who have kept their pets are not stinting on what they spend to feed them."

Nestle went on to point out that "premium" brand foods cost three to four times more than supermarket brands, yet no valid research provided evidence of the added value to health and longevity.

"There is, however, ample evidence that, despite claims to the contrary, both dogs and cats "are perfectly able to digest grains if they are cooked," Dr. Nestle said.

http://www.nytimes.com/2010/06/01/health/01brod.html?_r=1

Dr. Nestle also confirmed what many food companies do not want the consumer to know:

"*All pet foods are made from the byproducts of human food production,*" Dr. Nestle explained. "*No matter what the package says, your dog is not getting whole chicken breasts, but what remains after the breasts have been removed for human food.*"

This subject has been a matter of great debate, particularly between the pet food manufactures Blue Buffalo ® and Purina ®. On May 6, 2014, Purina filed a lawsuit against Blue Buffalo for false advertising after testing revealed the presence of poultry by-product meal in some of Blue Buffalo's top selling pet foods.

Blue Buffalo ®, whose food sells for $1.26 – 2.59 per pound (compared to 62¢/lb for Purina ® Dog Chow), offered a "True Blue Promise" that states that its food "contain NO chicken (or poultry) by-product meals, NO corn, wheat or soy, and NO artificial flavors, colors or preservatives."

Unfortunately, it did. After a year of denial, Blue Buffalo ® admitted that "substantial" and "material" portion of Blue Buffalo ® pet food sold to consumers contained poultry by-product meal, despite pervasive advertising claims to the contrary. However, Blue Buffalo asked the Court for additional time to file an Amended Complaint in the litigation, naming its ingredient suppliers as Defendants.

Blue Buffalo ® is no stranger to complaints of misleading advertising practices. Hills ® the makers of Science Diet ® and Hills ® Prescription Diets, has filed several complaints to the National Advertising Division (NAD) of the Better Business Bureau. Each time NAD ruled largely in favor of Hills ® Pet Nutrition.

"Dr. Joseph Wakshlag, a Cornell University College of Veterinary Medicine nutritionist, speaking as an observer, said, *"I'm shocked that Purina is filing a lawsuit, but I'm not surprised that the Blue Buffalo ingredients are not exactly what they say they are."*

In 2005, while working at a veterinary clinic in Connecticut, Wakshlag remembers Blue Buffalo salespeople coming in to introduce their products. He recalls them telling this tale about the company's origin: The owner's dog, Blue, had died of cancer, so the owner set out to make better food to save other pets from dying of cancer.

"We asked, *'Where is the proof of all this?'*" Wakshlag recounted. "*'Where is the data that shows it increases my dog's life span?' They'd say, 'Look it's got blueberries!'*" http://news.vin.com/VINNews.aspx?articleId=32011

Dr. Wakshlag went on to say in an interview for the New York Times, "*Often the higher-cost foods have had a "more cerebral" thought process put into their formulation, whether your dog needs some of these nutrients is debatable, particularly the "kitchen sink" foods, as I like to call them. These foods add every know vegetable, fiber source, probiotic and herb into the mix to catch your attention.*" http://dinersjournal.blogs.nytimes.com/2011/01/21/q-and-a-with-a-pet-nutritionist/

This begs two questions, in what other ways have we, as consumers and pet parents, been deceived and what type of pet food is really good nutrition for our pets??

Homemade Pet Foods and the BARF diet: Are they safe and nutritionally complete?

A trend that began in the mid 1980's and was boosted by the food scare of 2007, was the move away from pre-packaged pet foods.

The two most common approaches was homemade cooked food and raw food.

Making nutritionally correct cooked food is a challenge. The percentage of protein, carbohydrates, fats, vitamins and minerals must be carefully considered.

"The University of California, Davis, School of Veterinary Medicine tested 200 recipes, many written by vets. The researchers found most of the recipes were short on some essential nutrients. " http://pets.webmd.com/dogs/guide/homemade-dog-food

Raw diets, most commonly known as the BARF diet (Bones and Raw Foods or Biologically Appropriate Raw Food), was introduced in 1993 when it was suggested by an Australian veterinarian Ian Billinghurst that pet food should be based on what the animals ate prior to domestication.

This diet has been very controversial and its nutrition questioned. The diet rules out all grains, focusing on protein. While some raw food supporters suggest supplementing with vegetables, others do not.

The strictest raw diet feeders feed only raw meat, bones, and eggs, but no fruit, vegetables, or grains. Often these diets do not include supplements to make them balanced or complete.

The recommended meal content for these raw food purists is 80% meat, sinew, ligaments, fat, and can also include heart meat, 10% edible bone, 5% liver, 5% other organ meat.

Exaggerated health claims regarding the diet include, but are not limited to the following:

- The diet will prevent illness as it creates a healthy immune system
- The pet will have no tooth decay, periodontal disease, or gum infection.
- The body's immune system will fight off parasites and your pets will never have to be dewormed.
- The pet will have no metabolic diseases
- The pet will have sweet smelling skin and will rarely require bathing.
- The pet will have a better balanced character, more energy, and better concentration.

While good food does support a healthy immune system, no diet can make these blanket promises. According to Dr. Kate KuKanich DVM, PhD, DACVIM, *"there is no evidence-based research to support any of these health claims."* http://veterinarycalendar.dvm360.com/pros-and-cons-raw-food-diets-proceedings?rel=canonical

In fact, Dr. KuKanich cautions against the possibility of additional health concerns including, gastrointestinal obstruction, perforated bowel, and broken teeth from the raw bones.

The premise of the raw food diet for dogs is based on the idea of what dogs ate before they were domesticated 10,000-15,000 years ago, and what the gray wolf eats today.

A few of the arguments of pro-raw food proponents include:

- Domestic dogs and gray wolves share 99.7 % of their genes
- Domestic dogs are of the order Carnivora, proving they are strictly carnivores

- Domestic dogs can interbreed with wolves proving they are the "same" species

- The dentition (teeth) of the domestic dog, proves they are carnivores.

- Buying meat "fit for human consumption" rules out bacteria/parasite potential.

- Domestic dogs have natural enzymes called lysozyme that destroys bacteria, proving they can handle a raw diet.

- Dogs with healthy immune systems can fight any parasite or bacteria encountered in raw diets.

While it is indeed true that domestic dogs and gray wolves share 99.7 % of their genes and descended from a shared ancestor, http://news.discovery.com/animals/pets/dogs-not-as-close-kin-to-wolves-as-thought-140116.htm this does not make dogs small wolves. Humans share 96-99 % of their genes with chimpanzees, but that doesn't make us chimps and no one expects us to eat a chimpanzee diet.

Dogs are also from the order Carnivora. This order includes the wolf, coyote, jackal, dingo, and wild dog. It also includes giant pandas, who are almost exclusively herbivorous.

Wolves are known by their scientific name, Canis lupus. There are 40 subspecies of the Canis Lupus. All members of this group can interbreed and produce healthy litters. This does does mean they are the same exact animal with the same exact needs. It only means they are related. Domestication has caused changes in the dog that separate the dog from the gray wolf. Like wolves, dogs have sharp canine teeth, however they are smaller than wolf teeth and less pronounced.

"Wolves' canine teeth are very large and they are more curved and thicker than the typical domestic dogs teeth are, they can reach lengths up to just over a couple inches long. They are adapted to crush huge bones in one crunch. Claws and jaws work together to hold down the meat, (claws which also can rip up hide) and jaws to cut/slice, shred, and break bone." http://yamnuskawolfdogsanctuary.com/resources/wolf-to-woof/physical-differences-between-wolves-and-dogs/

Many omnivores and even herbivores have sharp canine teeth. All primates for instance, have sharp canines. Even humans have retained sharper canine teeth than most none-primate herbivores.

In regards to primate herbivore teeth of gorillas, Peter Emily of the Peter Emily International

Veterinary Dental Foundation, said the following:

"First off, teeth aren't just for chomping flesh. Gorillas eat a lot of heavy twigs and bark, which requires tough teeth—particularly molars—to grind all that tough plant material....[Gorilla canine teeth are] used for display, in particular "to defend against external threats, as well as fend off other male gorillas competing for dominance."
http://news.nationalgeographic.com/news/2015/02/150207-animals-gorillas-elephants-teeth-science-dentistry/

So, the dentition of the mammal, does not always determine the dinner.

There are other important factors that separates the dog from the wolf. Wolves skulls are larger, wider, and longer than the domestic dog. The nails are thicker and larger, making ripping off tough animal hides easier. As pups become full grown wolves, all of their nails turn black in color.

Also, unlike the domestic dog, female wolves only go into estrus once yearly, and the male's testicles will be peanut size and infertile, until the female goes into heat.

These are just a few of the differences between dogs and wolves.

Perhaps the most important distinction, and a subject of some recent studies, is the digestive process differences between the wolf and dog.

The domestication of dogs and the evolution of humans, closely paralleled one another over the past 10,000 - 15,000 years. Domesticated dogs began to eat a more varied diet along with their humans, eventually resulting in an important genetically identifiable characteristic: the ability to digest starch.

Evolutionary geneticist Erik Axelsson led a study which sequenced DNA from 12 wolves from around the world and from 60 dogs belonging to 14 breeds.
http://www.nature.com/nature/journal/v495/n7441/full/nature11837.html

One hundred twenty-two genes were located that could have contributed to the dogs evolution.

A most surprising difference between the wolf and dog was genetically revealed in this study. Domestic dogs are far more capable of digesting starchy foods such as grains, potatoes, rice, peas, and corn.

"Dogs had four to 30 copies of the gene for amylase, a protein that starts the breakdown of starch in the intestine. Wolves have only two copies, one on each chromosome. As a result, that

gene was 28-fold more active in dogs, the researchers found. More copies means more protein, and test-tube studies indicate that dogs should be five fold better than wolves at digesting starch, the chief nutrient in agricultural grains such as wheat and rice."
http://news.sciencemag.org/plants-animals/2013/01/diet-shaped-dog-domestication

This genetic study disproved what many in the raw food world believe.....the dog digestive system is not the same as the wolf.

The safety of raw foods is most certainly in question. While raw food proponents disagree, scientific studies have supported this concern. In a study conducted by the FDA called **"Investigation of Listeria, Salmonella, and toxigenic Escherichia coli in various pet foods,"** *researchers found that "one-third of samples of raw dog or cat foods ordered online were positive for Listeria organisms."*
https://www.avma.org/News/JAVMANews/Pages/141015j.aspx

Raw diet proponents claim that dogs have a unique enzyme in their saliva and digestive tract called lysozyme that destroys any bacteria. Dogs do have this enzyme, but so do humans. No one would recommend that their human child be fed raw foods even though that child has the same bacteria-destroying enzyme as dogs.

In fact, this claim is addressed directly in the study, **"Bacteriological evaluation of commercial canine and feline raw diets"**
http://www.ncbi.nlm.nih.gov/pmc/articles/PMC1140397/.

The researchers state:

"One major proponent of raw diets has suggested that bacterial pathogens that may be found in raw foods are not able to cause disease in the dog because of the unique adaptation of its intestinal tract (2). There is no evidence to support this supposition and cases of salmonellosis in dogs and cats fed homemade raw diets have been reported."

During the study twenty-five pre-packaged raw diets from 8 different manufacturers were evaluated.

Escherichia coli (e coli) was identified in 16 diets (64% of the total), and monophasic *S.* Typhimurium was detected in 5 diets (20% of the total). *Salmonella* was detected in samples containing beef, lamb, quail, chicken, and ostrich. Sporeforming bacteria were identified from 4 diets (16% of the total). *Clostridium perfringens* was identified in 5 (20%) of the samples taken. *Clostridium difficile* was found in one turkey-based food.

The study concluded with the following:

"There is currently inadequate information regarding the safety of raw diets in terms of both animal and human disease. However, considering the variety of infectious and potentially zoonotic pathogens identified here and in other studies, the potential risks must be taken seriously. Given these safety concerns, the absence of any scientific data indicating beneficial health effects of raw diets, and nutritional deficiencies that have been reported with such diets, it is difficult to recommend their use at this point."

The claim that utilizing "human grade" meat does not rule out bacterial contamination. *"The CDC estimates that each year roughly 1 in 6 Americans (or 48 million people) get sick, 128,000 are hospitalized, and 3,000 die of food borne diseases."* Most of those foods are cooked.
http://www.cdc.gov/foodborneburden/

An important consideration in the raw-food debate, is that the method of delivery of raw food to the domestic dog is far different from the delivery of raw food to the wolf. In the wild, the prey is killed and eaten in a short amount of time. Today, animals are killed in slaughterhouses, shipped to processors and finally to the store shelves where it may sit for days before being consumed. This latter process leaves plenty of opportunity for cross-contamination and gives opportunistic organisms plenty of time to multiply. Only cooking to a proper temperature can kill those organisms.

The American Veterinary Medical Association (AVMA) *"discourages the feeding to cats and dogs of any animal-source protein that has not first been subjected to a process to eliminate pathogens because of the risk of illness to cats and dogs as well as humans. Cooking or pasteurization through the application of heat until the protein reaches an internal temperature adequate to destroy pathogenic organisms has been the traditional method used to eliminate pathogens in animal-source protein.... Several studies reported in peer-reviewed scientific journals have demonstrated that raw or undercooked animal-source protein may be contaminated with a variety of pathogenic organisms, including Salmonella spp, Campylobacter spp, Clostridium spp, Escherichia coli, Listeria monocytogenes, and enterotoxigenic Staphylococcus aureus. Cats and dogs may develop food borne illness after being fed animal-source protein contaminated with these organisms if adequate steps are not taken to eliminate pathogens; secondary transmission of these pathogens to humans (eg, pet owners) has also been reported. Cats and dogs can develop subclinical infections with these organisms but still pose a risk to livestock, other nonhuman animals, and humans, especially children, older persons, and immunocompromised individuals."*
https://www.avma.org/KB/Policies/Pages/Raw-or-Undercooked-Animal-Source-Protein-in-Cat-and-Dog-Diets.aspx

It must be recognized that the nutritional requirements for both dogs and cats are not simple. If these requirements are not met or are given in excess, severe problems can occur. For example, diets deficient in protein can cause brittle bones, lack of growth in puppies or kittens, lethargy, chronic infections, slow healing wounds, and mood changes. **Too much protein produces large amounts of ammonia that can encourage the formation of bladder and kidney stones and even shut down the kidneys.** The Merek Veterinary Manual, referring to a study of Dalmatians fed a high protein diet reported:

"Dalmatians fed a diet high in animal protein excrete a net acid load in the urine, and urinary ammonium output is subsequently increased. The combined high concentration of ammonium and urate in urine increases the risk of formation of ammonium urate stones. The excretion of acidic metabolites of an animal protein diet is believed to be important in this process, because urinary ammonium excretion is enhanced and ammonium urate is insoluble....Urine alkalinization minimizes renal ammonia production; the goal is to achieve a urine pH >7..... This can be accomplished by feeding a low-purine, low-protein commercial diet."
http://www.merckvetmanual.com/mvm/urinary_system/noninfectious_diseases_of_the_urinary_system_in_small_animals/urolithiasis_in_small_animals.html

If raw food guideline recommendations for both dog and cat include: 80% meat, sinew, ligaments, fat; 10% edible bone; 5% liver; and 5% other organ meat, how is it possible to avoid too much protein? http://rawfeddogs.org/rawguide.html and http://www.rawfedcats.org/practicalguide.htm

Other BARF (Biologically Appropriate Raw Food) supporters do recommend some vegetables, but continue to insist that all starches are inappropriate, in spite of genetic testing that proves otherwise.

To give you an idea of the nutritional needs of your pets, consider the following from the National Research Council:
http://dels.nas.edu/resources/static-assets/banr/miscellaneous/dog_nutrition_final_fix.pdf

Nutritional Needs of Dogs

Protein:

Total Protein Minimal Requirement - 2.62; Recommended Daily Allowance - 3.28
Amino Acids:
Arginine Minimal Requirement - 0.092; Recommended Daily Allowance - 0.11
Histadine Minimal Requirement -0.048; Recommended Daily Allowance - 0.062
Isoleucine Minimal Requirement -0.098; Recommended Daily Allowance - 0.12
Leucine Minimal Requirement -0.18; Recommended Daily Allowance - 0.22
Lysine Minimum Requirement - 0.092; Recommended Daily Allowance - 0.11
Methionine Minimum Requirement - 0.085; Recommended Daily Allowance - 0.11
Methionine-cystine Minimum Requirement - 0.17; Recommended Daily Allowance - 0.21
Phenylalanine Minimal Requirement - 0.12; Recommended Daily Allowance - 0.15
Phenylalanine-tyrosine Minimal Requirement - 0.19; Recommended Daily Allowance - 0.24

Threonine Minimal Requirement -0.11; Recommended Daily Allowance - 0.14
Tryptophan Minimal Requirement -0.036; Recommended Daily Allowance - 0.046
Valine Minimal Requirement -0.13; Recommended Daily Allowance - 0.16

Fat:

Total Fat (g) - Adequate Intake - 1.3; Recommended Daily Allowance - 1.8; Safe Upper Limit - 10.8
Fatty Acids:
Linoleic Acid (Alpha Linolenic Acid) Omega 3 (g) Adequate Intake - 0.14; Recommended DailyAllowance - 0.12; Safe Upper Limit - 1.4
Arachidonic Acid Omega 6
Eicosapentaenoic & Docosahexaenoic Acid Adequate Intake - 0.03; Recommended Daily Allowance - 0.03; Safe Upper Limit - 0.37

Minerals:

Calcium Minimum Requirement - 0.059; Recommended Daily Allowance - 0.13
Phosphorus Adequate Intake - 0.10; Recommended Daily Allowance - 0.10
Potassium Adequate Intake - 0.14; Recommended Daily Allowance - 0.14
Sodium(mg) Minimum Requirement - 9.85; Recommended Daily Allowance - 26.2
Chloride(mg) Adequate Intake - 40; Recommended Daily Allowance - 40
Magnesium(mg) Minimum Requirement - 5.91; Recommended Daily Allowance - 19.7
Iron(mg) Adequate Intake - 1.0; Recommended Daily Allowance - 1.0
Copper(mg) Adequate Intake - 0.2; Recommended Daily Allowance - 0.2
Iodine(μg) Minimum Requirement - 23.6; Recommended Daily Allowance - 29.6
Zinc (mg)Adequate Intake - 2.0; Recommended Daily Allowance - 2.0
Manganese(mg) Adequate Intake - 0.16; Recommended Daily Allowance - 0.16
Selenium(μg)Adequate Intake - 11.8; Recommended Daily Allowance - 11.8

Vitamins:

Vitamin A, (μg retinol) μg Adequate Intake - 40; Recommended Daily Allowance - 50;Safe Upper Limit - 2,099 (IU)
Vitamin D3, (Cholecalciferol) μg Adequate Intake - 0.36; Recommended Daily Allowance - 0.45; Safe Upper Limit - 2.6
Vitamin E, (alpha tocopheral), mg Adequate Intake - 0.8; Recommended DailyAllowance - 1.0
Vitamin K, (menadione) mg Adequate Intake - 0.043; Recommended Daily Allowance - 0.054
Thiamin, mg Adequate Intake - 0.059; Recommended Daily Allowance - 0.074
Riboflavin, mg Minimum Requirement - 0.138; Recommended Daily Allowance - 0.171
Pyridoxine, (B6) mg Minimum Requirement - 0.04; Recommended Daily Allowance - 0.049
Niacin, (B3) mg Adequate Intake - 0.45; Recommended Daily Allowance - 0.57
Pantothenic Acid, (B5) mg Minimum Requirement - 0.39; Recommended Daily Allowance - 0.49
Folic Acid, (B9) μg Minimum Requirement - 7.1; Recommended Daily Allowance 8.9
Biotin, (B7) aka, Vitamin H; For normal diets not containing raw egg white, adequate biotin is probably by microbial synthesis in the intestine. Diets containing antibiotics may need supplementation
Vitamin B12 (Cobalamine) μg Adequate Intake - 0.92; Recommended Daily Allowance - 1.15
Choline mg Minimum Requirement - 45; Recommended Daily Allowance - 56

Nutritional Needs of Cats

Protein:

Total Protein Minimal Requirement - 3.97; Recommended Daily Allowance - 4.96
Amino Acids:
Arginine Adequate Intake - 0.19; Recommended Daily Allowance - 0.19
Histadine Adequate Intake -0.064; Recommended Daily Allowance - 0.064
Isoleucine Adequate Intake -0.11; Recommended Daily Allowance - 0.11
Leucine Adequate Intake -0.25; Recommended Daily Allowance - 0.25
Lysine Minimum Requirement - 0.067; Recommended Daily Allowance - 0.084
Methionine Minimum Requirement - 0.033; Recommended Daily Allowance - 0.042
Methionine-cystine Minimum Requirement - 0.067; Recommended Daily Allowance - 0.084
Phenylalanine Adequate Intake - 0.099; Recommended Daily Allowance - 0.099
Phenylalanine-tyrosine Adequate Intake - 0.38; Recommended Daily Allowance - 0.38
Taurine Minimum Requirement - 0.0079; Recommended Daily Allowance - 0.0099
Threonine Adequate Intake -0.13; Recommended Daily Allowance - 0.13
Tryptophan Adequate Intake -0.032; Recommended Daily Allowance - 0.032

Fat:

Total Fat - Adequate Intake - 2.2; Recommended Daily Allowance - 2.2; Safe Upper Limit - 8.2
Fatty Acids:
Linoleic Acid (Alpha Linolenic Acid) Omega 3 Adequate Intake - 0.14; Recommended Daily Allowance - 0.14; Safe Upper Limit - 1.4
Arachidonic Acid Omega 6 Adequate Intake 0.0005; Recommended Daily Allowance - 0.0015; Safe Upper Limit - 0.049
Eicosapentaenoic & Docosahexaenoic Acid Adequate Intake - 0.0025; Recommended Daily Allowance - 0.0025

Vitamins:

Vitamin A, (µg retinol) µg Adequate Intake - 19.8; Recommended Daily Allowance - 24.7; Safe Upper Limit - 2,469 (IU)
Vitamin D3, (Cholecalciferol) µg Adequate Intake - 0.14; Recommended Daily Allowance - 0.17; Safe Upper Limit - 19
Vitamin E, (alpha tocopheral), mg Adequate Intake - 0.74; Recommended Daily Allowance - 0.94
Vitamin K, (menadione) mg Adequate Intake - 0.025; Recommended Daily Allowance - 0.025
Thiamin, mg Adequate Intake - 0.11; Recommended Daily Allowance - 0.14
Riboflavin, mg Adequate Intake - 0.079; Recommended Daily Allowance - 0.099
Pyridoxine, (B6) mg Minimum Requirement - 0.05; Recommended Daily Allowance - 0.06
Niacin, (B3) mg Adequate Intake - 0.79; Recommended Daily Allowance - 0.99
Pantothenic Acid, (B5) mg Minimum Requirement - 0.11; Recommended Daily Allowance - 0.14
Folic Acid, (B9) µg Minimum Requirement - 15; Recommended Daily Allowance 19
Biotin, (B7) aka, Vitamin H, µg Adequate Intake - 1.5; Recommended Daily Allowance - 1.9
Vitamin B12 (Cobalamine) µg Adequate Intake - 0.44; Recommended Daily Allowance - 0.56
Choline mg Minimum Requirement - 60; Recommended Daily Allowance - 63

Minerals:

Calcium Minimum Requirement - 0.040; Recommended Daily Allowance - 0.071
Phosphorus Minumum Requirement - 0.035; Recommended Daily Allowance - 0.063
Potassium Adequate Intake - 0.13; Recommended Daily Allowance - 0.13
Sodium(mg) Adequate Intake - 16.0; Recommended Daily Allowance - 16.7
Chloride(mg) Adequate Intake - 23.7; Recommended Daily Allowance - 23.7
Magnesium(mg) Minimum Requirement - 4.9; Recommended Daily Allowance - 9.5
Iron(mg) Adequate Intake - 1.98; Recommended Daily Allowance - 1.98
Copper(mg) Adequate Intake - 0.119; Recommended Daily Allowance - 0.119
Iodine(μg) Minimum Requirement - 31.6; Recommended Daily Allowance - 35
Zinc (mg)Adequate Intake - 1.9; Recommended Daily Allowance - 1.9
Manganese(mg) Adequate Intake - 0.119; Recommended Daily Allowance - 0.119
Selenium(μg)Adequate Intake - 6.95; Recommended Daily Allowance - 6.95

Needless to say, making a home made diet is more complicated than it seems.

Common Sense Pet Nutrition

With all this information, we have to ask, what is common sense nutrition?

It is important first, to clarify common types of pet food and the brands often associated with that category. Companies identify themselves as "premium", "organic", "holistic", among others. These terms do not guarantee the quality of nutrition.

Categories of pet food:

- Off-brand and store brand foods (Everpet ® Ol'Roy ® Special Kitty ®)
- Supermarket brands (Purina ® Cat Chow, Beneful ® , Pedigree ®)
- Exclusive economy or premium feed store brands (Retriever ® 4 Health ®, Sportmix ® , Diamond ®)
- Premium brand name foods (Innova ®, Wellness ® Blue Buffalo ®)
- Prescription Diets available only through veterinarians (Hills ® Prescription Diet, Royal Canin Veterinary Diet ®)
- Home cooked food
- Raw diets freeze dried/frozen/home prepared (Primal ®, Instinct Raw ®)

In a "Consumer Reports" article, Dr. Joseph Wakshlag DVM Ph.D, assistant professor of clinical nutrition at the Cornell University College of Veterinary Medicine, and diplomat at the American College of Veterinary Nutrition said the following:

"There's no scientific evidence that any food is better than the next......Pets can thrive on inexpensive food or become ill from pricey food. If your animal is active and healthy, the food is

doing its job. A higher price could mean better ingredients and better quality control during and after manufacturing. But you might also be paying for pretty packaging, marketing, or a fancy name." **http://www.consumerreports.org/cro/magazine-archive/march-2009/money/pet-food/overview/pet-food-ov.htm**

Yet when we ask the question, what is an "ideal" diet for our pets, we will get different answers depending on who we are talking to. Raw food enthusiasts are certain that raw food is healthier and more natural. Home cooking fans will say that their diet is superior because there are no "mystery ingredients". Premium brands may insist that only foods with no bi-products or grain are healthy.

The ones to question are those who spend every day studying and improving our pet food: Board certified animal nutritionists.

When a similar question was posed to the animal nutritionists and veterinarians at Cummings Veterinary Medical Center at Tufts University and The Ohio State University Veterinary Medical Center, they offered the following information:

- Pet foods with an AAFCO (Association of American Feed Control Officials) statement on the label saying that the diets have undergone **animal feeding trials** are preferred to those formulated by computer to meet the AAFCO nutrient profile. Feeding trials are groups of 10 adult dogs, for example, being fed for 6 months. Based upon lab work, maintaining outer signs of good health, and maintaining body weight, the food is given the AAFCO seal of approval. This means that the food can sustain the pet without gross deficiencies. Food trails are expensive to perform. Interestingly, many companies that do not conduct animal feeding trials claim instead that they are "cruelty free" because they do not "test" on animals.

- Some manufacturers may add ingredients to diets solely for marketing purposes, to increase the appeal of the diet to consumers. These ingredients may have unproven benefits, be present in minuscule amounts and provide nothing to the diet but added expense.

- The phrase "human grade" has no legal meaning in the pet food industry. Once a product is destined for inclusion in pet food, it is no longer fit for human consumption by definition. Moreover, ingredients sourced from the human food chain are not necessarily any more nutritious, wholesome, or safe than ingredients initially destined for pet food. Therefore, manufacturer's claims of human grade ingredients should not be over interpreted.

- Despite anecdotal reports from pet owners and even some veterinarians, there is currently no evidence that raw diets offer any benefits over cooked diets. However, there is substantial evidence that these diets may be associated with dental fractures, bacterial and parasitic infections and other health concerns in pets. All raw meat, regardless of source, should be considered to be contaminated until proven otherwise.

- Whole grains, rather than being fillers, contribute valuable nutrients including vitamins, minerals, essential fatty acids and fiber to diets while helping to keep the fat and calories lower than if animal products were used in their place.

- By-products (mainly organ meats and entrails) often provide more nutrients than muscle meats on a per weight basis and are important components and even delicacies of human diets in other countries. The term by-product comes from the fact that they are the leftovers from animal carcasses once the desirable (for Americans) muscle meat has been removed. AAFCO definitions of mammal by-products specifically exclude hair, hooves, horn, hide trimmings, manure and intestinal contents, as well as anything that is not specifically part of the carcass.

- There are currently are no regulations or legal definitions for labeling a food "holistic". Foods are considered "organic" if they contain ingredients grown without the use of pesticides, synthetic fertilizers, sewage sludge, genetically modified organisms, or ionizing radiation. Animals that produce meat, poultry, eggs, and dairy products do not take antibiotics or growth hormones. "Organic" has nothing to do with the nutritional value of a food.

- Whole meat is not necessarily better than meat meal. Meat meal is actually a more concentrated source of protein due to the fact that it does not contain the water content of
whole meat, and therefore can be added in greater quantities to dry foods to achieve a higher protein content.

- Regarding allergies, the problem in patients with allergies is with the immune system of the individual rather than with any external substance, which has no effect on those with healthy immune systems. If a pet is allergic to beef, he is allergic to all beef regardless of the source or "quality".

- "Fillers" are ingredients with no nutritional value at all. Corn is a grain that offers nutrition while being successfully digested. Corn is not a filler.

http://vet.tufts.edu/nutrition/faq/frequently-asked-questions-about-general-pet-nutrition/ and

http://vet.osu.edu/vmc/companion/our-services/nutrition-support-service/myths-and-misconceptions-surrounding-pet-foods

A concern that applies to human food and pet food equally, and not mentioned in these two articles, is the use of artificial food dyes in our food. Dyes are added to food and treats to make it appear more palatable to humans. It has no advantage for the pet. In fact, dyes have been identified as allergy triggers, and there is some concern that dyes are possibly carcinogenic (having the potential to cause cancer).

In the early 1900's, 80 dyes were used in human food. At that time, the only commercially available pet food was a dog biscuit introduced in England by the American James Spratt in 1860. http://www.petfoodinstitute.org/?page=HistoryofPetFood

The *Pure Foods and Drugs Act,* was passed by Congress in 1906, and scientists began testing the safety of each dye. Today, only 7 dyes remain in use in the US, and many of those are in question and/or illegal in other countries.
http://www.forbes.com/sites/rachelhennessey/2012/08/27/living-in-color-the-potential-dangers-of-artificial-dyes/

The publication, "Food Dyes: A Rainbow of Risks" a report of the Center for Science in the Public Interest, concluded that the "nine artificial dyes approved in the United States likely are carcinogenic, cause hypersensitivity reactions and behavioral problems, or are inadequately tested." https://cspinet.org/new/pdf/food-dyes-rainbow-of-risks.pdf

The FDA denies this claim. However, considering the tainted history of food dyes, it would behoove the pet parent to consider a food free of dyes.
http://onlinelibrary.wiley.com/doi/10.1111/j.1541-4337.2009.00089.x/pdf

According to the National Research Council, both dogs and cats need amino acids from proteins, fatty acids and carbohydrates, vitamins, minerals, and water to survive.

With this in mind, dog pet parents should focus on providing the following:

- A good source of animal protein. Dogs can survive on a vegetarian diet as long as they receive adequate plant protein and vitamin D. The pet should be monitored closely by a veterinarian for any nutritional inadequacies.

- Food free of dyes, or as few dyes as possible.

- Essential fatty acids found in animal fats and seed oils.

- Carbohydrates for energy, found in grains and legumes.

- Vitamins and minerals. Found in most commercial foods. If a good quality food is fed, supplementation should not be required.

- Fresh water always provided

Dogs require a minimum of 20-15% protein. Cats require 34-40% protein, a much higher percentage. Animal protein digests easier than plant protein. This makes it even more unwise to try to force a vegetarian diet on a feline.

Dietary protein provides 10 essential amino acids that neither the cat or dog can create on its own. Deficiencies of any one of those can lead to serious health problems.

Special Dietary Considerations for Cats

Cats have other unique nutritional issues. For example, insufficient arginine in the cat diet can cause a toxic buildup of ammonia in the bloodstream.

In the 1970s, a correlation was made between urinary tract disease in male cats and a high an ash content in cat food. Ash, is a generic term for a combination of minerals such as calcium, phosphorus, magnesium, sodium, potassium, chloride, iron, zinc, copper, manganese, selenium and iodine.

Later, it was determined that it was specifically the magnesium in ash, that caused the problem. The high magnesium in the food that was supplied by plant proteins created an urinary environment that was too alkaline. As a result, struvite crystals are able to form causing deadly blockages of the urinary tract.

The term "ash" is not usually included in the list of cat food ingredients, however many of the minerals themselves are listed. It is best to keep the total number of minerals at, or under, 8%. Many pet food manufacturers responded by lowering the ash content and increasing the amount of meat protein in some of their food brands. Today, these foods can often be identified as "urinary tract formulas".

If taurine, a chemical compound found only in animal protein, is deficient in the diet, it can lead to metabolic disorders, blindness, deafness, heart disease, and more. In the 1980's, the importance of taurine in the cats diet was evident and pet food companies began adding the supplement to their dry and canned food.

When cats began transitioning to a dry kibble as it came onto the market, a valid concern was the lack of moisture in dry food. A average cat's daily water requirement ranges from **5 -10 fluid ounces per day** compared to the dog which requires on average (depending on size) between **8.5- 17 ounces of water per 10 pounds.**

Cats eating canned food will receive much of their daily water needs from its food, since canned food is about 70 to 80 percent water. In contrast, dry food is only 7 -10 % water. Pet parents feeding dry food are encouraged to monitor their cat's water consumption and to encourage it by use of pet water fountains or bubbler bowls.

What the cat pet parent should focus on is providing the following:

- A food higher in animal protein than plant protein.
- A food low in ash, magnesium, and carbohydrates
- A dye-free food.
- The proper water intake found in canned foods and water bowls.
- Proper pH
- Regular feedings and monitoring

A food that is higher in animal protein rather than plant protein will have meat as the main ingredient.

Like ash, carbohydrates are also not listed in the nutrition information, however, Dr. Jennifer Coates has a common sense approach to estimate the number of carbohydrates in the food. http://www.petmd.com/blogs/nutritionnuggets/cat/jcoates/2013/sept/calculating-carbohydrates-in-your-cats-food-30887

According to Dr. Coates:

"Pet food labels must list the minimum crude protein percentage, minimum crude fat percentage, maximum crude fiber percentage, and maximum moisture percentage. They will also sometimes include a maximum value for ash. If this is not present, I use an estimate of 3% for canned foods and 6% for dry. Once you add up protein, fat, fiber, moisture, and ash, the only thing left is carbohydrate."

For cats to have a healthy urinary tract, they require an acidic environment throughout the urinary tract. Keeping in mind that the lower the pH number, the more acidic the urine, a number of 6.0-6.5 is ideal. A number above that, which is more alkaline, can encourage the formation of struvites or magnesium ammonium phosphate crystals. Nature loves balance, so when the urine gets too acidic, calcium oxalate crystals can form.

Foods are available that help encourage a proper pH environment. Another alternative is adding **potassium citrate with cranberry** or **cranberry extract** to the food. Tubs of this supplement can be purchased online for $10-15 per tub.

The pH of the urine can be tested with urine test strips as described in Chapter 15.
While some pet parents believe in regular food fastings have health benefits for their dogs, cats should never be fasted. In fact, a cat that is fasted, either by parental choice or illness, is at great risk of hepatic lipidoses, known commonly as "fatty liver disease". This is an emergency, that if not treated, can lead to death. It is important to monitor the eating habits of each cat in the home. Otherwise, it may not be noticed until it is too late.

Cats do not metabolize medicines or supplements in the same way as dogs do. For that reason many supplements can be harmful to cats.

Many products recommended for cats contains brewers yeast, yet this supplement contains magnesium which is one of the culprits in urinary tract disorders in cats. Vitamin C is an antioxidant that can cause urinary crystals to develop, and cause mouth and stomach issues if given in high doses. Calcium and Vitamin D can be potentially toxic and hard to balance a correct dose. Garlic and onion can both lead to anemia, yet I have read home made diets for cats calling for one or both.

There are some supplements that are healthy for cats and others that are safe for some cats. Potassium citrate with cranberry I mentioned earlier is one of those. Not only does it support urinary health, it contains essential fatty acids for a healthy coat. Digestive enzymes and probiotics are both safe and they can help your cat recover from digestive issues or resupply the necessary gut bacteria that is often destroyed by antibiotics. Brewers Yeast, often a component in many calming formulas, among others, can be safe for a cat that has had no history of urinary problems.

Comparison of Pet Food Ingredients

With all the things we have learned from animal nutritionists and unbiased veterinarians, it is helpful to compare common foods from the least to most expensive. As pointed out by the animal nutritionists, the more expensive brands add some unusual ingredients with little nutritional value to the pet including pomegranate, kelp, and oil of rosemary. While beneficial to humans, the benefit to the dog and cat are questionable. Are we buying these foods because the ingredients sound more appealing to us?

For full disclosure, at T.Paws Rescue & ARFanage, we most often use Diamond ® and Diamond Naturals ®, but we do not turn down any food donated to the rescue.

DOG FOOD

The ingredients in Purina Dog Chow ® Cost $26.99/42 lbs (64¢ per lb)

Whole Grain Corn, Meat and Bone Meal, Corn Gluten Meal, Animal Fat Preserved with Mixed-Tocopherols, Soybean Meal, Poultry By-Product Meal, Egg and Chicken Flavor, Whole Grain Wheat, Animal Digest, Salt, Calcium Carbonate, Potassium Chloride, Dicalcium Phosphate, Choline Chloride, Zinc Sulfate, Yellow 6, Vitamin E Supplement, L-Lysine Monohydrochloride, Ferrous Sulfate, Yellow 5, Red 40, Manganese Sulfate, Niacin, Blue 2, Vitamin A Supplement, Copper Sulfate, Calcium Pantothenate, Garlic Oil, Pyridoxine Hydrochloride, Vitamin B-12 Supplement, Thiamine Mononitrate, Vitamin D-3 Supplement, Riboflavin Supplement, Calcium Iodate, Menadione Sodium Bisulfite Complex (Source of Vitamin K Activity), Folic Acid, Biotin, Sodium Selenite

The ingredients in Diamond Naturals ® Chicken and Rice Adult Dog Food. Cost $31.99/40 lbs (80¢ per lb)

Chicken, chicken meal, whole grain brown rice, white rice, cracked pearled barley, chicken fat (preserved with mixed tocopherols), oatmeal, dried plain beet pulp, egg product, flaxseed, natural chicken flavor, fish meal, salt, potassium chloride, choline chloride, vitamin E supplement, iron proteinate, zinc proteinate, copper proteinate, ferrous sulfate, zinc sulfate, copper sulfate, potassium iodide, thiamine mononitrate, manganese proteinate, manganous oxide, ascorbic acid, vitamin A supplement, biotin, niacin, calcium pantothenate, manganese sulfate, sodium selenite, pyridoxine hydrochloride (vitamin B6), vitamin B12 supplement, riboflavin, vitamin D supplement, folic acid.

The ingredients of 4 Health Grain Free Whitefish and Potato Dog Food: Cost $37.99/30 lb bag ($1.26 per lb)

Whitefish, Fish Meal, Pea Protein, Dried Peas, Tapioca, Whole Potato, Sunflower Oil (preserved with Mixed Tocopherols, a source of Vitamin E), Dried Plain Beet Pulp, Whole Flaxseed, Natural Flavor, Salt, Potassium Chloride, Fish Oil (preserved with Mixed Tocopherols, a source of Vitamin E), Zinc Proteinate, Vitamin E Supplement, Iron Proteinate, L-Ascorbyl-2-Polyphosphate (source of Vitamin C), Choline Chloride, Manganese Proteinate, L-Carnitine, Copper Proteinate, Niacin, D-Calcium Pantothenate, Biotin, Sodium Selenite, Vitamin D3 Supplement, Riboflavin Supplement, Thiamine Mononitrate, Vitamin A Supplement, Vitamin B12 Supplement, Calcium Iodate, Pyridoxine Hydrochloride (source of Vitamin B6), Folic Acid.

The ingredients in Blue Buffalo ® Life Protection Adult Dog Chicken & Brown Rice: Cost $51.99/30 lbs ($1.73 per lb)

Deboned Chicken, Chicken Meal, Brown Rice, Barley, Oatmeal, Chicken Fat (preserved with Mixed Tocopherols), Tomato Pomace (source of Lycopene), Peas, Flaxseed (source of Omega 3 and 6 Fatty Acids), Natural Flavor, Potatoes, Alfalfa Meal, Calcium Carbonate, Salt, Potassium Chloride, Potato Starch, Dried Chicory Root, DL-Methionine, Caramel, Mixed Tocopherols (a natural preservative), Sweet Potatoes, Carrots, Garlic, Choline Chloride, Vitamin E Supplement, Ferrous Sulfate, Iron Amino Acid Chelate, Zinc Amino Acid Chelate, Zinc Sulfate, Yucca Schidigera Extract, Oil of Rosemary, L-Lysine, Parsley, Kelp, Blueberries, Cranberries, Apples, Spinach, Blackberries, Pomegranate, Pumpkin, Barley Grass, Turmeric, L-Ascorbyl-2-Polyphosphate (source of Vitamin C), Copper Sulfate, Copper Amino Acid Chelate, Glucosamine Hydrochloride, Nicotinic Acid (Vitamin B3), Calcium Pantothenate (Vitamin B5), Taurine, Biotin (Vitamin B7), Manganese Sulfate, Vitamin A Supplement, Manganese Amino Acid Chelate, L-Carnitine, Thiamine Mononitrate (Vitamin B1), Riboflavin (Vitamin B2), Vitamin D3 Supplement, Vitamin B12 Supplement, Pyridoxine Hydrochloride (Vitamin B6), Beta Carotene, Dried Yeast, Dried Enterococcus faecium fermentation product, Dried Lactobacillus acidophilus fermentation product, Dried Aspergillus niger fermentation extract, Dried Trichoderma longibrachiatum fermentation extract, Dried Bacillus subtilis fermentation extract, Folic Acid (Vitamin B9), Calcium Iodate, Sodium Selenite

CAT FOOD

The ingredients in Purina Cat Chow ® Cost: $12.78/16 lb bag (80¢ per lb)

Poultry by-product meal, ground yellow corn, wheat flour, corn gluten meal, soybean meal, brewers rice, beef tallow preserved with mixed-tocopherols (source of vitamin E), fish meal, brewers dried yeast, animal digest, phosphoric acid, potassium chloride, calcium carbonate, tetra sodium pyrophosphate, calcium chloride, choline chloride, dicalcium phosphate, salt, taurine, zinc oxide, ferrous sulfate, vitamin supplements (E, A, B-12, D-3), L-Alanine, riboflavin supplement, niacin, calcium pantothenate, manganese sulfate, biotin, thiamine mononitrate, folic acid, pyridoxine hydrochloride, copper sulfate, citric acid, menadione sodium bisulfite complex (source of vitamin K activity), calcium iodate.

The ingredients in Diamond ® Maintenance Cat Food: Cost $17.99/20 lbs (90¢ per lb)

Chicken by-product meal, whole grain ground corn, wheat flour, chicken fat (preserved with mixed tocopherols), corn gluten meal, brewers rice, dried plain beet pulp, natural chicken flavor, flaxseed, fish meal, sodium bisulfate, potassium chloride, choline chloride, DL-methionine, taurine, zinc proteinate, vitamin E supplement, niacin, manganese proteinate, copper proteinate, zinc sulfate, manganese sulfate, copper sulfate, thiamine mononitrate, vitamin A supplement, biotin, potassium iodide, calcium pantothenate, riboflavin, pyridoxine hydrochloride (vitamin B6), vitamin B12 supplement, manganous oxide, sodium selenite, vitamin D supplement, folic acid.

The ingredients of 4 Health ® Grain Free Whitefish, Potato, and Pea Cat food. Cost: $21.99/16 lb bag ($1.37 per lb)

Whitefish, Fish Meal, Salmon Meal, Turkey Meal, Whole Potato, Dried Peas, Pea Protein, Tapioca, Poultry Fat (preserved with Mixed Tocopherols, a source of Vitamin E), Dried Egg Product, Turkey, Natural Flavor, Dried Plain Beet Pulp, Whole Flaxseed, Potassium Chloride, Salt, Dried Carrots, Choline Chloride, Dried Cranberry, Vitamin E Supplement, Taurine, Zinc Sulfate, Ferrous Sulfate, Niacin, Fish Meal, L-Ascorbyl-2-Polyphosphate (Source of Vitamin C), Manganese Sulfate, Copper Sulfate, Thiamine Mononitrate, D-Calcium Pantothenate, Vitamin A Supplement, Sodium Selenite, Riboflavin Supplement, Vitamin D3 Supplement, Biotin, Pyridoxine Hydrochloride (Source of Vitamin B6), Menadione Sodium Bisulfite Complex (Source of Vitamin K activity), Vitamin B12 Supplement, Folic Acid, Cobalt Sulfate, Potassium Iodide.

The ingredients in Blue Buffalo ® Indoor Health Salmon and Brown Rice Cat Food: $36.99/15 lbs ($2.47 per lb)

Deboned Salmon, Turkey Meal, Chicken Meal, Brown Rice, Barley, Chicken Fat (preserved with Mixed Tocopherols), Peas, Tomato Pomace (source of Lycopene), Powdered Cellulose, Natural Flavor, Flaxseed (source of Omega 3 and 6 Fatty Acids), Potatoes, Calcium Carbonate, Alfalfa Meal, Choline Chloride, Potassium Chloride, Salt, Potato Starch, Dried Chicory Root, Caramel, Taurine, DL-Methionine, Cranberries, Mixed Tocopherols (a natural preservative), Sweet Potatoes, Carrots, Zinc Amino Acid Chelate, Zinc Sulfate, Ferrous Sulfate, Nicotinic Acid (Vitamin B3), Iron Amino Acid Chelate, Vitamin E Supplement, Yucca Schidigera Extract, Oil of Rosemary, L-Lysine, Parsley, Kelp, Blueberries, Apples, Spinach, Blackberries, Pomegranate, Pumpkin, Barley Grass, Turmeric, L-Ascorbyl-2-Polyphosphate (source of Vitamin C), Thiamine Mononitrate (Vitamin B1), Copper Sulfate, Biotin (Vitamin B7), Vitamin A Supplement, Copper Amino Acid Chelate, Pyridoxine Hydrochloride (Vitamin B6), Calcium Pantothenate (Vitamin B5), Riboflavin (Vitamin B2), Manganese Sulfate, L-Carnitine, Manganese Amino Acid Chelate, Vitamin D3 Supplement, Beta Carotene, Vitamin B12 Supplement, Folic Acid (Vitamin B9), Calcium Iodate, Dried Yeast, Dried Enterococcus faecium fermentation product, Dried Lactobacillus acidophilus fermentation product, Dried Aspergillus niger fermentation extract, Dried Trichoderma longibrachiatum fermentation extract, Dried Bacillus subtilis fermentation extract, Sodium Selenite

11

Fleas and other Ectoparasites

The Flea Life Cycle

The flea life cycle is important to understand as it gives you the advantage in the fight for flea control. A blood meal, which comes from a host (generally your pet), is necessary to begin the cycle. Once the adult female has consumed the blood meal, she can lay her eggs. The eggs are smaller than a grain of sand and can me laid in your pet's fur where they often fall off into the environment such as the carpet or furniture in your home. A single adult female can lay about 40 eggs per day. In one month 10 female fleas can produce 200,000 fleas. It only takes one single bite from a flea to produce an incredible allergic reaction in some pets.

Depending on environmental factors, it can take anywhere from two days to two weeks for the egg to develop. Cold and dry conditions will slow down the process. Once the eggs hatch, the flea larvae emerge. They are blind and avoid light. The larvae feed off the flea dirt which is really predigested blood, often called "flea poop" that is left behind by adult fleas. They are at most ¼ inch long, nearly transparent, and have no legs. When conditions are favorable, they will spin their cocoon which moves the cycle to the next phase, pupae. Until conditions are favorable, the pupae will remain in the cocoon where it is protected. The cocoons are sticky and sweeping and vacuuming doesn't always remove them. This stage could be weeks, months, and even years. Until a host is detected by vibration, rising carbon dioxide levels, and the presence of body heat, the pupae will remain in stasis.

This is why I experienced a population explosion of fleas the summer I moved back to Tennessee. All my pets were on Frontline ® (fipronil), but favorable warm conditions encouraged a mass emergence of new fleas whose pupae had been left behind by the previous owner. Once my entire rescue of about 25 animals arrived on the scene and spring transitioned to the warm, humid conditions of summer, it was an absolute perfect environment for the flea population.

The flea battle plan is designed to stop fleas at all stages of development and in all areas where they may be hiding. Ignoring one step of the plan can make it useless. The most commonly ignored step is treating the environment. While you may put flea preventative on your pet, the flea must first bite your pet to be affected. One bite for some pets means an itchy allergic reaction.

Pet parents often think that because they have not seen fleas in the environment or on the pet, that they are not present. Its important to remember that the female fleas only have to be on your pet long enough to get a blood meal. All other times, she may be in the carpet, or inside your furniture with other fleas. The classic sign of fleas and flea allergies is irritation near the tail of your dog. If you can spread the hair or use a flea comb, chances are, you will find flea dirt. This means no matter how much you want to deny it, there are fleas in your environment.

Fleas are tenacious in finding a host. If your pet is protected using a product such as fipronil, but there are fleas still in the environment, guess who else the fleas can focus on? You and your human family. So the importance of treating the environment can not be overstated.

No matter what flea product you use, the steps in the flea battle plan never changes. Those steps include:

- Remove the pets from the house and treat the inside
- While the pets are outside, treat the pet
- Move the pets inside, and treat the outer environment

We now use more natural, chemical free methods when possible, but when the flea population explosion occurred in 2008, I felt I had no choice but to turn to an indoor flea fogger such as Raid ® Flea Killer Plus and Bio Spot ® Yard and Garden Spray for the outside.

I removed all my pets from the home, covered all food and dishes, put a fogger in each area including the basement and garage. Once all the foggers were activated, I kept the animals outside for 2 hours. During that time I treated them with fipronil, the generic version of Frontline Topspot ®.

Once the two hours were up, I opened the doors and windows to let the home air out any excess fogger. After 30 minutes, I took my pets inside. Next, I applied the Bio Spot ® Yard and Garden Spray to the grass. The pets were not allowed outside for several hours until the spray had time to dry. I continued to apply fipronil to all the pets for the remainder of the summer, and had no further problem.

Choosing a Safer Flea Preventative

There are a lot of products available for flea prevention, making it very confusing sometimes for the pet parent. Fipronil, a spot-on topical I believe to be one of the safest available, was once only available under the brand name Frontline Topspot ® Now that fipronil is available in generic forms, the original manufacturer has discontinued production of Topspot and focused their energy on Frontline Plus ® . There are generic forms of Frontline Topspot ® and Frontline Plus ® including Sentry Fiprogard ®, Pet Armor ®, and Sargent's Pronyl ®. At one time these generic products contained the exact ingredients as their predecessor. However, in 2011, a patent dispute forced generic supply companies to find a second ingredient. While they can use fipronil, the second ingredient is no longer S-methoprene.

Chemicals used to replace S-methoprene include cyphenothrin, etofenprox and permethrin. Cyphenothrin is toxic to cats, while etofenprox is *"less toxic for cats than other synthetic pyrethroids"* according to the Safety Summary for Veterinary Use: http://parasitipedia.net/index.phpoption=com_content&view=article&id=2682&Itemid=3044

Another has added permethrin. According to the ASPCA Animal Poison Control Center, *" Cats are more likely than dogs to develop pyrethroid toxicosis"* from permethrin, while *"smaller dogs seem to have a greater risk of toxicity".* http://www.vspn.org/Library/misc/VSPN_M01289.htm Both permethrin and etofenprox are found in many inexpensive over-the-counter products, including, Hartz ® and Adam's ® Flea topicals.

A 2010 EPA report in regards to side effects from spot-on (topical) treatments found the following: *"Chihuahuas, shih tzus, miniature poodles, Pomeranians and dachshunds had the most reported incidents, according to the EPA report released Wednesday. For products containing cyphenothrin, those breeds accounted for 33 percent of the reported problems. For products containing permethrin, shih tzus, bichon frise, chihuahuas, yorkshire terriers and maltese were involved in more than 25 percent of the incidents. K-9 Advantix for Dogs contains permethrin and some Sergeant's products and Sentry's Pro XFC contain cyphenothrin."* http://www.scientificamerican.com/article/small-dogs-susceptible-flea-poison/

As if there wasn't enough to worry about, Cipla, the makers of Pet Armor ®, refused to reveal the inert ingredients in their products. This was made public during the 2011 patent dispute. Complaints of ineffectiveness, chemical burns, allergic reactions, and even tremors and seizures have been reported as occurring anywhere from a few minutes to 24 hours after application. Many times, the side effects are caused by the inert ingredients. As a result of the changes in these generic fipronil products, I have chosen to use Frontline Plus ® name brand.

Over-the-counter flea preventatives aren't the only ones to be linked to dangerous side effects. Some prescription flea treatments have been named in several cases of illness and even death.

In addition to the Frontline ® and its generics, there are many other brands on the market. Most require a prescription, with Frontline ® and Advantage ® being the exceptions. Some kill, repel, or control, not only the fleas, but their eggs and larvae as well. In addition, they may kill lice, mosquitoes, and even heart worm and intestinal parasites. While many are spot-on topical drops, others are chewables or tablets. All must be given or reapplied monthly with the exception of Bravecto ® and Serestro ®. A few are safe for exotics and some are safe for pregnant or lactating pets.

Name Brand	Ingredients	Species	Parasites killed, repelled, or controlled	Earliest age/size safe to use	Price range per dose
Frontline Topspot ® (discontinued; generics available)	Fipronil	Dog, cats, some exotics	Fleas, ticks, lice (safe for pregnant or lactating pets)	8 weeks	$5.00-6.70 topical
Frontline Plus ®	Fipronil/methoprene	Dogs, cats	Fleas, flea eggs, flea larvae, ticks, lice, mosquitoes (safe for pregnant or lactating pets)	8 weeks	$13.34-15.00 per topical
Advantage II ® (original Advantage discontinued)	Imidacloprid/pyriproxifen	Dogs, cats, some exotics	Fleas, flea eggs, flea larvae	7 wks (pups) 8 wks (kittens)	$11.25-12.50 per topical
K9 Advantix ®	Imidacloprid/permethrin/pyiproxifen	Dogs only	Fleas, flea eggs, flea larvae, repels mosquitoes and flies	7 weeks	$8.33-9.16 per topical
Advantage Multi ®	Imidacloprid/moxidectin	Dogs, cats, ferrets	Fleas, hookworms, roundworms, whipworms (dogs only) heartworm, and earmites (cats only)	7 wks (pups) 9 wks (kitten)	$15.00-18.33 per topical
Comfortis ®	Spinosad	Dogs	Fleas	14 wks and 5 lbs	$14.17-17.50 per chewable
Trifexis ®	Spinosad/milbemycin	Dogs	Fleas, hookworms, roundworms, whipworms, heartworms	8 wks/5 lbs	$18-20.00 per chewable
Revolution ®	Selemectin	Dogs, cats, some exotics	Fleas, ticks, roundworms, hookworms, heartworms, sarcoptic mange (safe for pregnant or nursing pets)	6 weeks	$16.00-25.00 per topical
Sentinel ® *	Lufenuron/milbemycin	Dogs	Fleas, hookworms, roundworms, whipworms, heartworms	4 wks/2 lbs	$7.17-10.50 per chewable
Sentinel Spectrum ® *	Lufenuron/milbemycin/praziquantel	Dogs	Fleas, hookworms, roundworms, whipworms, heartworms, tapeworms	6 wks/2 lbs	$10.00-12.50 per chewable
NexGard ®	Afoxolaner	Dogs without history of seizures	Fleas, ticks	8 wks/4 lbs	$20.00-26.67 per chewable
Activyl ®	Indoxicarb	Dogs, cats	Fleas, flea eggs, flea larvae	8 wks/4 lbs(pups), 2 lbs (kittens)	$11.67-15.00 per topical
Bravecto ®	Fluralaner	Dogs	Fleas, ticks for 12 weeks (safe for pregnant and lactating pets)	6 months and 4.4 lbs	$47.50 per chewable
Serestro ®	Flumethrin/imidacloprid	Dogs, cats	Fleas, ticks for 8 months, water resistant only	7 wks (pups), 10 wks (kittens)	$50-70 for one collar

- **Never give spinosad in combination with ivermectin.**

Above is a comparison of the most popular brands, including a price range per dose. Some products are topicals, sometimes called "spot on treatments. Others are in chewable form with one product being a collar. The larger the pet, the higher the price per dose will be for that product. The prices quoted are from 1-800-Pet-Meds. Prices may differ at your local veterinarian. While some veterinarians will sell single doses of the product, many will only sell by the package. The package sizes vary from 2-4 doses.

Before buying any flea product, research reviews of the products. This can provide you information of the efficacy and safety of the product by people who have actually used it. 1800Petmeds.com collects reviews from across the internet, including the good and bad. If you decide on a generic or over-the-counter product, be sure to read the ingredients. Reading the ingredients is more important than reading the brand name. It is the only way to know exactly what you are giving your pet. If you don't recognize an ingredient, look it up.

Of all the products available, only two have a special property that can cut the cost of flea preventatives exponentially. This is especially true if you have multiple pets: Frontline ® and Advantage ® .

Topical Tricks of the Trade

While there are many topical flea preventatives on the market, **only two are unique in that it is the same basic formula for dogs and cats.** The only difference is the dosages in the packages. In other words, the cat formula is the same as the dog formula, only a different measurement.

The advantage in this is being able to buy an extra large dose sold for large breed dogs and split it properly using a tuberculin syringe and a chart. The dosage chart was supplied by the makers of the product.

Two name brand products that are safe to use with the syringe and chart method are **Frontline Plus® and Advantage II (not to be confused with Advantage Multi or Advantix II). Frontline Topspot ® is no longer available. The generic form of Frontline Topspot ®, fipronil, is available, but may contain other ingredients that may make it unsafe using this method.**

The original Frontline Topspot ®, contained only fipronil and inactive ingredients. It killed adult fleas within 24 hours. Frontline Topspot ® was discontinued when the patent expired, allowing other companies to sell Topspot ® in generic forms.

Frontline Plus ® combines fipronil plus S-methoprene, which kills eggs and larvae in addition to adult fleas. Both dog and cat formulas contain S-methoprene. However, the percent in the dog and cat dose is not the same. For dogs, the formula is fipronil 9.8% and S-methoprene 8.8%

and for cats it is fipronil 9.8% and S-methoprene 11.8%. Notice the dosage of S-methoprene is actually higher for cats, making it safe to use the formula packaged for dogs on cats.

Advantage II has the same ingredients for both dogs and cats: Imidacloprid 9.10% and Pyriproxyfen .46 % with the remainder being inactive ingredients.

It is easy to dose either flea preventative among your pets. Once your order arrives, open all the vials at once and put them in a container such as a plastic squeeze bottle or empty pill bottle. It is important that the container seal properly to avoid evaporation. Fipronil has no expiration date but it will evaporate if not kept sealed. **Never mix Frontline ® and Advantage ® together.**

One dose (not boxes) of fipronil or Frontline Plus ® (fipronil/S-methoprene) extra large dog, could treat 8 cats or 5 small dogs. If you have only one cat, one vial would treat your cat for 8 months. One vial could treat your small dog for 5 months.

To give you an example of the savings, assume you have one cat. You have the choice to purchase the 3 vial pack marketed for cats or the 3 vial pack marketed for extra large dogs:

Product	Cost	Number of Applications or Number of Months Protected	Price Per Application
3 Pack Frontline Plus ® for Cats	$35.00	3 applications or 3 months of flea protection	$11.66/application
3 Pack Frontline Plus Extra Large Dog	$36.00	24 doses or 24 months of flea protection	$1.50/application

If you don't wish to purchase 24 doses, single vials of the extra large dog dose can be purchased on Ebay, usually with a needle-free syringe with it. Make sure that you know the exact product you are purchasing if you chose this option. Not all fipronil products are created equal. Use a tuberculin syringe, not an insulin syringe. For larger dogs, you can use a 3 ml syringe.

Weight of Pet	Dosage of Fipronil/Fipronil Plus in Milliliters
Cats (no matter the weight)	0.5 ml
Dogs: 0-22 lbs	0.7 ml
Dogs: 23-44 lbs	1.35 ml
Dogs: 45-88 lbs	2.68 ml
Dogs: >89	4 ml

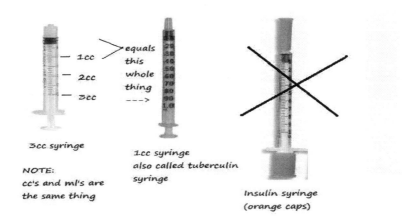

Advantage II ® (not any other form of Advantage ®) is safe to dose in a similar fashion, but the milliliters are not the same. The correct dosage is charted below. Using a tuberculin syringe, I dose as follows:

Weight of Pet (cat or dog)	Dosage of Advantage II in ml (milliliters)
0-10 lbs	0.4 ml
11-20 lbs	0.8 ml
21-30 lbs	1.2 ml
31-40 lbs	1.6 ml
41-50 lbs	2.0 ml
51-60 lbs	2.4 ml
61-70 lbs	2.8 ml
71-80 lbs	3.2 ml

Advantage II ® for dogs has a caveat "Not for cats". However close inspection of the ingredients in all of Advantage II ® packages shows the same exact percentage of ingredients. Imidacloprid 9.10% Pyriproxyfen 0.46% and other inactive ingredients.

Other commercial flea preventives

As you could see in the flea product comparison chart, there are a lot of products to choose from. As the patent protection ends on older products such as Frontline Topspot ® , original Advantage ® , and Program ® (Lufenuron), other companies are then allowed to make and sell the drug.

When it is no longer profitable for the original manufacturer to make the product, they discontinue the product and release a new product with a new ingredient that allows them to again, be under patent protection. Merial ® added S-methopren to create Frontline Plus ®, Bayer added pyriproxifen and released Advantage II ® . Novartis added milbemycin, and Program ® became Sentinel ®. More recently Merial has released a brand new drug and named it NexGard ®. Bayer released K9 Advantix ® , which kills ticks by adding permethrin to Advantage II ® . They also created Advantage Multi ® which contains the ingredients in Advantage II, plus moxidectin. In 2013 they also introduced the Serestro ® collar, which is said to have a time release property that lasts for 8 months. Norvartis also added praziquantel to their Sentinel ® ingredients and sold a second product under the name Sentinel Spectrum ®. (Norvartis has recently been acquired by Elanco/Eli Lily who has sold their Sentinel ® products to Virbac)

For the pet parent, it was an improvement on an already good product. For the consumer, it kept or increased the cost of the original product.

Additional products such as Comfortis ® and Trifexis ® have been introduced to the market by the drug company Elanco/Eli Lily. Merck, another drug company, released Bravecto ® in 2014. It claims to protect dogs from fleas and ticks for 12 weeks. One chewable can cost between $45-65 each.

Since its introduction, Trifexis has taken a particularly hard hit in reports of negative side effects and even death caused by their product. Trifexis is a combination of spinosad (found in Comfortis ®) and milbemycin (found in Sentinel ®). Milbemycin has also sold for years under the name Interceptor ®, a heart worm and intestinal parasite drug.

On its website, Elanco says the following concerning Trifexis ® :

"Trifexis has been demonstrated to be safe in pure and mixed breeds of healthy dogs when used according to label directions for dogs and puppies 8 weeks of age and older and five pounds of body weight or greater. You should discuss the use of Trifexis with your veterinarian prior to use if your dog has a history of epilepsy (seizures). Puppies less than 14 weeks of age may experience a higher rate of vomiting."

There are a few key things to recognize before even discussing pet parents' reports. First, Elanco says Tri-fexis ® is safe in *healthy* animals, not in animals with a compromised immune system or pre-existing conditions. Second, it should never be given to a dog with a history of seizures. By including that statement, the company recognizes that at least one of the animals the drug was tested on had a seizure after taking Trifexis ® . Next, they admit that in their studies, puppies less than 14 weeks old may experience a *"higher rate of vomiting."* There is no question that it causes vomiting, it just causes more vomiting in puppies under 14 weeks old.

So it should come as no surprise when pets experience vomiting and seizures when taking this drug. The company plainly admits there is a possibility of adverse side effects if used on young puppies and unhealthy dogs (immunocompromised or those with pre-existing conditions).

That being said, these types of warning are on nearly every medication on the market: e*very* medication. That includes the medications we take ourselves and those we give our pets.

So far, there is no absolute positive correlation between Trifexis ® and death of healthy animals. A demonstrative positive correlation is a cause and effect relationship. (A) causes (B). What we have are many pet parents who have reported the death of their pet after taking Trifexis ®. However, some are reporting death months, not days, after giving the drug.

Elanco hired an "independent" veterinarian to look for a positive correlation, however his ability to be unbiased has been put into question and he only looked at pathology reports, not the actual pets.

One thing we can do is look at the other products that contain the same ingredients as Trifexis ®. Comfortis ® contains spinosad as well. Precautions for spinosad include the following:

Comfortis ®/spinosad *"are for use in dogs and puppies 14 weeks of age and older. Use with caution in breeding females [and] dogs with a history of seizures"*. It goes on to say *"If vomiting occurs within an hour of administration, redose with another full dose"*. http://www.fda.gov/downloads/AnimalVeterinary/Products/ApprovedAnimalDrugProducts/FOIADrugSummaries/UCM326907.pdf

Milbemycin is the other ingredient in Trifexis ® and is the main ingredient in Interceptor ® heart worm preventative.

Adverse reactions include: Depression/lethargy, vomiting, ataxia, anorexia, diarrhea, convulsions, weakness and hypersalivation. http://www.accessdata.fda.gov/spl/data/8511b388-6827-4573-b401-c444238e26e2/8511b388-6827-4573-b401-c444238e26e2.xml

These are most of the side effects reported by pet parents: Vomiting, seizures, lethargy, ataxia (the loss of full control of body movements), anorexia, diarrhea, and convulsions.

Perhaps it is the combination of the drugs, but frankly, as of this writing, the results are inconclusive. Does Trifexis ® cause death? We can't say with 100% certainty. What we do know without a doubt, are the statements regarding side effects given by the drug company itself. This example stressed the need to read the label and warnings prior to giving anything to your pet.

Food Grade Diatomaceous Earth (DE)

I am a fan of using natural products any time it is possible, but only if they are effective and safe.

Food grade diatomacious earth is a product that can be used to treat fleas as long as it does not get wet. Moisture robs it of its efficacy. Incidentally, it is also mixed in with animal food as a very effective dewormer. Food grade DE is also safe for humans to consume and has been used as a natural dewormer and treatment for Irritable Bowel Syndrome.

DE is actually a sedimentary rock that is fossilized remains of diatoms, hard shelled algae. It is crumbled into white powder and is sold as either pool grade DE or food grade DE. The difference between the two is very significant. Food grade DE must not contain more than 10mg/kg of arsenic and no more than 10mg/kg of lead. It also contains less than 1% crystalline silica.

Diatomaeous earth kills fleas by drying out the waxy outer layer of the flea called the exoskeleton causing the flea to dehydrate and eventually die. Water makes DE ineffective.

Diatomaceous earth is very dusty and a mask should be used while applying it to the yard or pet. It is safe to apply on pets as long as the eyes are avoided and rinsed out afterward. I found that it dried out the sensitive skin of some of my dogs, so I use it only on the yard on a sunny day.

Pool grade DE is easy to find, but it is imperative that you purchase the food grade product. It is available in small containers in the chicken aisle at Tractor Supply for around $8.99 or in 20 lb bags in the livestock section for about $12.99.

I found it most useful applying the DE to recently mowed grass in the areas the pets frequented most outside. I also applied it in the dog and cat building. Generally, by applying it one to two times per month, and continuing to use Frontline Plus ® or Advantage II, the flea population remain well under control.

Beneficial Nematodes

Beneficial nematodes are basically tiny pest hunters that live underground. They control about 250 different types of insects, fleas being one of those. They do not harm the insects we need in our lawns and gardens, nor do they hurt earthworms. They are completely natural and one hundred percent organic.

The only drawback to using the name brand product is the cost. One million nematodes to cover 2000-3000 sq. ft. is nearly $40, while enough to cover an acre is nearly $70, and that is the cost if you do it yourself. To have the company itself come to your home and apply the nematodes is even more expensive.

My research found a affordable choice. Dr. Pye's Scanmask Beneficial Nematodes ® sold for about $18, including shipping online. For that price you can order 7 million nematodes, which is enough to cover about 12,000 sq ft. They now come in a form that is much easier to apply. Simply add to a garden sprayer.

Borax Powder

The same company that made using nematodes popular also makes a powder to be used inside the house. It is essentially borax powder (not to be confused with boric acid) and diatomaceous earth. The product is said to have a low pH level to be safer than using plain borax powder. It must be applied to the entire carpet, including moving furniture. It is left for 24 to 72 hours and then vacuumed. It is said to be safe as long as it is not digested.

For homes with hardwood floors, this borax powder and diatomaceous earth mixture, can be applied in areas of the home not easily accessible by your pets. These areas may be under furniture, under dog crates, under the sink, behind the washer and dryer, among other places.

Other Natural Alternatives

A friend of mine, and farmer, had a particularly difficult time with fleas last year. A pregnant dog wondered on to his property, and since he couldn't find her owner, he took her in. Within days, she gave birth to puppies. Over the summer he fought fleas with everything he could think of including the most expensive veterinary flea treatments on the market. He alsoused all the solutions in the first edition of **Secrets of a Vet Tech**. One of his big problems was the huge round bales of hay on the property where all his cats and livestock were fed. It was the perfect hiding place for fleas. There was simply no winning the battle.

Then he decided to try two things. One was apple cider vinegar and the other was garlic. He added both to the water. He said he noticed that the dogs smelled like garlic, but the flea population reduced significantly. So I decided to do some research.

I consulted "**The Whole Dog Journal**" and found the following regarding apple cider vinegar:

"There are pros and cons to adding cider vinegar to a dog's drinking water, with the recommended dose usually 1 teaspoon to 1 tablespoon per 50 pounds of body weight. "People often talk about adding ACV to water bowls," says canine health researcher Mary Straus. "My feeling is that if so, you should also offer plain water, just in case your dogs don't want to drink the water with the ACV in it. You wouldn't want to risk their drinking less water and possibly becoming dehydrated."

"Is a daily dose of apple cider vinegar good for your dog? Unless your dog is allergic to apples, he or she isn't likely to suffer a serious reaction, and within a month you should be able to tell whether the addition is helping. Commonly reported benefits include improvements in skin and coat condition, a reduction of itching and scratching, the elimination of tear stains on the face, fewer brown or yellow urine spots in lawns, increased mobility in older dogs, reduced flea populations, and an improvement in overall health." (http://www.whole-dog-journal.com/issues/15_01/features/Pet-Uses-Of-Apple-Cider-Vinegar_20435-1.html?pg=3)

I have heard mixed opinions about the use of garlic in dogs. Most pet poison hotlines list garlic as being poison to dogs. Garlic is still considered toxic to cats.

However, in the study "Hematologic changes associated with the appearance of eccentrocytes after intragastric administration of garlic extract to dogs" found that it was very difficult to bring a dog to a toxic level of garlic." http://www.ncbi.nlm.nih.gov/pubmed/11108195

The NCBI seemed to concur with this study as garlic being LESS toxic to dogs than onions, for which they share similarities. http://www.ncbi.nlm.nih.gov/pmc/articles/PMC2984110/

"Garlic (Allium sativum) is considered to be less toxic and safe for dogs than onion when used in moderation. Allicin and ajoene, pharmacologically active agents in garlic, are potent cardiac and smooth muscle relaxants, vasodilators, and hypotensive agents...Lee et al. studied whether dogs given garlic extract developed hemolytic anemia. Garlic extract was administered intragastrically (1.25 ml/kg of b.wt. (5 g of whole garlic/kg) once a day for 7 days). Compared with initial values, erythrocyte count, haematocrit and hemoglobin concentration decreased to a minimum value on days 9 to 11. Heinz body formation, an increase in erythrocyte-reduced glutathione concentration, and eccentrocytes were also detected, however, no dog developed hemolytic anemia. Eccentrocytosis appears to be a major diagnostic feature of garlic-induced hemolysis in dogs. "

Garlic extract is often sold in conjunction with Brewer's Yeast as a flea preventative and healthy coat supplement. A drawback I found in my research besides possible toxicity is the smell. Just as with humans, we eat garlic, we smell like garlic. The same result occurs with dogs.

In my opinion, the research is inconclusive. While I may give the apple cider vinegar a try, I plan on steering clear of the garlic for now. With a cat/dog mixed population, I'm not sure I want to take a chance on their safety, or deal with the smell.

Other Ectoparasites

An ectoparasite is any organism that lives on the outer body of its host, but does not contribute in any way to the survival of the host. Fleas are the most common ectoparasite. Others may include the following and are often species specific.

- **Ticks:** Scientifically known as parasitic arachnids (think spiders). The most common tick is the brown dog tick. Ticks feed on the blood of the host until they are engorged. Infestations can lead to anemia and weakness, particularly in immunocompromised animals. Ticks are also the carriers of Lyme disease, Rocky Mountain Spotted Fever, as well as other diseases and complications. Ticks are fairly easy to spot and should be removed manually with tweezers by grabbing nearest to the mouth and pulling back in one quick motion. Most spot on flea treatments also have something to repel ticks. Although most veterinarians frown at flea collars, many sell Virbac's Preventic ® Tick Collar. This is made with amitraz which is the main ingredient in Mitaban Dip ® used for the treatment of demodex mange.
- **Lice:** Lice are tiny parasites that live on the host and, depending on the species, either chew on the skin, or suck the blood of the host. Lice can cause intense itching, hair loss, anemia, and other issues. They are usually species-specific meaning, the lice on a bird will not jump over to your dog. The most common treatment now is fipronil (Frontline ®) or selamectin (Revolution ®. For reptiles, herpetoculturists often dilute ½ ml of 1 %

ivermectin to a quart of water, spraying the cage and pet. Before attempting this, however, be sure your particular species can tolerate it.

- **Mites:** There are a lot of different species of mites. In the canine, there are demodex mites and sarcopic mange mites. In the bird, you will find feather mites, quill mites, burrowing mites, and surface mites. Rabbits are even susceptible to fur mites, sarcoptic mites, and ear canker mites. Reptiles can suffer from snake mites, chigger mites, and the list goes on. Depending on the mite involved treatment can be ivermectin, lime-sulfur or Mitaban ® dips, and others. Revolution ® and Advantage Multi ® are both effective against sarcoptic mange. The FDA does not label Advantage Multi ® for sarcoptic mange, but other countries do.

- **Flies/Maggots:** Although flies don't generally live on the host, flies can cause what is typically called "fly strike". Most commonly found on the ear tips of dogs who live near livestock or are tied up or in a small outdoor enclosure and cannot get away from the flies. In a situation where the pet is kept in a small outdoor area, feces usually attracts the flies first, so frequent cleanup is imperative. When the flies move in for a blood meal, it is most frequently on the ear tips. Pet parents notice bumps, bleeding, hair loss and general irritation around the tips of the ears. In addition to the pain of multiple fly bites, anywhere flies are found, maggots, or fly larvae, are not far behind. Fly larvae eggs of the common housefly are laid in places that will provide a food source upon hatching. Sometimes that source is on a cut or sore of a live animal. Matted animals are frequently at risk as the tightening of the mats rip the flesh. Turtles and tortoises are also at particular risk when their shell has been cracked. As the eggs hatch, they feed on the flesh. If left untreated, they can eat their way through layer after layer of flesh attracting more flies to lay their eggs. They can cause pain, flesh and organ destruction, and sometimes death. During warm weather, any open wound, no matter the cause is perfect breeding grounds for flies, so frequent exams of your pet are very important. Fly repellent ointment is available in brands such as Farnam ® SWAT Clear Fly Repellent or VIP ® Fly Ointment. If you are unable to get to the store, apply petroleum jelly to the ear tips. If you have human-grade insect repellent that you apply to yourself, consider adding a bit to the petroleum jelly.

- **Leeches**: Leeches feed on the blood of its host. They are most common in exotic aquatic pets. Leeches must be manually removed.

FLEA (not to scale)   TICK (before feeding)   DEMODEX MANGE   SARCOPTIC MANGE

12

Heartworm Prevention

One of the most important lessons in saving money on animal care, is not to let your pet get sick in the first place. If there are things you can prevent, do it. One of those things is keeping your pet properly dewormed.

Both intestinal parasites and heartworms can do major damage to pets. Intestinal parasites such as roundworms, hookworms, tapeworms, and protozoa such as giardia or coccidia can cause diarrhea, loss of appetite, lethargy, wasting away, anemia, and more. Heartworms can easily kill animals and the treatment for heartworm, called Immiticide, has limited availability.

Heartworms and Transmission

Heartworms are a variety of roundworm called *dirofilaria immitis*. The journey the heartworm takes to infect a dog, cat, or ferret, is one completely dependent on the female mosquito. There are 3500 species of mosquito, only about 185 in the United States, and only certain species that

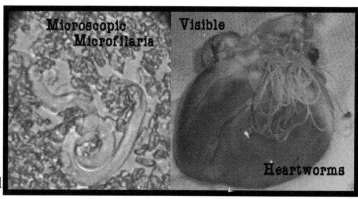

"allow" the development of worms in her cells. Only female mosquitoes bite and they are only active in temperatures above 50 degrees. http://www.megacatch.com/mosquitofacts.html.

In order for the heart worm cycle to begin, the female mosquito must bite a mammal in the first of three stages of development. Once she does this, over the next 10-14 days, the microfilaria will develop into larvae within the mosquito unless it is interrupted by a drop in temperature under 50.

If the larvae make it this far, once the female mosquito bites the dog, cat, or ferret, the journey continues. The infected larvae travel from the bite, through the tissue, and into the bloodstream. Over the next 6-7 months, the larvae will mature into adult heartworms. They will mate, producing microfilaria, thus, completing the life cycle. As the worms mature and propagate, they can over-burden the heart, eventually leading to heart failure.

At one time, it was believed that pets living in dry, arid, regions were unlikely to contract heart worm, because the mosquitoes could not propagate. However, thanks to human habitation which resulted in the introduction of standing water from sprinklers and other sources, animals living in these areas now have a higher chance of contracting this deadly parasitical infestation. To see the impact of this, the following link shows the reported incidences of infections or infestations in the United States in 2013.
https://www.heartwormsociety.org/veterinary-resources/incidence-maps

Preventing Heartworms

The term "heartworm prevention" is a misnomer. Actual prevention can only occur when there are no mosquitoes that allow the heartworm life cycle to take place. Drugs sold as preventatives are preventing the microfilaria or larvae from becoming adult heartworms by killing them before the process is completed.

So what can be done to stop the heartworm life cycle? First, reduce the chances of mosquito propagation and two, administer heartworm prevention to your pet. Mosquitoes propagate in stagnate warm water. Outdoor water bowls, buckets, old tires, bird baths, and kids swimming pools can all collect rain water or water from your sprinklers can be a perfect breeding area for mosquitoes.

Once eggs are laid, they will hatch within 24-48 hours. Even though mosquito larvae are tiny, they are visible to the naked eye. Depending on the species, they will usually grow to about 5 millimeters. Most breathe through an air tube and their movement is in a quick, jerk-like rhythm. Seven to ten days after hatching, the larvae will move to the pupae stage. If you have outdoor pets that you need to provide water for, keep the bowls out of the sun and change the water often to break the life cycle.

The first heart worm preventative sold contained the drug diethylcarbamazine and was sold under the brand name Filaribits ® . It was a once-a-daily chewable tablet. When monthly preventatives came onto the market, Filaribits ® lost their popularity. However, some veterinarians recommend it for dogs sensitive to monthly preventatives and those with autoimmune diseases, so it is still available under the name brand Dimmitrol ® .

Today, heart worm preventatives are most commonly available in three forms:
- Ivermectin
- Milbemycin oxide
- Moxidectin

Interceptor ® , the brand name for milbemycin oxide, was discontinued in 2011, when an FDA inspection revealed some issues at its Novartis manufacturing site. Thankfully, now that

Elanco/Eli Lily has acquired Novartis, Interceptor ® returned to the market in 2015.

Another drug, created by Fort Dodge, was pulled off the U.S. market in 2004. The drug was moxidectin, marketed as a 6 month slow release injection called Proheart 6 ® . Moxidectin is also found in Advantage Multi ®.

When Proheart 6 ® was released in 2001, it was given en masse to dogs, without consideration of their health status. Severe reactions and even deaths were reported, so Fort Dodge voluntarily pulled Proheart 6 ® to do further research. Other countries did not pull the drug including Canada, Japan, Australia, and most of Europe.

The FDA allowed Proheart 6 ® to return to the United States market in 2008 with strict guidelines.

- Blood work was required prior to administration
- Only pets younger than 7 years old were allowed to have the injection
- Proheart 6 ® could not be given the same day as vaccines
- Dogs with a history of weight loss were disqualified
- Caution was advised for any animal with any type of allergies.
- Vets have to have a one hour training session online and pass a test
- The pet parent had to sign an authorization stating they had been informed of any possible side effects and permitted the vet to administer the injection. (This requirement has since then been changed and an authorization is no longer acquired). http://veterinarynews.dvm360.com/risk-requirements-eased-proheart-6-injectable-heartworm-control

On the following page is a comparison of most of the heartworm preventatives on the market. A The price ranges for these products were taken from the 1-800 Pet Meds website. The range of parasites killed or controlled affects the cost of the products. Each pet parent should consider all factors including cost, safety, and health of their pet before deciding on what drug to use.

Multi-pet households and rescues may benefit from using extra-large doses of generic Frontline ® , Frontline Plus ® or Advantage ® for fleas dosed according to the chart as discussed in Chapter 11 . Adding oral ivermectin with pyrantel pamoate or fenbendazole for heartworm and intestinal parasites, can kill or control every parasite listed with the exception of mange mites. While ivermectin can kill most mange mites, it is given at a different dosage and only for a short period of time. Pet parents with certain breeds should have their pet tested for the MDR1 gene, discussed later. The presence of this gene can make the pet intolerant of ivermectin and toxicity can occur.

Medications	Ingredients	Species	Parasite killed	Dosage administration	Warnings or Indications	Monthly Cost
Dimmitrol ® or Filaribits	Diethylcarbamazine	Dogs	Heartworms	Daily	Best for dogs w/ autoimmune diseases or sensitivity to monthly preventatives	$7-17 for 100 tablets
Heartgard ® Heartgard ® for Cats	Ivermectin	Dog/Cat	Heartworms	Monthly	For dogs with the MDR1 gene including collies and herding dogs, use with caution.	$8-10 per dose
Heartgard Plus ® Iverhart Plus ® Triheart Plus ®	Ivermectin/pyrantel pamoete	Dogs	Heartworms Hookworms Roundworms	Monthly	For dogs with the MDR1 gene including collies and herding dogs, use with caution.	$8-10 per dose
Interceptor ®	Milbemycin Oxime	Dogs	Heartworms Hookworms Whipworms Roundworms	Monthly	None	$8-10 per dose
Sentinel ® Sentinel Spectrum ®	Milbemycin Oxime/Lufenerone Sentinel Spectrum ® also contains praziquantel	Dogs	Heartworms Hookworms Whipworms Roundworms Fleas Tapeworms (Spectrum only)	Monthly	None	$9-16 per dose (Sentinal ®) $10-17 per dose (Sentinal Spectrum ®)
Trifexis ®	Milbemycinoxime/spinosad	Dogs	Heart worms Hookworms Whip worms Roundworms Fleas	Monthly	Some concern with side effects of this drug combination. More research needed.	$22-23 per dose
Advantage Multi ®	Moxidectin/ Imidocloprid	Dogs	Heart worm Hookworm Whip worms Roundworms Fleas	Monthly	None	$19-21 per dose

Proheart 6 ® injection	Moxidectin	Dogs	Heart worm Hookworm	Every 6 months	Used only with a strict protocol. See page ___ for more info	$42-60 per dose plus cost of labwork
Revolution ®	Selamectin	Dogs Cats	Heart worm Hookworm Roundworm Whip worm Fleas Ticks Sarcoptic mange (dogs) ear mites (cats)	Monthly	None	$20-22 per dose
1 % Ivomec ® for Cattle given orally rather than by injection	Ivermectin	Dogs Cats	Heart worms	Every 30-45 days	Tuburculin syringe and dosing chart required. Must be diluted for cats and drug sensitive dogs including those with the MDR1 gene	8-80 ¢ per dose

The Drug Sensitivity Gene and Heartworm Prevention

Research has shown that certain dog breeds have a gene that causes drug sensitivity. The gene is called the MDR1 gene which stands for "multi-drug reaction". Although veterinarians knew since the early 80's that some, but not all, Collie breeds, had a sensitivity to ivermectin, it wasn't until 2001, that Katrina Mealey, DVM, PhD, DACVIM, DACVCP, of Washington State University's Veterinary Clinical Pharmacology Laboratory, discovered the gene.

Only $1/200^{th}$ of the normal safe ivermectin dose in normal dogs, causes toxicity in dogs with the MDR1 gene.

The protein encoded in this gene, P-glycoprotein (PGP), is unable to do its job which is to keep potential neurotoxins from entering the brain. As a result, the toxins build up in the brain. One dose of ivermectin, or dosing over a longer period of time, may cause toxic levels to be reached.

Breeds found most commonly with the MDR1 gene include: Collies, Border Collies, Australian Shepherds, English Shepherds, German Shepherds (white German Shepherds show a higher frequency of the gene), Old English Sheepdogs, Shetland Sheepdogs, Silken Windhound, McNab, Long Haired Whippet, herding breed mixes and some other mixed breeds.
http://vcpl.vetmed.wsu.edu/affected-breeds

The only way to know for sure if your dog has the MDR1 gene is to be tested. Washington State University's Veterinary Clinical Pharmacology Laboratory offers the test for $60-70 with discounts for multiple pets. http://vcpl.vetmed.wsu.edu/

The Wisdom Panel ® 3.0, not only includes the MDR1 gene test, but the genetic information of your pet. The cost for this is $85. http://www.wisdompanel.com/

Other drugs, in addition to ivermectin, can seriously affect dogs with the MDR1 gene. These most common ones include: Acepromazine, a sedative, butorphanol (Torbugesic), a pain reliever, and loperamide (Imodium) an anti-diarrhea drug. Some pre-anesthetic, chemotherapy, and anti-parasitic drugs (including other heart worm preventatives) can also affect dogs with the MDR1 gene. Erythromycin, an antibiotic, can also cause a problem.

Topical, spot on flea and tick medications, including some with heartworm preventatives added seem to be safe for MDR1 dogs. According to WSU-VCP scientists:

"While the dose of ivermectin used to prevent heart worm infection is SAFE in dogs with the mutation (6 micrograms per kilogram), higher doses, such as those used for treating mange (300-600 micrograms per kilogram) will cause neurological toxicity in dogs that are homozygous for the MDR1 mutation (MDR1 mutant/mutant) and can cause toxicity in dogs that are heterozygous for the mutation (MDR1 mutant/normal)."

In regards to other anti-parasitics including selamectin, milbemycin, and moxidectin, these same scientists said: *"these drugs are safe in dogs with the mutation if used for heartworm prevention at the manufacturer's recommended dose. Higher doses (generally 10-20 times higher than the heart worm prevention dose) have been documented to cause neurological toxicity in dogs with the MDR1 mutation. "*

As I mentioned before, I was concerned about using ivermectin with Casey, my golden/collie mix, but she had taken ivermectin in the form of Heartgard ® long before I had known about the MDR1 gene.

Ivomectin for Heartworms

When I and my rescued pack returned to Tennessee in 2008, I knew that heartworm preventatives were going to be even more important in the humidity of East Tennessee . I also knew that $60-65 per month to buy Heartgard Plus ® or Interceptor ® was going to be very difficult to afford.

I found that ivomectin 1%, marketed as an injectable for cattle, could be given orally. Ivermectin 1% was the same ivomectin found in Heartgard ®. Heartgard ® certainly tasted better in its chewable form and also contained pyrantel for intestinal parasites. However, the dose of liquid ivermectin necessary for prevention was so small, I could put it in the dogs' food, (dry kibble mixed with canned food) along with pyrantel.

Using the dosage chart below, a tuberculin syringe, and an 18 gauge needle, I drew the proper amount from the bottle of ivermectin 1% for Cattle and Swine, and mixed it in the food once monthly.

Note that other forms of ivermectin are available including 0.8 % Sheep Drench. Never use any other form of ivermectin other than 1% for Cattle and Swine. It is sold most commonly under the name Ivomec ® but generic liquids, such as Noromectin ® 1% Injectable. Never buy Ivomec Plus ® , Noromectin Plus ® or any that contain additional dewormers.

For dogs *without* the MDR1 gene, the following dosages apply:

Weight of Dog	Dosage of Ivermectin
Up to 10 lbs	0.1 ml
11-20 lbs	0.2 ml
21-30 lbs	0.3 ml
41-50 lbs	0.5 ml
51-60 lbs	0.6 ml

Although the Washington State studies showed that dogs with MDR1 can tolerate the proper dosage of ivermectin found in Heartgard ® and other ivermectin brands, some veterinarians are recommending smaller dosages for pets with the gene. The concern is making sure they are given enough for heart worm protection, but not so much that it becomes toxic to them. I would recommend testing for the gene if you have a herding breed or hunting breed mix, and talking to your vet to get his or her recommendations.

Ivomectin 1% can still be used in the same manner as above, but in a more diluted form. For dogs with the MDR1 gene, it has now been recommended to dilute the ivermectin with food-grade (USP) glycerin or propylene glycol, if you plan to store it. Vegetable oil can serve as a substitute for propylene glycol. However, it must be used the same day as diluted and any remaining mixture discarded. http://www.dogaware.com/health/ivomec.html

For small dogs with the MDR1 gene, a ratio of 30:1 is used when diluting ivermectin. That would be, for instance, 1 ml of ivermectin mixed with 3mls of glycerin, propylene glycol, or vegetable oil. Shake well before using. This method makes 33 mcg (micrograms) per 0.1 ml, which is roughly half of the usual dosage found in Heartgard ®. The proper dosage is then 0.1 ml (not 1 ml) per 10 lbs of body weight as found in the chart above. Since the rate of the MDR1 gene is low in toy and small breeds, I would recommend testing for the gene before using this diluted dosage, otherwise, you may not be giving enough for heart worm protection.

For large dogs with the MDR1 gene, the ratio is 9:1 or 9 parts glycerin, propylene glycol, or vegetable oil (0.9 ml) to 1 part ivomec (0.1 ml). To make a larger amount to store in the refrigerator, mix 3mls of ivermectin to 30 mls of glycerin or propylene glycol and shake well. Do not use vegetable oil if the mixture is to be stored.

Using this formula changes the dosage given in the chart for dogs without the MDR1 gene. For large dogs, the following applies:

Ivermectin dosage for large dogs with MDR1 gene using 9:1 mixture

Weight of the dog	Ivermectin dosage
19-36 lbs	0.1 ml
37-73 lbs	0.2 ml
74-110 lbs	0.3 ml
111-147 lbs	0.4 ml

To give you an idea of the savings, having no dogs with the MDR1 gene, I use a total of 2 milliliters (mls) of undiluted ivermectin per month. I purchased a 50 ml bottle of Ivomec (ivermectin)1% at Tractor Supply in 2012 for $40. That $40, using 2 mls per month equals **25 months worth of heartworm protection for $1.60 per month for all 12 dogs**. ($1.60 for all 12 dogs, not $1.60 each).

To get 25 months of heartworm protection using Heartgard ® and similar brands, we would have paid $1960 or $78.40 per month for 12 dogs. **That's a total savings of $1920.**

Now that I have found generic ivermectin (Noromectin ®) online for less than $30, we are paying only $1.20 per month. Once we changed to a new dosing protocol (as I will explain later in the chapter), we saved even more.

Using the more expensive of the two brands (1% Ivomec, purchased for $40), the cost of heartworm prevention per pet/per month is about 8-80 cents.

It should be noted that Heartgard ® includes pyrantel, which kills intestinal parasites, while ivermectin alone does not. However, as you will see in the following pages, my cost for pyrantel was minimal.

If you only have a small dog that only uses 0.1 ml of ivermectin per month, a 50 ml bottle would expire long before you have finished it, so it may be in the best interest of the single pet household to buy Heartgard ®, Interceptor ® or similar.

Possible evidence of resistance to heart worm preventative

According to the American Heartworm Society, there have been an unusual number of cases of dogs on heartworm preventative being diagnosed positive for heartworm infestation, particularly in the Mississippi Delta. https://www.heartwormsociety.org/newsroom/in-the-news/81-heartworm-preventive-resistance-is-it-possible

This caused a concern about a possible resistance to macrocyclic lactones, the term for drugs like ivomectin and milbemycin oxime, used to kill microfillaria, or baby heartworms.

In my research, I found that while the American Heartworm Society was being conservative in its conclusion that a resistance was occurring, Dr. Jennifer Coats of PetMD was very concerned and cited the following case:
 http://www.petmd.com/blogs/fullyvetted/2013/aug/resistance-to-heartworm-prevention-medications-in-cats-dogs#.UmqYZxCtbMI

"The case report I mentioned above details the case of a dog that was rescued in New Orleans after Hurricane Katrina. The dog tested positive for and had symptoms consistent with heartworm disease. It was treated with four doses of melarsomine dihydrochloride [brand name: Immiticide], which killed the adult worms living in its heart and lungs. So far so good, but an equally important part of treatment is the use of a macrocyclic lactone to kill the microfilariae circulating in the blood stream. The microscopic worms can cause damage to the kidneys and other organs and are responsible for the transmission of heartworm disease from animal to animal through mosquito bites."

"The dog in question received three treatments (one should suffice) with high doses of macrocyclic lactones — once with milbemycin oxime and twice with ivermectin, all to no avail. The researchers performed a genetic analysis on the surviving microfilariae and identified the mutation that is most likely responsible for this case of drug resistance. It looks like the heartworms have mutated so that the proteins in their cell membranes no longer allow macrocyclic latones to enter their cells."

I had to ask myself why the AHS, who recommends year around prevention no matter where you live, was so conservative on the issue. Then I realized that all the sponsors of the AHS are large pharmaceutical companies that manufacture heartworm preventatives.

This made me wonder about resistance. We know that in humans, for instance, our resistance to certain antibiotics have occurred because of overuse and eating antibiotic-laced meats. (http://www.cdc.gov/drugresistance/threat-report-2013/)

So have we been exposing heart worms to macrocyclic lactone so much that a resistance is building up? Some veterinarians seem to think so.

When tested, the heartworms themselves were found to have mutated into a new strain the scientists called the MP3 strain.

Some veterinarians believe that the shortage of Immiticide ® (melarsomine dihydrochloride), the only approved treatment for heart worm infestation contributed to the mutation. (http://www.dogaware.com/articles/newsimmiticide.html).

The shortage of Immiticide ®, a drug which includes arsenic, began around 2009. In 2011, Merial, the manufacturer of the drug, reported it was completely out of the drug because of technical difficulties with production. Now, in 2015, the drug is again being made, but is on back order. http://news.vin.com/VINNews.aspx?articleId=36880

Immiticide ® works very quickly comparatively speaking. Immiticide ® is an injection given under very controlled conditions. Generally it is given in one or two separate treatments. The dog must be kept confined for several weeks to prevent a possible embolism, which in itself, can kill the dog. Still, it is the only drug we have that can kill adult heart worms.

When the drug was no longer available, veterinarians turned to what is called the "slow kill" or "soft kill" method. Most used heartworm preventative....ivomectin. Ivomectin kills the larvae stage of the worm, but not the adult worms. Their hope was that by preventing the larvae from becoming adults, they could keep the number of adult worms to a minimum until they died of natural causes. Adult heartworms can live for more than 5 years and grow a foot in length. During that time, they can do severe damage to the internal organs.

Several veterinarians also began adding the antibiotic doxycycline. Although an unexpected drug, according to a 2008 study, doxycycline kills an organism called wolbachia that lives inside the heart worm, weakening the heart worm and making them sterile. http://www.ncbi.nlm.nih.gov/pubmed/18930598

The ivomectin/doxycycline therapy is much cheaper than Immiticide ® by about 50-75%. Some argue that is it also safer for the individual pet.

Other veterinarians argue that it is this "slow kill" treatment is actually not in the pet's best interest if Immiticide ® is available.

Dr. Byron Blagburn, presented the possibility of resistance in April of 2011 in his paper and webinar " **Emerging issues in heart worm disease,**" and other veterinarian agree. http://files.dvm360.com/alfresco_images/DVM360/2013/11/19/8d168467-a4f8-4b2b-bd13-1ff20e7f2d9a/article-32691.pdf

Charles Thomas Nelson DVM cited three problems with the slow-kill method:

- Nothing is done to mitigate the possible damage to the body when the worms die.

- If this damage occurs, the dog is going to need emergency care that is very expensive and could be life-threatening.

- It might add to selective pressure of the organisms. (Selective pressure is any factor that can alter the health of an organism within its environment. Selective pressure is the driving force in the evolution of resistance. If an organism develops the ability to survive a drug, it passes that ability onto its offspring. If selective pressure is great enough, resistance can develop.)

http://www.veterinarypracticenews.com/May-2013/Not-The-Heartworms-You-Used-To-Know/

In other words, the slow kill method may have contributed to the resistance creating the MP3 strain.

Dr. Blagburn tested the efficacy of several common heart worm preventatives including Heartgard Plus ® (ivomectin), Interceptor ® (milbemycin oxime), Revolution ® (selamectin), and Advantage Multi ® (moxidectin), against the MP3 heart worm strain. Only moxidectin proved 100 % effective with ivomectin, milbemycin oxime, and selemectin having only a 12.5 % efficiency. http://veterinarynews.dvm360.com/heartworm-preventive-efficacy-study-results-revealed-navc

While there is still more research to do, Dr. Blagburg recommends yearly testing for heartworms and year around heartworm prevention.

According to the American Heartworm Society, (who, according to their website, is sponsored by the makers of most heart worm preventatives):

"The fact is that heartworm disease has been diagnosed in all 50 states, and risk factors are impossible to predict. Multiple variables, from climate variations to the presence of wildlife carriers, cause rates of infections to vary dramatically from year to year—even within communities. And because infected mosquitoes can come inside, both outdoor and indoor pets are at risk." https://www.heartwormsociety.org/pet-owner-resources/heartworm-basics

However, several reputable sources disagreed:

"Many species of mosquitoes die off when the weather turns cold, leaving only eggs which lie on the ground like seeds, waiting for warmth and spring rains to hatch and produce a new generation. Except in the warmest part of their range, these adult mosquitoes actually do only live in the summer and disappear in winter. Other species survive cold weather by hibernating.....Mosquitoes that hibernate need warm weather to become active, while mosquitoes that spend the winter as eggs need rainfall to flood the eggs and make them hatch." http://www.mosquitoreviews.com/mosquito-cold.html

So, can mosquitoes live during the winter in areas below 50 degrees? According to many entomologists, including those at Purdue University the answer is no.

"Over-wintering females shelter in sites such as caves, culverts, and human dwellings. An extended period of cold (equivalent to the passage of winter) is required before delayed-hatching eggs that have gone through a period of being dry are capable of hatching. An extended period of cold also is required before over-wintering females are capable of developing eggs." http://extension.entm.purdue.edu/publichealth/insects/mosquito.html

Still, the Companion Animal Parasite Council (CAPC), advocates year-round heart worm prevention for cats and dogs.

"This recommendation is based on parasite and vector characteristics and human behavior:

- *Heartworm transmission occurs throughout the year in portions of the United States.*
- *Mosquito presence and ability to transmit heart worm microfilariae are often unpredictable, making it impossible to pinpoint potential transmission seasons.*
- *More pets are traveling with their owners, often to and from heartworm-endemic areas during transmission season.*
- *Year-round prevention may help improve client compliance and efficacy of preventatives."*

http://www.capcvet.org/expert-articles/are-we-doing-enough-to-prevent-heartworm-infections/

While I agree that pets that travel to warm areas in winter should be on yearly heartworm preventative, I believe the real reason for universal monthly heartworm preventative use is "client compliance". If you give the preventative the same day every month, twelve months out of the year, you are less likely to forget.

With all that information in mind, it seems that the following would have to happen in winter in cold climates for a dog, cat, or ferret to acquire the heartworm larvae:

The temperature would have to stay above 50 degrees for several weeks. Hibernating mosquitoes would need time to come out of dormancy and the likelihood that they would bite would be minimal.

http://www.megacatch.com/mosquitofacts.html

Eggs laid the previous season would require water to hatch and at least a 10 day span of continued warm weather to metamorphosis into adult mosquitoes. Then a female mosquito of a proper species must bite a mammal in the early stages of heart worm, be given an additional two weeks for the microfilaria to become larvae, with the temperatures never dropping below 50 degrees. If she gets that far, then she can transfer the larvae to your pet by biting him or her.

The chances seem remote in areas that experience any winter below 50 degrees.

Elizabeth Miller of Mosquito Review, said, *"Since weather makes such a difference, mosquito activity can begin at different times each year, and even in the same year, some species may become active before others. Still, it's possible to estimate roughly when mosquito season will begin and end, depending on what part of the country you live in.*

http://www.mosquitoreviews.com/mosquito-season.html

So, it seems that if we are attentive to the weather and the reminder to begin heart worm preventatives when it warms above 50 degrees, we should be able to give preventatives only during the active-mosquito months.

Long Term Affects of Monthly Heartworm Preventatives

It has been said that the best defense against disease is a strong and healthy immune system. This is the premise under which holistic veterinarians practice. It is a good premise.

There are several valid questions asked by myself, many holistic and even some conventional veterinarians:

- Have we over-exposed heartworms to ivermectin and other anti-parasitics causing the heart worm to build up an immunity to conventional drugs?

- Are we damaging the immune system's ability to function with monthly doses of anti-parasitics? (Holistic vets refer to conventional anti-parasitics as "toxins")

- Are we seeing a rise in immunologic diseases and cancer? Did we cause this by exposing our pets to environmental "toxins" including heartworm preventatives?

- Are there really long-term consequences to the conventional approach of monthly dosing?

As of today, there are no studies, long-term or otherwise, to determine if monthly dosing is causing harm. However, some veterinarians expand what they know from earlier research into the possible negative effects of vaccines, to apply to heartworm preventatives.

According to Jean Dodds, DVM, *"In the last few decades, veterinarians and animal fanciers have recognized that immunologic diseases have significantly increased in the dog population. At the same time, the ongoing linebreeding and inbreeding practices of dog fanciers tend to promote the genetic susceptibility to disease. More than 40 diseases are known to have an autoimmune basis (i.e. where the body reacts against itself producing antibodies that destroy various tissues), and susceptibility to almost all of them is influenced strongly by a specific small group of genes in people and animals."*

http://drjeandoddspethealthresource.tumblr.com/post/46289883129/dodds-heartworm-preventives#.VZ2mO_ldjNV

In fairness, we have to ask: Is there an actual increase confirmed by accurate record keeping or studies, or are we simply testing for and recognizing these autoimmune diseases? Are we seeing more illness because animals are living much longer than before?

The study most cited for the "attack" on the immune system by "environmental toxins" (vaccines, heartworm and flea preventative) is the Purdue Vaccination Study mentioned earlier in the discussion of vaccines.

The study tested the hypothesis that over-vaccinated dogs would produce auto-antibodies that would lead to auto-immune diseases. While auto-antibodies were detected, Dr. HogenEsch, in his email to me, made clear that *"none of the dogs became sick or had any clinical evidence of autoimmune disease or allergies."*

In other words, although there was an increased concentrations of antibodies, there was no definitive proof that this increased concentration caused health problems. However, the scientists did believe that their results showed a possible genetic predisposition to autoimmunity. As Dr. Dodds said in an earlier quote, " *ongoing linebreeding and inbreeding practices of dog fanciers tend to promote the genetic susceptibility to disease.*"

After all this research, we really find that none of our original questions can be answered. There has not been enough research to say that properly dosed monthly heartworm preventatives harm your pet unless your pet has the MDR1 gene. Nor can we say beyond a doubt that year around use of the preventatives has caused heart worms to build immunity to ivermectin or any other anti-parasitic. All we have is anecdotal evidence, not hard science.

A middle ground approach, suggested by Dr. Jean Dodds, that takes into account the possibility of some negative effects of anti-parasitics, but does not rule out the need for them.

"Foremost, I recommend administering heart worm preventive every 45 days instead of every 30 days, but only if this interval is strictly adhered to. If it's difficult to keep track with a reminder calendar, then your dog may need to stay on the medication every month.

Spinosads are found in Trifexis, a monthly heartworm/flea preventive, as well as Comfortis for flea prevention. While I believe these are effective for flea prevention and killing, spinosads are contraindicated in epileptic or seizure prone dogs and should not be given to these dogs. Unfortunately, this is generally unknown and should be shared with your veterinarian, friends and family.

Overall, the temperature needs to be above 57 degrees for approximately two weeks and mosquitoes are prevalent. Please use the temperature as your primary guide."

http://drjeandoddspethealthresource.tumblr.com/post/46289883129/dodds-heartworm-preventives#.VZ2mO_ldjNV

Conventional vs "Natural" Heartworm Prevention: Defining "Toxicity"

Over the course of my research, I noticed that many holistic vets referred to conventional medications, particularly vaccines and anti-parasitics, as "toxins". Anything not "natural" or "herbal" seems to count as a toxin.

According to Dr. Herschel Lessin, *" People seem to think that if something is "natural" then it must be completely safe. If only it were true. If "natural" means coming from herbal or other sources arising in nature, then most of our prescription drugs (made by the "evil" pharma companies) are "natural"."Natural" medicines, sold in "health food" stores, online, and in pharmacies are not without serious side effects ,and are not sold without profits in mind."* https://survivorpediatrics.wordpress.com/2011/05/18/is-word-natural-on-products-mean-the-product-is-safe/

One such example Dr. Lessin uses is the heart drug, digitalis. Digitalis is made from the foxglove plant and was used as a "natural" medicine for years. However, eat too much foxglove, and one will suffer cardiac arrest. Digitalis is "natural", yet it can cause death.

Essential oils are toxic to cats and many essential oils can be toxic to dogs including wormwood and pennyroyal used for parasites.

I found a shocking example when reading **The Nature of Animal Healing** by one of America's top holistic veterinarians, Martin Goldstein. (Published April 6, 1999, Knoft, 1st edition)

Dr. Goldstein, who does not recommend conventional monthly heartworm preventatives, does recommend using black walnut, *"an herb known to kill parasites"* (page 223). *"For clients who insist on a more active form of prevention, "* Dr. Goldstein says, *"I suggest doses of black walnut given two to three times a week, as I've actually reversed clinical heartworm with it"* (page 223).

The problem is black walnut is also known to kill dogs and horses. Black walnut is on the ASPCA's list of poisonous substances just like foxglove. http://www.aspca.org/pet-care/animal-poison-control/toxic-and-non-toxic-plants/black-walnut .

While the nut itself is not poisonous until it starts to decompose, this potential of toxicity is never mentioned in the book or in most holistic websites I read. Dr. Goldstein does say he administers black walnut in liquid form and I can only assume it is prepared from fresh, and not decomposing nuts.

In regards to black walnut use, Dr. Shawn Messonnier, also a well known holistic vet, says *"Black walnut is usually considered to be too toxic to use without veterinary supervision. There are reports of toxicity due to fungal contamination. The tannins and alkaloids may lead to vomiting and diarrhea. Most conventional dewormers (and other herbal deworming preparations) are much safer. "*(page 217)

http://www.totalhealthmagazine.com/Pet-Health/BLACK-WALNUT-for-Pets.html

In his book, **8 Weeks to a Healthy Dog** (Published September 13, 2003, Rodele Books)**,**

Dr. Messonnier states:

"I've read some reports where doctors tried using black walnut for heartworms. The doctors admitted that black walnut didn't work, so they gave the dog a conventional drug. When the conventional drug got rid of the worms, the doctors claims that the black walnut "weakened" the worms, making conventional medication more effective." (page 72)

If black walnut wasn't bad enough, Dr. Goldstein goes on to recommend homeopathic nosodes for heartworm.

According to "Dogs Naturally," *"Nosodes are specialized homeopathic remedies that are prepared by taking actual diseased matter from a sick animal such as diseased tissue or nasal discharge. The preparation of a nosode involves a lengthy process of succussion and dilution of the original material using traditional homeopathic protocols until virtually no molecules of the crude substance remain, rendering the nosode safe for use. This process, called potentization, inactivates the original disease substance and converts the material into a bioenergetic remedy which interacts with the body's energy field. The final product is a potent remedy that is an energetic blueprint of the actual disease.* "http://www.dogsnaturallymagazine.com/nosodes-can-they-replace-vaccines/

Simply put, diseased matter is diluted with alcohol until no more diseased matter remains. All that is left behind is alcohol.

As Dr. Luc De Schepper, MD, DI Hom., CHom., Lic.Ac answered when asked if nosodes have side effects, *"No, again because we are talking energy, not molecules. When you use potencies over 24c there is not even one molecule of the original substance left, and then when you put it in water it is even more dilute."* http://www.drluc.com/homeopathy-basics.asp

So, according to followers of holistic medicine, some type of "energy" left behind is responsible for the cure. This substance is then called a "homeopathic vaccines". However, as a result of stricter standards enacted by the Natural Health Products Directorate, these "homeopathic vaccines" must now read *"This product is not an alternative to vaccination."*

In his defense, Dr. Martin Goldstein does recommend adding the conventional daily heart worm pill for animals living in heartworm endemic areas. He says "I recommend adding to this regimen [of homeopathic heart worm nodoses], the conventional daily heart worm pill given three times weekly." https://tr.im/AoPiH

The daily heartworm pill he refers to is generic diethylcarbamazine known as its name brand Dimmitrol®.

If Dr. Goldstein had full faith in nosodes, why recommend a conventional heartworm preventative?

Other veterinarians agree with the holistic approach to heartworms. Dr. Jeffery Levy believes a whole dog approach is necessary and we are missing the point of heart worm prevention and treatment.

"*The objective of treating a dog with heart worm should NOT be to get rid of the heart worm. You're not treating the heart worm, you're treating the dog... It makes a lot more sense to measure the treatment by looking at the dog's quality of life. So, he is positive for heartworm. The fact is, heartworms have been around forever and dogs and heartworms have been coexisting for all eternity. It's actually a relatively recent phenomenon that dogs are dying from heartworm. Heartworm is not, by any means, the death penalty it's made out to be.* **The dogs that die from heartworm are the dogs that are being vaccinated, fed processed pet food and are being treated with suppressive drugs for every little thing that comes along".*" -Dr. Jeffery Levy (http://www.thewholedog.org/heartworm.html)

The "Whole Dog Journal" article goes on to say, "*Dr. William Falconer, a veterinarian with a homeopathic practice in Austin, Texas states: "The heartworm has been out there forever as far as we know, but we don't read reports of wolves and coyotes being wiped out by heartworm, and yet domestic dogs are falling prey to it."*

The problem is, none of the holistic doctors in any of the books or online articles I read cited any scientific study to back up their claims. There was no study on the effectiveness of homeopathic heartworm nosodes. No one provided proof that only vaccinated dogs fed processed foods die from heartworm. No statistic was cited for evidence that wolves and coyotes do not fall prey to heartworms.

Dr. Levy does the reader a disservice by claiming that dogs from previous generations did not die from heartworm. Heartworm, or dirofilaria immitis, was discovered in Italy in 1626. The first case in the United States was reported in 1847. Beyond that, no consistent records were kept as to the number of wolves, coyotes, dogs, or cats that have died as a result of a heartworm infestation.

In the introduction of this book, I discussed at length the "proving methods" for nosodes, and found it to be seriously lacking. However, that doesn't seem to stop the market for heartworm nosodes and other "natural" heartworm products.

A "natural heartworm protection formula" is sold on the internet. This formula is said to be made from "extracts of herbs well known for their mosquito repelling properties, and others well known for their anti-parasitic properties." http://www.pet360.com/product/55618/only-natural-pet-hw-protect-herbal-formula

Again, no studies are cited proving that the herbs are effective mosquito repellents or have anti-parasitic properties.

In fact, a caveat is including in the description: *"An herbal approach to heart worm prevention is not like a traditional heartworm pharmaceutical preventative, which chemically kills all heart worm larvae, but it may be an effective and more natural method to prevent heart worm infection."*

As I read this, the statement seems to be saying "while traditional pharmaceutical preventatives actually kill heart worm larvae, this *might help* prevent it." And, then again, it might not.

Cats and Heartworms

It was once believed that cats are not affected by heartworms, but we have found that this was not true. We are also finding that it is more common than previously thought.
http://www.prnewswire.com/news-releases/new-study-reveals-pathology-of-feline-heartworm-disease-proves-existence-of-hard-57901652.html

The difference is in the way the heartworm reacts in the cat rather than the dog. Heartworms were intended for dogs. They know how to make their way through the body and to the heart of a dog and they know how to get passed the immune system.

Since the cat is not a natural host, the heartworm is generally unable to complete its cycle and make its way to the heart. The heartworm is in a strange land, and usually, the cat's immune system can detect and destroy the heartworm microfilaria. If microfilaria make it through the cat's defenses they tend to migrate to the lungs where they can cause serious health conditions. The cat is much less likely to be heartworm positive than the dog. Any heartworms that do survive live about 2-3 years in cats compared to 4-5 years in dogs. The damage heartworms do during that time can be extensive.

Symptoms include a persistent cough, lethargy, vomiting and difficulty breathing. Often the cat will be misdiagnosed with asthma, bronchitus or upper respiratory infection. The diagnosis for this is now called heartworm associated respiratory disease or HARD.

Unlike in dogs, you will not find microfilaria under the microscope when doing a simple direct smear heartworm test. Antigen testing is necessary.

Treatment with Immiticide ® is not an option, as Immiticide ® is toxic to cats. At this point, there is no approved method of treatment for heartworm found in cats. However, some veterinarians are using the option of treatment with ivermectin and doxycycline, the "soft kill" method I mentioned earlier. Some prefer to wait out the lifespan of the worm and give supportive care in the meantime. Prednisone is used to open the lungs and make breathing easier.

If left untreated, the result can be severe damage to the respiratory system, kidneys and liver. Heartworm can cause sudden death.

Now, with all this said, exactly how prevalent is feline heartworm disease?

"Studies of heartworm infection in southeastern U.S. cats obtained from shelters indicate a prevalence of 2.5 to 14 percent. This approximates or exceeds prevalence of feline leukemia virus and feline immunodeficiency virus infections. A 1998 nationwide antibody survey of more than 2,000 largely asymptomatic cats revealed an exposure prevalence of nearly 12 percent."
http://www.capcvet.org/expert-articles/are-we-doing-enough-to-prevent-heartworm-infections/

"Following the Gulf Coast hurricanes in 2005, researchers explored the question of whether abandoned animals might have a higher incidence of heart worm infection related to a lower level of veterinary care. The prevalence of heartworm disease among rescued animals was found to be similar to that of the general population in the region."
https://www.avma.org/News/Journals/Collections/Pages/AVMA-Collections-Heartworm-disease-summary.aspx

There are heartworm preventatives available for cats. Heartgard ® which is oral ivermectin is around $35 for a 6 month supply. The heartworm preventative ingredient is the same (ivermectin) used in dog heartworm preventatives. However, the dosage of ivermectin is 55 *micro*grams for small cats. (Notice MICROgrams, not MILIgrams)

To make monthly heartworm prevention for cats using the same 1% Ivomec sterile solution I used for my dogs, you would mix .55 ml ivermectin using a tuberculin syringe to 5 ml propylene glycol or vegetable oil to obtain a 55 mcg per ml solution. Each cat would get 1 ml monthly. Do not store the mixture if made with vegetable oil.

This would be suitable for the cattery or rescue but for a one cat household **Advantage Multi ®** would be my choice. Advantage Multi ® is a topical and sells for about $69 for a six month supply, but it controls fleas, heart worms, ear mites, hookworms and roundworms.

Testing for Heartworms

In the early days of laboratory heart worm detection, a drop of blood was put under the microscope and the veterinarian or technician searched for microfiliaria. This processed was improved by centrifuging the blood, thereby concentrating the microfilaria to make detection easier. This was called the Knott's test. Later, filtration and staining tests made detection even easier.

Unfortunately, none of these tests detected larvae or adult heart worms. This presented a problem, because microfilaria will not be present in the blood until the larvae has matured into adult heartworms, who then propagate and produce the microfilaria. If a pet was tested during this stage, the test results would be a false negative.

Tests were then created to detect antigens. Antigens are small protein and carbohydrate components of the heart worm in the bloodstream. These are the common snap tests used in most veterinarian's office. Although more accurate than earlier tests, the antigen tests only show a positive if female heartworms are present.

Serologic tests were then created to detect the antibodies. Antibodies are produced when the body has been exposed to an invader. While this solved the problem with detection of only female worms, it only proved the pet had been exposed to the heartworm, not necessarily infected with it.

So each test has its positive and negative aspects. The microfilaria test can be done at home if one learns the skill. Antigens tests are available to buy in bulk and I recommend it to rescues.

A Final Note on Heartworm Prevention

While the choices and debates in the world of heartworm prevention can seem daunting, some things are common sense and quite simple. The best way to prevent heartworm, is to prevent mosquitoes.

Make sure there is no standing water around your home allowing mosquitoes to breed and multiply. If you have outside pets or leave water out for the birds, change the water every few days. Look for areas where even a small amount of water could gather, such as in the creases of old tarps or upturned garbage lids. Mosquitoes are very active in the evening. Bring pets inside when mosquitoes are at their worst. While there are some essential oils that may repel mosquitoes, be careful in their use. Essential oils can be toxic to cats and ingesting essential oils can make dogs ill or become toxic to them as well. Check with your vet before using essential oils.

13

Intestinal Parasites & Protozoas

Unless the mother of puppies and kittens has been properly dewormed while pregnant, your puppy and/or kitten will more than likely have intestinal parasites. It's a fact of life. There are several types of parasites and protozoas that can effect dogs and cats. Other common pets, such as bunnies, rats, reptiles, etc, can also be carriers and suffer from intestinal parasites and protozoas. Whether you are talking about a dog or a snake, most often **the general and specific signs of parasitism are about the same.**

- Anorexia (no appetite/not eating)
- Weight loss/emaciation (potbellied appearance in some)
- Lethargy/overall depression
- Failure to thrive
- Vomiting/Diarrhea
- Dehydration
- Dull coat/Skin

Types of Intestinal Parasites and Protozoas:

There is terminology when discussing this subject that can be very confusing when it is really rather simple.

All parasitic worms are called helminths. Animal medicine is most concerned with two groups of helminths classified by their shape: round and flat. Nemotodes are unsegmented worms, that have a long cylindrical (round) bodies. They include ascaris (which we often call "roundworms"), hookworms, whipworms, and heartworms.

Flatworms are comprised of tremotodes (flukes) and cestoda (tapeworms). The difference in the two is how they acquire and digest their food. Flukes have a digestive system. Tapeworms, on the other hand, absorb their nutrients through their skin. They have no need for a digestive system.

Protozoans are not helminths or worms, but single celled parasites that can only divide and reproduce in a host. They are often divided by their shape. Amoebas have no defined shape and use a pseudopod (fake appendage) to move. Flagellates on the other hand, use a hairlike appendage that is whipped back and forth to propel themselves. Ciliates have hundreds of tiny hairs that move in unison to create locomotion. They are all protozoans, but function differently. The two most common protozoans treated in animal medicine is giardia and coccidia.

All of these technical terms are simply for classification. What you need to know is how to recognize them and their symptoms, and what is used to eradicate them.

Only a few of these parasites can be seen with the naked eye. This includes ascaris (roundworms) and tapeworm segments. Most worm eggs and some protozoas can be easily seen under the microscope. The pictures below are not to scale, but serve as an example of what can be found under the lens of a microscope.

The intestinal parasites and protozoas listed below can affect most types of common pets including dogs, cats, rabbits, rats, ferrets, and reptiles.

Helminths:

- **Roundworms/Ascaris:** In the feces, these worms resemble spaghetti noodles, and are probably the most common worm seen. They are often passed from mom to pup/kitten or picked up from contaminated soil or prey. They can cause a potbellied appearance, diarrhea, lethargy, poor 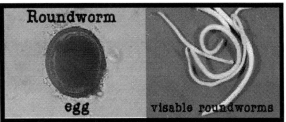 development, poor skin coat, coughing, and other symptoms. Other species can also be affected by some form of roundworms including most exotics. Treatment is with pyrantal or fenbendazole.

- **Hookworms:** Since hookworms are much smaller than roundworms, you will not see these in the feces. They can also be passed from mom to pup/kitten and picked up from soil or prey. They have the added skill of being able to burrow into the feet or skin of the pet while on the ground. Hookworms attach themselves to the inner lining of the intestine and feed off the blood, so a common symptom, particularly in puppies/kittens is anemia and weakness. This is where checking the color of the mucus membranes comes in handy. Diarrhea is also common. Some reptiles 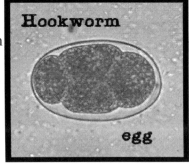 may also become infested with hookworms. Treatment is with pyrantel or fenbendazole.

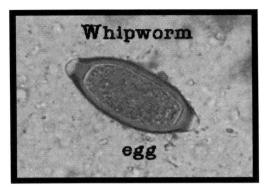

- **Whipworms:** Even smaller than hookworm, this is another type of worm you will not see in the stool but that can cause extremely severe symptoms in young or immunocompromised animals. The eggs lay dormant in the soil until picked up by the pet, usually through self grooming. They also attach to the lining of the intestine and can cause severe bloody diarrhea. If left untreated, death can occur. Whipworms are not killed by pyrantel, but are killed by fenbendazole and Interceptor ® which is now back on the market.

- **Tapeworms:** Tapeworms resemble grains of rice. What you are actually seeing are tapeworm segments, not the entire tapeworm. Tape worms come from fleas that carry the eggs to your pet. Those segments that you see carry eggs and the method tapeworms keep their life cycle going. Though you will usually not see many symptoms associated with tapeworms, it is imperative that the cycle be broken. Anything that can compromise your pet's  immunity needs to be dealt with. Sometimes fly larvae (maggots) can be mistaken for tapeworms, and are much more lethal. Unlike tapeworm segments found around the rectum, maggots can be found anywhere there is a skin lesion. They are generally larger than tapeworm segments and demonstrate much more movement. Treatment for tapeworms is praziquantel.

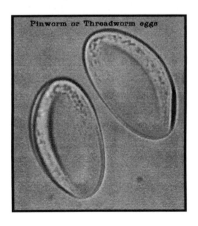

- **Pinworms:** Also called threadworms, these are a type of roundworm most commonly are found in rabbits, rodents, and reptiles. There are different types but all belong to the nemotode class. Treatment is usually pyrantel.

Protozoans:

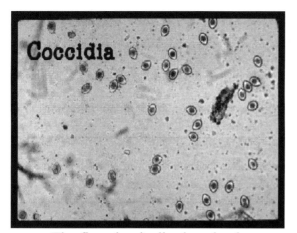

- **Coccidia:** This is a protozoa, or a one celled animal that you cannot see with the naked eye. It is one of many that can affect your pets. Pups, kittens, bunnies, ferrets, and many reptile species are susceptible. Most commonly seen in stressed puppies or kittens, coccidia is an opportunistic protozoa. In other words, most likely there is another reason the immune system is not working as it should. Environment also plays a major factor. Poor sanitation allows them to reinfect themselves over and over. The first sign is diarrhea that becomes more and more severe until it is mucus-like and tinged with blood. If not treated dehydration can quickly occur. Albon ® is the most common treatment.

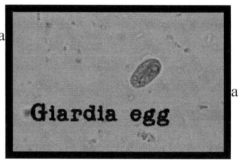

- **Giardia:** This is also a protozoa, most specifically a flagellate. It is often picked up by dogs in contaminated water. Streams and puddles are common sources. Oftentimes, vets will see it after particularly hard rain that floods the yards where the pets are kept. Typically, you will see large amounts of diarrhea that is often watery or as described by some as resembling a "cow pile". Weight loss can occur. Other species are susceptible to forms of giardia including birds, lizards, and rodents. Treatment is metronidazole.

The following protozoas are not commonly diagnosed in the veterinarian in-house lab. If the veterinarian suspects one or more protozoans in a patient, a stool sample and other lab work may be sent to a laboratory for further testing. Exotic veterinarians may be more experienced with detecting protozoans such as amoebas or tricomoniasis in a fecal sample.

- **Toxoplasmosis:** Although dogs can be carriers, the preferred host is the cat. This is the protozoa that makes pregnant mothers panic and give up their cats instead of just wearing gloves and a face mask when they clean the litterbox. Most cats show no symptoms unless they are immunocompromised and when they do it is usually lethargy, loss of appetite, and weight loss. Treatment for both dogs and cats is clindamycin.

- **Cryptosporidium:** This is actually a very nasty strain of coccidia. It produces severe diarrhea. It comes from contaminated drinking water and wild prey. Although related to coccidia, pets generally are unresponsive to the same treatment. Cryptosporidium can also affect birds, lizards and snakes. Antibiotics for this include clindamycin, azithromycin, and tylosin

- **Amoebas:** These are protozoan organisms most often found in lizards and snakes than in dogs and cats. Since amoebas generally require warm temperatures found in tropical and sub tropical regions, it is not of particular concern in most of North America. However, if a pet, (most often a reptile) is shipped from a tropical area to the U.S., amoebas can be a problem. Treatment is generally metronidazole.

- **Trichomoniasis:** Found in several exotic species, tricomoniasis often does not present any gastrointestinal signs in reptiles. For this reason, it is important to do yearly fecal tests. It is sometimes known as "canker" or "trich" in birds and can cause problems in the intestinal and respiratory systems. The most common treatment is metronizole

Below, you will find two charts listing some of the internal and external parasites and protozoans that can affect your pet. Some animals serve as immediate hosts and are sickened by the parasite, while others can be carriers. The parasite, although often called by the same generic name (such as roundworms), may be different sub-groups that only target specific pets.

Its important to note that pets kept indoors are more isolated and much less likely to contract a parasite. Guinea pigs and rabbits purchased by a reputable source and kept indoors will probably rarely, if ever, have to worry about most of the parasites listed on the following page.

In the exotic pet trade, many pets are wild-sourced (wild-caught). Although this is changing and more are bred in captivity under more controlled conditions, pet parents should be aware of where their exotic pet comes from. It should be assumed that all wild-sourced exotic pets have some type of external and/or internal parasite. A fecal and exam should be performed on all wild-sourced pets by a qualified exotic veterinarian.

Parasite/Protozoa	Dog	Cat	Guinea Pig	Rabbit	Rodent	Ferret
Giardia	X	X	X			X
Coccidia	X	X	X	X	X	X
Toxoplasmosis	X	X				
Cryptosporidium			X		X	X
Roundworms	X	X	X		X	X
Hookworms	X	X	X			X
Whipworms	X					
Lungworms		X				

Parasite						
Pinworms				X	X	X	
Tapeworms	X	X		X	X	X
Heartworms	X	X				X
Fleas	X	X	X			X
Ticks	X	X				
Lice	X	X	X		X	
Fur Mites			X		X	
Ear Mites	X	X	X		X	X
Mange Mites (Includes Sarcoptic, Demodex, Notedric, among others)	X	X	X		X	X

**The "Rodent" category is generalized and includes rats, mice, hamsters, and gerbils

The number of exotic pets makes it difficult to be specific about the parasites of each sub-group of each species. The chart on the following page is a representation of the most common parasites found in many exotics. It is important to note that within the species, some may be terrestrial or land dwellers, while others are aquatic. Leeches, for example, will not affect (or be less likely to affect) a terrestrial species compared to an aquatic species.

Amphibians include frogs, salamanders, and newts. Chelonia include turtles, tortoises, and terrapins.

Parasite	Bird	Amphibian	Chelonia	Lizard	Snake
Giardia	X			X	
Coccidia	X	X	X		X
Tricomoniasis	X	X	X		X
Criptosporidium	X			X	
Amoeba				X	
Roundworms	X	X	X	X	X
Hookworms				X	X
Pinworms				X	X
Tapeworms	X		X		X
Ticks			X		X
Mites	X		X		X
Fly Larvae			X		
Leeches		X	X		X

Types of Dewormers and Protozoa Treatments

There are many anti-parasitic drugs on the market that treat a wide array of parasite and/or protozoa infestations. They are sold under generic as well as trade names, marketed for dogs and cats, exotic, and livestock, and dosages vary. It can be very confusing and intimidating when the pet parent is trying to determine what anti-parasitic is best for their pet's condition and what is the most effective option.

In the following pages, anti-parasitics will be listed by their scientific/generic name and most common trade names.

Pyrantel Pamoete (Strongid ® /Nemex 2 ®)

Years of reading fecal samples under the microscope taught me that the most common worms found in dogs and cats were roundworms and hookworms. That's why most veterinary hospitals use pyrantel pamoete as their drug of choice for deworming. Over-the-counter pyrantel is sold in a 4.5 mg/ml solution. Veterinarians purchase the 50 mg/ml liquid. The difference in cost is phenomenal.

An important note and a possible source of confusion is the difference between pyrantel pamoete (Strongid, Nemex 2) and pyrantel tartate (Stongid C). Tartate is a medicated feed sold primarily for horses. Tartate is not for use in a dog or cat.

To treat a 10 lb. dog using the pet store purchased pyrantel, you would be using 5 mls of liquid, but only 0.5 mls using the livestock liquid (see chart on the following page). You would treat once now, and again in 2 weeks.

The same bottle of pyrantel pamoete that your vet can acquire can also be purchased at local feed stores or online. I purchased a 16 oz (1 pint) of pyrantel recently for $20.93 with free shipping. That's about 4¢ per ml. To treat all of our dogs and cats using pyrantel, It costs 93¢ for the first dose, and another 93¢ in 2 weeks.

To have your pet treated with this same pyrantel at a veterinarian clinic, it would cost around $15, not including the office call and fecal exam.

If you will recall from a previous chapter, to prevent heartworm in all 12 dogs using ivermectin, our cost is only $1.20 per month. To get the same exact protection against heartworm and intestinal parasites found in Heartgard Plus ®, our monthly cost for all 12 dogs (not each dog) is only $3.06. If we had to purchase Heartgard Plus ®, our monthly cost would be $78.40.

Pyrantel is very safe and difficult to overdose. Pyrantel is safe for both dogs and cats and is well received. Most veterinarians dose at 1ml per 10 lbs using the 50 mg/kg bottle. On the following page is the dosage for dogs and cats. This same information will be provided in a later chapter for exotic species.

Weight of Dog or Cat	Amount of Pyrantel in milliliters (ml)
Under 5 lbs	.25-.5 ml
10 lbs	1 ml
20 lbs	2 ml
30 lbs	3 ml
40 lbs	4 ml
50 lbs	5 ml
60 lbs	6 ml

The pet should be treated once, and repeated in 2 weeks with the same dose. Pyrantel does not control whipworms.

Fenbendazole (Safeguard ® /Panacur ®)

Fenbendazole is the generic term for Panacur ® or Safe-guard ® . Fenbendazole treats all the same things as Pyrantel plus whipworms, some forms of tapeworms, and giardia. Another advantage is not having to buy an entire quart, but plenty to do the job. An 125 ml bottle can be purchased for around $20 at feed stores. At Tractor Supply, it is marketed under Safe-Guard Goat Dewormer. I pay about 0.16¢ per milliliter, which is an excellent price.

The disadvantage of fenbendazole, is that it has to be given once daily for 3 days. It also has a higher dosage requirement. So, dogs should be dosed, according to weight, for three days. However, fenbendazole does not have to be repeated in two weeks as pyrantel does.

Weight of Pet	Dosage of Fenbendazole in milliliters
5 lbs	1 ml
10 lbs	2 ml
15 lbs	3 ml
20 lbs	4 ml
25 lbs	5 ml
30 lbs	6 ml
35 lbs	7 ml
40 lbs	8 ml
45 lbs	9 ml
50 lbs	10 ml

Fenbendazole can be given by mouth using a syringe, or it can be mixed with canned food. I now deworm with fenbendazole every three months. This protocol has proved very successful.

Praziquantel (Droncit ®)

Fenbendazole will kill some forms of tapeworms, but not *Dipylidium caninum* the most common tapeworm and the only one transmitted by fleas. These tapeworm segments often resemble tiny pieces of dried rice near the tail. The only dewormer lethal to *Dipylidium caninum* is called praziquantel, the generic name for Droncit ®.

Treatment for this species of tapeworm can be expensive. A single tablet of Droncit ® can cost between $8-9. Over-the-counter tablets marketed for dogs and cats costs about $7 each.

The same praziquantel marketed for fish and with no prescription necessary is only about $1 per capsule. For less than $30, we can purchase enough capsules of praziquantel on Ebay to treat everyone at T.Paws Rescue.

Weight of DOG	Dosage using 34 mg capsule of Praziquantel
5 lbs and under	½ tablet
6-10 lbs	1 tablet
11-15 lbs	1 ½ tablet
16-30 lbs	2
31-45 lbs	3
46-60 lbs	4
Over 60	5

The average cat only requires about 23 mg of praziquantel. Unfortunately, the 23 mg is only marketed for cats, not fish, and is much more expensive. My solution was reached by opening the capsule up. One whole capsule equals 34 mg, half of the capsule is 17 mg, and ¾ of a capsule is about 25 mg. When my cats require a dose of praziquantel, I dose *the cats* using the chart below, breaking open a 34 mg capsule, and adding it to their canned food:

Weight of CAT	Dosage using 34 mg capsule of Praziquantel
Up to 10 lbs	½ capsule
10 lbs	¾ capsule
Over 10 lbs	1 capsule

Deworming once is enough using praziquantel unless there is a re-infestation from another flea bite.

Remember, when shopping for these products at Tractor Supply, do not look in the pet supply section, but rather the livestock aisle. These products are much cheaper and comes in larger quantities, and often at higher milligram so less is needed.

Sulfadimethoxine 12.5 % solution (Albon ® /Di-methox ®)

Albon ® is a prescription used to treat certain bacterial infections in dogs and cat. Albon ® is also the preferred treatment for coccidia, a protozoa that can cause diarrhea. Coccidia is especially devastating for kittens and puppies, as it can dehydrate them so quickly. I nearly lost a foster kitten to coccidia once.

The primary ingredient in Albon ® is sulfadimethozine 12.5% which is sold at many feed stores under the name Di-methox. The taste is pretty unpleasant so it is often mixed with V.A.L Syrup ® (recently discontinued), Dyne ® (dogs only), or Pet-tinic ® (dogs and cats) . These syrups provide a highly palatable source of vitamins and minerals that help a pet recovering from illness. **It is important to note that Dyne ® can be toxic to cats.**

In order to create a palatable form of generic Albon ® using these syrups and sulfadimethozine, mix **5 oz of either syrup (not all), to 4 oz of sulfadimethozine**. The first dose is higher the first day and cut in half for the next four days. Its is given once daily.

To purchase smaller amounts of sulfadimethozine that is already compounded for better flavor, a one ounce, two ounce, or eight ounce bottle can be purchased for $15-89 at the following website: http://www.beautifuldragons.com/Albon.html

Weight of Pet (Dog and Cat)	First Dose of Albon	Next four doses
< 5 lbs	2.5 ml	1.25 ml
10 lbs	5 ml	2.5 ml
20 lbs	10 ml	5.0 ml
40 lbs	20 ml	10 ml
80 lbs	40 ml	20 ml

Toltrazuril (Baycox) ® : Albon ® Alternative #1

An alternative to Albon ® that was given to me by a reader, is Baycox ® or its generic, toltrazuril. Toltrazuril is used to treat coccidia in many types of animals including dogs, cats, and rabbits, although it is not marketed for that. At present, it is not sold in the United States. However, it can be purchased at http://search.vetproductsdirect.com.au/search?w=baycox%20piglet.

It is not a cheap drug, so it would be more helpful for the shelter or rescue. On the website mentioned, it is $140 per bottle.

The plus side is that only a single dose of toltrazuril is required compared to many dosages over several days. According to Dr. Bruce Kilmer of Bayer ® Canada:

"The toltrazuril will kill all single cell stages of coccidiosis. Once an animal has diarrhea and you can find oocysts on fecals, the drug can not penetrate the oocysts so technically it is too late to treat. In the actual clinical cases, treatment is still worthwhile to shorten the length and severity of the diarrhea as there is still development of the life cycle in the small intestine that will be controlled." http://www.bullmarketfrogs.com/2013/07/coccidia-puppies-kitten-baycox/

It comes in two forms when ordering from abroad: a 5% Solution (50mg/ml) or a 2.5% solution sold for poultry. **You must order the 5% solution.**

The dosage is 0.1 to 0.2 ml per pound of body weight.

Toltrazuril has a foul taste and if given alone, will make the pet foam at the mouth. Toltrazuril can be mixed with Linxotinic ®, Pet-tinic ® or chicken broth.

Ponazuril (Marquis ®) : Albon ® Alternative #2

A similar drug to toltrazuril that is available in the United States is called Marquis ® and is marketed for horses. Marquis ® is also expensive, at about $100 per tube, but thanks to the UC Davis Koret Shelter Medicine Program, http://www.sheltermedicine.com/library/internal-parasite-control-guidelines we have the following dilution and administration information:

*"Dilute one syringe of paste (127 grams at 150 mgs/gm., 120 ml volume) in 21 mls of water or other carrier (e.g. Val syrup) results in a solution of 135 mgs/ml. This can be dosed at 1 ml/10 lbs (30 mgs/kg). The solution should be stored in a light proof container and thoroughly shaken before administration. Dosage is **1ml per pound of body weight with a second dose recommended 10 days later.**"*

Metronidazole (Flagyl ®/ Fish Zole ®)

Although there is no FDA approved drug for giardia, treatment of diarrhea caused by giardia, is most often metronizole. This drug is also used to treat amoebas in reptiles. The dosage is the following:

- **Dogs**: 3-23 mg per pound of body weight by mouth 1-4 times per day for 5-7 days
- **Cats**: 5-23 mg per pound of body weight by mouth 1-2 times per day for 5-7 days
- **Reptiles**: 12-25 mg per pound of body weight by mouth once daily for 5-7 days
- **Rabbits**: 10 mg per pound of body weight by mouth twice daily for 3 days.

HOME PHYSICALS AND LAB TESTS
"Until one has loved an animal, a part of one's soul remains unawakened"~Anatole France

14

The Home Physical Exam: Learning to be a Good Pet Health Detective

One of the best things you can do for your pet is to know every inch of him or her. While not the easiest thing to do with two dozen animals, I have tried to learn how to do a proper physical exam on each of my pets and to do it regularly.

If you pay attention when you go to the veterinarian, the doctor examines your pet in almost the same exact way each time. This exam method is a practice ingrained in the veterinarians to make sure they never miss examining any part of your animal.

The things a layperson can do is a bit different from the doctor. However, if the pet parent does this exam often enough, he or she will know when something has changed. This exam is what each pet parent should learn and focus on.

Doing an exam like this from the time the pet is a puppy or kitten, makes it easier to know what is normal. For adult pets, having a baseline exam performed by your veterinarian, will be the best place to start.

On the following page is a diagram showing how to do an at-home physical. As I said, it is not the exact same physical your vet will do. For instance, the vet can feel the abdomen and be more comfortable knowing if there are any abnormalities for that species. You, on the other hand, if you familiarize yourself with your pet's abdomen, can know if there are any abnormalities for your pet. This is just as important.

The most vital thing is to examine your pet often. Pay attention when you are petting him. Observe what his normal comfortable stance looks like so you will know when he is uncomfortable. Notice the color of her gums when she is feeling well, so you know when it looks discolored when she is ill. The more you recognize what is normal, the quicker you will recognize what is abnormal. Trust your instincts to tell you when something just "isn't right".

I always refer to the "**physical exam train**" (**PET**), when teaching someone how to examine their pet. Start at one end and work your way to the other. The exam works basically the same for all pets, regardless of species.

A simple diagram of the external anatomy of the canine is below. Common terms, rather than medical terms are utilized. Cat anatomy is basically the same.

Pet Exam Train (PET)

The **PET** is not intended to replicate the exam performed by an experienced vet. There are parts of an exam that take years of training and experience in order to evaluate correctly. What our purpose is in an examination is to know what is normal for your pet so you will have no question when something is abnormal. The exam teaches a pet parent to know what questions to ask regarding each system. Consider yourself a **Pet Health Detective** and get your notebook out. I recommend keeping notes of all your observations and when you visit your veterinarian, take your notebook with you. A baseline is a term that refers to what is normal for your pet. So what you will be providing is that baseline. The baseline will be very helpful in assisting your vet in diagnosis.

Common Note Shortcuts:

If you've ever peeked at the notes while a vet tech or doctor is asking questions you will usually see common note shortcuts used in veterinary medicine. Understanding those note shortcuts may make taking your own notes a little easier. Throughout the pet exam train, you will become more comfortable with the terms.

BAR: Bright, Alert, Responsive. The pet is alive and well, not in immediate distress, and is responsive to you

EENT: Eyes, Ears, Nose, Throat: If all is good, this acknowledges that it has been examined

CRT: Capillary Refill Time

MM: Mucous Membrane Color (gum color)

HR: Heart Rate

TPR: Temperature, Pulse (the presence of a pulse means the pet is alive and it helps you determine the HR), Respiration (# of breaths per minute)

BCS: Body Conditioning Score. A BCS helps evaluate if the pet is too thin, a healthy weight, or obese.

WNL: Within Normal Limits indicates that the rate or condition is within the normal range for that species.

Mouth and dentition

While the eyes are the window to the soul, the gums and teeth are a window to the health of the pet.

A healthy mouth is free of gum disease, full of strong teeth that are free of calculus and tartar, and the gums are a nice shade of pink. There should be no strong odor. The teeth are strongly anchored to the gums and not loose. The gums are not a dark shade of red, pale white, or sickly yellow.

So what does the gum color indicate?

- Red, inflamed gums, may indicate gum disease.

- White or pale gums may indicate that the pet is anemic or that the blood is not pumping properly.

- Brick colored gums may suggest a bacterial infection, or sepsis.

- Blue gums are very serious and indicate that your pet is not getting enough oxygen.

If you see any of these colors, contact your vet immediately. Keep in mind that some breeds may have a black pigment on their gums. The more you look at the teeth and gums when your pet is young and healthy, the easier you will recognize when there is an abnormality.

Periodontal disease is a serious issue. Not only can the pet lose teeth, but the infection can affect the heart, kidneys, and liver. Much like an open sore on the skin is an opening to allow infection to invade the body, so too is the mouth.

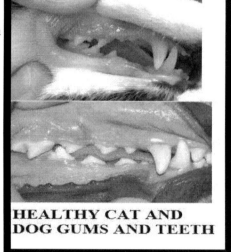

HEALTHY CAT AND DOG GUMS AND TEETH

When the mouth is filled with bacteria and infection, each time that pet swallows, the infection spreads. This is the importance of constant maintenance and observation of the teeth and gums.

I have seen veterinarians and long time technicians gag when trying to clean up a neglected mouth. Most of the time, a pet in this condition did not come from an unloving home, but from pet parents who didn't think to check the condition of the mouth.

In a perfect world, we would all brush our pet's teeth, yet few of us do. Normally, one way to guess at pet's age is the condition of the mouth. Over the years, I've gotten pretty good at determining age. Then last year, I met a dog who I thought was a young dog of two to three years by the condition of his teeth, only to find out he was eight years old. I was absolutely stunned. His mom had brushed his teeth since the first day she adopted him as a puppy. He had never had to have a dental because of her diligence.

If you do chose to brush your pet's teeth, never use human toothpaste. A paste that is safe and palatable for your pet is available at pet stores.

We've discussed the significance of the color of the gums, now on to **capillary refill time**. CRT is done by pressing onto the gum and letting go, counting how many seconds it takes for the now-white gum to return to its original color. What you are doing is forcing the blood out of the capillaries by pressing down, and allowing them to refill by letting up. The **normal refill rate for both dogs and cats is 1.5 seconds.** Anything above that can indicate that the heart is not pumping and flowing as it should or that the pet is dehydrated. Dehydration is common in a pet that is in shock.

Questions to ask:
- What color are the gums?

- What is the capillary refill time?
- Is there an unusually foul odor?
- Is there a sweet smell to the breath? (can indicate diabetes)
- Are there broken teeth?
- Is there calculi/tarter present, or are the teeth bright and white?

Muzzle/Nostrils/Eyes

Before humans began shaping the genetics of dogs and cats by selective breeding, the shape of the face of both species was best suited for survival. Recent molecular evidence and very detailed genetic analysis, for instance, has proven that all dogs and the gray wolf descended from a common ancestor. http://news.discovery.com/animals/pets/dogs-not-as-close-kin-to-wolves-as-thought-140116.htm

Cats, on the other hand descended from wild African cats (*Felis silvestris lybica*) in the Middle East. (http://www.nytimes.com/2007/06/29/science/29cat.html)

This is important to know because the interference of humans, whether good or bad, has changed the face of the dog and cat significantly in some cases. The longer muzzle made breathing and even eating easier as adults. Selective breeding has produced cats and dogs with little to no snout. These are called **Brachycephalic** breeds. As an article in the German journal "Pneumologie" states:

"Selective breeding for exaggerated features caused in many brachycephalic dog and cat breeds virtually a loss of the nose, with serious anatomical and functional consequences. In addition to respiratory and olfactory tasks, in dogs the nose is of vital importance for thermoregulation. As obligatory nose breathers, dogs suffer far more than humans when their nasal ventilation is restricted"
https://www.thieme-connect.com/DOI/DOI?10.1055/s-0030-1255513 (Original)
http://www.ncbi.nlm.nih.gov/pubmed/20632241 (Translation)

Examples of these breeds include canine English Bulldogs, Pugs, and Pekingese and feline Himalayan, Persian, and Scottish Folds. Since these breeds are so popular, it is necessary to discuss the added difficulties and challenges they face so you know what is normal and abnormal for these breeds.

Brachycephalic Airway Syndrome

- **Stenotic nares:** This is the scientific name for narrow nasal passages. These very narrow air passages are not uncommon, particularly in English Bulldogs. Surgery is often required to open up the passages and make it easier to breathe. Its not a matter of convenience, but of survival.
- **Elongated pallate:** The same amount of teeth, gums and flesh have to fit into the mouth of the brachycephalic breed as any other breed. There are 42 teeth in the dog and 30 in the cat. This number is not reduced when breeding forces less and less space to put the teeth. Nature's only solution is to have the soft palate, the flap of tissue that separates the oral cavity from the nasal passages, hanging loosely in the throat.
- **Tracheal stenosis:** The trachea itself is too narrow in some places.
- **Everted Laryngeal Saccules:** The larynx (voice box) has two small pockets called saccules. The effort required of those with chronic breathing difficulties can turn the saccules inside-out causing even more difficulty breathing.

These issues all lead to difficult challenges for the brachycephalic pet. Heat stress and heat stroke is common.

Regardless of the size of the snout, there are some **universal conditions regarding the nose and eyes.**

As mentioned, both **dogs and cats should be able to breath through their nose**. Dogs pant to cool off, but cats do not. A panting cat is a cat in deep distress. Another important health consideration is that a cat who cannot smell her food, often will not eat, leading to fatty liver syndrome, and, if left untreated, death.

Contrary to popular belief, the level of dryness of the nose, does not indicate the body temperature. This measure of moistness of the nose should never be used as a determination of health.

The nose should remain **clear of debris**. There may be some clear drainage present, but frequent sneezing or excess drainage should elicit concern. **Yellow or green discharge may be an indication of infection and your vet should be notified.** Also look for any foreign bodies such as **foxtails** which are spike-like parts of weeds that burrow into noses, eyes, ears and skin. This tends to be a bigger concern in the western part of the U.S., however, briers and thorns can be a problem anywhere.

Some dogs develop a condition called **hyperkeratosis.** This is a thickening of the nose fibers that creates a cracked, dry appearance. There is no cure, but to make it more comfortable for the pet, you can apply Vasoline ® to soften it. Be sure not to cover the nostrils and restrict air flow.

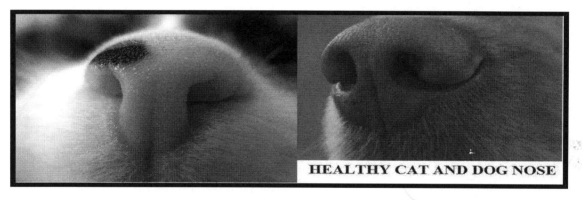

HEALTHY CAT AND DOG NOSE

Much like the nose, **eyes** should be clear of debris and discharge. Some breeds of dogs and cats have a constant clear discharge that stains the hair around the eye. **Excessive tearing or discharge that is yellow or green is an indication of an infection. Squinting is often a symptom of a foreign body or injury.**

Other signs to look for are a **cloudy or hazy appearance** to the eye or a bloodshot eye. Look for **uniform sized pupils**. Uneven or abnormal pupil size can be an indicator of many things and need to be pointed out to your vet immediately. Also notice if the eye has a bright, shiny appearance or if it is dull and dry.

Questions to be asked:
- Do I observe any discharge from they eyes or nose?
- If so, is it clear? Yellow? Green?
- Do I notice any pawing at the eyes or nose?
- Are the eyes bright and clear, or do they appear dull and dry?
- Can my pet breathe comfortably through his/her nose?
- Do you notice any sneezing?

Outer and Inner Ear

The ears of our pets vary. Some are floppy, while others are erect. For the most part, however, **there should be no unusual thickness to the pinna (outer ear flap) and it should be malleable** (able to bend it without causing damage). **There should be no unusual odor, nor should there be an excess of material in the ear canal.** Breeds that have excess fur in the ear canal may require regular plucking of the ear hair.

The ear canal in most of our pets is not a straight line from outer ear, to ear drum. It is an "L" shape. Debris and foreign objects can be easily missed. This image shows you what a healthy clean ear looks like:

HEALTHY, CLEAN DOG AND CAT EARS. IN BOTH IMAGES, THE EAR PINNA IS BEING POSITIONED FOR CLEAREST IMAGE OF THE ENTRANCE OF THE EAR CANAL.

While dogs are more likely to have bacterial and yeast infections in the ear, cats are more likely to have ear mites. The debris is typically black and often resemble black sand. Suspicion of ear mites can be confirmed using a microscope. It is important to clean the ears before applying any medication for ear mites.

Some pets naturally keep beautifully clean ears, but most often, pets need assistance to maintain clean ears. It is not that unusual to have two or more pets who help keep each other clean. One of our chihuahuas, Athena, insists on keeping her two closest friends, Pearl and Onyx, clean from head to toe. Willow, our cat, has a special love for Mr. Blue and she diligently keeps his ears clean.

When a fellow canine or feline companion doesn't do the job, it is up to the pet parents to maintain a healthy ear environment with frequent exams, weekly cleaning and plucking if necessary. Doing so prevents ear infections, ensures the comfort of the pet, and saves money in the long run.

Questions to be asked:
- Is my pet shaking his/her head or pawing at the ears?
- Does the outside of the ear look swollen?
- Is there any debris inside?
- If so, what is its appearance?
- Are there any foreign bodies or any parasites such as ticks

Trunk: Withers, Back, Abdomen and Rump

The trunk is the area between the neck and the tail. The trunk is composed primarily of the withers, back, abdomen, and rump. Examination of the trunk focuses on any unusual posture or signs of pain.

The task of examining all aspects of the trunk is primarily hands-on. Before beginning, however, observe the posture of your pet. Your pet should have a relaxed posture. Look from both the side, front, and back and note the natural curvature of the spine.

Telling if a pet is in pain, is difficult, unless you know what to look for. **Nature has taught animals that to show weakness is a sure way to be targeted for attack, so most dogs and cats will not show pain until it is extreme.** This is where close observation and a hands-on approach is vital.

Universal Signs of Pain:
- Limping
- Holding one leg up
- Weaving when trying to walk/run
- Holding head down
- Not turning head normally
- Back is rounded and the pet has a "hunched over" appearance
- The animal cries out when pressure is put on either area of the spine

There are tried and true ways to test for pain and to narrow down the particular area affected.

The best methods to test for pain include:
- Stand to the side of the pet. With one hand on the neck, and the other on the muzzle, slowly and gently turn the head side to side, then up and down. Resistance can indicate pain.
- Standing in front of the pet, lift his/her front legs up. I call this the *"dance position."*

- Notice if the pet stands comfortably on the back legs.
- Lift one front foot up and observe if the animal is comfortable putting pressure on the opposing foot. Repeat with all legs.
- Beginning on a front leg, examine the paw pads for briers and cuts. Note the length of the nails. Longer nails on one side may mean pet is unable to apply pressure to that foot. Repeat with each leg.
- Again, beginning with a front leg, gently squeeze the paw, moving up to the body. Repeat with each leg.
- To test for nerve issues, turn each paw upside down with the nails facing toward the back. Release and observe how long it takes the pet to put the paw back in its original position. If the pet does not seem to notice and does not return the paw to its original position, there is possible nerve issues.
- Stand to the rear of the pet. Pick up both back legs with your hands near the body, in a wheelbarrow position. Notice if pet seems comfortable with all the weight on the front legs.

For a very specific method of doing these tests, as well as what to do to relieve any pain, please refer to Dr. Daniel Kamen's book **The Well Adjusted Dog: Canine Chiropractic Methods You Can Do.**

Skin and Fur

The next focus of the exam is on the skin. Run your hands through your pets fur feeling for any abnormalities. Do this from the front to back, then back to front. **Note any lumps that you find**. Also look for black specks of **flea droppings** near the base of the tail. If you see no droppings but the area is red and inflamed, you most likely have fleas in your environment.

Note if the coat is shiny or dull. Is it oily or dry? One wants a shiny coat that is neither oily or dry. Oily can be a sign of thyroid dysfunction.

Look for mats in the fur. Mats are a much more serious issue than people realize. Mats are not simply an inconvenience that you cannot brush through. The hair twists, pinching and even ripping the skin. In the summer months, these matted, torn areas are the perfect place for flies to lay their eggs, and guess what that means? **Maggots**. A maggot infestation can go unnoticed until the smell is so overpowering, the pet parent begins to look for the source of the odor. During that time, the maggots can bore deep into the tissue. I have seen it many times in my years working with animals, and it can take a very long time to clean and remove all the fly larvae from an open wound. It is painful for the pet and a dangerous source of infection. So if you see a mat, shave it off. Never allow it to rip open the skin.

Notice if the hair appears groomed. Cats, in particular, are fastidious in their grooming habit, keeping their fur clean and nails nice and sharp. When a cat doesn't sharpen their nails, the sheath of the nail grows. This growth thickens the nail. This can be normal in a very old cat, but younger cats should never allow this. If they do, there is a very good reason, and you have to find out why the cat doesn't feel well enough to groom him/herself. When your older cats no longer groom themselves, it is important to trim their nails and remove the outer sheath. Helping them in this way makes them more comfortable in their later years.

Next, look at the rear by lifting up the tail. Note any redness or lumps. Check the anal glands to see if they are full (more on that later). In the female dog, check for any discharge from the vaginal area and surrounding tissues. Note if it is yellow. This may indicate an infection and should be pointed out to your veterinarian.

On both the dog and cat, **notice if there are any signs of tapeworms on the fur** surrounding the anal area. These look similar to a grain of rice.

Now have your dog or cat **lay on his/her back** if possible. A good belly rub is good for the soul! While doing, this search for anything unusual as you did on the upper torso.

Extremities

Check the **legs and paws** for signs of burrs, fox tails, or cuts. Lightly squeeze the legs and paws and notice anything that could indicate pain. Sometimes, burrs, fox tails, or cuts are not visible. Check the pads on the elbows, as well as the pads of the paws. In hot weather the paw pads can burn on hot asphalt, and in winter, they can suffer from frostbite. The elbow pads, particularly on large breed senior dogs, can become tough as the pet grows older and can sometimes benefit from an application of Vaseline ®.

Next, move your attention to **the nails**. Do they need to be trimmed? Are any nails broken? Has the dewclaw grown into the skin?

Don't forget to **check the tail** itself. Make sure it has not been damaged by being shut in the door or other method.

Questions to be asked:
- Do I notice any signs of pain or discomfort?
- Do I observe any signs of parasites on the skin?
- Do I feel any lumps and if so, has the lump changed since the last exam?
- Does the skin feel oily or excessively dry? Does she seem to be grooming herself?
- Are there any mats? Are they tightly pulling the skin?
- Do I see any burrs, fox tails, or other foreign objects attached to the fur?

- Are there any cuts or abrasions on the paws?
- Are the nails too long or broken?
- Any feces on the fur?
- Does the tail look normal?

Vital Signs: Temperature, Heart Rate, Respiratory Rate & Body Weight

Next you will want to record vital signs. I have added body weight to this category and recommend weighing a pet several times a year. Since we are with our pets daily, it can be difficult for us to notice a gradual change in weight. What seems to be a small change in weight to us, can be significant for our pets. Weight gains and losses can sometimes be indicators of disease.

Traditionally, vital signs include the temperature, heart rate, and respiratory rate.

While the pulse rate can be determined by feel, listening to the heart with a stethoscope is interesting and preferred. The only advantage to a non-medically trained person listening to the heart is hearing what your pet's heart beat sounds like. **If you know what it *should* sound like, you will know when it doesn't sound right.**

It takes practice to learn to count the beats per minute of the heart. Ask your veterinarian or veterinary technician to get you started.

The beat of the heart is a two-part sound. "Lub-dub, lub-dub, lub-dub", so count "1 lub-dub, 2 lub-dub, 3 lub-dub." If you don't have a stethoscope, you can feel the pulse in femoral artery. The pulse is located near the groin area where the rear leg meets the body. You can also feel the heart beat on the left side of the chest. A good trick to find it is to pull the pet's elbow back and see where it meets the chest. Count the heart beat for 15 seconds and multiply by 4 or if the pet will let you, or count for a full minute. Either way, you have your beats per minute.

Respiratory rate determines how many breaths a pet takes in one minute. Just like the heart beat, breathing is performed in two motions...inhaling and exhaling Count "one inhale-exhale, two inhale-exhale". Again, count for 15 seconds and multiply by 4 or simply count for a full minute.

Last, but not least is the temperature. Unfortunately, this is a rectal procedure. Ear thermometers are rarely effective because of the "L" shape of the ear.

Normal Vital Signs for the Dog and Cat:

Temperature   (dog or cat) 100.5-102.5 degrees
Heart rate   Dog – 80-160, Cat 110-200 beats per minute
Respiratory rate (breathing rate) Dog 15-30, Cat 20-40 breathes per minute

With that, you are finished! Give your pet a treat and one for you too! The Pet Exam Train has arrived at the station.

How to make grooming part of the physical exam

A great time to do a physical exam is when you are grooming your pet. Grooming can include brushing, bathing, hair trim or shave, nail trim, ear cleaning, and anal gland expression.

A grooming exam allows you to look for parasites and growths that you might not see otherwise. Grooming also makes it easier to spot and to remove matted fur.

As I mentioned before, people often underestimate the damage matted fur can cause. During my time as an animal cruelty investigator, I came across so many animals who had been left un-brushed and matted. Many of those animals were unable to defecate as the fur was so tightly matted in the rear, it held the feces inside. Others were unable to move properly without pulling at the fur and skin, causing rips and tears. In the summer, we would shave the mats from these dogs to find maggots eating into their tissue.

Brushing the fur regularly serves several purposes. Grooming and brushing is an excellent bonding experience for pet parent and pet. Grooming is an opportunity to examine your pet. It can prevent mats that can lead to serious health problems and pain. Regular grooming also saves money because you can catch small problems before they become big problems. The cost of professional grooming of a matted pet is much higher than grooming a dog or cat whose fur has been well maintained.
The question often asked is, "How often should I bathe my dog?" Stephen L. Zawistowski, PhD, an animal behaviorist and science adviser to the American Society for the Prevention of Cruelty to Animals (ASPCA) offers an answer.

"If your dog stays fairly clean with regular brushing, you might get away with fewer baths, Zawistowski says. But in general, dogs need to be bathed about every 3 months, according to the ASPCA.

If your dog gets dirtier, for example, by romping outdoors, consider lathering up more often. Always use a puppy or dog shampoo, not a people shampoo, Zawistowski says. Shampoos made for people aren't toxic, but they may contain fragrances and other ingredients that irritate pets' skin.

Though frequent brushing may do wonders for your dog, the same is not true of baths. Don't overdo it. "Most people bathe their dog more often than they need to," he says, sometimes weekly or every other week. Too many baths will strip the coat of natural oils that protect the skin, and your dog's coat will lose some of its shine and luster. However, there are dogs that will need more frequent, medicated baths, but only if your vet recommends it."
http://pets.webmd.com/features/pets-bathe-groom-important

Shaving

A way to save some money can be learning some grooming techniques you can use at home. Utilizing clippers and the proper scissors can create an acceptable cut. Although it may not make a professional look, a little practice makes for pretty good results.

A

The easiest grooming technique is a simple shave down. shave down is created using a clipper with a #10 blade for the shave, and a #7 blade to blend the fur. There are many good instructional videos on YouTube and grooming books with instructions to help you learn the technique.

A shave down requires a good quality set of clippers. Less expensive clippers come with one blade that cannot be removed but combs can be attached. These clippers wear out quickly, pull the fur, and are not worth the money you pay for them. Once the blade dulls, most have to be thrown away.

By paying more initially for good quality clippers, you can detach the blade for cleaning, interchange blades, have the blades resharpened and buy new blades anytime you need to.

I shave my pets in the late spring/early summer. There is actually some controversy over whether summer shave downs are in the best interest of the pet. It is said that the fur helps to keep the pet cool and prevents sunburn. My experience has shown the shave down to be a lifesaver. When I shaved my dog, Scrappy one spring, a growth was revealed that would not have been seen otherwise. The growth was pre-cancerous, and I was able to have it surgically removed in time.

In all the years I have been shaving my dogs, I have never had a dog experience sunburn. I provide plenty of shade for the dogs. For dogs that go on frequent walks with their pet parents in the heat of the day, the possibility of a sunburn may be a concern.

The dogs love the shave downs and even Peaches, one of our cats, gets in line to be shaved.

Nail Trims

Dogs and cats should be taught from the time they are small to allow the pet parent to touch their paws. Many pet parents do not have that training advantage when they adopt an adult pet. Newly adopted pets and their pet parents learn to trust each other by interacting. Petting the dog or cat while watching television, going for a walk, or feeding the pet by hand, all create a loving, trusting relationship. Once pet parents feel comfortable, he or she should begin to touch and hold the paws, followed by a treat, praise, or a few minutes of playtime.

Each individual pet is different and it may take some experimentation to find a method of nail trimming that works. Some pets handle trims better if one pet parent holds the pet, while the other trims the nails. Other pets may be calmer, if only one pet parent both holds, and trims the nails.

When training a pet to allow a nail trim, never make a big show of getting the clippers out and preparing the for trim. This overt preparation can build a sense of anxiety in the pet. Treat the nail trimming as just another part of your pet's healthy grooming, such as daily brushing. If the pet is sitting on your lap, as you watch television, trim a nail and give a belly rub. Later, trim another nail. Trimming becomes less scary this way.

When Haseleah used to take her dog Abigail to her veterinarian for nail trim, Abigail would start resisting as soon as the car turned up the hill to the clinic. Inside the clinic, she protested all the way to the treatment area. Haseleah warned me when she moved to T.Paws Rescue, that trimming Abigail's nails would be a struggle. One day as Abigail sat in my lap, I picked up the small nail trimmers (as seen in the picture below) and started trimming. There was absolutely no drama. Abigail has trusted me to trim her nails ever since that day.

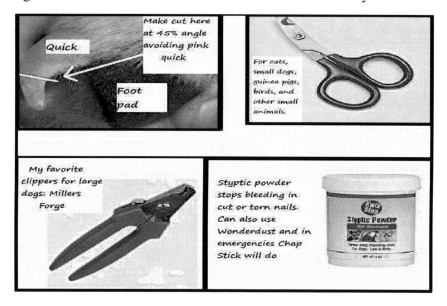

Buster, my basset hound that passed away in 2013, always loved nail trim time. He associated it with tummy rubs and treats. His positive association made nail clipping a breeze.

The picture above shows the appropriate angle to trim nails. Most nails are slightly transparent and allow you to see the quick of the nail. Clipping into the quick causes pain and should be avoided. Occasionally, you will come across a black nail that doesn't allow you to see the quick. If the pet has any clear nails, assume that the quick in the black nail will be in approximately the same place as the clear nail. If no clear nail is visible, clip in small increments. When the nail begins to feel more spongy and thicker, you are probably close to the quick.

For nails that are extremely long but also have a long quick, you will need to clip the nails more often for a while. When you clip close to the quick, it will recede. Each time you clip again, the quick will recede more. **Do NOT intentionally quick the nails**. If you have ever "quicked" or torn a nail, you know how much it hurts. Intentionally quicking a nail is cruel. Anyone who offers to quick a nail on a conscious pet should be avoided.

If a rescued pet has nails with quicks so long they are impeding the pet's ability to walk comfortably, the nails can be clipped and quicked under sedation. A good idea is to combine the nail trim with another procedure, such as a dental cleaning. Request a pain injection be given before the pet wakes up so she will not wake up in pain. Ask that oral pain medication be prescribed to last 24-48 hours. Just because an animal doesn't show pain, does not mean that the pet doesn't hurt.

Cats love to sharpen their claws and often do it on the sides of our couches and chairs. For me, it is easier to trim the nails of a cat, than a dog, as the demarcation between the nail and quick is much clearer. You do have to press behind the cat's nail to extend so the nail can be trimmed.

Ear Cleaning

The process of ear cleaning is fairly easy, particularly if the ear cleaning is done on a regular basis. Cleaning the ears of a dog is a fairly easy procedure. Keeping the ears clean and healthy is made easier by maintaining an acidic environment in the ear canal. This discourages yeast and bacteria from growing.

Perhaps the most effective method of maintaining this environment is to clean the ears with a 1:1 ratio apple cider vinegar/water mixture (1:1 means 1 part vinegar to 1 part water). Combine ½ cup of apple cider vinegar to ½ cup of water. If the ears are not inflamed or red, the water can be replaced with rubbing alcohol which dries the ear environment even more.

Put the mixture in a squeeze bottle or use a large syringe.

Holding up the ear flap, use a 6 cc or larger syringe, or the squeeze bottle, to gently force the fluid into the ear canal. The pet will want to shake her head, so flush quickly, put the ear flap down, and immediately massage at the base of the ear. Let the pet shake. If there is no debris, repetition of the process is not necessary. Clean all remaining debris with a cotton ball.

Normally, cats will not tolerate this type of ear flushing as well as the dog. Instead, clean the outer ear with a cotton swab drenched in the apple cider/water mixture. Use a cotton tipped applicator to clean between the folds of the ear.

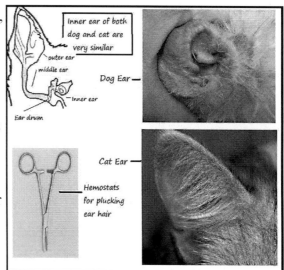

In certain dog breeds, hair grows densely in the canal and can trap debris and wax. Some veterinarians recommend keeping the ear hair shaved as much as possible. Others suggest regular plucking of excessive ear hair. While plucking does remove the hair, it can also irritate the ears and encourage an infection. However, shaving still leaves hair behind that can trap particles and debris leading to an ear infection.

If wax has built up in the canal and if a thorough cleaning is being impeded by the hair, plucking may be necessary. Clean the ears with diluted apple cider vinegar prior to plucking and dry the ear as much as possible. Boric acid powder (not the same as Borax ®), commonly used as an antiseptic and even a pesticide, can be applied to the ear canal. Not only does boric acid make the hair easier to grip, it provides a gentle antiseptic to help heal the skin after plucking and discourages infection. Plucking with the fingers is preferred as it reduces the chance of pinching the skin, however, some veterinarians do use a hemostat.

Consult with your veterinarian on what is best for your dog.

Cats do not need ear plucking. The hair on the ear of the cat in the photo above is normal.

If your pet has frequent problems with excess ear hair and infections, consider having the pet sedated for a through ear hair plucking and ear flush. If the pet is being sedated for other reasons, such as a dental cleaning, request that the ears be flushed and plucked while under sedation.

While pricked and semi-pricked ear breeds do get ear infections, pendent-ear breeds, like those found in the hound and retriever group, have restricted air flow to the inner ear that can encourage infections. Considering that retriever breeds also like the water, the possibility of recurring infections rises. Regular exams and cleanings are even more important for these dogs.

Maintaining a dry acidic environment in the ear with diluted apple cider vinegar, followed by boric acid, will help discourage bacteria and yeast.

Anal Gland Expression

If you have ever seen your dog scooting his booty on the carpet, chances are his anal glands are full. As far as we know, the purpose of anal glands is to mark territory. However, as evolution and selective breeding changed the dog from a wide undomesticated canine to a lhasa apso, the anal glands seemed to lose their importance in marking and became a big pain in the behind for many dogs and their pet parents.

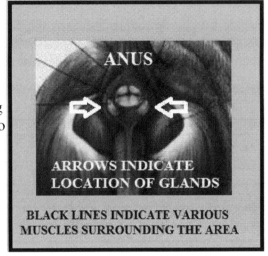

The illustration to the previous page shows the location of the anal glands. Often, pet parents mistake this carpet scooting as a sign of worms, and a swollen anal gland as a hemorrhoid.

If the anus is imagined as a clock, the anal glands are located on both sides of the anus at about the 4 and 8 o'clock position.

The glands fill up with a vile fluid, that, if it fills in excess or with fluid that is too thick, it will abscess. Somewhere around the gland pocket, the abscess may rupture, leaving a hole. The abscess is a terribly painful condition that requires that the dog be anesthetized and the abscess flushed. Prescription pain medication and antibiotics will also be necessary.

Although the idea of expressing anal glands is off putting, it can save your pet from this experience and save you money.

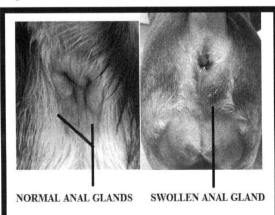

In the picture below, compare a normal looking anal area and one with the right anal gland about to rupture.

In this image, you will see on the left that the area of the anus is flat and even a slightly concave. The anal glands are being emptied by the dog on a regular basis as nature intended. The image on the right is very different.

At this point, the area is so swollen that attempting to empty the glands at home would be extremely painful and probably result in rupture. The pet would need to be sedated and treated by a veterinarian.

That's why it is best to regularly check, and if need be, empty the anal glands.

One suggestion to make this easier is to keep the area around the anus shaved. Shaving keeps the area more sanitary and makes it easier to check the glands.

Express the anal glands each time you bathe your dog. Cats rarely have an anal gland problem.

Fair warning: Be sure, when expressing or emptying the glands, to put a paper towel over the area and point it away from your face.
If possible, have a vet tech, veterinarian, or groomer demonstrate the procedure before trying it on your own.

There are two ways to express the anal glands. Always wear latex gloves (or similar if you are allergic to latex).

The external method:
This is the most common method used by pet parents, and if at all possible by vet techs as well. Put your gloves on, and with your non-dominant hand pick the tail up so that it is pointing upward. This helps to expose the glands. Imagine the area like a clock. The glands are at 4 and 8 o'clock. Using a paper towel in your dominant hand, place your index finger at 4:00 and your thumb at 8:00. Gently squeeze as you push up slightly. The fluid is brown in color and can be thin or very thick. The thicker the fluid, the more likely the fluid has been there a while. Once you have emptied the glands, clean the area thoroughly. Remove your gloves, wash your hands, and give your pet a treat and you a treat too!

The internal method:
The method is similar to the external method only a little more in depth, shall we say. While wearing gloves, lube your index finger with KY Jelly ® or something similar. Insert your lubed finger into the anus. If the glands are full, you will feel a bulge to each side. You will be squeezing similarly to the external method, but the index finger will be inside and the thumb outside. Use your non-dominant hand to hold the tail up as well as draping the paper towel over the area to protect yourself. Do this method gently as to not exert too much pressure on the glands. You don't want to rupture them in the process. Once the glands are empty, clean the area, and throw your gloves away. Wash your hands and give yourself a high five for having the nerve to go where no one but veterinary technicians generally go. Give your pet a treat, because you really need to make up after that.

15

In-Home or In-Rescue Lab Tests

Pet parents, animal shelters, and rescues must use what money is available to them to take care of their pets. Utilizing that money in the most efficient way possible can help the pet parent afford care that would not have been feasible to the parents before. Animal shelters and rescues can save more animals if the cost of caring for each animal is reduced.

One way to save a significant amount of money, particularly for the shelters and rescues, is learning to perform some simple laboratory tests themselves.

I was taught on-the-job how to do the lab test in this chapter. Its easier having the support of other techs and doctors to help you, but thanks to the internet, there are many websites that you can refer to in order to teach yourself. Those websites are included in this discussion. Unless you have many pets as I do in my rescue, it is best, and probably more cost effective to have these tests performed at your veterinarian.

Fecal Test

Fecal tests allow you to test the feces of your pet for intestinal parasites. I recall a day when it only cost $5 to get one at my local vet, but times have changed. Now a fecal test will cost around $15 each and you often have to pay an office call. Learning to do it yourself can save a lot of money.

A simple microscope can be purchased on Amazon or Ebay for $25-100. The microscope should be able to read 10X to 40X. In other words, the image would be magnified times 100 or 400.

The next thing needed would be a liquid product that allows the feces to sink while the worm eggs float to the top. Most vets use a product called **Fecal-Sol ®**. However, by using water and Epson salt, you can make a similar product.

To make a fecal float solution, use the following procedure:
Using a large mason jar, fill it about halfway up with warm water. Next, pour just a bit of Epson salt in at a time, and stir until each one fully dissolves. When the salt no longer dissolves, the mixture is ready. The solution can be kept for several months.

If you would prefer to purchase a fecal flotation solution instead of making it, the solution can be found at Lambert Vet Supply under "medical supplies" as can many other useful products.

Microscope slides and slide covers can be purchased from Drs. Foster and Smith for about $5 and are also available on Ebay. You can purchase fecal vials, but it is much cheaper to use empty pill vials.

Steps for preparing and reading the fecal sample:
To acquire fecal samples, follow your pet your pet outside. Once the pet defecates, use a tongue depressor or popsicle stick to pick up a piece of fecal matter less than half the size of a penny.

Fill your vial about half full of fecal float solution, put the feces in the liquid and stir. Then fill the vial to the top with the solution until it is nearly overflowing. You need to make it slightly higher than the vial edge for the liquid to touch the slide cover. Then place the slide cover on the top. If you have filled your vial properly, putting the slide cover on will make a bit of the liquid overflow. Wait at least 10 minutes for the feces and eggs to separate.

Once the 10 minutes are up, take the slide cover off and place it in the center of the slide and place the slide on the microscope stage. Starting at a power of 10x, scan for eggs.

To learn what parasite eggs look like under the microscope, go to http://www.pet-informed-veterinary-advice-online.com/fecal-float.html . It takes practice to learn the difference in an air bubble and a parasite egg. The more you practice, the better skilled you will become.

For another step-by-step guide (including images) for doing fecal testing go to http://www.pet-informed-veterinary-advice-online.com/fecal-flotation.html#float-performed

Heartworm test by Direct Smear and SNAP test

Doing a heartworm test by a direct blood smear is the old school way to test for heartworms. Direct smear tests are no longer the preferred method of detection. The test is limited, as it only detects microfilaria, the larvae stage of the heartworm. A direct smear does not detect adult heartworms.

The antigen test is much more reliable but more expensive. The most common test is called the SNAP ® test and is made by Idexx Laboratory. Antigen tests can be purchased online. While some individuals sell the tests singly, most companies sell them in bulk. Animal shelters and rescues can save money by purchasing these and performing the tests in-house. Pet parents may find it just as economical to have the procedure done by their veterinarian. While the cost of having the test performed by your veterinarian varies, one can expect the test to be $25-45 each.

SNAP ® Antigen heartworm tests can be purchased online at Lambert Vet Supplies. The cost at present for the heartworm test is $169 for a 15 count kit. Vetscan ® heartworm tests are found on Allivet for $125 for 25 tests ($5 per pet) . That is a huge savings for shelters and rescues. Individual heartworm tests can be found on Ebay for about $20. Instructions are included in the kits.

Learning the Skill of Venipuncture (Blood Draw)

For tests requiring a small sample of blood, the cephalic vein, located in the foreleg, is the most practical vein to use. Every veterinary assistant or technician has learned this skill by on-the-job training. It takes time and practice to become proficient and it should always be taught under the supervision of a qualified individual.

Venipuncture takes two people to do the blood draw. The assistant will restrain the pet while simultaneously holding off and rotating the vein to present it for blood draw. This method takes the place of a tourniquet. Some venipuncturists prefer to use the tourniquet, only using the assistant to restrain the pet. Having an assistant confident in restraint techniques makes all the difference. Youtube has many videos demonstrating the proper techniques and the CTP Veterinary Assistant page offers very good instructions.
http://www.gatlineducation.com/demo/Vet_Assist_DEMO/JSCTP/html/L21/L21CH03P01.html

Step-by-step online instructions for learning to do a simple blood draw can be found online as well. http://www.slideshare.net/DrAlana/lec-04-venipuncture-of-dogs-and-cats)

Since such a small sample is required, a 1 ml tuberculin syringe or 3 ml syringe with a 22 gauge needle is all that is needed. Less than 1 ml is needed for the heartworm test.

Animal shelters with euthanasia technician have an advantange in that their technicians are already proficient with finding the cephalic vein to administer the pentobarbitol. Those same technicians can use this skill to learn to draw blood for in-house tests.

Performing a Heartworm Test and Reading the Results

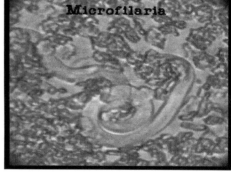

Direct smear tests, although not preferred, are still used in some veterinary practices. Once the blood is available to the technician, a small drop is place on a slide, and a cover slip is placed on top of the sample. It is not necessary to wait to read the results as you did in the fecal test.

Much like acquiring the skill of recognizing intestinal parasites, learning to recognize microfilaria under the microscope takes time and practice. Looking at images available online is a good place to start.

http://www.coulterah.com/site/view/223863_HeartwormTesting.pml

Normally a direct smear heartworm test is read with a microscopic strength of 40x.

Antigen heartworm tests require a small drop of blood in the well and the test snaps into place. After a short amount of time one dot will appear. If no other dots appear, the test is negative. If two dots appear, the test is indicating heartworms are present. It is recommended that a positive test be repeated.

SNAP ® antigen heartworm tests can be purchased online at Lambert Vet Supplies. The cost at present for the heartworm test is $169 for a 15 count kit. Vetscan ® heartworm tests are found on Allivet for $125 for 25 tests ($5 per pet).

Due to cost, shelters and rescues should consider doing their own testing as a way of managing donated money more efficiently. Having someone trained in drawing blood for either the direct smear or antigen test could potentially save the rescue hundreds of dollars per year.

FeLV and FIV tests

Also available online for shelters and rescues are feline leukemia (FeLV) tests and feline immunodeficiency virus (FIV) antigen tests. They are available individually and as a combo test. These tests, however, are much more expensive than heartworm tests.

Feline Leukemia (FeLV) is more common in cats than feline immunodeficiency virus (FIV). Any cat who has been vaccinated for FIV will show positive for it on antigen testing, so I hesitate to recommend to shelters and rescues to test for FIV. A positive result can be an automatic death sentence in some shelters. The cat may have simply been vaccinated for FIV, and not have the disease.

FeLV-only tests are significantly less expensive for the FeLV/FIV combo test. A 30 count of the combo Idexx SNAP ® test is $600 whereas the FeLV-only test is $200 cheaper. Synbiotics Assure(R) FeLV test is available from Revival Animal Health for $270 for 25 tests. That's just a little more than $10 per test. All tests come with directions.

While probably not cost effective for the pet parent, these tests are very cost effective for the animal shelters and rescues who have someone available who is qualified to perform venipuncture.

Parvo tests

Parvo tests are also available online. Parvo tests are cost effective for the animal shelter or rescue. The test is a type of ELISA test. ELISA stands for Enzyme Linked ImmunoSorbant

Assay and is based on a similar technology used for home pregnancy tests. The most common ELISA test to identify parvo is the Idexx SNAP ® test that uses feces rather than blood. If pet parents do purchase this test and the results are positive, the pet should be taken to the veterinarian for treatment.

Skin Scrape for Sarcoptic or Demodex Mange

The presence of either sarcoptic or demodex mites can be determined with a skin scrape. If a dog is suspected of having mites, a skin scrape, properly performed can reveal the culprit of the itchy skin. Demodex mites are present on every dog. When the immune system is compromised, the population can explode.

To prepare for a skin scrape, a microscope, microscope slide, surgical steel blade (dulled), and mineral oil is required. Next, focus on a patch of hair loss or lesion, most often found near the ear flap (pinna) or elbow. The blade is first dipped in mineral oil and the excess oil scraped onto the microscope slide. If you have groomer's clippers, it is best to shave the testing area first. Once done, squeeze the shaved skin (to push up the demodex mites from inside the hair follicles, if present). Scrape the skin in one direction several times. Be sure that you are not using the blade to cut the skin, but scrape it. Repeat in several areas placing all results on one slide. A great tutorial for this procedure is found at http://youtu.be/CSmLmAbmxQ4.

Blood Glucose Test

One of the things I did while a pet sitter and vet tech in California, was to go to homes on behalf of a local veterinarian and take blood samples. Usually, this was for pets who were very scared or aggressive when at the vet and who were calmer at home. The most frequent testing I did was for
blood glucose levels on diabetic animals.

The same glucometer sold for human diabetics works well on cats or dogs. The only difference is the method of blood retrieval. Although a small sample is required, the typical finger stick used on humans will not work on dogs or cats. The blood must be taken from the vein in the same way as for heartworm tests. If the pet parent can learn from a skilled technician how to pull a small blood sample, he or she can help monitor the pet with more consistency and provide the veterinarian with blood results from a pet much calmer at home than at a veterinarian office. Proper glucose levels are between 80-150.

Urine Test Strips

Sometimes, the pet parent feels that something isn't quite right with their pet. Urine test strips may provide information to confirm if your instinct is correct.

Urine test strips are small paper strips onto which the urine of a pet (or human) can be tested for the following: Glucose, Bilirubin, Ketones, Specific Gravity, Blood, pH, Protein, Urobilinogen, Nitrite, Leukocytes, and Ascorbic Acid.

For home purposes, this should be considered a generalized test that will help you rule out certain conditions. A high leukocyte (white blood cell) count can indicate an infection. High or low glucose levels suggest the possibility of hyperglycemia (high glucose levels/diabetes) or hypoglycemia (low blood sugar).

Another use of the urine test strip is to monitor the pH levels of the urine. This is important because certain uroliths or bladder stones form in more alkaline urine while others develop in more acidic urine. If your pet has a history of either of these stones, and you know what type of stone your pet is prone to, testing the pH of the urine frequently helps you to utilize diet to avoid the conditions that encourage formation of the stones.

Urine is typically collected by taking your pet outside on a leash with an assistant that is prepared to catch the urine as the pet squats or lifts his leg. Usually an old spoon ladle can be re-purposed for this procedure.

In general, most urine test strip results providing the following information:

- **pH value**: The lower the number the higher the acidity. A high number means that the urine is more alkaline and can indicate inflammation of the kidneys

- **Protein**: High numbers can indicate kidney disease as healthy kidneys do not allow protein to pass through their filters.

- **Glucose**: Also known as blood sugar. High numbers (over 120) can indicate possible diabetic issues.

- **Nitrite**: If nitrites are present in the urine, it is a good indicator that an infection is present. A positive result indicates that the cause of the infection is a gram negative organism, most commonly Escherichia coli.

- **Ketone**: Positive ketone levels are usually present when the blood sugar is high.

- **Bilirubin**: When red blood cells break down, bilirubin is the result. A high level can indicate that the liver is not working properly.

- **Urobilinogen**: This is the product of the breakdown of bilirubin. A high count or positive result supports the fact that the liver is not functioning as it should.

- **Red blood cells**: Another term for red blood cells is erythrocytes. The presents of these in the urine can indicate a problem with the kidneys or blood.

- **White blood cells**: Known as leukocytes, their presents indicates infection.

- **Blood**: If there is any evidence of blood in the urine, it may indicate bladder or kidney stones. Call your veterinarian.

Test strips are limited in their efficacy by the time read, expiration dates, and other factors. Again, the use of this test at home should be limited to confirming your suspicions that your pet has a problem, or any other procedures as determined by your veterinarian. A negative result does not indicate that your pet is perfectly healthy, and if you still feel something is wrong with your pet, further testing should be conducted by your veterinarian.

Ear Mite Tests

Ear mites are most common in cats. They leave a signature debris in the ear and cause excessive itching. However, to be certain you are dealing with ear mites, a sample can be taken and confirmed using a microscope.

Prepare a slide by putting a drop of mineral oil in the center of the slide. Using a cotton tipped applicator, take a small sample from your cat's ear. Roll the debris-covered applicator tip into the mineral oil spreading out the sample, making an even field. You may place a slide cover over the area. Scan your field with the microscope until the entire field has been searched or you have found an ear mite.

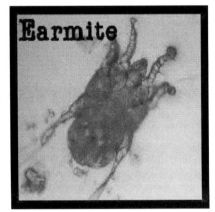

16

Essential Tests Only Your Veterinarian Can Perform

When you are on a strict budget, doing what you can do at home makes it easier to afford those things you cannot do yourself. Preventative medicine includes good nutrition and exercise, but it also includes preventative screenings which I recommend at least once yearly.

Complete Blood Count (CBC)

To get a picture of the condition of your pet's immune system, complete blood counts and chemistry panels are necessary. While the values (number) are different depending on species, these are the same tests your own human doctor performs.

For most people, a complete blood count (CBC) consists of unfamiliar words, numbers, and percentages. Taking what I explained about immunity, here is what you can learn with a complete blood count:

There are three basic parts of the blood:
- White blood cells (WBC) also called leukocytes
- Red blood cells (RBC)
- Platelets

White blood cells are important for fighting off infection. If you have a high WBC count, there is a very good chance there is a bacterial infection somewhere. There are different types of WBC that are in charge of different things. The number of each can show a vet a little more detail. For instance if the monocytes are increased, the infection may be caused by an allergic reaction to something.

Red blood cell counts tell you approximately how many red blood cells are in the body. These RBC's are in charge of getting oxygen throughout the body and carbon dioxide out. If the count is low, you may be anemic and your body is having difficulty getting oxygen. However, it is not good for the values to be too high, because too many RBC can block the oxygen from getting through to the rest of the body. There are other values within a RBC count that tell you specifics such as how dense the RBC count number is, and how good of a job the RBC's are doing of carrying the oxygen.

Platelets are in charge of blood clotting. Proper clotting requires a delicate balance of the correct amounts of platelets in the blood stream. If there are insufficient amounts of platelets, the body cannot clot the blood appropriately. However, if there are too many platelets, the potential for dangerous blood clots increases.

Chemistry Profiles

Blood chemistry tests are often called chemistry profiles or internal organ profiles (IOP). The results of these tell you how well each organ is working. All organs affect each other. Performing a full chemistry profile provides a picture of how an illness is affecting all major organs.

The cost of this profile is about $100-150. While this may seem expensive, the information it provides is invaluable. Focusing the profile on just one organ (for example, if a urinary problem is suspected, performing only a BUN and creatinine), does not cost significantly less than a full panel. It is in the best interest of the pet and the pet parent to have a full chemistry profile performed.

The test analyzes the following:

Liver: Alkaline Phosphatase, ALT (SGPT), Total Bilirubin, Cholesterol
Kidney: BUN, Creatinine
Pancreas : Blood Glucose, Lipase, Amylase
Electrolytes: Sodium, Potassium, Chloride, Magnesium
Proteins: Albumin, Total Protein, Globulin

Reading a CBC and chemistry profile is an art unto itself. Veterinarians are taught to analyze the big picture. This is why I say I must acknowledge that this is something I cannot do myself.

While I performed hundreds of these tests in my career, I still do not have the skill it takes to read the tests with the same educated perspective a veterinarian has. I can't tell you how many times I have taken the results of a chemistry profile to the on call vet expecting bad news only to hear "Ok, not bad."

So, I can guarantee you, taking the results of your pet's lab work home, getting on the internet and trying to translate the values, will only serve to scare you or confuse you. Trust your vet's interpretation and don't feel intimidated to ask questions if you want to understand more fully.

Thyroid Test

The thyroid glands are responsible for the metabolism along with other functions. The thyroid test results can be too low (hypothyroidism) or too high (hyperthyroidism). There are a number of tests that evaluate the function of the thyroid. The most common is the T4. If it indicates an issue, further testing should be done.

Many people do not realize the affects of a low or high thyroid. For instance, with low thyroid (hypothyroidism) the following symptoms may occur: lethargy, weight gain (with no increase in appetite), hair loss, dull coat, chronic itchy skin, dry skin, frequent skin infections, cold temperature intolerance, slow heart rate, frequent ear infections, behavioral changes, and depression.

High thyroid (hyperthyroidism) symptoms are: weight loss (with increase in appetite), restlessness and hyperactivity, increased heart rate, increase in frequency of defecation and size of stools, increase in thirst and urination, matting of the fur with a greasy coat, reddening of the mucous membranes.

Although thyroid tests are not inexpensive, in the long run the test can save you money. The pet parent may make repeated vet visits with their pet for chronically itchy skin, spending hundreds of dollars. If the thyroid test had been performed when the vet first suspected a thyroid problem, perhaps the thyroid could have been treated long ago. Once the thyroid becomes balanced, many problems resolve themselves.

Radiographs (X-RAY)

While an x-ray may seem self-explanatory, knowing a few facts about x-rays is important for the pet parent.

First, radiography for pets has come a long way in recent years. Now that digital films are available, the images are crisper, clearer, and the veterinarian can adjust the film on the computer to make it lighter, darker, and even magnified to get the best view possible.

For people stretching their budget to afford an x-ray, this advancement is a good thing. The fewer images required, the more economical the price. However, even with all this advancement, one view (image) is rarely enough.

X-rays look at a three dimensional object on a two dimensional film. In order to envision the body in three dimensions, you need a lateral and ventral/dorsal (v/d or d/v) view. So two different images are required.

Typically, when taking an x-ray of the abdomen, for example, the pet must rest on her side, normally right side down. This image is called a lateral view. Next, the pet is positioned either on her back (v/d) or less commonly, on her abdomen (d/v) and another x-ray is taken. The images are shot from directly above the pet.

The veterinarian puts those two images together in her mind, compares them, and realizes that either:

- Everything looks normal
- Things appear abnormal and medication can be prescribed
- Things appear abnormal and further study needs to rule out an obstruction, or torsion

Some things cannot be seen in a typical x-ray. If your pet eats your socks, the chances of the sock showing up on the x-ray are slim. Most soft objects cannot be seen in an x-ray unless they contain some type of metal. An important piece of information that may be gathered by these two x-rays is that the food is not moving through the digestive system as it should. The food the pet parents fed twelve hours ago may still be in the dog's stomach. The vet may assume that there is a blockage. To confirm this she may order a barium series.

Barium is a liquid that can be seen on an x-ray. Barium series radiographs work on a time lapse. The pet is given barium liquid by mouth, and a lateral and/or v/d film will be taken every 15-30 minutes. If the barium passes through the stomach, small and large intestine, and colon, a foreign body can usually be ruled out. However, it stops, the pet needs surgery immediately.

Radiographs can visualize a broken bone, find kidney or bladder stones, detect an enlarged heart, confirm a diaphragmatic hernia, or show chest congestion. The importance of an x-ray cannot be overstated.

Other diagnostic tools such as ultrasounds, EKG's, and ear cytologies are just a few other diagnostic tools available to your veterinarian that you simply cannot do at home. Learn to work with your vet by sharing the information you can gather with at-home tests and physical exams and trust your vet to help further the diagnostic process.

Emergencies and Common Illnesses

"Petting, scratching, and cuddling a dog could be as soothing to the mind and heart as deep meditation and almost as good for the soul as prayer." ~Dean Koontz

17

Emergencies

Physical exams can reveal a lot of important information. Determining what is an emergency or non-emergency, takes practice. **Learning what is normal is essential to learning what is abnormal.**

The ability of calmly assessing a situation is a valuable skill. A second valuable skill is reacting without panic. The more upset you are, the more frightened your pet will be. The best way to avoid panic is to educate yourself and be as prepared as possible when emergencies occur. Always have your veterinarian's phone number available as well as the nearest emergency animal hospital and poison control center. Know the quickest driving route to both hospitals.

In this chapter, I have attempted to cover the most common emergencies and what you can do. My hope is that this information will help you feel confident so that in an emergency, you will respond in a calm fashion to do the best thing for your pet.

Acute Allergic Reaction

Severe, unexpected allergic reactions can occur after a vaccine, bee sting, application of an insecticidal shampoo or flea product.

Symptoms of acute allergic reaction can include:

- a swollen muzzle and eyes
- difficulty breathing
- ataxia (loss of control of body movements)
- hives
- burning of the skin
- collapse

The reactions occur within 15-20 minutes of exposure.

A vigil pet parent who observes swelling taking place can give diphenhydramine (Benadryl ®)

as soon as symptoms appear, unless the pet has collapsed or cannot swallow. Your veterinarian should be contacted immediately.

Benedryl ® dosing guidelines are 1 mg per lb of body weight for dogs and 0.25-.50 mg per lb of body weight for a cat.

If your pet has a history of severe vaccine reactions, talk to your vet about giving diphenhydramine prior to the vaccine.

Some pets have allergic reactions to topical flea products. Most of the time, the reaction is to the alcohol or other inert ingredient. The pet's skin will appear to have a chemical burn. The pet will normally be very restless and try to reach the area that is in pain.

Call your vet for instructions. If a veterinarian is not available, the topical product should be washed off immediately with a cool (not cold) bath. Allow the water to run over the affected area to soothe the pain. Apply aloe vera if available. An alternative to aloe is one or two cool, wet, tea bags (black tea only). The tannic acid in the black tea pulls heat from the burn, making it less painful.

Never use ice on a burn. Call your vet as soon as he or she is available to see if further action is required.

Burns

By far, the worst burn I ever saw on a dog was intentionally caused. The owner, tired of her chained up dog barking, took a pot of boiling water and threw it on the dog. Most of the dog's head and back was covered in second and third degree burns.

Most pet parents would never intentionally harm their pet, but accidents do occur.

It is important to know that burns can actually be worse than they look.

"Even what looks like only a mild burn can become much worse over time. This is particularly true for thermal burns, which may be caused by heat lamps, water blankets, or even hot water from a garden hose that was used for bathing. The skin may look red initially, but then may turn black, crusty, and become quite painful with these burns," says Dr. Alison Diesel, lecturer specializing in dermatology, at the Texas A&M College of Veterinary Medicine and Biomedical Sciences. https://vetmed.tamu.edu/news/pet-talk/pet-burns

Burns can occur from a number of sources:

- Chemical Burn (discussed above)
- Sunburns
- Electrical burns

- Hot water or oil
- Open flames (candles, fireplaces)
- Hot metal surfaces such as car engines
- Hot asphalt or tar
- Hot electrical heating pads or hairdryer
- Heat lamps or heat rocks (particularly for exotic pets)

Thermal and chemical burns are categorized as follows:

- **First degree**: These burns are superficial, involving only the top layer of skin. An example is a sunburn
- **Second degree**: Deep partial thickness burns involving deeper layers of skin. Blisters appear on the skin surface and it is very painful. A veterinarian should be consulted immediately.
- **Third degree**: This full thickness burn involves the destruction of all skin layers. The skin is our largest protector from bacteria and other invaders. Once it is charred and destroyed, bacteria begins to invade the body. Blood circulation and immune response is delayed or completely blocked by the burn. Sensation is lost in the area. The pet should be rushed to the veterinarian.

Most burns are too serious to be treated at home. Sunburn causes reddening of the skin and pain. Sunburn usually occurs in pets chained outdoors, or those who have a summer shave but are unable to find shade. Most sunburns are first degree burns. The pet should be kept out of the sun until the body heals. Cool oatmeal baths may help relieve the discomfort.

Electrical burns are most often focused in and around the mouth, while asphalt burns can show up more readily on the paws.

The severity of the burn can take 24-48 hours to show. For this reason, it is recommended that the pet parent contact his or her veterinarian immediately for instructions.

Never treat a burn with ice, ice packs, or very cold water.

Choking

Witnessing a dog choking is one of the most frightening and helpless experiences of my life. I've always wondered if I knew then what I know now if my dog Pepper would still be living. So I want to give you the tools you need to help you in a situation like this.

Although choking is possible in cats, they rarely choke in the way dogs do. Cats are more particular about what they put in their mouths. Cats will sometimes start playing with a string or piece of tinsel from a Christmas tree and swallow it. Sometimes the string is swallowed only part of the way, leaving some of it still sticking out. Be careful about pulling on it. Strings, tinsel, or fishing wire have been known to be tied around the tongue and partially swallowed. Strings, tinsel, or fishing wire can restrict blood flow to the tongue, causing the tongue to die. Call your veterinarian immediately if you suspect your pet has swallowed a foreign object.

There is a difference between a backward or reverse sneeze and actually choking. This is something that may confuse some pet parents. A backward sneeze is a layman's term for mechanosensitive aspiration reflex and this reflex is fairly common. A backward sneeze is caused by a spasm of the throat and soft palate. Many things can cause a backward sneeze and the sound and reaction of the dog is much scarier than it really is. Generally during an episode, the mouth will be closed and instead of the air being forced out of the nose as it would in a normal sneeze, air is being forced in. It is not life threatening and there's nothing to do but to hold your pet and try to calm her down until the episode is over. I rub the throat of my pet, but there's really no proof that rubbing the throat helps. If rubbing the throat does nothing else, the action makes me feel like I'm doing something to help.

A pet that is actually choking will most likely not be able to move the amount of air as they would with a reverse sneeze.

A dog or cat that is choking may exhibit the following signs:

- The mouth will probably be wide open with little or no air passage
- He/she may be pawing frantically at the mouth
- He/she may appear in deep distress
- He/she may be attempting to vomit
- The mucus membrane color will turn blue

If your pet is conscious, give him a chance to see if the item will dislodge with the pets own efforts. Many dogs who seem to inhale their food will do this, take the food to another location, and vomit it up in another place.

If the item is not dislodging and the pet seems in extreme distress then you will have to take it a step further. If someone is with you, and your dog is a larger breed, have that person hold the dog. If not, take the dog to a well lit area and put the pet near a wall. This helps you maintain a little more control of the body. The wall works like an assistant.

Keep in mind that the dog may be panicking like any of us would in this situation. Use your non-dominant hand on the top of the muzzle, and your dominant hand on the bottom and open the mouth. Look for the object. If you can, take your index finger on your dominant hand dislodge the object. Be careful not to push it further down the throat or to get bitten.

If this doesn't dislodge the item, you will need to do a Heimlich maneuver.

There are several versions of this process depending on the pets size and if the pet is conscious. I'm going to give you several options. Don't give up until you have tried them all.

Heimlich Maneuver for Dogs and Cats:

If your dog is a **large or medium size dog, conscious, and standing**:

- Stand behind the dog
- Wrap your arms around the dog placing your fist on the abdomen just below the ribs. Wrap your other hand around that fist.
- Give one sharp, quick thrust in toward the backbone and up toward the head. If the item dislodges, then stop. If not then...
- Repeat 5 times.
- Check between each thrust to see if the item has dislodged

If your dog is a **toy size dog or a cat that is conscious, and standing**:
- Place your pet on a table.
- Put two knuckles on the abdomen just below the ribs and place your other hand on the back of the dog
- Give one sharp, quick thrust in toward the backbone and up toward the head. If the item dislodges, then stop. If not then....
- Repeat 5 times.
- Check between each thrust to see if the item has dislodged

If this doesn't work and the pet has become unconscious, and you can get to the vet within a couple of minutes, GO. If not have someone drive you and the dog to the vet as you try the following:

- Pick up the dog with the head facing down and the back against your chest. The reason for this is to have gravity in your favor.

- For a small dog or cat, instead of putting your other hand on the back, put it over your knuckles to help with the sharp, quick thrusts. Repeat thrusts.
- If the dog is too large for you to pick up, lay the dog on his/her side. Kneel near the tail or in any position that will give you the best balance to perform the procedure. Place one hand on the back and make a fist with the other hand. Repeat thrusts.
- If the item dislodges and your pet is still unconscious, you may need to perform CPR

Dehydration

Dehydration can be caused by many things. Insufficient water intake (often seen in pets living on chains), severe diarrhea or vomiting, heat stroke, and chronic kidney disease are some common causes.

Dehydration has to be addressed fast before symptoms get any worse. Dehydration causes dizziness, weakness, and nausea. A lack of appetite, lethargy, and a sunken-eye appearance can be indicators of dehydration.

Dehydration is often the cause of death in puppies with the parvovirus. Puppies will want to drink water, but cannot hold the water down. Often the first indication that a small puppy has parvo is finding her by her water dish staring at the bowl.

Dehydration is also common in the elderly cat. Kidney disease is almost inevitable in senior cats. When encouraging the cat to drink does not suffice, often your vet will subscribe subcutaneous fluids to be given daily or several times weekly. Most veterinarians will teach you how to do this procedure at home.

To determine if your dog or cat is dehydrated, perform a **hydration test.** The hydration test is the most important part of the exam. Gently lift the skin between the shoulder blades and let go. If the pet is not dehydrated, the skin should snap back quickly into place. If the skin doesn't respond in this manner, the pet is dehydrated. The longer it takes the skin to return to its normal shape, the more dehydrated the animal is. This is called the **skin turgor** and is the reflection of the elasticity of the skin.

Veterinarians use a **dehydration assessment** based upon a physical exam. The things they look for is amount of skin turgor, the dryness of the mucous membranes, the condition of the eyes, and the pulse rate. **Enophthalmos** refers to a sunken eye appearance and may be present during severe levels of dehydration. Tachycardia refers to an excessively rapid heart rate and can be a symptom of severe dehydration.

Dehydration Assessment Score	Symptoms Presented
Mild (~5%)	Minimal loss of skin turgor, semi-moist mucous membrane, normal eye.
Moderate (~8%)	Moderate loss of skin turgor, dry mucus membranes, weak and rapid pulse, enophthalmos
Severe (> 10%)	Considerable loss of skin turgor, extremely dry mucus membranes, severe enophthalmos, tachycardia

http://www.catvets.com/public/PDFs/PracticeGuidelines/FluidTherapyGLS.pdf

There are three ways to treat dehydration:

- Orally (only for animals who are not vomiting)
- Subcutaneous fluids (given under the skin)
- IV fluids (given by catheter directly into the vein of the pet)

Oral treatment for dehydration can be with water only, or an electrolyte solution. If the pet can drink water, give it in small frequent amounts. Don't allow a quick intake of water as a fast water intake may cause vomiting, leading to more dehydration.

To make an electrolyte solution that is taken more readily by the dog and cat compared to Gatorade ® or Pedialyte ®, use an animal electrolyte solution such as Bounce Back ® or ReSorb ®. Mix as directed, substituting some water with reduced sodium chicken broth.

If the pet is already vomiting, and the hydration test reveals dehydration, get the pet to the vet immediately for IV fluids.

Your vet will determine the amount of fluids to give your pet. This number is dependent upon the percentage of dehydration and the body weight of your pet in kilograms.

Percent of dehydration X body weight of pet = hydration deficit

For example, if your vet determines that your 5 kg pet is 8 % dehydrated, she has a 400 ml hydration deficit.
http://www.veterinarypracticenews.com/January-2011/Fluid-Therapy-Can-Be-Lifesaver-If-Done-Right/

For severe cases, the fluid will be given intravenously over a period of hours. If hospitalized, it is rare to treat dehydration with subcutaneous fluids. An IV catheter is the preferred route of administration.

If given subcutaneously, the veterinarian may give the fluid in two or more sessions throughout the day. This method of fluid administration is often referred to as the "sub-q" method. The same bag of fluid with an administration set is required. However, no IV catheter is used. Instead the fluid is put under the skin of the patient. The skin of dogs and cats is more elastic than human skin, allowing the skin to stretch. The administration set should be attached to the fluids, and the fluid hung higher than the treatment area of the pet. Gravity will make the task much easier. To ensure there is no air in the line, open the line completely with the flow control valve. Allow the fluid to run in a sink, shaking the line a bit if necessary, to remove all air bubbles. The air removal should only take 1-2 seconds.

Attach an 18 or 20 gauge needle to the end of the administration line. The higher the gauge number, the smaller the needle. An 18 gauge needle will allow the fluid to flow faster than a 20 gauge. However, for a small kitten or puppy, the veterinarian may choose a 20 gauge needle.

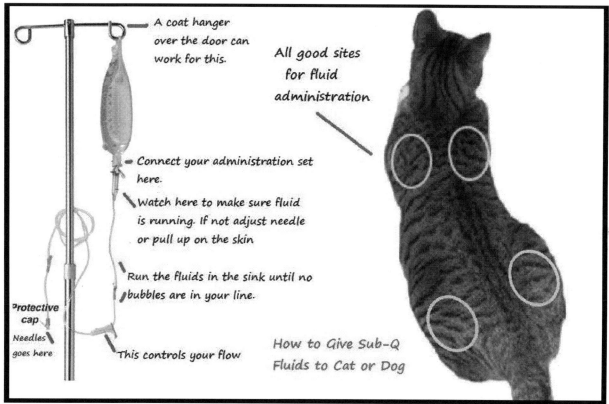

In the image above, the circles indicate areas of some of the most elastic skin and the ones used most often by veterinarians. For a detailed photograph instruction guide, see the following link: http://www.vetmed.wsu.edu/ClientED/cat_fluids.aspx

Perhaps the best area for subcutaneous fluids is the area between the shoulder blades. This is done by pulling the skin up in a "tent" fashion, inserting the needle in the "door" of the tent, being careful not to puncture though to the other side. The position of the needle should be nearly parallel to the body. Once the needle is properly inserted, the veterinarian or technician will continue to hold the skin up to prevent the skin from blocking the flow of the fluids. The flow control will be turned all the way on. If properly placed, one can see the fluid drip into the fluid reservoir. If the fluids run too slow, the needle should be adjusted by pulling back on the needle or re-positioning it.

Normally 50-100 milliliters of fluid can be put in one area. Filling too full can be painful, however, the more fluid in one area, the fewer needle sticks are necessary. Doing this properly is a common sense balancing act.

Utilizing gravity and the proper needles allows the process to go much faster. This is to the advantage of the pet and the fluid administrator.

Dizziness or Vertigo

Sudden onset of dizziness or vertigo most commonly occurs in senior dogs and cats.

The pet may appear drunk, stumble when attempting to walk, and lose all sense of balance. The head may tilt, the pet may appear disorientated walking in circles, and the eyes may jerk erratically.

The most likely cause is **idiopathic vestibular disease,** a disease once referred to as "old dog syndrome."

The diagnosis of idiopathic vestibular disease is reached when other causes have been ruled out. These causes may include inner ear infection, hypothyroidism, injury or trauma, tumors, and toxicity.

"Old Dog Disease" can be successfully treated. Our dog, Casey, was diagnosed and treated this year and has fully recovered.

When the pet parent cannot afford the necessary tests to rule out these potential causes, the vet may reat with steroids, antibiotics, and meclizine (Bonine ®, Dramamine II ®). Recovery may take weeks.

Other conditions can mimic a vestibular disease to the untrained eye. This may include cardiac collapse (for pets in congestive heart failure) and seizures.

Heat Stroke

There's always an idiot who leaves their pet in the car in the middle of summer thinking that rolling the windows down will keep the pet cool enough. Perhaps your dog is one of the short nose breeds, that even with panting, can't cool down enough. Or maybe you tie out your dog to enjoy the sunshine but forgetting that he needs shade and water too. Whatever the case, heat stroke can be deadly.

Symptoms of heat stroke include:
- excessive panting
- bright red tongue
- thick sticky saliva
- weakness
- unsteady gait
- vomiting
- coma

If you witness a dog in this condition, the first thing to do is to remove the pet from the hot environment. Wet the patient down with cool water, or for smaller pets, lukewarm water. Cooling the body too fast can be counterproductive and dangerous. If you are able to get the pet to the vet, do so after wetting him/her down. If the patient is comatose, make sure that he/she does not inhale the water as this can cause aspiration (water in the airway) or even choking. If you are unable to get the pet to the veterinarian, take the pets temperature. Anything above 103°F is too high. Temperature below 99° F is too cold. **Normal temperature is 100.5-102.5°F for cats and 101-102.5°F for dogs.**

If the pet is still above 103°F, you will need to continue to wet the pet down and/or put a cooling pads around the dog. At the vet office, we either froze leftover IV fluids or water in an empty soda bottle and kept them ready for a situation like this.

A fan can be used to help cool the pet, but take the temperature every few minutes. Once the temperature is just below 103°F, stop your cooling process. When the pet is conscious, you will need to provide electrolytes and re-hydrate the animal.

Do not attempt to force fluid down the throat.

High Fever

High fever is a symptom of a larger problem. **Normal temperature is 100-102.5°F for cats and 101-102.5°F for dogs. The temperature or level of dryness of the nose is not an indicator of normal or high fever.**

The temperature of any pet appears unwell, should be taken rectally. In a dog or cat that has not been exercising, the temperature should not exceed 103°F.

There are many reasons for a fever. It is not uncommon for pets to have a low grade fever for 24 hours or so after vaccinations. High fevers accompany heat stroke as well as many infections.

A high fever should be investigated immediately. A thorough exam may discover an abscess or infected tooth, for example. Contact your veterinarian as soon as possible.

Applying ice packs, wetting the coat down, and wiping the paws with alcohol swabs, can help bring down the fever until the cause can be identified. Putting the pet in front of a fan may also help, but the temperature should be monitored closely.

Hypoglycemia/Low Blood Sugar

Hypoglycemia is low blood sugar. If the blood sugar is low enough, the pet can collapse.

Normal blood sugar, or glucose, in the fasted dog and cat is 75-120 mg/dl.

Diabetes, also called hyperglycemia, occurs when the blood sugar is significantly higher in a fasted animal than it should be.

Hypoglycemia is low blood sugar and can occur in diabetic animals when they have not eaten and have been given insulin, or when they are given too much insulin. Hypoglycemia can also occur in puppies (rarely kittens), particularly in teacup and toy breeds.

Signs of hypoglycemia include:

- Unbalanced, wobbly walking and lack of muscular coordination
- Disorientation
- Weakness/lethargy
- Pale gums
- Head tilt
- Collapse
- Seizure like activity
- Glassy eyes, staring off into the distance
- Coma

Cats have also been reported to have made unusual vocalizations when hypoglycemic.

The treatment for this condition is glucose, or sugar. If the pet is conscious, you can feed the pet corn syrup, honey, or liquid glucose (you can purchase at the pharmacy). If she is not eating it by choice, you can put some on the tip of the nose, and most cats/dogs will lick automatically. You can also fill a syringe with corn syrup and slowly squeeze it into the mouth. Be careful not to aspirate the liquid into the airways.

If the pet is unconscious, it is important to get to the vet. On your way, you can put a little syrup on the tongue, but be careful not to block the airway or the pet can aspirate it into the lungs. Once the pet is at the vet, if there is no improvement, your vet may need to put in an IV catheter to deliver the glucose more directly.

Intestinal Blockage, Bloat and Gastric Torsion

Intestinal blockages occur when an object, such as a toy, sock, or bone gets stuck in the digestive tract, allowing nothing, or very little, to pass through the intestinal tract.
Signs of intestinal blockage may include:

- Drooling
- Vomiting (sometimes projectile)
- Lethargy and weakness
- Abdominal pain and distention
- Loss of appetite
- Dehydration

Bloat can be caused by a pet quickly consuming lots of food or water causing a gas buildup. This gas buildup causes the stomach to expand. This stomach expansion can cut off the blood supply to vital organs, cause a tear in the stomach wall, and make breathing difficult.

The stomach can twist, particularly in deep chested dog, causing a condition known as **gastric dilatation volvulus or gastric torsion.**

Signs of gastric torsion include:

- Restlessness, unwilling to lay down
- Anxiety
- Drooling
- Attempting to vomit/dry heaves
- Arched back
- Swollen, painful abdomen

- Rapid Breathing

Both of these conditions are intensely painful emergencies that cannot be treated at home.

Your vet should be contacted immediately. Ask your vet about giving simethicone (Gas-X ®) by mouth on the way to the animal clinic.

Cats are less likely to experience gastrointestinal blockage than dogs, but it is possible. Common causes include digestion of a foreign body (string, string with sewing needle, tinsel, rubber bands), and hairballs. Symptoms of intestinal blockage is much the same in the cat and dog. Prevention is much cheaper than the cure.

Hairballs can be prevented by feeding small amounts of pumpkin regularly. Hairball remedies such as Laxatone ® are a tasty paste that some cats prefer.

Being aware of things in your pets environment that could cause potential problems can save your pets life.

Preventative actions to avoid gastrointestinal emergencies include:

- Keeping food stored where your pet cannot reach it. Some pets will eat every last morsel of food causing a build up of gas
- Never allow your pet to gulp water in large amounts after exercising.
- If your dog likes to gulp his food, slow him down by using a commercial slow-feed bowl sold in pet stores. You can also put a ball in the food that he must move in order to eat his food. Make sure the ball is too big to be swallowed.
- Do not purchase toys with small parts that can be swallowed, or can be easily torn apart by the pet. If you have a cat and dog, keep in mind that the bell in the cat toy could easily be swallowed by the dog.
- Do not use tinsel on your Christmas Tree.
- Keep your cat out of your sewing room or be vigilant about putting your sewing needle, thread or yarn away.
- Do not give rawhide to dogs who consume it too fast. Always stay with your pet when giving a treat.
- Consider the unusual things that pets consume such as coins, socks, towels, and paper clips, and keep them away from your pet.

Minor Wounds

No two wounds are alike. In my time as a technician and animal cruelty investigator, I have assisted with treating bite wounds, scrapes, cat scratches and bites, and wounds caused by tight collars (particularly chain prong collars), and wounds resulting from matted fur.

Universal practices for responding to minor wounds include:

- Make sure the pet is in a safe place to avoid further injury
- Keep the pet as calm as possible. A high heart rate can encourage faster blood loss.
- If the wound is bleeding, apply pressure with a clean towel
- Shave the hair around the wound with clean, disinfected clipper blades
- Clean the wound with a 1:2 Nolvasan ® solution mixing one part Nolvasan ® with two parts warm water.
- Apply a triple antibiotic ointment
- If a bandage is required, used a non-stick gauze pad.

If bleeding is severe, most likely stitches will be required and the pet should be taken to the vet immediately.

The pet parent should also consult with her veterinarian to see if oral antibiotics are necessary.

Orphaned Animals

Many of us have found ourselves with orphaned pets or those that need artificial nursing. Perhaps a mother bird escapes the cage, a mother dog has more puppies than she can feed, or a cat mother is hit by a car and killed.

Whatever the cause, we are left with the responsibility of raising their offspring and it is no easy task. Orphaned animals are an emergency, because, without our help, they will die. This section is dedicated to raising the most common among the domestic animal kingdom: puppies, kittens, and birds.

Puppies and Kittens:
A common postpartum problem in a nursing canine is hypocalcemia, (also called eclampsia). This is a lack of calcium that occurs as a result of nursing and inadequate feeding prior to whelping and after. (Expectant and new mothers should eat a high quality puppy chow). Milk contains a lot of calcium and as this mother nurses, she is depleted of this necessary mineral. Unless that calcium is replaced, she can die. It is an absolute emergency. Once it occurs, typically the veterinarian will instruct that the humans take over the nursing duties.

For both puppies and kittens, avoid cow's milk and soy milk. Buy a milk replacer made specifically for the species or goat's milk. Other milks can cause severe diarrhea. When you purchase your milk replacer, also buy a bottle too as it has the correct nipple size.

One week old puppies and kittens require feeding about every two hours (including night-time). As they age, the intervals between the feeding times will increase. After the first week, feed every three hours for the next three weeks.

Mix small amounts for each feeding as instructed on the milk replacer. Use warm water, not cold, in the mixture. If the milk is warmed in the microwave, be careful as this can make it much too hot. Shake the milk and test it on your own wrist to assess the temperature.

Allow the puppy or kitten to suckle as long as he is willing. If he or she is not willing to suckle, it is often helpful to use a syringe (with no needle) to introduce the milk to the animal. Be careful not to give too much at one time as they pet can aspirate.

Once finished, take him, her to the sink, and using a warm, soft wet cloth, wipe the anal area. This simulates the mother's licking and will stimulate the puppy or kitten to potty. This stimulation should be done after every feeding.

The young of both species should be kept in a small box or whelping bed. The box or bed should be placed away from any drafts. Put a heating pad on low on one side of the box, or if a heating pad is not available, you may heat up a small water bottle. Be sure the water bottle is not too hot, wrap it in a towel and monitor everyone carefully. Be sure that the water bottle cannot roll around. For the ones I have cared for, I always added a stuffed animal in the box for the babies to cuddle with.

Often orphaned puppies and kittens will be infested with fleas. You can bathe the orphans in warm water and a gentle baby shampoo. Using a flea comb available at pet stores, comb any fleas out of the fur. You can rinse them down the sink. Do not use a flea soap or flea drop (like Frontline ®) until 8 weeks of age or later as indicated on the box. The one exception is Frontline ® Spray (not drops and no other brand) which can be used as early as 2 days.

Around four to five weeks of age, the feedings can alternate between milk replacer and puppy/kitten food. Using the highest quality dry kibble you can afford, mix it with warm water to the consistency of oatmeal. Decrease the milk feedings and increase the wet kibble feedings. If the young do not respond well to the wet kibble, use a high quality canned food, but be careful as not to encourage diarrhea with the increased water content. As the puppies and kittens begin to teethe, you can gradually decrease the water content in the wet kibble and allow them to eat dry kibble.

Deworm both puppies and kittens at 2 weeks old and every two weeks thereafter, for a total of four dewormings. Most veterinarians use pyrantel for this purpose.

Kittens can be introduced to the litter box after the first couple of weeks. Remember kittens' eyes do not open until about 10 days old.

Keep the young ones isolated to protect them from disease. Normally they get their initial immunity to disease from their mother's milk. Bottle fed puppies and kittens do not have that advantage.

Watch for any sign of blood in the stool, unusual eye discharge, sneezing, and lack of appetite. Contact your vet if any of these occur. A common killer of puppies and kittens is coccidia, a protozoa that causes severe intestinal distress. Coccidia can kill in a matter of hours by dehydration. Albon ® is the initial treatment for coccidia, but the patient may also require subcutaneous fluids if it is severe.

At six weeks vaccinations can begin. Take care in exposing your pets to other pets whose vaccination and deworming status are in question. Also keep in mind that many diseases and parasites can live in the ground and your bottle fed baby can be very susceptible to those.

Birds
Raising baby birds can vary greatly depending on the type of bird. For this reason, I highly recommend the book **Hand-Feeding and Raising Baby Birds: Breeding, Hand-feeding, Care and Management** by Matthew Vriends. Although this book is more comprehensive and written for those interested in breeding, the book has all the necessities for hand rearing.
My personal experience was in hand feeding zebra finches.

For an excellent article on feeding finches for the purpose of taming them, an excellent blog article can be found at
http://www.finchinfo.com/submissions/guide_to_hand_feeding_finches.php

Even though feeding specifics can vary by species, here are some general guidelines to follow:

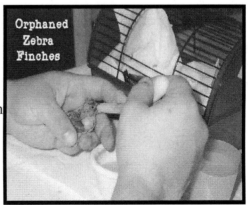

- **Know the specific nutritional needs of your baby birds**: With the exception of the lorikeet, a nectar feeder, and mynah birds, an animal protein eater, most baby birds can be fed Kaytee's Exact Hand Feeding Formula ® or Lafeber's Instant Nutri-Start Baby Bird Formula ®. Mix the formula as directed on the product label. Make sure that the formula is not too hot. Appropriate food temperature is between 100-106°F. The formula must also be able to pass through the syringe properly without any extra air in the syringe. Small birds will only eat 0.1-0.2 cc while a large bird may eat 1.0 cc at the first feeding. Some recommend adding elecrolytes to the formula in the form of clear Pedialyte ®. Be careful not to aspirate the bird by pushing the plunger of the syringe too fast. To encourage the bird to eat, tap the tip of the syringe lightly on the beak. Additional encouragement may be necessary such as gently opening the beak to allow a tiny amount of food in. Once the bird begins to eat, allow him or her to eat until full. You can clearly see the crop fill up. Throw away any unused formula. Never save excess formula and reuse the formula later. Using a warm cotton ball, clean each bird after feeding.

- **Use the correct equipment**: Depending on the size of the bird, you will need to purchase the correct size syringe for feeding. Finches will use a tuberculin syringe (1 cc) while larger birds can use a 10 or 12 cc syringe or perhaps even larger. Many syringe sizes can be found at your local drug store or feed store. You may have to ask your veterinarian for a 1cc tuberculin syringe if you are feeding finches. If feeding more than one bird, use one syringe per bird and wash them thoroughly after use. Medicine droppers can also be used as long as it has not been used previously for medication. New droppers can also be purchased at drug stores.

- **Environment**: Birds need to stay warm and away from drafts. You can keep them in a small shoe box ventilated with holes. Line the bottom with paper towels and add additional paper towels around the birds to help warm them. It may be a good idea to put the box on a heating pad on low. Make sure that it is not too hot. I prefer to have two boxes. One for the birds to rest in before feeding and a clean one to put the birds in after they are fed. After feeding, clean out the first box and prepare the box for next feeding. Since I had other animals in the house, I was not comfortable keeping my birds in a shoe box. I purchased a very tiny cage. It made it easier taking the birds to work and I was able to keep them warmer by covering them with a small kitchen towel. If a heating pad is unavailable, you may use an incandescent bulb on a swivel desk lap as a heat source. Be careful not to put it too close to the birds and test the temperature of the environment.

- **Feeding Schedule**: The intervals between feedings depends on the age at which you have to begin feeding. Most professionals recommend feeding every two hours for hatchlings and nestlings. Hatchlings (1-3 days old) may need help holding their heads up and keeping their neck stretched out, in order to feed. Be very gentle in doing so. Once the bird has fed, you can see if the crop is full. Empty crops indicate the need for another feeding. Fledglings, (about 3-4 weeks old), birds will begin to show interest in eating on their own and leaving the nest. They should be transferred to a small cage with perches at this stage. Adding a small millet spray to the cage will give the fledglings an idea of what is to come next. They should begin to peck on the millet. A soft egg food such as Cede is a good beginner food for juvenile birds and should be provided in the cage along with water. During this transition, birds do depend on their parents, and may require intermittent feedings from you.

Pain

It took a long time for humans and even those in the vet industry to admit that animals experience pain. When they did admit that animals feel pain, for a while they thought it was a good thing because the pain limited activity, allowing the pet to heal faster.

In an effort to come to a consensus on what animal pain looks like, several hundred veterinary professionals, from veterinarians to technicians were asked "what criteria did he/she use to determine if an animal was in pain?"

The answers as reported in **Small Animal Emergency and Critical Care: A Manual for the Veterinary Technician** by Andrea M. Battaglia are as follows:

- Vocalization (crying out, whining, etc)
- Increased heart rate
- Increased respiratory rate (including panting)
- Restlessness
- Increased body temperature
- Increased blood pressure
- Abnormal posturing (involuntarily extending arms and legs indicating possible brain damage)
- No appetite
- Aggression
- Unwillingness to move
- Frequent changes in position (inability to get comfortable)
- Facial expression
- Depression
- Insomnia
- Anxiety
- Nausea
- Enlargement of the pupils
- Licking, chewing, or staring at site of pain
- Poor mucus membrane color
- Excess salivation
- Head pressing (standing near a wall or corner face first without moving)

I cite this report in an effort to make pet parents more aware of the signs of pain in their pets.

Unlike us, pets cannot point to the pain chart and report their pain level on a 1-10 scale. A sign that wasn't mentioned, but that is very relevant for the pet parent, is a pet that is hiding.

Knowing these indicators of pain does not mean you know what is causing the pain. There is a lot to take into account in determining where the pain is coming from and what to do. Determining pain is just a piece of the puzzle in figuring out the big picture. An important rule of thumb: if you recognize multiple signs of pain in your pet, call or get to your vet as soon as possible.

I do have to take this opportunity to tell you a true story that happened at our rescue. This is an example of recognizing pain and distress and trying to figure out what kind of emergency I was dealing with.

One year, in the late spring, I had stepped out to run an errand. Most of the dogs were together in the dog room and could run outside through a dog door leading to an outside fenced area. Since it was not warm enough to turn the air conditioning on, I had a box fan blowing so the dogs could lay comfortably in front of the fan.

When I came home, I found that someone had chewed through the electrical wire and the area around the wire was wet. I unplugged the cord immediately hoping not to be electrocuted in the process.

I began counting dogs to see if everyone was okay. I noticed Onyx, my beautiful black female chihuahua, didn't look quite right. She looked anxious and stiff. Her pupils were huge as if frightened. I took her into another room to assess her. Her right rear leg seemed to levitate on its own as her back contorted into a strange shape. At first, she ran and tried to hide. I considered if she was having some sort of seizure after being electrocuted. The vet was closed, so after retrieving her from her hiding place, I held her, checked her mucus membranes (noticing no signs of burning that could have been caused by the electrocution) watched her breathing, and felt the stiffness in her back. I pressed gently along her spine to see if she had any sharp reaction to pain. She tensed when I pressed in an area about 2 inches above her tail. I felt a very tight muscle and massaged it until it loosened up.

I went back to check on the others dogs. I realized that the liquid on the electrical cord was urine. I noticed that Teddy, my mid-sized mixed breed dog refused to come back in the house. I went outside to check on him. Knowing his tendency to assert his authority by sometimes urinating, I checked his penis. He pulled back in pain, obviously not wanting me to touch it. He was distracted from my exam by a toy and I watched him until he went to the nearest bush and urinated. I had a feeling that Onyx wasn't the only dog at fault.

Over the next several days, Onyx's right leg suddenly seemed to levitate on its own. Onyx appeared as if she was a towel and someone wringing her dry. Onyx would run to hide, displaying a painful look on her face.

I found that if I placed Onyx on a table in front of me and started a deep massage along the spine mid-back toward the tail, that her stiffness would relax. The "levitating" leg would return to its normal position, and in a few minutes she would be fine. She had one heck of a charlie horse.

I don't know if I ever fully solved the mystery, but I believe Onyx may have chewed on the wire, and Teddy, in his alpha dog way, urinated on the wire causing electricity to travel up the urine trail and straight to his penis.

Because I knew what pain in my pets looked like, I was able to help Onyx even in my confusion, and to assess Teddy.

I have learned never to allow electrical wires anywhere near my dogs and I hope Teddy learned a very valuable lesson. If nothing else, he earned his alpha dog status that day. At times I look at Teddy and giggle, shake my head, and be very thankful that it turned out as well as it did.

The two books which taught me to assess pain and methods of massage and manipulation to relieve pain are Dr. Daniel Kamen's **The Well Adjusted Dog: Canine chiropractic methods you can do** and Dr. Michael W. Fox's **The Healing Touch: The proven massage program for cats and dogs.**

With this information, do not make the mistake that all pain can be treated with massage. While it is good for arthritic animals and situations such as Onyx's charlie horse, pain can be a sign of much more. For example, a hunched over appearance does not necessarily mean that the back is hurting. A hunched over appearance can be a sign of severe abdominal pain caused by something that may not be able to be treated at home. If you have any question in your mind regarding the severity or cause of the pain, contact your vet as soon as possible.

Pancreatitis

The pancreas is responsible for producing several important hormones that help in digestion and regulate blood sugar. These hormones including insulin, glucagon, and somatostatin. The exocrine gland, secretes pancreatic juice containing digestive **enzymes** that pass to the small intestine. The pancreas is part of a complex digestive process that seeks to break down proteins, triglycerides, and complex carbohydrates. This process also produces bicarbonate to buffer stomach acid.

Pancreatitis can be chronic (long term) or acute (sudden). Chronic pancreatitis is more common in cats and acute pancreatitis is more common in dogs. Siamese cats and miniature schnauzers seem to be genetically prone to suffer from pancreatits.

Certain drugs, viruses, and bacteria can cause the inflammation of the pancreas, a condition known as pancreatitis. The most common cause of acute pancreatitis in dogs is the consumption of fatty human foods such as pork, beef, and other fatty human foods.

Veterinary hospitals frequently see an increase in acute pancreatitis immediately after Thanksgiving and Christmas celebrations. Perhaps the pet parents, wanted their pets to join in the holiday, and shared their turkey and/or ham with their dog or cat. Dogs who frequently get into the trash, a condition many veterinarians refer to as "garbage gut" are also prone to the acute form of pancreatitis.

When a pet eats fatty foods, the pancreas releases enzymes and other substances into the surrounding area of the abdomen rather than secreting it properly through the digestive system. The secretions cause localized inflammation that damages the pancreas and nearby organs. This can become a serious, life-threatening condition that can lead to diabetes, kidney failure, and intestinal obstruction. A pet not properly treated for this condition, if he recovers, can be more likely to have pancreatitis again, or develop the chronic form of the disease.

Symptoms of pancreatitis in dogs include:
- lack of appetite
- lethargy
- fever
- diarrhea
- vomiting
- painful abdomen
-

Symptoms of pancreatitis in cats differ and include:

- lethargy
- poor appetite
- dehydration
- lower body temperature
- increased respiratory rate
- possible hepatic lipidoses (fatty liver syndrome) that causes the mucus membranes to turn yellow in color

Pancreatitis treatment is similar for the dog and cat. Your veterinarian will take away all food and water to rest the digestive system. The pet will be put on IV fluids. Pain medications, anti-vomiting medication, and sometimes, antibiotics will be administered through the IV line. With treatment, it can take several days for the inflammation to subside. Only then will your vet begin offering small amounts of water, and begin a bland diet. Once the pet has shown that he can eat without ill side effects, the pet will be sent home on a bland diet such as Hills ® Prescription I/D. The vet will have the pet parent slowly transition the dog to his regular food over a period of one to two weeks.

Pancreatitis is very difficult to treat at home. Some of the symptoms such as diarrhea can be improved with over-the-counter medications. If the pet can drink without vomiting, dehydration can be prevented with an oral electrolyte solution. However, there is nothing you can give your pet to help with the severe abdominal pain.

Considering the possible severe outcome, it is recommended that you prevent pancreatitis rather than treating it at home.

Methods of prevention of pancreatitis include:
- Feed a steady diet
- If changes in foods are required, do it slowly over several days by adding a small amount of the new food to the old food, until the new food has completely replaced the old diet
- If you decide to add approved vegetables and fruits to your pets diet, add only a small amount at a time. Keep in mind that a small amount for a Chihuahua is different than a small amount for a Great Dane.
- If you make your own canned food or meat-based home made diet, add only boiled low fat meats (such as chicken). Avoid high fat meats as well as spices.
- Keep your garbage in a secure place that your dog or cat cannot access.

Poisoning

Our pets have metabolisms that are different from ours. For this reason, things that are not poisonous to us can be poisonous to them. Things that are not poisonous to a dog can be poisonous to a cat. The same goes for exotic pets. Here is a list of the most common toxins.

Food/Drinks Toxic or Problematic to Dogs:

- **Chocolate:** Bakers chocolate is the most toxic chocolate. Ingestion of chocolate can cause seizures and death
- **Caffeine products like coffee/tea :** Caffeine causes a similar affect as chocolate and can be toxic

- **Grapes and Raisins:** Both fresh grapes and raisins can cause liver damage
- **Macadamia Nuts and Walnuts:** These nuts can cause weakness and paralysis. Pet parents should avoid sharing nuts with their pets in general, however, the occasional serving of peanut butter does not seem to have a negative affect on dogs.
- **Onions and Onion Powders:** Onions destroy red blood cells causing anemia
- **Xylitol:** A sweetener in many chewing gums, some peanut butters, and gummy bear-like products including vitamins. Xylitol can cause liver failure
- **Pits of Fruits such as peaches, cherries, and apples:** These pits contains cyanide. The rest of the fruit is non-toxic
- **Tomato plant and/or green tomatoes:** Tomatoes are members of the nightshade family and can cause heart problems
- **Avocados/guacamole:** Avocados can cause breathing difficulty and fluid accumulation
- **Alcohol:** Alcohol causes liver damage in dogs and humans. Alcohol is much more toxic in dogs because dogs are much smaller.
- **Fatty meats:** Meats in very limited amounts are are usually not harmful, but sudden ingestion of a fatty meat in larger quantities for the pet, can cause pancreatitis. Moderation is important.
- **Yeast dough:** Dough is especially bad for dogs prone to bloat as it can expand in the stomach and cause torsion
- **Mushrooms:** It is best to assume most of the mushrooms in your yard are poisonous to your pets and remove them.

Food/Drinks Toxic or Problematic for Cats:
- **Milk:** Most cats are lactose intolerant. Milk can cause major stomach upset. According to Linda P. Case, MS, adjunct assistant professor at the University of Illinois College of Veterinary Medicine and author of **The Cat: Its Behavior, Nutrition, and Health.** The only time cats are exposed to lactose is while they are nursing, so, much like humans, as they get older they can develop lactose intolerance. The issue can cause acute diarrhea. (http://pets.webmd.com/cats/guide/cats-and-dairy-get-the-facts)
- **Tuna:** Although put in some cat foods, giving straight canned tuna on a regular basis can lead to yellow fat disease (steatitis). It can also lead to mercury poisoning. Most vets say a little bit occasionally is okay, but a regular diet of tuna is not.
- **Liver:** Moderation as too much liver can lead to Vitamin A toxicity.
- **Onions, Chives, Garlic:** While garlic and chives simply cause stomach upset, onions can cause anemia and should be avoided.
- **Grapes and Raisins:** Fresh grapes and raisins can cause kidney failure in cats.
- **Caffeine and Alcohol:** Both of these substances can be deadly to cats, and there is

really no antidote. Very small amounts of caffeine or alcohol can cause death.
- **Chocolate, Candy, Gum:** Theobromide in chocolate is life threatening. Xylitol, found in candy, gum, and gummy bears can be extremely toxic, eventually leading to liver failure if severe enough
- **Raw eggs, meat and fish:** The dangers of raw eggs, meat, and fish, are its effects to the absorption of the vitamin. These raw foods also destroy an important component of vitamin B. one affecting the absorption of Vitamin B and the other destroying an important component of Vitamin B
- **Raw Yeast Dough:** Once dough is consumed, the dough swells in the stomach and can cause a lot of pain. Another interesting component of this is that the process to digest dough turns it into alcohol which can cause alcohol poisoning.

For more information regarding what cats can and cannot eat, please go to: (http://pets.webmd.com/cats/ss/slideshow-foods-your-cat-should-never-eat)

Medications Poisonous to Pets:
- **NSAIDS**: Non-steroidal anti-inflammatories like Aleve ® (naproxin) and Advil ® (ibuprofen), can cause kidney failure and severe intestinal upset.
- **Acetaminophen**: Tylenol ® can cause liver damage and damage of red blood cells which help supply oxygen.
- **Anti-anxiety and sleep aids**: Klonopin ® (clonazapam), Xanax ® (alprozolam), Ambian ® (zolpidem), and similar drugs can cause liver failure. Lunesta ® (eszopiclone) a common sleep aid, has the opposite affect in pets and can cause hyper-excitement and agitation.
- **Anti-depressants**: Effexor ® (venlafaxine), Wellbutrin ® (buproprion), and similar drugs, can have a stimulant affect The drugs can raise the blood pressure, heart rate, and temperature. These drugs can also cause seizures and other neurological issues and death. While some anti-depressants are used in treating cats and dogs, all anti-depressants should be considered toxic until a veterinarian confirms otherwise.
- **Birth Control**: Estrogen found in birth control can be potentially dangerous to your pet in high dosages. Estrogen can cause bone marrow suppression and hemorrhaging, among other things.
- **ADD/ADHD Medications**: Ritalin ® (Methylphenidate) and Adderall ® (amphetamine and dextroamphetamine) are stimulants that can raise blood pressure, heart rate, and temperature that can lead to seizures, tremors, and death.
- **High Blood Pressure Medications**: Ace inhibitors like Zestril ® (Lisinopril), Altace ® (Ramipril) are less dangerous than beta blockers such as Tenormin ® (Atenolol), Toprol ® (Metoprolol), Coreg ® (Carvedilol). While ace inhibitors will decrease the blood pressure and cause dizziness, beta blockers can cause severe decreases in blood

pressure, dangerously low heart beat, and death, even in small doses.
- **Decongestants**: Sudafed ® (pseudoephedrin), Actifed ® (chlorpheniramine and phenylephrine), Tavist-D ® , Allegra-D ® (the "D" always indicates "decongestant") are all toxic to pets. Chlorphenarimine by itself is safe for dogs.

If you see your pet take the pill(s) or see a recent indication that they have, most veterinarians will recommend the pet parent induce vomiting. This can be done by using a large syringe and forcing the pet to drink hydrogen peroxide. Generally, you give small amounts (3-5 mls) until the pet vomits. Be careful not to cause the liquid to aspirate into the airway. Its best to call your vet or poison control first for instructions.

Plants Poisonous to Pets

The toxic plant list is about seven-hundred entries. It is far beyond what can be covered here. The entire list can be found at the ASPCA website link listed below. The list at the ASPCA website offers photos when possible and the list is divided into plants poisonous to dogs, cats, or horses. If you think your pet may have been poisoned, you can call their 24-hour emergency poison hotline directly at 1-888-426-4435. Better yet, get your pet to the vet if at all possible.
http://www.aspca.org/pet-care/animal-poison-control/toxic-and-non-toxic-plants

If you are an avid gardener or love indoor plants, please consult the list before choosing your plant, and never assume you have the plant in an area safe from your pet. All lilies are poisonous to cats, while bulbs are often a deadly temptation for dogs. Many of the most common household and landscape plants are the deadliest. Aloe vera, bird of paradise, many palm trees, privets, types of holly, and yews are included in this list.

The toxic effects of most plants are similar and include vomiting, diarrhea (sometimes bloody), tremors, and even seizures. Death can occur without treatment.

Other Common Poisons:
- Rat Poison
- Insecticides (Including some OTC flea treatments)
- Household Chemicals
- Slug and Snail Bait
- Metal Toxicity (including coins)
- Antifreeze
- Essential oils. Most essential oils are toxic or potentially toxic to cats. Several are toxic to dogs. Never give essential oils internally and do not apply essential oils to the skin where a dog can lick. Assume the oils are toxic until it is confirmed safe by your veterinarian.

NEVER induce vomiting with any of these poisons. Pets should be immediately taken to the vet along with a sample of the substance that was ingested. If for any reason you cannot get to a vet, contact the Poison Control Center Immediately. 1-855-764-7661.
http://www.petpoisonhelpline.com/

Seizures, Seizure-Like Activity and Collapse:

I get more desperate Facebook inbox messages for this topic more than any other topic. It usually happens late at night when no veterinarian office is open.

In my experience there are several basic reasons for seizure like activity and collapse including the following:

- **Epilepsy**: Generally a dog with epilepsy will start showing signs around 2 years old. A typical seizure is a very frightening scene, indeed. The pet will salivate, appear unsteady, and the eyes will have that far off, unfocused look. The pet will collapse, begin shaking, often urinate and/or defecate. Often the muscles will become rigid and the extremities stiff. Epilepsy is not something that can be treated at home. Epilepsy is an ongoing disease that requires specific drugs to control. Phenobarbitol will need to be prescribed by your vet. During a seizure, however, panic is the last thing you need to do. The more panicked you are, the worse you make the situation. Your job during a seizure is to keep the pet from hurting herself and others. Dogs in seizure will sometimes have a biting response caused by muscle spasms. Get any children or other pets away from the seizing patient. Clear anything away from the environment that the dog can knock into and if possible, sit on the ground with the dog, holding the pet until the seizure subsides. Calm the dog and place her in a quiet area to recover. Recovering from a seizure can take hours, if not days. The pet will be very tired and often, unsteady. Do not encourage activity soon after, and call your vet as soon as possible.
- **Poisoning**: Some poisonous substances and plants can cause a seizure. Look around your house for rat poison and similar substances. If you find what your pet ingested, proceed to your vet immediately. you can call poison control. Take the substance or plant to the vet with you as this will help your veterinarian know what treatment will be needed to save your pet. Prevention is the one thing you can do. Never, ever, put out poison and don't assume your pet (or child) cannot get to the poison.
- **Congestive Heart Failure (CHF):** CHF is the inability of the heart to provide adequate circulation generally because of a weakened heart muscle. The collapse is often misinterpreted to be seizures or a stroke by pet parents. The pet collapses and the tongue is usually blue. The collapse generally happens during a time of increased activity or anything that gets the heart rate to increase. Coughing is an early signal of CHF. The pet appears lethargic and has difficulty getting up. Found most often in older dogs, CHF

finally results in the death of the pet, medications such as enalapril and lasix can be prescribed by your doctor to lengthen the life of your dog. The medications are not expensive and can greatly improve the quality of life for your pet.

- **Lack of oxygen and over heating**: As I mentioned before, pets bred to have short or pushed in noses have a harder time breathing. As a result, they often succumb to over heating, heat stroke, and collapse. Pet parents of brachycephalic pets must be mindful that their pet has more difficulty cooling his body temperature. The pet parent should use care when when playing or walking in warm conditions. Leaving a pet in a hot car or in direct sun, can also cause heat stroke. If you suspect overheating, you can confirm it by taking the pet's temperature. If confirmed by thermometer, (104°F or more), take immediate action. Cool the pet by applying cool, but not cold water. If you have a fan, direct it at the pet. If the pet has collapsed and is unconscious, do not try to force water down his throat. If he is conscious, offer small amounts of water. Large amounts of water can cause the pet to vomit, encouraging dehydration. Ice packs can be applied to the pet. Call your vet to have the pet examined as soon as possible.

Saddle Thrombosis

There are emergencies that frighten you, then there are those that terrify a pet parent. Usually its collapse in a dog, and saddle thrombosis in a cat. As I've said throughout the book, when a cat shows pain and begins panting, that cat is in an emergency situation.

The saddle is where the aorta, the major blood vessel of the heart, splits to deliver oxygen rich blood, ultimately, to the rear legs Saddle thrombosis occurs when a large blood clot formed in the heart travels down the aorta and blocks the path at this juncture.

The blood supply to the back legs is slowed or stopped, the muscles of the rear legs become hard and cold, and the paws develop a bluish tent.

The cat is unable to use one or both of the legs, but often drags himself to a hiding place and begins to pant. The pain is extreme and the cat goes into shock. Many pet parents assume that the cat has broken his/her back because of the paralysis.

There is no question about getting this cat to the vet. Do it immediately.

In most cases, this may be the first sign of heart failure. There is absolutely no way to treat this disease at home. Generally you have two options:

- Hospitalization: Intensive care in which the cat is usually placed in an oxygen chamber and given an IV to administer fluid and medications. Pain medication is through the IV port or injection. Additional medications to dissolve the clot, treat the heart failure and

shock, are administered. Tests confirm whether or not there is significant heart failure.
- Euthanasia: This is an issue where choosing to take the pet home to die "naturally" is outright cruelty. There is no "wait and see". As hard as it is, you have to make the decision to treat or euthanize.

Shock and CPR

Shock is a condition that can be caused by many things such as being hit by a car, heat stroke, allergic reactions, and blood loss.

Whatever the cause, the process is the same. *Something* causes a once well functioning body, to suddenly be unable to provide sufficient oxygen rich blood to the organs. This can be a heart that is not pumping adequately, insufficient blood flow, or volume and pressure. The respiratory system may not be working properly or may be blocked. This is the internal picture of shock.

If not properly treated, the body itself will try to compensate by increasing the heart and respiratory rates. If the volume of blood or oxygen is not sufficient, the body, in its survival mode, will use what it has, but faster. If this process is allowed to continue, the organs will eventually shut down. Internal organs are used to a balanced jog, not a clumsy sprint.

Early signs of shock may simply appear as an overly excited animal, with bright red gums, but late shock is another story. Do not administer any medicines, food, or fluid if you suspect shock.

Signs of late shock are similar in the dog and cat. Symptoms include:
- weakness and/or collapse
- cool extremities and ears
- pale and cool gums
- slow capillary refill time
- weak pulse but rapid heart rate
- rapid but shallow breathing

As shock progresses, the body cools, breathing may become slow and shallow, and the pulse will be weaker. The gums will become more pale and capillary refill time will be even slower. The pet may have a fixed stare with dilated pupils.

Assuming the pet is still breathing and the heart beating, keep the pet warm by wrapping the patient in a towel or blanket. Do not use heating pads as they can divert blood flow from important organs. If the pet is losing blood through an injury, control bleeding by applying pressure to the wound.

Remain calm or you may make things much worse. Keep the head *below* the heart to make it easier for blood to pump from the heart to the brain. Massage the body and extremities to encourage blood circulation. If you suspect a broken bone, do not massage that extremity and be very careful when applying pressure to the wound. If the pet is still conscious, you may be bitten. Be careful.

If you can get to the vet, GO.

If you cannot, then the rest is up to you. Stay calm in order to think clearly.

No layperson can properly set a bone if that is the cause of shock. It takes sedation, a series of xrays, and experience, to be sure it is positioned correctly. Unless an open fracture (one that has broken through the skin) has cut a blood vessel, more than likely, you will not need to apply pressure to the break. Concentrate on saving the life first.

More than likely, a pet in severe shock will be unconscious. Continue to monitor the pulse and breathing. Make sure your pets airway is clear. If the animal is completely unconscious, you should be able to open the muzzle to remove anything blocking the airway. Pull the tongue forward to open the airway and allow it to rest to the side.

If the shock progresses, your pet may stop breathing and his heart stop beating. Its time for CPR. **CPR** in dogs and cats is similar to humans. The one difference is the small dog, large dog with a funnel shaped chest, or cat needs to be laying on the side, not the back. The other alternative is to lay
the animal on the back and do compression from both sides. I prefer right side down.

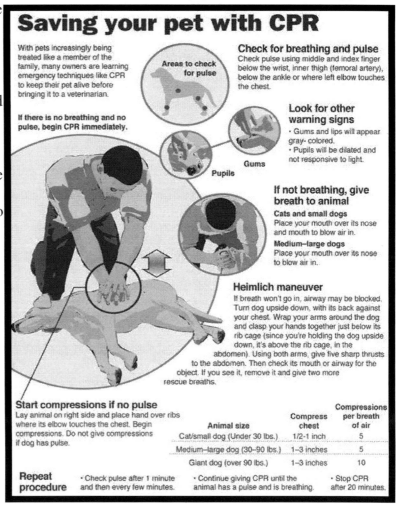

220

If you have followed the instructions so far, you have already cleared the airway of any obstructions. Extend the head a bit, close the mouth, and if the dog is large, breathe into the nose. If the pet (dog or cat) is small, you should be able to fit both nose and mouth with your mouth as you breathe. Give 2 breaths and notice if the chest is rising.

Next begin chest compressions. The size of the pet determines how many compressions you give per minute. The smaller the pet, the faster the compression. The recommendation is to give pets 10 lbs or less, 120 compressions per minute (CPM), dogs 11-60 lbs=80-100 CPM, and pets over 60lbs, 60 CPM.
Another recommendation that I find easiest is to do 30 compressions followed by 2 breaths. Continue until the pet revives, you get the pet to a vet, or you realize there is nothing else you can do.

The American Red Cross offers classes that will teach you how to properly perform CPR on your pets. The CPR diagram on the previous page is courtesy of The American Red Cross.

Strains & Sprains

Strains are injuries to the tendons that connect the muscle to bone. Sprains injure the ligaments that connect bones to bones which can cause damage to the joint. Either way, they are painful.

Many strains and sprains may be simply an over-use injury similar to what humans might get in the gym. Other times, injury is caused by slips, falls, or missteps during regular play. Jumping down from the couch, or stepping into a hole are additional causes for these painful injuries.

Strains are most common in the hip and thighs while sprains most often affect the knees and wrists. Damage to the cruciate ligament of the knee is often mistaken as a break. This is an example of an strain or sprain that must be surgically repaired.

Initial symptoms of straining or spraining may include limping or holding the leg up. The pet may experience muscle spasms and cry or whimper in pain.

Sprains and strains are not limited to the extremities. The neck and back can also be affected by sprains and strains as well as pulled muscles. Pets with neck injuries will often hold their head down and avoid turning it to the right or left. Pain in the back can often be detected by gently pressing down along the spine, looking for any reaction from the pet.

Alternating ice and heat on the strained or sprained area can be helpful. Do not leave your pet alone with either ice or heat.

Broken bones must be ruled out when displaying the symptoms mentioned above. The only sure way to tell if an injury is a strain/sprain or a bone fracture, is with an x-ray. There are four physical symptoms that are unique to broken bones and can help you as you gather information regarding the injury.

Physical signs of broken bones:

- Visible bone

- Misshapen appearance of the area

- The pets extremity is completely non-weight bearing

- Numbness or change in temperature of extremity (if blood flow is cut off from extremity by a break, it will begin to feel cold)

If you are not able to seek immediate professional help and your pet experiences a sprain, strain, or closed break to an extremity, you may need to apply a light bandage for support. Breaks to the humerus (upper arm bone) or femur (upper leg bone) cannot be helped with a bandage.

Pets in pain can be aggressive, so a muzzle made with gauze wrap can be applied. An assistant can retrain the pet using proper restraint techniques.
http://www.vetmed.wsu.edu/ClientED/dog_restraint.aspx

To apply a bandage, you will need a roll of cotton gauze, first aid tape, a Popsicle ® stick (or something similar), and Vetrap ®. Vetrap ® is a self-adhering wrap that provides support and compression.
Vetrap ® can also be used as the outer layer of bandages for open wounds.

Once, my Pomeranian Panda, a hyper and bouncing dog, bounced a few too many times, injuring his front leg. I bandaged it by using first aid tape to make stirrup strips on the front and back of the leg (taping parallel to the leg). The tape strips were made twice as long as the leg and a Popsicle stick was put between the excess tape to keep it from sticking. I wrapped the leg a few times with cotton gauze and then again with Vetrap ®. I then twisted my stirrup tape and stretched it up the leg to keep the bandage from slipping.

To the right is an image of the simple bandage I made for Panda. It provided compression and support, however, I limited his activity until he was well. I kept him in a large crate and let him out to potty and spend a few minutes with me.

Bandages like the one I made, should be monitored to make sure it is not rubbing

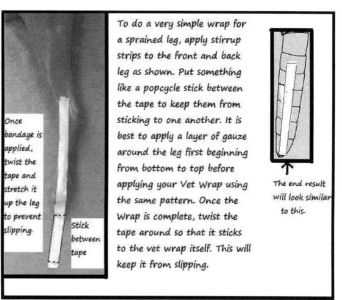

and causing more harm than good. I made sure to monitor the bandage to make sure it didn't cause any rubbing. The bandage can be changed if it becomes soiled and if it is causing sores, it should be removed.

With the wrap and the reduced activity, Panda was better within a week.

Vomiting and/or Diarrhea

There are so many different causes for both vomiting and diarrhea, that it can be difficult to pin down the origin of the illness.

Some of the most common causes of vomiting and diarrhea:
- Viral disease in puppies and kittens (parvovirus or feline distemper)
- Intestinal parasites or protozoans (roundworms, hookworms, whipworms)
- Bacterial infection (salmonella, e-coli)
- Intestinal bloat, blockage, or gastric torsion (usually associated with vomiting only)
- Pancreatitis (inflammation of the pancreas often caused by eating greasy or fatty foods)
- Sudden food change (any food changes should be done over a period of a week)
- "Garbage gut" (eating spoiled food from the trash)
- Anxiety
- Toxicity (poisonous substance or plant)
- Kidney, liver disease or diabetes (usually in senior pets)

As you can see, vomiting and diarrhea are often symptoms of a larger problem.

The most common cause of both vomiting and diarrhea in puppies and kitten is viral disease such as the parvovirus (dog) or feline distemper (cat) and intestinal worm infestations. Time is of the essence for these small animals, and a fecal test should be done to rule out intestinal parasites. A parvo test should be performed on the puppy. Both the kitten and puppy should be examined by a veterinarian.

In adult pets, once intestinal parasites and protozoans are ruled out or eliminated, a thorough exam and history can provide your vet more clues as to the cause.

When to take your adult pet to the vet:

- Stool is bloody, tarry, or black
- Toxicity is suspected. Pet is found with rat poison, poisonous plants, or gum made with xylitol

- Pet has a fever, is depressed
- Pet is dehydrated
- Mucus membranes are white or yellow
- Pet appears in pain
- Vomit is blood-streaked, or looks like coffee grounds
- Pet is attempting to vomit, but is unsuccessful.
- Abdomen appears bloated, hard, or painful

Isolating the part of the digestive system most involved, can help your vet speed up the diagnosing process. Problems can be related to the small or large intestine. Taking a sample of the stool with you to the veterinarian will allow the staff to test for intestinal parasites or certain viruses. Photos of the stool may also be helpful.

Location	Symptoms
Small intestine	Increased stool volume; frequency of bowel movements is normal or slightly increased; not straining when defecating; no obvious blood seen in stool, but stool may be black/tarry; no mucus present in stool; possible weight loss, vomiting, and/or increased gas
Large intestine	Volume of stool is changed only slightly; frequency of bowel movements is greatly increased; straining is common; blood is seen in stool; usually no noted weight loss, vomiting, or gas

Vomiting is common in both dogs and cats. There are primary causes such as disorders and diseases of the stomach and upper intestinal tract. Secondary causes of vomiting are disorders of other organs that result in an accumulation of toxic substances in the blood. These substances trigger the vomiting response in brain. Kidney disease can cause vomiting as the body's ability to get rid of waste is compromised.

Regurgitation is often mistaken as vomiting and should be ruled out. Regurgitation is the ejection of the contents of the esophagus or the organ leading from our mouth to the stomach. There are characteristics that differentiate regurgitation from vomiting:

Condition	Characteristics
Regurgitation	Food is expelled with little effort. Food is undigested, covered in mucus and may have a tubular shape. Pet may try to eat what was just regurgitated.
Vomiting	Pet heaves to vomit. Food partially digested. Vomit may contain yellow bile.

Frequent regurgitation may indicate a mega-esophagus, a condition in which the esophagus loses its muscle tone. The contraction of the esophagus forces the food down into the stomach.

When muscle tone is lost, it is not able to do its job properly.

Before jumping to the conclusion that your pet has a mega-esophagus, know that many dogs will gulp their food, take it to a quieter, safer location, and regurgitate the food back up to chew it. This purposeful regurgitation is a problem we have at T.Paws Rescue.

We feed six dogs in one location, four dogs in another. Two dogs are fed alone. The arrangement is based on the eating habits of each dog. Bojangles, an older chihuahua, came to us after numerous chihuahuas were dumped at the shelter by an unethical breeder. The dogs were all in poor condition and terrified of humans. After several years, Bo still has behaviors associated with his experience. He will swallow his food whole, move away from the pack, and regurgitate it. He then takes his time eating. After some experimentation, we found that if he is fed out of sight of the other dogs, he will eat slower with no regurgitation. I simply feed him around the corner from his pack-mates.

Hairballs in cats will also cause vomiting. The hairball itself is a blockage, most often at the pylorius, which is the transition point from the stomach to the small intestine. Cats will often vomit up their food, but not the hairball. However, the motion created by the process of vomiting can dislodge the actual hairball and help with the digestive process. Hairball-related vomiting usually occurs within a few minutes of eating.

The color of the vomit can be important. Vomit can be clear, yellow bile, and in more serious cases, it may be streaked with fresh, red blood or look like coffee grounds. Take note of the color so you can provide good information to your vet.

Your vet will often order that a vomiting pet (and sometimes one with diarrhea) have all food and water taken away for 24 hours. This fasting method is called NPO for the latin "nil per os" and simply means "nothing by mouth". The purpose is the rest the digestive system and allow it to process the food within the intestines. Only pets that are on IV fluids will have both food and water removed.

If the pets symptoms are not severe enough to be on IV fluids, the pet will only be given water to avoid dehydration. However, the water will be given frequently and in small amounts. Too much water at one time can trigger more vomiting. Do not attempt to force-feed an animal who is vomiting.

After 24 hours, if vomiting and diarrhea have stopped, the pet can be given a small amount of water (for the pet on IV fluids). The food-only-fasted animal can begin eating a bland diet in small amounts. In the veterinary office, this bland diet is usually Hills ® Prescription I/D diet. At home, a boiled chicken and rice recipe can be served. Only a teaspoon of food should be given at first to avoid regurgitation or vomiting. If after an hour, there is still no vomiting, the amount of food can increase slowly. The transition to the pets regular diet should be done over several days.

Serious vomiting and/or diarrhea should have you contacting your vet immediately. Less serious cases in which the pet has no symptoms listed under "when to take your pet to the vet", can often be resolved with a food fast. Pets with severe diarrhea, vomiting, and refusal to eat or drink should be taken to the vet as soon as possible.

Loperamide(Imodium ®) is helpful for diarrhea in dogs and should not be administered to cats as it can cause hyper-excitement. One capsule or tablet tablet can be given to dogs every 24 hours. Loperamide is not weight dependent.

Pets whose diarrhea is bacterial or toxin related should not be given loperamide. Loperamide should be used with caution in older dogs, pregnant or lactating females, dogs with hypothyroidism, liver disease, or Addison's disease.

Some pets have acid reflux and will vomit a yellow bile. Veterinarians often prescribe famotidine (Pepcid ®) for these pets. Famotidine is also useful for treating ulcers. Dogs are dosed at 0.22 – 0.44 mg/lb every 12-24 hours. Cats are prescribed 0.22 mg/lb every 12-24 hours.

18

The Most Common Illnesses of the Dog or Cat

Some common illnesses and conditions are easily treatable, while others are more difficult to treat. For other illnesses, there is very little you can do without proper professional veterinary care. But there are actions you can take to prevent many common illnesses. You can educate yourself, be observant, and do regular home physicals on your pet. You can make sure your pet is protected against diseases with proper vaccination, feeding your pet a healthy diet, and making sure your pet gets exercise and mental stimulation.

I have chosen to cover the more common disorders, diseases, conditions, and illnesses seen by veterinarians. I hope to make the topic simple to understand. More detailed and scientific descriptions are available in other books and internet sites. This is an overview of the health challenges your pet might face.

This is not intended for you to self-diagnose. **Even if your pet has every symptom described, it does not mean that he or she has that disease or condition.** This chapter serves as a reference that teaches you what to look for, what to expect at the vet's office, and possible diagnostic and treatment options.

Abscesses

Abscesses occur most commonly in cats and is usually something you can see coming on gradually. Generally they are located in or around the face, but sometimes they are along the torso. Most often they are caused by the bite from another cat. The wound closes up and the infection builds up inside. The longer the abscess stays intact, the worse the infection can get and the sicker the cat will feel.

If you have multiple cats, or outdoor cats, sometimes the abscess can be overlooked. As soon as you notice it, it will need to be lanced, drained and flushed out by a veterinarian.

The abscess is prepared by the vet techs by shaving the fur surrounding the abscess with sterile clippers and a #40 or #10 clipper blade. Often, doing this procedure will open the abscess before lancing is needed. If not, proper sterile preparation will continue. A Nolvasan ® or Betadine ® mixture (1:2 parts warm water) is used to clean and disinfect the area to be lanced.

An additional bowl of Nolvasan ® or Betadine ® solution is made. Next, the following are opened and prepared for the veterinarian: A #10 or #15 surgical blade, a hemostat, and a 12 ml syringe without needle.

Many veterinarians will sedate the cat to perform this procedure. Other vets believe that the lancing, if performed quickly and properly, will hurt no worse than the injection to induce anesthesia. Once the abscess is lanced, the pain is minimal as immediate relief is given when the abscess drains.

The lancing of the abscess is performed quickly with the sharp, sterilized surgical blade. A small incision is cut near the bottom of the abscess to allow it to drain easily. The hemostats can be helpful in allowing the veterinarian to open up the incision if necessary for better drainage. Once it has drained as much as possible by gravity, the syringe is filled with the Nolvasan ® solution and the wound is flushed out by injecting the solution through the incision. Flushing the wound is performed several times. Once flushed, a triple antibiotic ointment may be put inside the incision, but the incision will not be closed.

Some veterinarians who sedate for the procedure may put in a drain, but most will not. The veterinarian will put the pet on an antibiotic such as amoxicillin or cephalexin for 7-14 days.

Arthritis

Arthritis, the inflammation of joints, is a disease that occurs in both dogs and cats. Large, older dogs are most prone to it. Older cats also suffer, but the signs are very hard to detect. Obese pets are also more likely to develop arthritis as a result of the extra pressure on the joints themselves. Pets who have had issues such as hip dysplasia or a luxating patella have an increased risk of arthritis in later years.

Symptoms include:
- Lameness or limping
- Difficulty getting up
- Stiffness
- Unwillingness or slow to climb stairs
- Slow, careful gait
- Less active and sleeping more

- May become more aloof or seek extra attention
- Temperamental changes
- Difficulty getting to litter box (cats) or reluctance to go outside to go to the bathroom (dogs).

It is possible to manage arthritis and help your pet live life in less pain. Daily exercise is important but those that require jumping are not recommended. A slow, steady walk is better. Swimming, especially in warmer water is an excellent exercise that is not only good for the joints but maintains a healthy weight. If your pet is obese, start him on a diet that will provide the necessary nutrients but help the pet lose weight. Reduce the amount of treats you give, or replace the treats with an occasional carrot. For more information on obesity in our pets, please refer to the topic on obesity in this chapter.

A warm, comfortable place to sleep is also helpful in making the pet less painful. Orthopedic beds are a great option for an arthritic pets . Beds can be purchased at pet stores or at great discounts on websites such as Groupon. Orthopedic beds can also be made using egg shell foam pads. Depending on the size of your pet, the size of the pads you purchase, and the thickness you want the bed to have, you could potentially make several beds for the price of one sold in pet stores.

Heating pads are useful for arthritic animals. Pets should not be left alone with a heating pad, particularly an electric one. Homemade heating pads with scrap fabric and uncooked rice. They can be put in the microwave to use as a heating pad, or put in the freezer for ice packs that can help bring down a fever or cool a dog that is suffering from heat exhaustion.

Massage can be very helpful. As I mentioned earlier, the book **Healing Touch for Dogs: The Proven Massage Program** by Dr. Michael W. Fox, has proven very useful in teaching me the proper techniques. For those interested in therapeutic massage for their pets, this book is highly recommended.

There are over the counter oral supplements to help with arthritis. The most common is **Glucosamine Chondrotin with MSM**. This combination of supplements maintains the joint cartilage, enhances the connective tissue, while preventing further damage by inhibiting destructive enzymes in the joints. Glucosamine Chondroitin is one treatment that both conventional and holistic veterinarians agree upon.

Buffered aspirin is an anti-inflammatory for use in dogs only. Aspirin can cause gastric issues including vomiting and ulcers. If you notice any signs of gastric distress, discontinue the medications immediately and see your vet. **Never give Tylenol ® , Aleve ® , Motrin ® , or any other over the counter pain medication to dogs with the exception of buffered aspirin and use aspirin with great care. Do not give ANY pain medications to cats that has not**

been prescribed by the veterinarian.

There are several prescription medications for arthritis. Since these medications are most often given to older pets and have the potential to effect the kidneys and liver, blood work may be required occasionally to make sure the medication is not doing more harm than good.

Some of those medications include Rimadyl ®, (generic carprofen), Dermaxx ® (deracoxib), Previcox ® (firocoxib). All of these are NSAIDs (non-steroidal anti-inflammatory drug) and are available in pills or chewable tablets. Another NSAID, Metacam ® (generic meloxicam) is also an option in treating pain, but comes in a liquid form.
Tramadol can be used in both dogs and cats but must be prescribed by a veterinarian. Neurontin ® (generic gabapentin) was originally created to treat epilepsy. However, it has been found to be a good alternative for pain in animals that do not tolerate NSAIDs well.

A last resort for pain relief would be corticosteroids. This is the "steroid shot" that is also given for itchiness and inflammation. Prednisone, prednisolone, or methylprednisolone are some of the prescription steroids a veterinarian may use. When oral steroids are sent home, the patient will begin with a dose and gradually tapered down until the pet is off the drug. Steroids can be overused and cause problems far greater than arthritis. For this reason, steroids must be used with caution. However, for those pets for whom nothing has worked, steroids have their place. Temporary use of steroids may also be appropriate to provide relief while other treatments have time to act.

Dr. Shawn Messonnier, DVM, a practitioner of holistic therapies and integrative medicine, comments in his book **8 Weeks to a Healthy Dog :An Easy-to-Follow Program for the Life of Your Dog (**Published September 13, 2003, Rodele Books, paperback):

"....*many natural remedies relieve pain and inflammation too. But sadly, instead of taking the time to try out natural therapies for arthritis and allowing for the four to eight weeks it can take for them to start working, many vets reach for the prescription pad.*" (page 175)

This is troubling. When considering treatment for chronic pain relief, the complimentary approach (a combination of conventional and holistic medicine) is appropriate and helpful. While long term use of corticosteroids may be ill advised, allowing a pet to stay in pain while waiting to see if a holistic approach is effective, seems cruel. Talk to your doctor about options for your pet.

Asthma and Bronchitis

Asthma and bronchitis are issues of the lower respiratory tract. Later I will cover the upper respiratory tract which includes the nose, throat, and trachea.

The lower respiratory tract begins at the end of the trachea (if visualized externally, the end of the trachea is near the bottom of the neck) and includes the bronchi, bronchioles, and alveoli. The bronchi and bronchioles branch out to each side of the lungs while the alveoli is responsible for the oxygen/carbon dioxide exchange.

Bronchitis is the inflammation of the bronchi and bronchioles. Bronchitis can be chronic (an ongoing issue) or acute (sudden, or short term). Acute bronchitis can be triggered by a virus such as that which causes kennel cough. Kennel cough can last a few weeks.

Chronic bronchitis is diagnosed when this inflammation is still occurring after 2 months. Cigarette smoke and house dust can cause continued irritation of the bronchi.

A sharp, dry cough is the hallmark of chronic bronchitis. Sometimes the coughing may produce sputum and be mistaken for vomiting. Keep in mind that a cough can be a sign of other issues including but not limited to heart disease. So before you assume you know what the problem is, it is important to have it formally diagnosed. The reason for this is without proper treatment, chronic bronchitis can lead to other chronic diseases that can eventually be fatal.

Veterinarians manage bronchitis with short courses of corticosteroids and medications such as theophylline which relaxes the breathing passages. Occasionally cough suppressants are used for exhausting coughing episodes, but should never be used on a long term basis.

Bronchitis and asthma are often confused. While both are inflammation of the airways, asthma goes a step further. The muscles surrounding the airway tightens and causes further restriction of air. Asthma can also be chronic or acute and is often triggered by allergens, air pollutants, perfumes, tobacco smoke, stress, or exertion.

Asthma is most often associated with the cat. An asthmatic episode can be very scary for you and your cat.

Symptoms of asthma include:

- Coughing and/or wheezing
- Hunched shoulders with neck extended, open mouth
- Rapid breathing
- Gasping for breath
- Blue mucous membranes
- Vomiting up foamy mucus

There is nothing you can do at home when an acute, severe episode like this occurs the first time. Asthma will not resolve itself. The pet should go to the vet immediately. Once you have the necessary tools (like medication and inhalers), then you can help manage the disease at home.

If your pet is diagnosed with chronic bronchitis or asthma, there are some things you can do to help.

What you can do to help your asthmatic pet:

- Reduce the pollution in the home.
- If anyone in the home smokes, **STOP**. Cigarette smoke is lethal to the asthmatic pet.
- Avoid the use of air fresheners or other aerosol chemicals.
- Change to a litter that is less dusty.
- Invest in an air purifier as well as a humidifier. Dry air makes the symptoms worse. However, make sure that the humidifier does not cause mold as this can be dangerous, not only to your pet, but you as well.
- While exercise is good, don't over do it.
- If your dog normally walks on a leash attached to a collar, change to a harness.
- If your pet is overweight, refer to the topic of obesity in this chapter and get the weight down.

Cancer

Our bodies, including those of our pets, are made up of cells that carry our DNA. When these cells become abnormal multiply out of control, the result is cancer.

Cancer can occur in any part of the body. The most common forms of cancer include abdominal (spleen, liver, intestine), bladder cancer, bone cancer, mammary tumors, cancer of the lymph nodes, skin cancer, mouth cancer, prostate, testicular cancer and leukemia in the cat.

Many cancers can be prevented. Feline leukemia, for instance is caused by a virus passed from cat to cat. A vaccine is available to protect cats from this virus. Cats that test positive for FeLV are 60 times more likely to develop lymphoma than cats that test negative for this virus, and cats that are FIV positive are five times more likely to develop lymphoma. Cats that test positive for both viruses concurrently are 80 times more likely to develop lymphoma. All kittens or cats should be tested for FeLV and FIV before coming into your home, particularly if you have other cats.

Before a vaccine for FeLV was introduced, it was the cause of most blood borne cancers in cats. During that time 2/3 of the cats with lymphoma were also infected with FeLV. With the introduction of the vaccine, blood borne cancers were reduced, but the rate of lymphomas

increased. The cancers were then found in other areas of the body, most often in the gastrointestinal tract. The answer as to why this occurred has not been found. Environmental toxins are high on the list, however.
http://www.petmd.com/blogs/thedailyvet/jintile/2013/aug/what-causes-cancer-in-cats-and-dogs-30787

An interesting fact related to FeLV vaccinations is the problem of feline postvaccinal sarcomas or cancers at the injection site. *"The only proven cause for injection site sarcomas in cats is prior administration of a killed, adjuvanted vaccine. Rabies and leukemia vaccines are the only ones with solid causal associations."* http://www.ncbi.nlm.nih.gov/pmc/articles/PMC3299519/

While this does not mean that you should not vaccinate your cat, it was one of the reasons I changed my vaccine protocol.

Mammary tumors or breast cancer are very common in unaltered female dogs. Spaying the pet earlier in life can prevent the cancer. **If a female dog is spayed before her first heat cycle, her chances of developing mammary tumors is only 0.5%. A kitten spayed before 6 months is 7 times less likely to develop mammary tumors later in life.**

Neutering male dogs prevents testicular cancer 100% as the testes are removed. Environmental toxins have been found to be linked to many cancers. In 2008, the Environmental Working Group tested dogs and cats and found that 48 out of the 70 industrial chemicals they tested for were present in those pets. We have to keep in mind that our pets can be exposed to environmental toxins even more than we can. When we walk, most of the time, we wear shoes. This gives us a barrier from the chemicals we have cleaned our floors with or the pesticides we use in our garden. Our pets on the other hand, walk on unprotected paws.

Instead of harsh chemicals, consider making spray and floor cleaners, hand soap, shampoo and more with concentrated Dr. Bronner's Pure Castile Soap. "Castile" refers to soaps made with vegetable oil rather than animal fat. It is very effective and protects our pets from exposure to harmful chemicals that can cause illness. A 32 oz of soap lasts us a long time because it takes so little of the concentrate. For a list of uses for Dr. Bronners soap and the dilutions, see http://www.lisabronner.com/dilutions-cheat-sheet-for-dr-bronners-castile-soap/

In addition to harmful chemical cleaners, it has been found that **pets that develop bladder cancer are more likely to live with a cigarette smoker. Pets belonging to smokers are also more likely to develop nasal tumors and lung cancer.** What was interesting is that the longer nosed breeds developed nasal tumors, while the short nosed breeds developed lung cancer. The nose is developed, not only in our pets, but in us, to trap particles when we breathe in. Short nose breeds are unable to trap the carcinogens from cigarette smoke, so they travel to the lungs.

Second hand smoke also causes cancer of the lymph nodes and mouth in cats. It is believed that the carcinogens in cigarette smoke is passively deposited on the fur of the cat. As the cat grooms the fur with his/her tongue, the carcinogens are transferred to the mouth, eventually causing cancer. As a veterinary technician, I can tell you that it is very obvious when a cat comes into the clinic. He reeks of cigarette smoke, so I do believe that hypothesis has merit.
http://www.petmd.com/blogs/thedailyvet/jintile/2012/oct/what_causes_pet_cancer-27780

A 2012 study that examined the application of lawn care products found that dogs that were exposed to professionally applied lawn care products had a 70 percent increased risk of developing canine malignant lymphoma. I think we have to ask ourselves if a perfectly manicured lawn is worth the lives of our pets.

A large 1981 study of 8,760 dogs at 13 veterinary teaching hospitals in Canada and the US found that dogs that lived in industrial areas were more likely to die of bladder cancer. Carcinogens from industrial operations were suspected as a key factor for the development of this type of cancer. http://www.alive.com/articles/view/23774/dogs_and_toxic_chemicals

Genetics also plays a part and there are breeds that are more susceptible to cancer than others. According to the US Canine Cancer Registry at Tufts University, Golden Retrievers, German Shepherds, Poodles, Boxers, Rottweilers, Dobermans, Shetland Sheepdogs, Beagles, Miniature Schnauzers, and Shih tzus are the most likely breeds to develop some form of cancer.
http://www.pethealth101.com/cancer/cancer_rates_by_breed.shtml

Certain cancers seem to be more prevalent in certain breeds and the reasons are not clear. Scottish terriers, for instance are 20 times more likely to develop bladder cancer than other breeds.

Since there are so many different cancers, there is no specific symptom to look for. There are some symptoms that can point to the possibility of cancer and should be addressed by your veterinarian. If your pet has one or more of the symptoms below, it does not necessarily mean that your pet has cancer. This only means that you should talk to your veterinarian about the need for further investigation.

Symptoms that can indicate the need of further investigation:

- Clear indication of pain
- Sudden changes in potty habits
- Lethargy
- Appetite changes
- Weight loss

- abnormal odors and/or discharge
- lumps

Actions you can take to prevent many forms of cancer in your pet:

- Spay or neuter your pet
- Get the appropriate type and amount of vaccines, but do not over vaccinate
- If you or anyone in your home is a smoker, **stop smoking.**
- Feed the healthiest diet you can.
- Change your household cleaners to more natural alternatives
- Have your kitten or cat tested for FeLV and FIV and keep your cat indoors
- Avoid pesticides in your lawn.
- Check the areas your pet stays most for environmental toxins.
- If you live in an area where chemical runoff into water supplies is a reality, consider bottled water for both yourself and your pet.
- Take your pet for yearly exams even if no vaccines are required. Request a CBC and Chemistry Panel be performed. These tests are excellent tools to catch disease early.

In the past, when a pet was diagnosed with cancer, the only answer was to euthanize. Today, however, there are some options. Depending on the type of cancer, surgery, chemotherapy, and radiation may be used in the treatment of the cancer. The cost can be high with chemotherapy drugs running into the hundreds or thousands over the course of the treatment. Pets seem to tolerate these treatments better than humans, particularly in relation to nausea.

While some look for holistic approaches to cancer, I could find none with reputable studies that produced positive results. Antioxidant treatment was cited in one holistic source as a natural alternative to traditional treatment. However, when I investigated the matter thoroughly, looking for the "Eastern European" studies given to support the treatment's success, I actually found the opposite. **Of 1300 studies reviewed by an independent agency, there was no evidence that manufactured anti-oxidants cured or prevented any serious disease. Diets rich in natural anti-oxidants on the other hand, have been shown to prevent certain diseases.**
http://www.euro.who.int/en/data-and-evidence/evidence-informed-policy-making/publications/hen-summaries-of-network-members-reports/do-antioxidants-prevent-disease

So again, this is where pro-active pet parenting comes into play. Boosting the immune system with feeding good quality foods, providing proper vaccinations and deworming, avoiding as many environmental toxins as possible can be a PREVENTATIVE measure. Expecting it to cure disease seems to be too little, too late.

Cognitive Dysfunction

Much like humans suffer from dementia in old age, dogs and cats experience cognitive dysfunction.

Before cognitive dysfunction can be diagnosed, other issues such as blindness or deafness need to be ruled out. Cognitive dysfunction can also occur in cats, and does more often, but perhaps because of the nature of the dog, it presents more profoundly in the canine.

Symptoms of cognitive dysfunction include:

- Becoming lost in familiar surroundings
- Staring into walls
- Getting trapped behind familiar furniture
- Easily startled
- Doesn't respond to his/her name
- Doesn't recognize familiar voices unwilling to play, go for a walk, or other usual activities
- Sleep schedule changes (sleeps during day, up at night)
- Previously potty trained dogs may urinate/defecate in the house
- Litter trained cats may urinate outside the box
- May tremble and shake
- May seek more attention or may become aloof
- Unusual pacing, particularly at night
- Unusual vocalization and behavior as if searching for something or someone.

Research on the disorder reveals certain changes in the brain that is similar in both the dog and cat. MRI's often show brain shrinkage. Other tests show that oxygen levels in the brain are decreased, and changes in various neurotransmitter chemicals are observed. Neurotransmitters are part of the pathway that allows the brain to fire chemicals that control most everything about us. When this pathway is changed somehow, the brain does not function at full capacity. Another change in the cognitive dysfunction dog is the overabundance of the protein B-amyloid. The presence of this protein forms plaque in the gray matter of the brain, killing cells and encouraging brain shrinkage. http://pets.webmd.com/dogs/cognitive-dysfunction-syndrome-dogs

"Researchers found that the overall prevalence of cognitive dysfunction was a little more than 14 percent, but only about 1.9 percent of cases are diagnosed. The same study found that the chances of having cognitive dysfunction increase with age, so that by the time dogs are 15 years old, 41 percent will have at least one sign consistent with cognitive decline. Neilson and Hart estimated the prevalence in geriatric dogs at 68 percent.

In a 2011 review, Gunn-Moore estimated that one-third of cats 11 to 14 years old has age-related cognitive decline, which increased to more than 50 percent of cats 15 years old or older.

Unfortunately, less is known about the cognitive effects of aging on senior cats than on senior dogs, but their management is similar." http://www.veterinarypracticenews.com/July-2013/When-Pets-Lose-Their-Sense-Of-Place/

Early detection can make it possible for you to help slow down this downward progression. Early detection is one of the principles of proactive pet parenting. Cognitive dysfunction is not a normal part of aging and shouldn't be ignored. The quality of life of your pet can be improved, so if you observe these symptoms, report them to your doctor. You may also find that one or more of the symptoms is caused by something altogether different. Urinating outside the litter box, for example, can be a sign of urinary tract infection, kidney disease, diabetes or simply a cat who would like her litter box cleaned more often.

There are several things that can help delay onset of this condition and to improve it when it does develop.

Just as with humans, consistent brain stimulation is essential to delay dementia type symptoms. Exercise, interactive and challenging toys, all help keep the mind stimulated. Indoor cats often get much less mental stimulation than outdoor cats. Putting up a bird feeder at your cat's favorite window or getting a fish tank can be easy ways to keep your cat's brain alert.

Hills ® Prescription Diets make a diet rich in anti-oxidants, called B/D that has been shown to help. It is very expensive, however, at $47-60 for a 17.6 lb bag. Hills ® Science Diet Age Defying Diet and Purina One ® Smartblend ® Vibrant Maturity are also good choices as each contain several of the supplements to help with brain function and overall health. Both of these diets can be purchased without a prescription at a much lower cost than B/D ®

Some over the counter supplements may help your pet with cognitive dysfunction. They include:

- SAMe (S-adenosylmethionine) is a supplement that has shown to slow down the decline of mental function.
- Melatonin may help your pet with anxiety and/or sleep and it is also a good anti-oxidant
- Omega 3 fatty acids such as fish oil and Omega 6 fatty acids promote cell membrane health

- α-lipoic acid and L-carnitine enhance mitochondrial function
- Plant-derived medium-chain triglycerides (MCTs) provide a good energy source for the brain
- Vitamin B helps enhance brain function

http://www.vetsonline.com/publications/veterinary-times/archives/n-44-16/dementia-in-geriatric-cats.html

Some name brand supplements sold specifically for dementia include Neutricks ® which contains apoaequorin; Novifit ® which contains S-adenosyl-L-methionine (SAMe); and Activait ® and Senilife ® , which contain phosphatidylserine and a mix of antioxidants.

Before giving your cat or dog any of these supplements, speak with your veterinarian.

Some prescription medications can help with cognitive dysfunction. Anipryl ® , L-deprenyl ® ,or the generic selegiline hydrochloride, is a prescription drug primarily used for Cushings in dogs, but it has shown promise for use in dogs with cognitive dysfunction. Fluoxetine (Prozac ®) is the drug of choice for feline cognitive dysfunction.

Routine is important for pets with cognitive dysfunction. Regular feeding, walking, sleeping schedules are helpful. Avoid moving around furniture as it will confuse the pet even more. Environmental stimulation such as play time, food-hunting games, companionship and interaction such as petting or massage, have been shown to help improve brain function.

Pay close attention to your pet and report any changes to your veterinarian.

Diabetes

Diabetes is found in both dogs and cats. Typically, increased thirst and urination are the first symptoms noticed by the pet parents. The dog may be urinating in the house when he/she has always been housebroken. The cat may seem grouchy and begin urinating on the bed instead of the litter box.

A quick glucose test may reveal very high glucose levels. **Normal glucose levels (when fasting) in both dog and cat are between 75-120 mg/dl which is similar to that of humans**. It is not unusual to find a glucose level in a diabetic animal to exceed 600 or more. That's when you understand why Kitty is so moody.

When diabetic, the body is either not producing enough insulin (Type I), or there is an incorrect response between the cells and insulin (Type II). In either the muscles and organs are not able to convert glucose to energy. All that glucose (some times referred to as blood sugar), then gets dumped in the blood system causing damage.

High glucose levels makes the body feel tired. The pet may become very hungry, yet lose weight. All that excess blood sugar is processed through the kidneys which is why you can detect high glucose levels on a urine test.

When blood sugar is out of control, the blood sugar causes damage every where it goes. The kidneys over worked. Blindness can occur. The body is unable to heal itself and wounds can take much longer to heal. The liver cannot process properly and keto-acidosis occurs as fat and protein is broken down in the liver. This can cause severe nausea.

Type I diabetes is the most harmful of the two and requires daily injections of insulin to control. It takes a pet parent willing to sacrifice, not only to purchase the insulin, but to feed the pet at a certain time and bring him/her to the vet for regular checks of the blood glucose level. Taking care of a diabetic pet is a lifetime commitment and may require changes in the family's schedule.

While any breed of dog can become diabetic, Poodles, Mini Schnauzers, Dachshund, Beagles, all are genetically prone to diabetes. Unspayed female dogs are at a higher risk, yet interestingly, male cats are more prone to diabetes than female cats, but the reason is, not yet, explained. http://www.2ndchance.info/diabetescat.htm

Unfortunately some pet parents are unable or unwilling to follow through with treatment. Ignoring the disease does not make it go away, but it does make the pet suffer. If you cannot afford the treatment, try to find a family who is willing and able to adopt the pet and treat for diabetes. If you cannot, the most humane action you can take is to have the pet euthanized. As hard as that decision is, euthanizing may be in the best interest of the pet. There is no good quality of life living as a sick, untreated diabetic pet.

The most important way to discourage diabetes and increase the lifespan of your cat or dog, is to prevent obesity.

Ear Problems

Although both dogs and cats can get ear infections, it is much more common in dogs. For cats, the typical issue is ear mites.

Otodectes cynotis, is the most common species of **ear mites** found in companion animals. Ear mite debris is characterized by a very dark, grainy appearance compared to relatively

smooth, brown ear wax. Ear infections cause itchiness, but rarely to the intensity that ear mites cause. Cats with ear mites, will scratch their ears intensely when the ears are touched by the pet parent or vet.

Proper diagnosis is done under the microscope.

Veterinarians will usually treat ear mites with a one time ear drop application of a prescription drug called **Acaraxx ®**. Acaraxx ® is 0.001 % ivermectin. Over the counter drops require multiple applications.

This same drug can be made at home using ivermectin 1% injection sold for cattle and swine. This is also the same ivermectin used in many heartworm preventatives.

To get 0.001% ivermectin from 1% ivermectin, the drug must be diluted. To do so, you will need a measuring cup and a 3 ml syringe. Pull up 1.2 ml of Ivomec 1% injection for cattle and swine. Add the ivomec to the measuring cup first. Add warm water to the ½ cup mark. This will be 118.8 ml of warm water.

Put contents in plastic squeeze bottle. Shake very well. Draw up 1cc of the mixture per ear. Apply to each ear holding ear closed once applied. The cat will attempt to shake, but it is best to hold closed at least thirty seconds. The application should not need to be repeated unless the cat is an outdoor cat that becomes reinfested. You can dispose of the remaining liquid or refrigerate for future use.

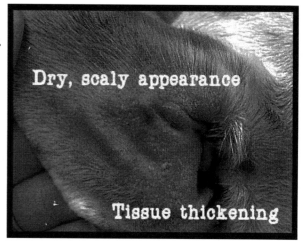

Dogs and cats can suffer from both **yeast infections or bacterial infections** of the ear. Certain characteristics can help to distinguish between these two types of infections.

Yeast infections commonly have a dry, flaky appearance. Often, yeast infections do not limit themselves to the ears, but other parts of the body.

Bacterial infections present with a wet, moist appearance accompanied by a very strong odor, redness and inflammation.

An ear cytology can be performed by your veterinarian. A cytology will reveal if the inflammation caused by bacteria or is allergy-related.

Food allergies can actually be a contributing cause to an ear infection. The ear is part of the largest organ of the body...the skin. Allergy related ear infections can be chronic and lead to thickening of the ear that may require surgery.

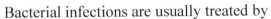

If these conditions are caused by a food allergy, having the pet diagnosed and switched to a non-allergic food can prevent these problems.

Certain breeds of dogs including Poodles, Shih Tzu, Bichons, and Schnauzers, need to have their ear hair plucked on a regular basis to prevent ear infections.

Bacterial infections are usually treated by shaving or plucking the surrounding fur on the underside of the ear. A Nolvasan ® solution (1:2 warm water) is made and drawn up into a large syringe. The ears are flushed using the solution. The debris is wiped out of the ear with cotton swabs and an appropriate topical medication applied.

Some animals, particularly dogs, that have very severe infections, may need to be sedated for the procedure as it may be too painful.

Dogs with ears that hang down, like basset hounds and cocker spaniels, are particularly prone to ear infections. Air flow is limited allowing moisture to build up. Add that issue to a dog like a retriever that loves to play in water, and you can have the makings of a lifelong ear infection. Cleaning them regularly with a vinegar solution will make the ear canal more acidic. An acidic environment is the enemy of yeast and bacteria.

The most common veterinary treatment for ear infections is called **Otomax** ®. The ingredients in Otomax ® includes an antibiotic (gentamicin sulfate), an anti-fungal/yeast (clotrimazole) and an anti-inflammatory (betamethasone) that is used twice daily for 7-14 days.

A similar product can be made at home using nitrofurazone, clotrimazole, and hydrocortisone cream. This formula will not be equal to Otomax ®, but may be of some help until you can see your veterinarian.

A homemade ear cream that may help bacterial and yeast infections, combines 1 part nitrofurazone, 1 part clotrimazole, and 1 part hydrocortisone cream. Mix thoroughly.

The cream can be put in an appropriate sized plastic squeeze bottle. Clip the tip off the bottle to allow the ointment to flow through.

In severe cases of ear infections that just are not getting better, some veterinarians will put dogs on an antibiotic, such as cephalexin if an ear cytology reveals it is more bacterial related, and even sometimes when bacteria is secondary to a yeast infection. Ketoconazole is used to combat yeast and fungal overgrowth.

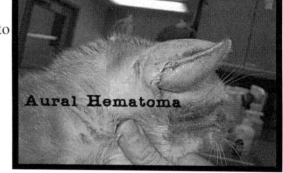

There are times when ear infections are secondary to other issues. Food allergies and thyroid issues are examples.

The presence of a **foreign body** can also lead to infection. In California and other parts of the country, spring brings fox tails and other similar weeds. .Fox tails are common weeds whose seed dispersal comes as a unit. They have a hardened tip and barbs that point away from the tip. Once on the pet, they can burrow anywhere including, but not limited to, behind the eye, between the toes, in the nose, and inner ear. Removal of fox tails usually requires sedation. Fox tails can also cause abscesses.

Constant scratching and shaking of the head caused by mites, foreign bodies, infection, fleas, or fly strike can lead to **aural hematomas**, a collection of blood that collects between the skin and cartilage of the ear. Both of these conditions can require surgery. During the surgery, the hemotoma is drained and the ear surgically stitched in such a way that it cannot fill up again.

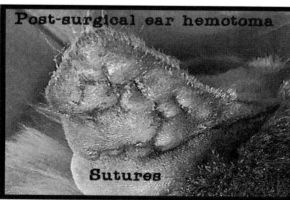

The repair and healing of the aural hematoma is a long process that requires multiple vet visits. Rarely will the ear look the same again.

While it is true that hemotomas will go away on its on over a period of weeks or months, there is not a consensus among veterinarians how painful aural hemotomas are to dogs and cats. Some believe it an inconvenience, while others see it as a terribly painful blood blister.

The picture to the above shows an aural hemotoma. The ear has been shaved in preparation for surgery. The swelling of the pinna (external ear flap) is painfully obvious. The photo to the left shows the ear post-surgery. Notice the lines of sutures throughout the pinna. These sutures are to prevent the fluid from flooding under the ear tissue.

Once a cat has an aural hemotoma, the ear flap will rarely look the same again. This is true even if the cat has the surgery.

To the right is a photo of our cat, Jerry several years after his surgery for an aural hemotoma. The difference in the ear flaps is clearly visible.

Eye Disorders

The most common illness of the eye of the dog and cat is called **conjunctivitis** or pink eye. The causes are many but the symptoms are generally the same including redness of the eye, swelling of the pink tissue or conjunctiva surrounding the eye itself. Another symptom, and the one most pet parents notice, is drainage from the eye.

Some dog and cat breeds commonly have a clear discharge, but when the discharge is yellow or white in color, there is cause for concern. If only one eye is effected and the pet is squinting, you must consider the possibility of a foreign object or a corneal ulcer. It can be difficult to see scratches in the eye without special tests and instruments, but it is something to keep in mind and take seriously. Both can be very painful and can cause permanent damage to the eyes.

A common opthalmic ointment once used by vets, but now sold over the counter, is Terramycin ®. It is a good ointment to keep in your pet medicine cabinet.

As our pet's age, their eyes begin to change, just like humans. It is more common to see advanced problems in dog's than in cats. As the eyes age, they develop a hardening of the lens which makes the lens appear gray. This is called **nuclear sclerosis** and it makes distance vision more difficult. It is of confused with cataracts.

Just as the lens appears gray in nuclear sclerosis, **cataracts** turn the lens a cloudy white. Cataracts are a clouding of the eye's natural lens, that lies behind the iris and pupil. Cataracts can gradually increase in severity over time.

Left untreated , a cataract may slip from the tissue that holds it in place, allowing it to float free around the interior of the eye. The cataract may settle and begin to block natural fluid drainage. This can lead to **glaucoma,** which is a pressure on the eye that can cause blindness, severe pain, and enlargement of the eye itself.

Glaucoma occurs when the fluid inside the eye, called the aqueous humor, cannot drain back into the blood stream as it should. If something blocks the eye's ability to drain, it is like a creek that has been dammed up. Fluid continues to pour into the creek (the eye)., but the liquid has no place to go. The fluid puts immense pressure on the eye. Dogs with glaucoma are not able to tell their pet parent that they are experiencing pressure in the eye or that they have a severe headache.

Generally, it is only during yearly check ups that the problem is discovered, or when the pressure has caused the eye to swell. I have seen eyes ruptured under the pressure of glaucoma and the only way to relieve the pain is to remove the eye.

Dogs generally adjust easily to blindness when it comes on slowly and their environment stays the same. Many dogs have gone blind without their pet parent realizing it until they rearrange the house, or bring in a new piece of furniture.

Medications for glaucoma tend to be expensive. The cost of one such medication, Dorzolamide HCI ® eye drops (which reduce the fluid production inside the eye), is about $75.

Even though the treatment is expensive, we cannot humanely allow our pets to be in intense pain. We can pretend it isn't happening because our pet's don't complain like we do, but our pets hurt just the same. Talk to your veterinarian about your options and do the most humane thing you can do.

There are certain conditions that can indicate a serious emergency. Uneven or abnormal pupil size is called **anisocoria** and can be an indicator of many things including trauma and neurological emergencies. **Nystagmus** is another eye condition in which the eyes make repetitive, uncontrolled movements. Nystagmus can occur with vestibular diseases, inner ear infections, or neurological disease.

Some pets are born with eye abnormalities. **Entropion** is a condition that causes the eyelids to roll inward, and is common in the Shar pei, Pekingese, Bulldog, and many other breeds. The eyelashes touch the cornea of the eye causing constant irritation, pain, corneal ulcers and erosion.

Ectropion causes the eyelids to roll outward. The eyes have a droopy appearance and the exposure causes the tissues to dry out resulting in conjunctivitis, corneal ulcers, and inflammation. Corneal scarring can eventually impair vision. The most common form of ectropion is congentital, meaning the pet is born with it. Breeds such as Cocker Spaniels, Basset Hounds, Bloodhounds, and St. Bernards are most frequently affected by ectropion. Facial nerve paralysis, chronic inflammation, and neuromuscular disease can result in acquired ectropion .

Cherry eye is the protrusion of the nictating membrane, also called the third eyelid. The prolapse exposes the gland, drying it out, and exposing it to bacteria. Cherry eye also obstructs the pet's vision.

All three of these conditions require surgery to repair.

The cornea is the protective outer transparent part of the eye and is made up of three layers called the epithelium, stroma, and Descemet's membrane (from outer to inner layer). **Corneal erosion** is the loss of a few layers of the epithelium. A **corneal ulcer** is the erosion into the stroma layer. If erosion continues deeper into the Descemet's membrane, the fluid of the inner eye leaks out, the eye collapses, and permanent damage occurs.

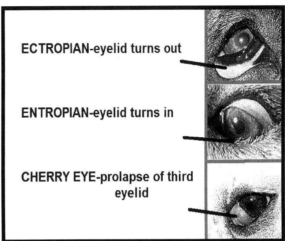

ECTROPIAN-eyelid turns out

ENTROPIAN-eyelid turns in

CHERRY EYE-prolapse of third eyelid

Dry eye is a serious concern and a common problem in Shih-tzu's and Cocker Spaniels. It is caused by reduced tear production or blockage of tear ducts. Dry eye is extremely uncomfortable for the pet. Pets with dry eye will have a dull appearance to the eye and this is usually accompanied by thick, yellow discharge. They're eyes should be cleaned frequently and drops which replace the tears applied.

Terramycin, or triple antibiotic ointment helps keep infection at a minimum, but dry eye requires medications that will keep the eye moist. Over the counter options include GenTeal Gel for Severe Dry Eyes ®, Systane Ultra Lubricant Eye Drops ®, and Refresh Tears Lubricant Eye Drops ®.

Hepatic Lipidosis (Fatty Liver Syndrome)

Hepatic lipidosis is an accumulation of fat in the liver that prevents the liver from functioning properly. Hepatic lipidosis is associated with many diseases, and is often associated with obesity. The condition is most common in older, obese cats, but can be seen in younger cats.

Stress, illness, or a sudden change in diet may trigger the cat to stop eating. This can lead to hepatic lipidosis. If left untreated, hepatic lipidosis can result in death.

Symptoms of hepatic lipidosis include:

- Lack of appetite
- Drooling, nausea

- Change of behavior such as hiding in unusual places
- Yellow color to the skin (jaundice)
- Dehydration
- Constipation
- Weight loss
- Muscle waste

Free feeding can, not only, make your cat obese, but make it more difficult to notice if your cat stops eating. A measured amount should be fed daily. As soon as it is noticed that the cat is not eating, the matter needs to be addressed promptly. Cats can be encouraged to eat by heating up a bit of canned cat food or tuna. If the cat still does not eat, contact your vet.

To the right is a photo of Biskit. She survived hepatic lipidosis by being fed through a feeding tube for two months.

Heart Disease

The heart is responsible for circulating blood throughout the body. The heart has a right and left side. The right side is responsible for sending blood that is oxygen poor and rich in carbon dioxide to the lungs. Once in the lungs, the carbon dioxide is released when we exhale. Inhalation brings oxygen to the lungs and to the blood, where it returns to the heart. Once there, the left side of the heart sends oxygen rich blood to all the organs of the body. Arteries are the pathways that blood uses to travel away from the heart and veins bring the blood back to the heart. Capillaries connect the arteries and veins.

The heart has four chambers with valves that only allow the blood to flow in one direction. This constant motion gives us life.

As the heart contracts, the valves open in succession. This closing and opening is the heart beat, and the reason why a heart beat is a two-part sound ("lub-dub"). As soon as one valve is closed, the other opens. Sometimes, you may hear a **heart murmur**. This is a sound of vibration that occurs if this timing of blood flow isn't working quite as it should. If you listen using a stethoscope you can often hear a "whooshing" or "swishing" sound.

Heart murmurs are rated by grades:

- I (1): barely audible

- II (2): soft, but easily heard with a stethoscope

- III (3): intermediate loudness

- IV (4): loud murmur that radiates widely, often including opposite side of chest

- V (5) : very loud, audible with stethoscope barely touching the chest; the vibration is also strong enough to be felt through the animal's chest wall

- VI (6): very loud, audible with stethoscope barely touching the chest; the vibration is also strong enough to be felt through the animal's chest wall

Often heart murmurs are inherited or congenital and of little consequence. A small heart murmur is not unusual to hear in a puppy under six months. Heart murmurs can also be acquired. For instance, our 18 (then) year old cat, Chloe was diagnosed as having hyperthyroidism. This disease caused a 5 out of 6 grade heart murmur. In addition to being prescribed medication for her hyperthyroidism, Chloe was also on medication for her heart until she passed away close to her 19th birthday.

Heart disease is any abnormality of the heart. The disease may be insignificant or serious.

Heart failure is a heart abnormality that makes the heart incapable of pumping enough oxygen rich blood for the body to function properly.

Several things happen in heart failure. The blood pressure is too low to pump the blood to other body systems in the consistent way the body did before. This causes the blood to "dam up" in the organs. In doing so, fluid leaks from the blood vessels and into tissues.

Commonly termed **congestive heart failure**, the symptoms in human and animal are similar.

Symptoms of Congestive Heart Failure include:

- Coughing more than usual, particularly after exercising, or at night.
- Loss of appetite

- Difficulty exercising
- Difficulty breathing, easily tired
- Pacing at bedtime and having a difficult time getting settled.
- Collapse or fainting, particularly during any situation that increases the heart rate.
- Swollen abdomen or extremities
- Bluish gray mucus membrane color
- Weight loss

There are two things that generally bring a pet parent to the vet with their pet in regard to the heart. One is coughing, the other is collapse.

In order to diagnose heart disease, your vet may need to do several tests such as x-rays, an EKG, urinalysis, and blood work including a heartworm test. X-rays allow the vet to look for an enlarged heart or other structural abnormality. The EKG lets them review the rhythm of the heartbeat. Urinalysis and blood work lets the doctor rule out other causes (like Chloe's hypothyroidism).

If your pet is not on heartworm preventative, heartworm needs to be ruled out as it can also cause coughing. Testing can get expensive, so be honest with your veterinarian about your situation. Discuss what the most important test is or if it is possible or safe to try the pet on medication to see if the situation improves.

Congestive heart failure can usually be treated and the quantity and quality of life improved. Lasix ® (furosomide), is given to assist with fluid retention. Enacard ® or Vasotec ® (enalapril), helps the heart beat more efficiently and prevents the build up of fluids. There are additional medications used in the treatment of heart failure, but these are the most common.

A low sodium diet might also be recommended. Again, prescription foods are available.

Above is a photo of Blue who is in congestive heart failure. Thanks to his medication, he is doing well.

Hypothyroidism and Hyperthyroidism

The thyroid gland produces several types of hormones that regulate many body functions. The two most common hormones are termed T3 and T4.

A proper functioning thyroid is essential for a properly functioning body.

The many jobs of the thyroid include:

- proper regulation of body temperature
- weight gain and loss
- skin condition
- muscle tone
- heart rate and cardiac output
- nervous system function
- growth and development of young pets
- metabolism of fats and carbohydrates.

The metabolic process creates a balance in the body of mammals. **Metabolism** is defined as series of chemical transformations within the cells that determine how an organism will react to their environment, grow and reproduce, and keep their structure intact. This process determines what your body finds nutritious or dangerous.

Metabolism determines, for example, how medications will react to an individual. The human metabolism deactivates acetylsalicylic acid (aspirin) in about four to six hours. That's why you can take another aspirin four to six hours after the first dosage. However with the different metabolism of the dog and cat, this same deactivation doesn't occur for nine to fourteen hours in the dog and twenty-two to forty-five hours in the cat. Give an aspirin too soon, and you can overdose the pet, leading to severe complications and even death.

When thyroid production lessens or increases, it throws the body's balance off. If the production is too little, one is said to have **hypothyroidism,** if too much is produced, **hyperthyroidism** is the diagnosis. (Hypo=too little, Hyper=too much).

Dogs are more likely to be diagnosed with hypothyroidism, while cats are more likely to be diagnosed with hyperthyroidism. The reason for this is unclear. Veterinarians have found that when dogs are diagnosed with hyperthyroidism, it is usually related to cancer or over medicating a dog with hypothyroidism.

Very little can be done to prevent either disease but recognizing the signs can get your pet the necessary treatment as soon as possible.

Symptoms of hypothyroidism in the dog include:

- Thinning of the fur along the torso

- Dull hair coat
- Excess shedding or scaling
- Weight gain
- Reduced activity
- Cold sensitivity
- Thickening of the skin and increased pigment
- Chronic ear problems
- Chronic skin infections
- Weakness

Symptoms of hypothyroidism in the cat include:
- Lethargy
- Inactivity
- Mental dullness
- Weakness
- Weight gain
- Unkempt appearance/matted, ungroomed fur
- Constipation
- Hair loss
- Low body temperature

Hormone replacement therapy will greatly improve the quality of life of the hypothyroid animal. Dogs and cat are usually given levothyroxine (Soloxine ®) or L-thyroxine for hypothyroidism. Some veterinarians see hypothyroidism in cats as a transitory (impermanent) condition and do not treat with hormones right away. If, however, the thyroid is removed, levothyroxine can synthetically replace the necessary hormone.

Symptoms of hyperthyroidism in dogs:
- Marked weight loss even while eating

- Excessive hunger and/or thirst
- Diarrhea
- Excessive urination
- Weakness
- Muscle atrophy/wasting away

Symptoms of hyperthyroidism in cats:

- Marked weight loss even while eating
- Increased appetite and/or thirst
- Restlessness, pacing, increased activity
- Aggressiveness
- Poor hair coat
- Periodic vomiting
- Increased amount of stool and urination
- Diarrhea
- Occasional weakness and depression

As mentioned, hyperthyroidism in dogs is likely to be caused by cancer. The treatment is more complicated than treatment of the hormone itself.

For some reason, unknown to scientists, there has been an increase in the cases of hyperthyroidism over the past 25 years. http://www.peteducation.com/article.cfm?c=1+2130&aid=218

Hyperthyroidism rarely affects cats younger than 8 years old. For those cats diagnosed with hyperthyroidism, there are three methods of treatment. The first, and most common, is the oral medication, methimazole (Tapazole ®). As with levothyroxine, the medication will need to be given for the rest of the pet's life. The second treatment is surgical removal of the affected thyroid gland. The third treatment is with radioactive iodine. All options should be discussed with your veterinarian.

Both hypothyroidism and hyperthyroidism require a thyroid panel to diagnose as well as to maintain the proper dosage in your pet as she ages. Many veterinarians will want to do a full chemistry panel yearly to make sure the thyroid disease is not damaging other organs. Although the cost may be seem intimidating, it will save money in the long run. Potential health problems can be caught earlier, medication can be adjusted, or the early signs of disease can be treated before it becomes a major health concern.

Treating the disease rather than the symptoms is just another way to save money and increases the quality and quantity of your pet's life.

Hypoadrenocorticism and Hyperadrenocorticism

Diabetes, hypo-and hyperthyroidism, and hypo-and hyperadrenocorticism are all diseases that affect part of the endocrine system. This system is a complex group of tissues that release important hormones. Whether we are talking about the pancreas releasing insulin, or the thyroid gland releasing a thyroid hormone, they are all a part of this vital system. Sometimes hormones will have a function that is polar opposite of another, but together, they provide an equilibrium or balance.

The adrenal glands are located just in front of the kidneys. The adrenal glands are work horses and responsible for so much in the body. The adrenal glands have two parts, the cortex and medulla, which have different functions. The cortex helps to balance the body's level of sodium and potassium salts, metabolize nutrients and even produce sex hormones.

The medulla is responsible for our responses to stress and low blood sugar. When a human, dog, or cat experiences stress or is exposed to a threat, there are two choices: fight or flight. The adrenals, particularly the medulla, kicks in, releasing epinephrine (also known as adrenaline) and norepinephrine to deal with this situation. The heart races, digestion slows down as blood is reassigned to the extremities, and blood pressure increases; all necessities in a fight or flight scenario. The "fight or flight" response is an important survival mechanism that we share with non-human animals.

The adrenal glands also control the body's amount of salt and sugar well as the water balance. In addition, the glands control the metabolism of fat and protein. The adrenal glands accomplish this by releasing hormones.

When those adrenal glands fail to produce the proper amount of hormones, **hypoadrenocorticism**, also known as **Addison's disease** occurs. Addison's disease is a deficiency of cortisol and/or aldosterone, hormones which help maintain proper blood pressure, kidney filtration, and a strong heartbeat. The deficiency of these hormone(s) cause the level of sodium and potassium to be abnormal resulting in a myriad of physical symptoms.

In most cases of Addison's, the disease is caused by an auto-immune response. Secondary adrenal insufficiency is also caused when the messenger hormone, ACTH, stops working properly. ACTH, is an acronym for adrenocorticotrophic hormone that travels from the pituitary gland in the brain, to the adrenals. ACTH is the messenger that signals the release of cortisol.

The most common cause of this secondary adrenal insufficiency is frequent prescription steroid use. In pets, steroids are often given in the form of an injection or pills for the treatment of inflammation and itchiness. These synthetic hormones such as prednisone and dexamethazone, cause an unintended response. The synthetic hormones begin to imitate the natural hormones, so the brain stops sending the ACTH signal to the adrenals to release much needed cortisol. The body is no longer balanced as it can no longer produce enough cortisol.

Although cats can develop Addison's, the disease is most commonly found in middle aged female dogs. Addison's does seem to affect certain dog breeds more often than others. Breeds more prone to the disease include Great Danes, Labradors, Rottweillers, Standard Poodles, Portuguese Water Dogs, Wheaten Terrier, and West Highland White Terriers.

Symptoms of hypoadrenocorticism/ Addision's disease include:
- lethargy
- vomiting and/or diarrhea
- increased thirst and urination
- weak pulse
- dehydration
- low temperature
- overall depression
- hair loss
- weight loss

The symptoms can be transient, meaning they come and go. Since the Addison's dog cannot produce enough cortisol, the symptoms may worsen under stress. Many of the symptoms are the same ones found in other diseases. To further complicate matters, about 5% of pets with Addison's disease will have other endocrine diseases such as diabetes or hypothyroidism at the same time.

Diagnosis takes more involved lab testing than many diseases. Generally a CBC, chemistry panel, and urinalysis are performed first. Perhaps one of the most telling results is a low sodium to potassium ratio of less than 23:1. Blood chemistry tests and a urinalysis will frequently show abnormally high potassium and calcium, liver enzymes ALT and AST, and urea (a build up of blood and waste products that should have processed out of the body.) Lower levels of chloride, sodium, and dilute urine are also common with this disease. These abnormal lab values can support your veterinarian's instinct to investigate further.

In addition to these usual biochemistry tests, an ACTH stimulation test will need to be performed. The initial needed blood sample is drawn as a baseline of the pets cortisol levels. An injection of adrenocorticotropin is given which will stimulate the adrenal gland if the pet is healthy. The hormone is given time to work and another blood draw is done to test the cortisol levels with the hormone stimulation. If the result shows a low amount of cortisol in the system post stimulation, the pet is diagnosed with Addison's Disease.

Often, Addison's is only diagnosed during an Addison's crisis when the pet is very ill. Pets in crisis usually require IV fluids. It is to the pet's advantage to be hospitalized to treat the symptoms and to begin treatment for the Addison's itself.

There are two basic methods of treatment. One is an injection of Percortin-V ® or the generic DOCP. This injection is given every 25 days. The other treatment method is Florinef® (oral fludrocortisone). Fludrocortisone helps replace the missing mineralocorticoids hormones. This treatment is the more expensive option. Talking honestly to your doctor about your circumstances and your pet's needs is important.

Hyperandrenocorticism, or **Cushing's disease**, is caused by one of two hormone glands. One, is the pituitary gland at the base of the brain, and second is the adrenal gland. Most often it is the result of a small tumor on the pituitary gland. The pituitary gland produces the adrenocorticotropic hormone (ACTH) which travels to the adrenal gland telling it how much cortisol to release. If the pituitary gland is malfunctioning and producing too much ACTH, the adrenal gland will produce too much cortisol.

Frequent use of prescription steroids, causes a condition that copies Cushing's disease symptoms. This is known as iatrogenic Cushing's.
Two types of Cushing's disease exist. One type is pituitary-dependent and the second is adrenal-dependent Cushing's disease. The former is caused by an overproduction of ACTH, and the latter and less common form is caused by a tumor on the adrenal gland.

Symptoms of hyperadrenocorticism /Cushing's include:

- a pot-bellied appearance
- increased thirst and urination
- increased appetite
- excessive panting
- hair loss
- reoccurring infections (skin, bladder)

As with Addison's, testing begins with a CBC, chemistry panel, and urinalysis.

Since the body is over-producing cortisol, the immune system is less capable of fighting infection. Cushing's dogs often have a history of skin infections.

Frequently the urinalysis will also reveal what is known as a silent infection of the bladder. A silent infection is one that was present, but did not show symptoms.

Laboratory tests may also show an increase in white blood cell count, cholesterol, blood sugar, and serum alkaline phosphtase, a liver enzyme. These results might indicate the need for further testing. X-rays will often reveal a enlarged liver. An ultrasound may reveal tumors on the adrenals. Specialty tests may be performed including a urine cortisol/creatinine ratio, low dose dexamethasone suppression test, high dose dexamethasone suppression test, and an ACTH stimulation test.

If the testing reveals adrenal-dependent Cushing's as a result of a tumor, the treatment is surgical removal of the adrenal gland.

Pituitary-dependent Cushing's does not require surgery, but does require medication that can be expensive. Since excessive steroid usage is often a trigger, steroid administration should be stopped.

Drugs used to treat Cushing's includes: Lysodren ® (mitocane) , Anipryl ® (l-deprenyl), or Vetoryl ® (trilostane).

Unlike hypo- and hyperthyroidism, pet parents have one powerful tool to help prevent Addison's and Cushing's: refusing overuse of steroids. The pet parent should insist on a second opinion when a veterinarian recommends repeated steroid treatment. In turn, the pet parent should be willing to work with the veterinarian to find the cause of the itchiness rather than just treat the symptom. While steroids may seem like a "quick cure", in the long run, they can be harmful to your pet and your wallet.

Obesity

Obesity is not a disease in itself, but a condition that can encourage and even cause disease.

The rate of obesity in dogs and cats has been on the rise for years and shows no indication of slowing down.

Proportion of hamburger & piece of bacon to full-sized human and full-sized chihuahua.

Small hamburger= 250 calories/10 grams fat
One piece of bacon= 44 calories/3.3 grams fat

It is hard for us to imagine that a pound or two of weight can cause health problems. However, a pound or two in our pets is equivalent to ten or twenty pounds in humans.

What is a small meal to us, can be an enormous meal to your pet. Consider the size of a hamburger and a piece of bacon compared to an adult human male and an average sized chihuahua:

"*According to recent findings by the Association for Pet Obesity Prevention (APOP), more than 45 percent of dogs and 58 percent of cats can be classified as overweight or obese.*"http://www.petmd.com/dog/nutrition/evr_multi_long_term_effects_of_obesity_on_pets

Obesity can cause or contribute to many health conditions including (but not limited to):

- Diabetes
- Heart disease and high blood pressure
- Difficulty breathing and heat intolerance
- Joint, bone, and ligament problems
- Lower immune system
- Digestive issues
- Skin problems
- Cancer
- Decreased tolerance and stamina
- Higher risk during anesthesia
- Shorter life span and quality of life

Pet parents must educate themselves on the nutritional needs of their pets. The nutritional needs of dogs differ from cats and both differ from humans.

In addition to proper nutrition, the rule of weight loss is the same for all: Expend more energy/calories than you take in.
If your pet is overweight, first make sure it is not caused by any disorder such as hypothyroidism. Talk to your vet to develop a plan that will help your pet lose weight and maintain good health.

Tips for helping your pet lose weight and maintain a healthy weight:

- If your pet is 40 lbs but should be 35 lbs, feed the required amount for a 35 lb dog according to the nutritional information and feeding directions on the bag of food you

already feed.
- Change to a diet high in quality protein and low in carbohydrates, fat, and calories. Some veterinarians will recommend Hills ® Prescription R/D, but if you cannot afford it, discuss other options with your veterinarian.
- Do not free feed, but measure the amount you feed based upon recommendations from the manufacturer or your veterinarian.
- Stop or reduce the number of treats you give or choose healthier ones.
- Find a way to incorporate some form of exercise in your pet's daily routine.
- If your pet is not obese, take a photo of the pet monthly and compare the present month photo with the past photos. Weight gain happens gradually and it is difficult to recognize for those who live with the pet daily.

A sudden change in diet and exercise is not recommended. Instead make the changes gradually, over a few weeks time. This will prevent digestive upset, sore muscles, and overuse injuries from exercise.

Veterinarian use a body conditioning chart similar to the one below to evaluate a pet's weight.

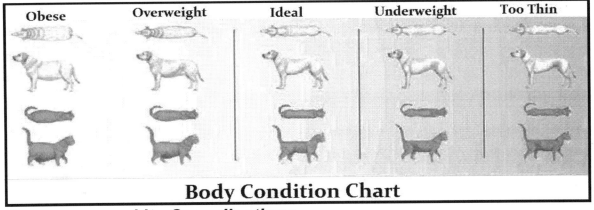
Body Condition Chart

Pregnancy and its Complications

If you are reading this book, I assume that you are an animal lover, love your own pet(s) and want what is in the best interest of all. As you read in the beginning chapters, not only is overpopulation a huge problem that leads to large number of euthanasias, but there are many health benefits to being spayed or neutered.

That being said, I do understand that pregnancies happen, and when they do, you need to know about the reproductive cycle of dogs and cats so you can make sure that the mom and babies are safe and healthy.

Female dogs generally go into heat (estrus) twice a year beginning around 6 to 8 months old.

The first stage of this cycle is called anestrus meaning "without estrus". Once certain hormones increase, they will stimulate the second stage to begin. This is proestrus and lasts about 9 days. Males will sense the heat cycle at this time, and but the female will not allow him to mount. It is during this time that one will notice a bloody discharge from the vulva as it begins to enlarge in preparation for mating. Estrous, the third stage, marks the time when the female accepts the male and mating can occur. This time period varies, but is about 9 days, on average. When mating does occur, the bulbus glandis of the male's penis swells inside the female's vagina, causing a breeding tie which locks them together for up to 30 minutes.

Post-estrus, is called diestrus and can last 2-3 months long. If the female becomes pregnant, the gestation period is about 65 days long.

If you suspect the female is pregnant, begin to feed her a puppy chow dog food, and continue until her puppies are weaned. Deworm the mother for intestinal parasites with Panacur ® (fenbendazole) as she can pass those on to her pups. Above all, consult with your veterinarian, particularly if you do not know who the father or fathers may be. Females bred to larger dogs can have pups too large to birth naturally and often die in childbirth.

8-24 hours before the delivery time nears, the rectal temperature of the female drops. During the first stage of delivery, the mother may appear anxious and restless. She may not eat and will probably pant. It is at this time that contractions begin, but are not visible externally. The cervix will begin dilating and the female may begin searching for a safe birthing place. She will need a quiet, familiar, enclosed, dimly-lit space away from high traffic areas. The expectant mother may feel safest in a whelping box.

Some expectant mothers appreciate your company, but only if visitors are quiet and calm. It is important to monitor and reassure her, but not to over-stimulate her. The mother can recognize anxiety in the visitors, which can make matters worse.

Stage two marks the beginning of obvious abdominal contractions. The placental water will break and one may notice a straw-colored fluid. Pups are usually delivered at an interval of 1-2 hours. The placenta, or afterbirth will usually be delivered before the next puppy is born.

The mother should begin licking the pup, not only to clean and dry the pup, but to stimulate the blood circulation and encourage the puppy to breathe. The mother should also chew the umbilical cord in two and eat the placenta. Do not interfere with the process unless the mother is neglecting her duties. First time mothers may need assistance. Some will ignore the pups or be overzealous.

Those prepared to assist with the birthing process should keep clean dishtowels, a suction bulb syringe, sharp, disinfected scissors, and a Betadine ® or Nolvasan ® solution nearby. Scissors with no plastic hand grip, can be disinfected by putting the scissors in boiling water for 5-10 minutes.

If the mother does require assistance, the remains of the placental sack should be cleared away. Next, pick the puppy up with the towel. Use the suction bulb syringe to remove any fluid from the nose and mouth. Vigorously and with care, stimulate the pup by wiping back and forth with the towel until he or she begins to cry. Repetition of the suctioning process with stimulation may be repeated, but it is essential for the assistant to remain calm.

If the puppy's umbilical cord has not been severed, it can be clipped with sharp, sterile scissors. Leave enough cord so that you can tie a knot in the cord to prevent bleeding and infection. Clean the cord with Betadine ® or Nolvasan ®. Once the pup is breathing and the umbilical cord clipped, tied, and disinfected, return the pup to the mother. She needs to bond with her puppies if she is expected to recognize them as her own and feed them like a good mother should.

There are several potential complications to the birthing process. Seek medical help if any of the following occur.

- Stage one lasts more than 24 hours. The female should start showing external signs of contractions and active labor within that time.
- There is more than 4 hours between delivery of the pups.
- Pups are born dead or near death.
- The mother shows extreme distress.

Some mothers need an injection of Oxytocin ® to stimulate the contractions to be strong enough to deliver the pups. The puppies may also be too big for her to deliver naturally, and a c-section may be required. If the mother is unable or unwilling to feed the puppies, you will need to do the feeding. I

For new mothers who can feed their pups, the burden of nursing can cause a significant drop of calcium in the mother's bloodstream. This is known as **hypocalcemia** and can be deadly. Hypocalcemia is most common in first litters and in toy breeds.

Symptoms of hypocalcemia include:

- restlessness
- disorientation
- unsteady gait

- muscle tremors
- convulsions
- vomiting
- dilated pupils
- rapid breathing
- high fever

It is imperative to get the mother to the veterinarian as quickly as possible.

Female cats also have an estrous cycle, but there is a particularly interesting thing required to stimulate the cycling to occur: 12 hours of sunlight. In the Northern Hemisphere outdoor cats will reproduce in spring and summer. Indoor cats will go into heat more often than outside cats. The labor and delivery process is much the same in both the cat and the dog and the same cautions apply. Begin feeding kitten food 2 weeks before delivery in cats and continue until the kittens are weaned.

Skin Disorders and Conditions

Skin disorders are among the top reasons pet parents take their dog or cat to the vet. Entire books can be written on the topic. Some of the most common are skin allergies, skin infections, hot spots, and alopecia (hair loss). It's important to keep in mind that things that make humans sneeze, tend to make our dogs and cats itch.

The skin is the largest organ of the body and includes the ears. While it may seem that skin disorders are external problems, many have internal causes. Histamine reactions, an improper functioning thyroid, and a weakened immune system are examples of causes of skin disorders.

The key to stopping the itching, hair loss, dry or oily skin is finding the cause. Is the cause an external issue caused by fleas or mites? Could the cause be an internally related problem with poor skin as just one of its symptoms? To find the answer requires a good external physical exam, knowing the right questions to ask, and possibly, lab work.

While some skin problems can be treated with over-the-counter medications (OTC), others require prescription medications (RX).

Below is a chart of common skin conditions, their characteristics, causes, and treatment options. A more thorough discussion follows.

Skin Condition	Characteristics & Causes	Treatment
Ectoparasite	Fleas, ticks, mange mites, fleas/flea dirt, and ticks can be seen with the naked eye, mites must be diagnosed with a skin scrape	Topicals, shampoos, dips, and oral parasite preventative
Allergic Dermititis	Irritation caused by allergens in food or the environment, itching of paws, abdomen, seasonal itching indicates and environmental allergy, continuous allergies may indicate a food allergy or endocrine disorder	Elimination diet, avoid environmental triggers, OTC medications, prescription medication, steriods
Endocrine Related	Skin infections are secondary to endocrine disease. May present as frequent pyoderma or yeast infections	Identify and treat endocrine disorder to eliminate or reduce skin problems
Pyoderma (Bacterial skin infections)	Red and raised white filled pustules, dry & flaky patches of skin, itching	Topical and oral antibiotics, medicated shampoos
Acute Moist Dermatitis (Hot Spots)	Localized area of inflammation, redness, and itching, usually caused by bacterial infection	Shaving surrounding fur, scrub, applying topicals, antibiotics, e-collar may be necessary, oatmeal baths
Yeast infections and overgrowths	Musty odor, thickened and discolored skin, scales & flaky skin, focused in ears, between skin folds, and toes, often a sign of underlying issues	Medicated Shampoos, ketaconazole, antibiotics for secondary infections
Ringworm	Fungus that causes round inflamed scaly patches of skin surrounded by hair loss	Topical anti-fungal medication, dips, shampoos, possible oral medications
Impetigo	Common in puppies, pus-filled blisters on hairless areas of the body	No treatment necessary unless severe, then topicals or oral antibiotics
Seborrhea	Greasy, flaky skin, may be genetically related and chronic or as a result of an underlying illness	Shampoos, discover cause of underlying illness
Acrael Lick Granuloma	Caused by compulsive licking of localized area most often on the extremities, possible neurologically or behavior related	Use of Bitter Apple ® to discourage licking, consult with vet to discuss possible use of oral medications for compulsive behavior, regular exercise.
Change in skin's color and texture	May change with no history of skin problems, skin may blacken from changing pigment, may be a signs of hormonal or metabolic diseases	Blood work to rule out underlying causes

Ectoparasites include the most common offenders including, fleas, ticks, and mange mites discussed in an earlier chapter. Ruling out external parasites should be your first step in determining the cause of the skin disorder.

Only fleas, flea feces, and ticks can be seen with the naked eye. The actual flea does not have to be present to cause flea allergy dermatitis. The saliva from one flea bite can trigger an allergic reaction.

One way to determine if there is a flea problem, is for the pet parent to use a flea comb, combing the fur near the tail and close to the skin. The pet parent may notice small dots of debris on the combed fur. To determine if the debris is flea feces, put the loose fur from the comb on a white paper towel and dribble water on it. Once wet, if there is flea feces present, the paper towel will turn blood red indicating you have a flea infestation, not only on your pet, but in your environment. Refer to Chapter 11 for the flea battle plan. While ticks do not cause itching, they can cause lyme disease, so should be removed as soon as possible.

Two other external parasites that can cause itching are **demodex and sarcoptic mange mites.** Neither can be seen with the naked eye. A skin scrape analyzed under a microscope is required to identify the parasite.

Demodex mange is an overgrowth of mites that are already normally on the body. Demodex is an immune problem that often resolves itself, but the cause of the low immune system should be investigated. Demodex does not spread from animal to animal, but siblings can both be affected. Hair loss is patchy and the skin normal looking. While demodex mites can cause itching, it is not the intense itching one sees with sarcoptic mange. Demodex is also not transmutable to humans like sarcoptic mange mites.

Treatment for demodex mites is two-fold. Since a lower immune system allowed the demodex mites to propagate, the reason for it should be addressed and measures taken to improve the immune system. Second, the dog should be bathed in a benzoyl-peroxide shampoo and then dipped in amitraz, also known as Mitaban ®. Do not towel off, but allow the pet's hair to air dry. Follow the directions carefully. This should be done once weekly until skin scrapes reveal no more mites.

While it is possible for sarcoptic mites to be passed to humans, after many years of petting, holding, bathing, and dipping affected dogs, the mite has never been transmitted to me.

Symptoms of sarcoptic mites are more extreme than other mites and include extreme itchiness, loss of hair and red, scaly skin.

Sarcoptic mange is treated with weekly baths and a lime-sulfur dip. Selamectin, which is sold as Revolution ®, is a topical that not only kills fleas and ticks but also helps kill the mites. Monthly use of Selmectin is recommended for at least for 2 months. For both demodex and sarcoptic mange, shaving the pet may be recommended during treatment.

If external parasites have been ruled out, the next thing to consider is an **environmental or**

seasonal allergy known as allergic dermatitis. Many are allergic to lawn grass and pollen. Problems seem to worsen during times of high pollen counts. The pet may start itching after rolling in the grass. Pet parents tend to notice their pets licking their paws, abdomen and other areas that touch the ground. Generally, environmental allergies are seasonal, not year round. However, some pets also have allergies related to the indoor environment such as dust and molds. Frequent skin and ear infections can be a sign of this type of allergy.

Over the counter treatments can sometimes help. Common ones include Benadryl ® (diphenhydramine), Chlor-trimeton ® (chloraphenaramine), and Allegra ® (fexofenadine). **Never give a pet any drug with pseudoephedrine as it is toxic to them.** This includes Allegra-D.

If over-the-counter drugs do not work, prescription medications may be your only option. Hydroxyzine is the most commonly prescribed drug for treatment of skin allergies. Atopica ® (cyclosporine) is an excellent drug but more expensive than hydroxyzine. Steroid injections or a course of short-term prednisone may be given by your doctor. Steroids reduce the inflammation of the skin, which relieves itching. Continuous steroid use can lead to more serious health problems such as Addison's and Cushing's disease.

Year around itching can often be associated with food allergies or a food intolerance. While many in the pet food industry have convinced us that grains are the most common culprit in food allergies, it is in fact, the protein source that causes allergic responses. True allergies are reactions to a specific protein. Allergies can affect many organs, including the skin. A food intolerance is often localized to the digestive system.

Itching is rarely localized and does not change with the seasons. Gastrointestinal problems may also occur. Cats with food allergies or a food intolerance will often scratch around their head and face. (Be sure to rule out ear mites in cats). Dog will scratch at their faces, chew on their feet, and may get frequent ear infections. Ideally, it is best to do some blood work to rule out other internal issues first, but if the cost is a barrier, and a food allergy is suspected, an ingredient elimination diet is the next step. This process is the best way to determine if the allergy is present, and if so, what kinds of foods the pet is allergic to.

Keys to an elimination diet:
- Note the ingredients of the food your pet is already eating
- Eliminate food dyes including Red 40, Yellow 5, Blue 1, Yellow 6 and even "caramel coloring", or "titanium dioxide"
- Look for foods with limited ingredients avoiding artificial ingredients as much as possible
- Change the meat source. If a dog is allergic to beef, he will be allergic to all beef, no matter the "quality" of the diet. "Organic" or "holistic" beef is still beef.

As mentioned in the discussion of nutrition, food dyes, have not only been linked to allergies and food intolerance, but as possible carcinogens.

For that reason, eliminating dyes from your pet food, may be a good step in determining the source of your pet's allergies. The elimination of dyes may also reduce any possible carcinogenic effects that these dyes may have.

When you are shopping for a new food for the elimination diet, choose one that has few ingredients. Once the artificial ingredients and dyes have been eliminated, focus on eliminating meat and carbohydrate sources. Beef has been shown to be the meat most likely to trigger an allergy. Eliminate it first. Other meats used in pet food include beef, chicken, lamb, fish, duck and venison. Carbohydrate sources include rice, potato, sweet potato, and peas.

Change diets slowly, to avoid stomach upset. Feed the new food for at least a month and monitor your pet for itching. If there is no change, move to another meat and carbohydrate source. My first choice has always been a salmon or potato or whitefish and rice combination.

Change the foods in succession monthly or bi-monthly until you have found a combination that does not stimulate an allergic response. If the itching continues, its time for the lab testing I recommended earlier.

Endocrine related skin problems are secondary to the endocrine disease itself. The body is regulated by several hormones, most prominently the thyroid and adrenal glands. While these hormones do not directly cause skin disorders, one of the symptoms of a malfunctioning gland is skin problems.

Hypothyroidism is one example of an endocrine related skin problem. A pet with hypothyroidism will normally show a loss of hair on the trunk, back of legs, and tail. The fur will be brittle, dull, and thin. The skin will probably be flaky, but not red and itchy. The skin may have black patches.

Hyperadrenocorticism, also known as **Cushing's disease,** can also manifest in bothersome skin conditions causing easy bruising, darkening of the skin, seborrhea, and scaly white patches on the skin and elbows.

Seborrhea occurs when the sebaceous (oil) glands produce too much sebum, and can make the skin excessively oily, dry and very flaky, or both. There is often an overabundance of scaling, dandruff, and blackheads. It typically occurs most along the back, but because it creates a positive environment for yeast and bacteria, problems can be anywhere on the body. Seborrhea can be related to other diseases, including Cushing's or seborrhea can be hereditary. Acquired seborrhea will often be resolved with treatment of the underlying disease.

The hereditary form of seborrhea are called primary idiopathic seborrhea. Dog breeds prone to this genetic condition include Cocker Spaniels, Labrador Retrievers, German Shepherds, West Highland White Terriers, Basset Hounds, Irish Setters, and Shar-peis.

Bathing can help seborrhea, and two recommended brands of shampoos include Virbac's Sebolux ® and Dermapet's DermabenSs ® . Application of apple cider vinegar diluted with water (1 part vinegar, 4 parts water) has shown some promise in the treatment of this skin condition. Never apply this solution to any area of open sores.

Skin disorders can be caused by **bacteria (pyoderma), yeast (candida) or fungus (ringworm).** While a definitive diagnosis requires certain lab tests, you can learn to identify some common characteristics of all three.

Bacterial infections or pyoderma usually present as pustules, hair loss, and redness. Pyoderma may present as open sores and the pet will constantly lick and scratch the area. Pyoderma can develop secondary to other issues such as a flea infestation and the pet may develop what is commonly known as a **"hot spot" (acute moist dermatitis).** A hot spot is an area of skin that has become so irritated, red, inflamed, and itchy, your pet can't leave it alone. The area may become raw and bloody with possible hair loss. Not all hot spots are caused by a bacterial infection, but hot spots can quickly become a bacterial infection.

Bacterial infections can be treated with oral antibiotics such as amoxicillin or cephalexin or shampoos such as Malaseb ®. Areas of hot spots should be shaved and the pet bathed in Maleseb ® or an oatmeal shampoo.

Pet parents should avoid all hot spot treatments that have alcohol in the ingredients as these products can be painful and cause additional irritation.
An alternative hot spot treatment to the burning over-the-counter treatments, is to gently scrub the inflamed tissue with a Nolvasan ® and warm water mixture (1:2 ratio). Once the pet is dry, Farnam's Wonderdust ®, or NFC Puffer ® can be applied. Either will help dry the wound. Do not apply apple cider vinegar to a hot spot.

A highly irritated and inflamed hot spot can make it difficult for the the pet refuses to ignore. However, licking and scratching a hot spot only makes it worse. Use of an e-collar or similar product might be necessary to give the hot spot time to heal.

Elizabethan collars (E-collars) are the lamp-shade-shaped plastic collars that you can purchase from a veterinarian or from local pet stores. The purpose of the collar is to ensure that the pet has limited, or no access to the wound. Many pets and pet parents dislike the typical e-collar that it is made of stiff plastic and makes it difficult for the pet to eat or drink.

Alternatives to the Traditional E-Collar:

1. **The Bite Not Collar ®** : Similar to a neck brace that prevents the head from turning, this collar is effective for pets that have lesions on the torso and upper limbs. The collar is rigid so the skin should be checked for chaffing on the neck.
2. **The Soft collar**: Made by several manufacturers, this collar is still, technically an e-collar but it is made of a pliable fabric or a thick paper material rather than stiff plastic. This collar works well for relatively relaxed pets.
3. **The Comfy Cone ®** : Made by All Four Paws, this collar is softer than the plastic e-collar, but more rigid than the soft collars. The cone is made with ½ inch foam that has been laminated with a durable nylon fabric. The original inventor of the collar made her first out of an exercise mat when using a typical e-collar was impossible for her Great Pyrenees.
4. **Inflatable collars**: Similar to neck rests we buy for a plane trip, these collars are inexpensive and fairly effective for wounds on the upper chest.

Feedback and reviews seem to choose the Comfy Cone ® as the best for comfort and durability. It has the sturdiness to prevent the pet from reaching most areas, but the flexibility that allows the pet to eat or drink and not knock down everyone in its path. The price runs from $13.99-28.99. However, it can be washed and used again and again.

Yeast infections differ in presentation from bacterial infections. Yeast infections generally occur in moist areas such as the skin folds. The skin tends to be a little more greasy and red, the smell is more pungent, and the skin tends to thicken in affected areas. Yeast infections are common to Bulldogs and Shar peis, both breeds that have excess skin folds.

Malassezia dermatitis is a common yeast infection that is caused by the overgrowth of a fungus malassezia pachydermatis. The fungus lives on the skin of dogs, cats, and even humans, but the immune system keeps an overgrowth at bay. Symptoms are common for yeast infections but can also imitate seborrhea.

Treatment may included medicated shampoos such as Malaseb ® and a topical cream like clotrimazole. Since yeast infections flourish in a wet alkaline environment, an apple cider vinegar and water solution (1:4) can be made and applied to the affected areas to make the environment more acidic. Once the tissue is dry, Farnam's Wonderdust ® can be applied to keep it dry and encourage healing.

If symptoms persist, an endocrine disorder should be ruled out.

Another common fungus is **ringworm**. Ringworm is more common on the cat than the dog and is not, interestingly enough, a worm. The term "ringworm" came from the small circular lesion it leaves. Ringworm may be difficult to diagnose without doing lab work, which can take several weeks to get results. Vets often use an ultraviolet light source called a woods lamp ® to see if the lesions fluoresce, but this does not give a definitive diagnosis. While ringworm can be transmitted to humans, ringworm is easily treated. The same treatment for yeast infections (Malaseb ® and clotrimazole) are very effective in treating ringworm. If the fungus is severe, covering much of the body, the drug ketoconazole may be prescribed.

Some pets lick, scratch, and bite out of nervous habit. Often these pets are bored, lacking exercise, suffering from anxiety, separation anxiety, or compulsiveness.

Lick granulomas, also known as **acral lick dermatitis,** are the result of compulsive licking of the lower portion of the legs until the fur is missing. Eventually the area will develop into thickened tissue.
Obsessive licking does not have to be limited to the legs to be considered compulsive, however.

One of the most simple treatments for this disorder, and the best place to begin, is regular exercise. A bored pet is going to be destructive. If he doesn't destroy his surroundings, he will turn that compulsion of destruction inward. A pet that has been entertained and exercised is a happy pet and instead of licking compulsively, the pet will sleep soundly. If you are not home for several hours a day, consider getting toys to keep the dog busy, or maybe a small fish tank to entertain the cat. Whatever you can do to stimulate the mind and body can help stop this destructive habit.

For some pets, however, additional treatment is required. Medical treatments include clomipramine (Clomicalm ®) and fluoxetine (Prozac ®). Royal Canin ® developed a food called Calm ® that is beneficial to the skin and helps maintain a sense of relaxation. Calming difusers such as Feliway ® for cats and Adaptil ® for dogs emit pheromones that are said to do the same.

Another issue of concern is a neurogenic condition in which the pet has no feeling in an extremity or tail. Once, while working for a vet in downtown New Orleans, a dachshund, who had nerve damage in his front right paw, chewed the paw nearly off. Not only did he need to be put on medication for the obsessive chewing, his paw had to be wrapped and eventually amputated. He adapted well after surgery and learned to function with only three legs. Today, wheelchairs are available for dogs and cats that makes the post-amputation experience easier. Wheelchairs for pets can be purchased online and can even be home made using pvc pipe. A good source of information and ideas is www.handicappedpets.com.

There are times when skin disorders are caused by a combination of reasons. My wife's dog,

Abigail, had been on hydroxyzine and prednisone for years for what seemed like a hopeless skin issue. Abigail had to be covered in shirts and sweaters all the time or she would pull out her fur. When Abigail and her mom joined our pack, I took her to my vet, Dr. Kitty. After a brief exam and discussion with Haseleah, Dr. Kitty put Abigail on fluoxetine, recommended she remain on hydroxyzine, but discontinue prednisone unless absolutely necessary. In no time, Abigail improved. Her coat is beautiful and full and she can go without clothing. She is calmer and happier. Sometimes it just takes a second opinion and a veterinarian with a new perspective to solve a problem.

Upper Respiratory Infections and Kennel Cough

One of the most common illnesses in the feline is an upper respiratory infection, often simply called a URI. A URI can be viral or bacterial in origin. Similar to our head colds, a cat with URI may sneeze, have nasal congestion and/or discharge, have eye drainage and even conjunctivitis (swelling of the mucus membrane or pink part of the eyelid).

There are generally four causes of URI. It helps to know the different symptoms so the best treatment and isolation can be assured.

Common causes of upper respiratory infections:

- Herpes: fever, depression, loss of appetite, drooling, eye ulcers, lethargy, sneezing, eye and nasal discharge. Discharges may be more prevalent with herpes.

- Calici:oral ulcers, lameness, signs similar to herpes, only milder

- Chlamydia:mild sneezing, serious eye infection, called conjunctivitis

- Bordetella: fever, sneezing, lymph node enlargement, nasal discharge, harsh lung sounds and cough.

Any animal showing any of these symptoms should be isolated from other animals.

Viral infections must run their course and are not treated with antibiotics. Supportive care is of upmost importance with any viral disease. Simple home treatments can often help matters until the immune system fights off the offending cause. However, if nasal or eye discharge turns a yellow color, the pet has difficulty breathing, or begins to run a fever, the pet may need to be prescribed an antibiotic. These could be symptoms of a secondary bacterial infection.

If a cat is experiencing nasal congestion, the pet parent can move the cat in a small room such as a bathroom, and use a humidifier and/or vaporizer.

For cats who have a stuffy nose, a saline nasal spray, such as Little Noses ® may help. One or two drops in each nostril once daily can be given. Never use nose sprays such as Afrin ® that have any medicated ingredients. Good nursing care such as wiping discharge away from the nose and eyes when needed, is very beneficial.

When cats become so stuffy they cannot smell, they usually will not eat and are at risk for developing hepatic lipidosis. To make the food more fragrant, the pet parent can microwave canned food for 10 seconds or less, making sure the food is not too hot for the cat.

Nutri-Stat ® is a concentrated nutritional gel for cats that can be beneficial during this time as it can, not only provide essential vitamins and minerals, but sometimes even encourage an improved appetite. If the cat will not lick it voluntarily, a small amount can be put on the tip of the cat's nose which usually triggers a licking response.

To encourage the cat to drink, the pet parent can make an electrolyte solution as described earlier and/or supplement it with warm, reduced sodium chicken broth, or tuna juice. Always keep a fresh bowl of water available. Cats are more likely to drink from moving water, so a Petmate ® water fountain can be very useful. An alternative is adding a bubble stone to the water powered by a small aquarium pump.

Viral infections must run their course and are not treated with antibiotics. However, with the immune system busy fighting the virus, secondary opportunistic bacterial infections may take advantage. The vet may prescribe a tetracycline or doxycycline antibiotic and request the pet be quarantined.

Dogs most often have kennel cough as an upper respiratory illness. This is a virus that can be prevented by vaccine. The virus itself does not respond to antibiotics, but often antibiotics are given to prevent, or treat, secondary bacterial infections. A dog with kennel cough should not be allowed to come into contact with other dogs until the virus has taken its course. Generally this takes two weeks to a month.

Urinary Tract Disorders

There are several urinary tract disorders. The most common include infections, stones, incontinence, and kidney failure.

Urinary tract infections (UTI's) are not uncommon in either dog or cat. These infections are typically caused by bacteria. Symptoms include painful urination, blood in the urine, unusual frequent urination and/or frequent attempts at urination without urine production, and urinating in inappropriate places.

Infection usually sets up in the bladder first, and if left untreated, will move up into the kidneys. Once in the kidneys, external palpitation near the kidneys will illicit a painful response. A high fever may develop, and a loss of appetite, vomiting, and excessive thirst may occur. This is a serious illness and can cause the kidneys to eventually fail.

Female dogs are more prone to infections than male dogs, but older unneutered males are more prone to infection of a nearby organ called the prostate.

If you suspect urinary tract infection, you can often confirm your suspicions by collecting a bit of urine in a small bowl as the animal urinates and then testing the urine with urine strips. (For more information, see the chapter on in-home or in-rescue lab tests).

The use of urine test strips are not a substitute for a urinalysis or additional blood work. However, it can tell you if your suspicions that your pet is not feeling well is correct.

Early treatment of a urinary tract infection are important. The bacteria can develop resistance to antibiotics. This is also why using the correct kind and dosage of antibiotics is vital. Pet parents should avoid the overuse or improper use of antibiotics and should complete the medication given by the vet. These are necessary steps to prevent resistance to antibiotics.

Two common antibiotics for urinary tract infections include amoxicillin and ciprofloxin. Often doctors will start a pet on one of these drugs as they wait for a more detailed urinalysis.

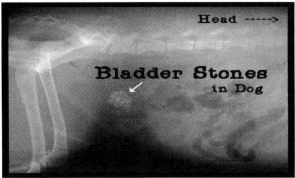

With inappropriate urination being one of the indicators of a urinary tract infection, it can be confused with **incontinence**. In older dogs in particular, incontinence can occur without an infection. As the body ages, the bladder becomes harder to control. Incontinence can have several causes including issues related to the muscles of the urethra, or the urethral sphincter. Generally the first drug that comes to mind with urinary incontinence is phenylpropanolamine (PPA), an inexpensive prescription drug that works in many cases.

Both dogs and cats can develop **urinary stones**, but they often have very different results. I have assisted in surgeries and have seen stones the size of golf balls in a small breed dog that had shown little complaint. On the other hand, I have seen male cats nearly die from a stone the size of a grain of sand. The difference, of course, is the width of the urethra.

Until the stones cause a blockage or irritation and the pet develops UTI symptoms, the pet parent often has no idea that there is a problem.

Radiographs (X-rays) or ultrasounds are often required to diagnose the problem. Whereas dogs can have kidney stones, cats tend to have stones (known as calculi or uroliths) in the bladder or the tube leading to the bladder or the one leading to the outside world.

This image shows the different sizes of stones found in one dog. The tiny specks are closer to the size you would find in a cat.

Unlike the dog, cats can develop small crystals in the urinary tract not associated with a UTI. These calculi are made when naturally occurring minerals in the urinary tract system, clump to form these crystals. Females are more able to pass the crystals, however, males can (and often do) experience blockage of the ureter. When this occurs, it is an emergency and if left untreated, the cat can die within 24-48 hours. It is important to note that both male dogs and cats are susceptible to urinary blockage. There is no treating this issue at home or "waiting it out". The pet must be sedated, and a catheter inserted to remove the blockage and allow for normal urine flow.

What we know about calculi, is how they develop, but not necessarily why.

Certain internal environmental conditions must be present including a prolonged high concentration of the calculi-forming materials and increased time of the presence of crystals within the urinary tract. That's why its important for your pet to drink adequately and be allowed to urinate on a regular basis. Expecting your pet to hold urine for extended hours is not healthy.

For the most common stones, improper pH of the urine can encourage stone development. Urinary tract infections, diet, and genetics may also play a part.

The environment of the urinary tract in cats and dogs needs to have a pH of approximately 6.2-6.5. Cats tend to have a more acidic pH. (The lower the pH, the more acidic while the higher the pH, the more alkaline) . Ranges too acidic (below 6.0) or alkaline (over 7.0) should be further investigated.

Uroliths or stones fall into three categories Knowing which stone is more prevalent is essential to knowing how to treat and feed the patient to avoid problems in the future. The most common stones or crystals are: **struvite (magnesium ammonium phosphate or triple phosphate), oxalate, and urate.**

Struvite crystals are the most common in both species. The best prevention for a cat is a diet low in magnesium and ash, and for dogs, preventing urinary tract infections.

Patients that have a history of stones are most often put on special prescription diets that are lower in protein to produce less ammonia. This is the standard treatment for dogs and cats who have suffered from a history of bladder stones.

Lower urinary phosphate and magnesium are also goals of prescription diets. which can help prevent certain stones. Calcium oxalate stones are unique in than they are more likely to form in urine that is more alkaline.

While prescription diets can be expensive, repeated surgeries and treatment of bladder stones are even more expensive. Care Credit ®, the health credit card that I highly recommend, will cover prescription diets, allowing you to pay for the food over time. Coupons are sometimes available as well.

Talk to your doctor about your alternatives. It may be possible to use certain urine acidifiers such as potassium citrate, cranberry, or Vitamin C to help maintain a healthy urinary

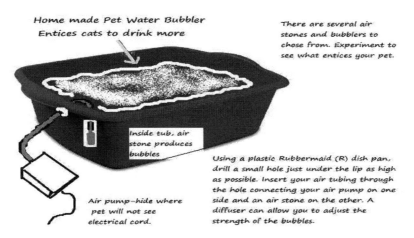

environment. In pets with a history of crystals or stones, never add acidifiers without consulting with your veterinarian.

One of the best preventatives for stone formation or urinary tract issues, is to make sure your pets drink plenty of water. Some vets recommend adding ¼ teaspoon salt to 1 pint of water (or 2 tsp per gallon) to encourage pet's to drink more. Salt is also added to some prescription foods for the same reason. I would recommend talking to your vet who knows the history of your pet before adding salt to the diet. Another method to encourage good hydration, is to feed good quality canned food rather than dry (or in addition to dry). Canned food has a high moisture content which can help keep your pet well hydrated. Most prescription diets are available in both dry and canned forms. Some pets like running water, particularly cats. Pet water fountains are available for cats that enjoy drinking from the faucet. A second option is an inexpensive home made water "bubbler" that can encourage stubborn cats to drink.

In cats, kidney disease most likely going to be part of the process in growing older. This is generally an issue that gradually occurs over a period of several years.

The kidney's main function is to process waste out of the body. If anything prevents that, the buildup of waste is not limited to the kidney, but throughout the blood stream. That is one reason why a person or pet with kidney disease is often nauseated. The name of this condition is azotemia. Issues other than kidney disease can cause azotemia, such as congestive heart failure and dehydration. Veterinarians classify kidney disease in stages.

Classification of kidney disease stages:

- Stage 1: No visible symptoms. This stage is only found by yearly urinalysis.
- Stage 2: waste starts to build up and the pet may urinate more often, but still no significant change is noticed.
- Stage 3: excessive thirst and urination begin to occur as the kidneys are working at only about 30-40 percent capacity. By this stage, the pet should be on a diet that does not put any undue strain on the kidneys. Often a prescription diet is required.
- Stage 4: vomiting, loss of appetite, and weight loss start to occur. The kidneys are functioning at only about 25 percent and more than likely, the pet will appear dehydrated and depressed. Often the vet will train the pet parents at this time on how to give subcutaneous fluids.

The treatment of end stage kidney failure if slightly different for the dog and cat. The similarities are encouraging fluid intake including supplying fresh water at all times as well as administering subcutaneous fluids. Medications may be given to assist with the nausea that often accompanies kidney failure. A diet change is a must, but the type of food differs for dogs and cats.

For dogs, this specialty diet needs to be low in protein, phosphorus, calcium, and sodium and high in potassium and omega 3 and omega 6 fatty acids. Thankfully, this complicated special diet is available from your vet.

Since the kidney cannot process phosphorus, phosphorus binders such as Epakitin ® may be added to the diet. Vitamin D supplements may also be added at the suggestion of your veterinarian.

Many pets may dislike this diet so it can be improved by adding a small amount of reduced sodium chicken or vegetable broth mixed with warm water. Add just enough to taste. Talk to your vet about other additives that are appropriate.

Cats also need a special diet, but their needs are different. The protein needs to be reduced but of a very high quality. This minimizes the levels of phosphorus and nitrogen the kidneys must process. Epakitin ® is not necessarily recommended in this case as it contains calcium which can be a problem for the cat in the later stages.

Vitamin B is lost in the cat in end stage renal failure, so it may be necessary to add it to the diet. There is a lot to consider when determining what vitamin B supplement is the best for your cat. Some contain alpha lipoic acid which can be toxic to cats. One recommended brand is Jarrow's B-Right ® which can be purchased online, but it does contain sugar and could be the wrong choice for a diabetic cat. It is best to consult with your veterinarian before choosing a vitamin B supplement.

Whereas special diets for dogs are often dry pellet food, it is better to feed end stage renal cats canned food as it stimulates the appetite and provides additional fluid to the diet.

UNDERSTANDING OUR PETS AND SOLVING BEHAVIORAL ISSUES

"If a dog will not come to you after having looked you in the face, you should go home and examine your conscience." ~Woodrow Wilson

19

Development of the Puppy and Kitten

Approaching the topic of animal behavior begins with understanding the physical, mental, and emotional development from birth. While the development of physical abilities (eyes opening, walking) varies depending on the breed, emotional skills develop at fairly consistent stages. This predictability gives us the opportunity to ensure that their social and coping skills develop well.

Puppies are born blind, deaf, and toothless. They are unable to regulate their own body temperature or urinate or defecate without outside stimulation from their mother or caregiver. They cry out when cold or lost in order for their mother to find them. Puppies will sleep most of the time, with their waking periods spent eating. It is important during this time that the puppy receive positive tactile stimulation. There is a concern regarding the effect tail docking has during this important period of 1-13 days old.

During the 13th-20th days following birth, the puppy's eyes and ears will open and the puppy will experience increased stimulation. He will begin to react to auditory and verbal stimuli. He will stand about the 15th day and be able to walk a few days later. The puppy will learn to interact with his litter mates and begin to play. It is exceptionally important that the puppy be handled by humans during this stage.

By 3-8 weeks, the teeth begin to erupt, and puppies will begin to eat solid food. During this time, the pet parents should feed some food by hand to discourage food aggression. The puppies movements become more coordinated, and they will begin to explore further from their mother. They also may interact will other dogs in the household (besides the litter mates). The puppies can identify their own species. Interestingly, however, puppies raised by cats will not recognize dogs as their species. During this time they they begin learning social skills as well as how to react to anxiety-provoking stimuli. Poor experiences can have a profound impact later in the lives of the puppies.

Weeks 4-12 are known as the socialization period. The puppy learns to bark around 4-5 weeks, and growl shortly afterward. The mother begins to wean the puppies between 4 to 6 weeks after birth. Puppies taken from their mother before this 6 week period, are not only socially challenged, but will not have the same immune system as a puppy who has been given the opportunity to be naturally weaned.

Puppies may go through a short period during which they react with fear, rather than curiosity at new things. During this period, the puppy should not be overstimulated with too many new experiences. Concentrate on a few experiences that the puppy will face often in the future. Encourage interaction with new people, for instance. Have friends come to visit and give him positive reinforcement. Fear of humans can be strongly imprinted during this stage of development.

Puppies always appreciate having their own safe place. If crate training is encouraged, he will have his own safe area and be easier to house break. Most puppies should be housebroken around 8 weeks of age.

As the pet progresses, he enters a period of intense curiosity. Puppies will usually seek to explore new environments. Play becomes rougher as the puppy becomes more confident. By 14 weeks, if puppies have not been allowed to explore new environments, they will cease to do so voluntarily and may become anxious and distressed if now forced to do so.

Around 20 weeks, dogs begin their journey to sexual maturity. Unneutered males will begin their marking behavior in earnest and females will begin the early stages of their first heat cycle.

Kittens begin life also blind, deaf, and toothless. That remarkable skill, purring, that humans love so much, develops by the second day following birth. They require outside stimulation by the mother or human caretaker, in order to urinate or defecate. By the 10th-14th day, the eyes open.

Separation from the mother or litter mates during this time can lead to fearful or aggressive behavior. Like puppies, kittens should be naturally weaned and kept with their mother until 6-8 weeks.

Between the 2nd-3rd week, the kittens can recognize their mother by smell and sight. The mother begins teaching them predatory behavior so they can find food in the future. By the 3rd week, the kittens can eliminate on their own.

About the 4th week, kittens are finally able to retract their claws.

Next, normal social play behavior begins and if exposed to other species such as humans or dogs, the kittens will show no fear. Exposure to humans is essential during this time. Again, having friends come over to your home during this time can help socialize the kitten.

At 5-6 weeks old, kittens can be easily trained to use the litter box and will begin using a scratching post if provided. Providing a post during this time can focus the kitten's scratching on an appropriate place, rather than on living room furniture.

All cats have a gape or flehmen response. This response is characterized by an open mouth, wrinkled nose, and raised chin, and its purpose is to facilitate pheromones from an area of interest to the vomeralnasal organ located in the roof of the mouth. This is usually done in response to other cat urine or feces, and provides needed information. By 7 weeks old, the kitten has this ability.
If kittens are handled during this seven week period, their confidence to approach new things increases. Handling by friends and family helps socialize the cat to be more comfortable with humans.

By 14 weeks old, social play is in full swing. Pouncing and stand up behaviors are more likely to initiate a response from another kitten. Play is more associated with predatory behavior and social fighting.

Kittens declawed during this time in particular, can experience profound behavioral changes, including developing aggression, biting, and urinating outside the litter box.

After 14 weeks, social play begins to decline. Males begin scent marking, and females can go into their first heat cycle between 4-10 months old. Kittens are normally spayed or neutered between 4-6 months.

20

Introduction to Miscommunication

While dogs and wolves descended from the same ancestor, dogs are not wolves. They are as genetically related to the wolf as we are to primates (between 96-99%). Those few percentage points make a great deal of difference.

For example, unlike wolves, dogs have evolved and have been bred to remain perpetually dependent on their family. Dogs are forever juvenile in that way.

We like to think of dogs as being "pack animals". We imagine the scene of the dominant alpha wolf ruling over the pack like a king. However, pack life is nothing like this. A pack is made up of a male and female (only one pair who are allowed to mate) and their relatives. The pack is a cooperative effort, not competition that makes them a successful, well-fed, hunting pack.

Animal scientist Dr. Temple Grandin takes it a step further in asserting that *"what the domestic dog (canis lupis familiaris) really needs is not a substitute pack leader but a substitute parent."*
http://www.fairfieldbeachaccess.org/coreemotionsofdogs.html

While domestic dogs share some of the same characteristics of the wolf, there is one huge difference: domestication. A domesticated dog has a brain that is 30 percent smaller than his ancestors.

In domesticating dogs, we changed the way dogs think, interact, look, and communicate with each other and with humans.

Cats on the other hand, have not changed all that much in regards to communication. Cats communicate with one another primarily by body language and cats communicate with humans by body language as well. We often misunderstand cats' body language and misinterpret the message, but the cats are consistent.

Both dogs and cats like to leave their scent on items to mark their territory, including us. The glands that do this can be found on the face, lips, head, paws, and anal area. The cat rubbing sweetly around our legs is leaving her mark on us. The dog who urinates on the freshly laundered bed is not doing it out of spite, but is returning a familiar comforting scent that you have washed away. The cat who marks the house, (including your bed) when you go on vacation isn't vindictive, but attempting to comfort him/herself just like the dog, with familiar, safe scents.

The more we understand how our pets think and communicate, the easier it will be dealing with all behavior problems. The lack of communication may be the only problem, but without seeing the world from the pet's perspective, we will never know. Meanwhile, more cats and dogs will be dumped at the shelter for misbehaving, when it was the pet parent who did not know how to communicate with the pet.

21

Perception: Seeing the World through their Eyes

In 1989 on **Star Trek: The Next Generation,** "The Ensigns of Command" episode, has a scene that was forever etched in my mind since it first debuted. In the scene, Counselor Deanna Troi, a half-human, half-Betazoid, with a gift to sense emotions, uses a very clear example of the difficulty of communicating with someone who does not speak our language:

Counselor Deanna Troi: "We are stranded on a planet. We have no language in common, but I want to teach you mine."

[she holds up her tea glass]

"S'smarith. What did I just say?"

Captain Jean-Luc Picard: "Cup... Glass."

Counselor Deanna Troi: "Are you sure? I may have meant liquid. Clear. Brown. Hot. We conceptualize the universe in relatively the same way. "

Captain Jean-Luc Picard: "Point taken."

So, when it comes to communicating with our pets, imagine what it must look like to our pets. We converse in complicated, symbol-driven, spoken word and our pets to understand us. Perhaps it is our failure that we have not attempted to understand how our pets communicate or how they perceive the world.

Imagine you and your dog go for a walk. Most humans view the world through our sense of sight. We look up ahead to see if there are any obstacles. We notice a couple lovingly holding hands, we gaze at the copse of trees near the park. We take in the beauty of the dew on the blades of grass. The fall colors reflect off the lake and the sun beams reach through the brilliant fall leaves and dances on the forest floor below. We are created to be sight dependent beings. Our eyes are made to focus on color, on detail, and to provide us with as much information as possible. We read the body language of those around us, to tell us if they are friendly or a threat. It is in this way that humans survive.

Humans have the ability to filter through sight, sound, and smell. While we are sitting in the park, we may not notice the bird sitting in the tree singing. We make a conscious effort to focus on that sound, and with effort, we can can see the forest for the trees. We can see individual trees. We can move close to the tree and observe the patterns on the bark.

Smell for humans is fairly insignificant compared to sight. Occasionally a smell will remind us of another time. The scent of a soap may remind us of summer camp years ago. Humans have a unique ability to adapt to a smell so much so, that they no longer sense it. Unless I have been gone from my home for a long time, I cannot smell the scent of the air freshener I use, or the welcoming smell that means dogs and cats live here. Yet, we don't depend on a sense of smell all that much compared to other animals.

Consider that you perceived the world through smell. Every thing that I see, my dog senses primarily through smell.

I see a leaf. My dog senses a leaf. The scent of the leaf will tell him how long its been since the autumn leaf fell to the ground; who has stepped on the leaf; and the breed of dog that has urinated on it. The scent also tells the dog that a cat passed by this way, and how long ago. The same type of information and more is coming from everything surrounding the dog. The dog is bombarded with information.

Humans have about six million receptor sites dedicated to smell. Dogs, depending on the breed, have many more receptor cells. The beagle, for example has over three hundred million receptor cells. While you may see a dog sitting perfectly still as bored, the nose is working, pulling in a world of information.

Cats "see" the world through their noses too which has 200 million receptor sites and a vomeronasal organ, otherwise known as a Jacobson's organ. The Jacobson's organ is located inside the mouth, just behind the front teeth. The organ connects to the nasal cavity. When you see your cat pull his/her lips back almost in a hiss, the cat is taking in the scent through the Jacobson's organ to better process it. This is called the Flehman response discussed earlier. You can guarantee there is definitely something interesting close by. Even indoor cats can detect cats outside by scent alone. No looking out the window required.

Dogs also possess a vomeronasal organ, but without the Flehman response.

Both dog and cats use their sense of hearing probably as a secondary sense in importance to the sense of smell. Human auditory range is from 20 hertz to 20 kilohertz. Compare that to the dog at up to 45 kilohertz and cats up to 65 kilohertz. Some dog breeds and most all cat breeds possess a pinna (outside ear) that functions as both a satellite and funnel. The ears can move back and forth to detect sound and funnel it inside to the eardrum.

Dogs with ears similar to that of the basset hound are not at a disadvantage, however. The droopy ears help stir up or even capture scents. Their ears enhance their sense of smell.

The eyes of the dog and cat work similarly. Cats are able to see in light that is six times our lowest limit. Dogs can see at about 5 times. One of the eye features called the tapetum, which is located at the back of the eye, is familiar to anyone who has pointed a flashlight at their pet only to see eyes that glow in the dark. Both the dog and cat possess larger pupils than humans and have more light detecting rods. Humans, in comparison, have more color detecting cones. This visual system allows both canines and felines to see in very low light and to detect the smallest movement and detail.

We see the forest. They see the trees.

Dogs and cats are also similar in the use of their whiskers which are called vibrissae. Vibissae have very sensitive touch receptors that serve as early warning signals as well as give the pet the added advantage when trekking in low light. Unfortunately, too often groomers will shave these sensitive receptors not understanding their importance.

Although there are some similarities, dogs and cats perceive the world differently from each other and even more profoundly from humans.

Alexandra Horowitz, in her book **Inside of a Dog: What Dogs See, Smell, and Know** goes into great detail regarding the canine perspective. Horowitz explains how experimentation supports this perspective and it is very helpful when it comes to training dogs.

Similarly, Dr. Myrna Milani, in her book **"The Body Language and Emotion of Cats: What your cat is trying to tell you."** opens the reader up to the world of cat communication.

22

Canine Body Communication

Dogs were kind enough to learn how we communicate, so it seems only fair that we learn the same about them.

We are often unaware of the importance of body communication because we are such vocal creatures. Yet we "read" one another every day. The "sixth sense" we attribute to some people is often just the ability to "read" human body communication very well.

This same communication is universal in mammals. Before we developed language and before dogs and cats learned to vocally communicate with us, there was body language.

Body communication among dogs is a universal language. Body language doesn't change between breeds or individuals. This form of communication is a combination of the facial expression, the position of the ears, tail, and fur.

A dog who is content often looks like he is smiling. The muscles of his face and body will be relaxed. His may have his mouth closed or slightly open and be panting softly. The natural upturn of the corners of his mouth give the impression of a smile. His ears are in their natural position and the eyes may be open and relaxed or give the impression he is about to fall asleep. His tail may wag in a soft circular motion.

If the dog suddenly stands up on all four paws, his eyes widen, and ears move forward, he is probably on alert and in search of the source of his concern. His tail will stop wagging and may fold over his back. He has an intense and focused appearance and his fur may start to raise. The dog may give a low growl, pulling his lips back, and turn his head and ears in the direction he senses the threat.

When it turns out that the dog has detected his buddy or his pet parent, he will remain on all fours, and may bow down indicating playfulness. The dog's ears may be up, his fur down, and his eyes bright. He will look at the dog or person that has peaked his interest, open his mouth and pant, or give a friendly bark and a happy tail wag. He may hop, leap, or run around the room. There will be no doubt that the dog is happy.

A frightened dog will tuck his tail between his legs and lower his head. The dog will lay close to the floor and do anything he can to make himself invisible or small. His ears will flatten and he will avoid eye contact. If you make a move, the dog may flinch and shut his eyes as if waiting to be hit. The dog will lick his lips and surprisingly, yawn.

The experience can go one of two ways based upon the dog's attitude. If the dog is submissive, he may roll over on his back to indicate he is not a threat. The dog may also urinate which is another sign of submission.

If the dog is fearfully aggressive, he will still make himself small, holding the ears down and tail close to the body. However, the dog will also pull back his lips in a growl and look at the source of the threat. Often the dog will lunge quickly with an open mouth and make a high pitched noise as if screaming. The dog will then retreat. Later on in the book I will tell you how to respond to a fearfully aggressive dog.

One other position of body language that is often times misinterpreted is mounting, a sign of dominance. In Tennessee, this humping behavior was grossly misinterpreted by the pet parent. The news read, "Tennessee man abandons dog for being gay." Thankfully the dog was adopted by a loving, well informed family.

Mounting is not a behavior exclusive to male dogs or to unaltered dogs. Spayed females may mount another dog as a sign of dominance, and many dogs will try to mount the leg of every visitor they meet. Our chihuahuas have even tried mounting Willow, our cat.

Hopefully this helps make it clear why it is so important to properly interpret canine body language.

23

Starting out on the Right Paw: Mistakes we Make from the Beginning

Pet behavioral issues are one of the toughest things for me to tackle. I deal with multiple pets in my rescue, most with issues that can make them unadoptable. I've rescued so long that the idea of a one pet home seems alien to me. Since we've stopped fostering to concentrate on the special needs pets we already have, our focus is on having a cohesive pack where everyone gets along and feels safe.

Behavioral problems are among the top ten reasons for surrendering pets to the animal shelter or giving them away. It is important to acknowledge that pet behavior is a two way street. Just as children need to be taught between right and wrong, so to must our pets be taught what is acceptable and unacceptable behavior.

Many times, the pet parent is not educated, prepared, or willing to provide that training. Most often it is our inability to learn to communicate properly with our pets.

It is very easy to adopt or buy a pet on a impulse. That kitten being given away for *free* is just so cute (and free!). Perhaps you going to the mall and come upon an adoption event and are reminded that the dog could be euthanized tomorrow if not adopted today. Maybe someone bought your child a pet for Christmas without even considering that your family may not be ready for the responsibility.

When pets are adopted, purchased, or gifted on impulse with a good-hearted intention, you often find yourself with issues you don't know how to handle. The expectations we have for that pet may be unreasonable, or you and the pet may simply be a bad match. Perhaps the breed is too energetic for you, or the cat doesn't enjoy being held.

So you have to ask yourself some questions and do some research before getting a new pet.

- What are you looking for in a pet? Are you looking for a pet who is very interactive with you or one who is more independent?
- How often are you home? If you are rarely home, do you really think its wise to get a

dog who needs to be taken outside to potty every few hours and who enjoys interacting with his human?

- What is your housing situation? If you live in an apartment and are gone all day, its difficult to expect many dogs to behave. Some breeds are meant to work. Putting a border collie or husky in a small apartment with nothing to do for hours, can mean a couch that is rip to shreds.
- What are you willing to invest in time and money? Will you take the time to walk the dog? If not, do you have the resources to have a fence installed in your yard or pay a dog walker? Are you willing to spend the money to take the pet to the vet when needed? How about professional training if needed? Do you have the time and money for training?
- What are your expectations for your pet? No shedding? Already potty trained? No barking? No getting on or scratching at the furniture?
- Would you enjoy a less interactive pet such as an aquarium full of beautiful fish?
- Who will be in charge of caring for the pet? If the answer is "the kids" expect problems. No matter how well intentioned that child is, he or she is a child and an adult should be ultimately in charge. If you are not willing to do that, then don't get the pet.
- Would you prefer a puppy or kitten you can train yourself, or an older dog that may already have some training?

You have to do research to see what is common in the pet you want. Different breeds of dogs were bred for different purposes and so have different needs and personalities. If you are a runner who wants a dog to exercise with, then you don't want a dachshund. If you love outdoor activities, labs and retrievers are great dogs for that. If you work long hours, having a dog may not be your best choice, so an adult cat has no problems sleeping the day away and then enjoying your company in the evenings.

Some things should be obvious. Long, heavy basset hounds are not physically created to run marathons with their pet parents. Chihuahuas are not created to be outside dogs who can be comfortable in the cold. Great Dane puppies are going to grow up to be huge.

However, the personality of a pet is not purely determined by their species or breed. While a certain breed of cat (like a Siamese) tends to be more vocal, not all Siamese cats are going to be. Most orange and white male cats are laid back and very friendly, but not all are. Like us, they are individuals.

No one is perfect. There are no guarantees. There are no guaranteed shed-free dogs, no perfectly potty trained puppies, no cat that will never be tempted to sit on your furniture or use it as a scratching post. If you expect perfection, don't get a pet. If you have no time to train a pet, adopt one that is already trained, but understand that you must do your part to keep a routine going. Think about how many times a day you have to go to the bathroom. What if you were allowed access to the bathroom only once, maybe twice daily? That is what is expected of many dogs. No wonder they soil the carpet. No wonder they get bladder infections.

Pets do not come to you with encyclopedic knowledge of proper behavior any more than a child does. Behavior is learned. You are the teacher. Acknowledge that perhaps you need more training and consistency and make it happen for you and for your pet.

24

Canine Behavior Problems

Excessive Barking

Excessive barking is probably one of the most common complaints from pet parents. The interesting thing is, barking may have been developed as a result of being domesticated by humans. Research has shown that in wolves, barks make up as little as 3 percent of wolf vocalizations. http://www.scientificamerican.com/article/what-are-dogs-saying-when-they-bark/

Dogs are social animals and they communicate with each other differently than they do with humans. Smell plays a big part (as anyone who has witnessed dogs smelling the rear of another dog can tell you). Not surprisingly, 33 % of a dogs brain is dedicated to smell compared to 5 % in humans. A sniff tells each dog where the other has been, what the other recently ate, if that dog has been recently anxious and scared. These are just a few of the things dogs learn in this process. Smelling is like a handshake and a five minute conversation among humans.

In their domestication, dogs became more vocal. Barking, whining, and howling are the three common vocalizations of the dog. Researchers have found that dogs use different barks for different situations. They recorded the "food growl" and "stranger growl" using a dog protecting a bowl of food and another at the approach of a stranger. They then put down a juicy bone, played each growl, and found that dogs were less likely to approach the bone when the "food growl" was played. Another experiment showed that dogs could differentiate from an "alone bark" and "stranger bark".

Humans are not very good at differentiating between the types of barking. In this same research study, researchers demonstrated that when these same kind of vocalizations were played for humans, most could only pick out the "stranger bark" among all of those provided. http://www.scientificamerican.com/article/what-are-dogs-saying-when-they-bark/

So it should go without saying that we, the humans, need to work on understanding the purpose of our dogs bark so we can find out what the excessive barking is all about.

So why do dogs bark?

The most common reasons for barking dogs include:

- Alert/Stranger: Normally this bark is loud and sharp warning that a stranger or threat is nearby.
- Excitement: This is usually the bark you hear when you come home or when its time to go for a walk.
- Anxiety: Dogs who experience separation anxiety will often have a high pitched bark. It is believed that this is a self soothing bark in an attempt to calm down.
- Boredom: The sound of a dog left in the back yard alone.
- Responding to neighborhood dogs: If you ever read or watched the movie **101 Dalmatians**, you should know that dogs will bark when they hear other dogs barking. Whether it is to pass important information about Cruella Deville, we may never know.
- Attention seeking: This is comparable to humans raising their hands in the air back and forth screaming "I'm here! I'm here!"

Dr. Temple Grandin in her book **Animals Make Us Human: Creating the Best Life for Animals** observed that dogs *"evolved to live and communicate with humans (barking is interpreted as a dog's attempt to mimic human language), are hyper-social and have evolved a hypersensitivity to the actions of humans: to the extent that dogs are not only easy to train but can train themselves. She writes that this is because our social reactions are reinforcing to dogs, and a dog becomes happy when his guardian is happy: over time, the dog notices what makes his guardian happy, and learns to behave in ways to evoke that response.* http://www.fairfieldbeachaccess.org/coreemotionsofdogs.html

In my experience in rescue, I have found that most dogs who were surrendered for excess barking, were bored, lonely dogs. Many had been on chains all their lives, or had little time with family or other pets.

Dogs are social creatures and most hate to be alone. When you adopt a dog, you become part of the dog's pack and the dog, part of your family. To be separated from that family is torture to a dog. This is why many rescues will not adopt to homes where the pet will be left outside in a kennel, fenced in yard, or on a chain. Living alone with little interaction is the worst possible life a pack animal can live. This is "doggie hell". So, why are we surprised when the dog barks?

Tips to stop excessive barking:

- Bring the dog in the home and make him part of the pack.
- Try to lessen the time the dog spends alone
- Give him/her interactive toys such as Kong ® brand toys

- Get your dog a friend. Two dogs can entertain each other if you are gone for long periods.
- Take your dog for walks. Go to the park. Dogs are full of energy and need a way to get rid of that energy. Replace the bored barking with an invigorating time at the dog park.
- Don't encourage excessive barking. Do not offer treats or petting to encourage silence. This tells the dog that you will reward her for barking.
- If the dog is barking, make a sharp sound such as a whistle or clap and redirect the dog's attention to something else. Once the dog is quiet, then offer a treat.
- Practice basic commands to get the dog to focus. If your dog sees you as the pack leader, then this will actually help calm him/her.
- If you need further assistance, a great resource is found here. https://www.aspca.org/pet-care/virtual-pet-behaviorist

We have an unadoptable rescued chihuahua named Bojangles. He came with four other chihuahuas when a backyard breeder dumped them all at the local shelter. The two male dogs, Rusty and Bojangles, were so terrified of people that we had to catch them with a slip lead in order to socialize them. Rusty, had a front leg that had been broken in multiple places and never reset. It was believed that the dogs had all been kept in a small cages all their lives.

Bojangles could not feel safe unless he was with a pack. Alone, he was terrified, but with a pack he seemed insulated from the fears of the world. Bo stayed with our established pack of medium to large size dogs and became a forever resident of T.Paws.

Bojangles has a barking problem. He will start barking and not stop until you get his attention. He doesn't seem to be barking at anything in particular. He just barks. It seems as if barking is what he does to calm himself.

Bo's best friend is Teddy, the most dominant dog in that pack. I believe it was Teddy and the pack that rescued Bojangles, not Haseleah and I. Teddy gives Bo confidence and one thing that seems to calm Bo the most: the daily howl.

Everyday, Bojangles stands up, puts his paws on Teddy's side, and together, they start what we call the "daily howl."

The daily howl is an unconventional ritual at T.Paws initiated by Teddy several years ago. Neither Haseleah or I initiate the howling. One by one, each dog joins in with Teddy and Bo, until all thirteen dogs are howling. It lasts less than a minute, sometimes a little more. When the howl is over, a wonderful sense of calm seems to embrace the entire pack, Bo included. Any disagreements they had during the day is forgotten, and they are a calm cohesive pack again. Thankfully, no neighbor is close enough to be disturbed by our daily howl.

Dogs love routine, and Bo loves the daily routine of the howl. He loves knowing that we wake up at a certain time, let everyone outside to potty, and begin making breakfast for all the T.Paws residents. They know that between 7:30-8 pm, everyone will get a snack. They are so connected to the rescue routine, they remind us when its time to do a scheduled task. Like clockwork, Abigail announces that it is treat time.

The idea of an instinctual need for routine makes me think that maybe barking is part of Bo's routine. If he was kept in a cage for the first several years of his life, all he had to do was bark. Take that away from him, and it causes anxiety. Averting his attention to something else seems to help without causing further stress.

It should go without saying that the beginning of a well behaved dog is structure. Teaching basic commands such as "sit" and "stay" are important in establishing boundaries for the dog. A dog without boundaries is like a teenager without boundaries. They will do as they please, when they please, and how they please. It makes for an obnoxious teenager and canine.

Having structure seems to have a calming effect on dogs much like routine does and it is very important in preventing unwanted behavior,

Potty Training

Potty training is another behavior that many pet parents have a difficulty with. As I have said, dogs love routine and if kept to a steady routine, they will potty train easier. Most dogs are also reluctant to urinate in the same place they sleep, making crate training a good method for potty training.

Puppies should always go outside after waking, playing, and before bed. Chose one spot in the yard where the puppy will go every time to go to the bathroom. As you go out, use a phrase such as "outside" or "go potty". The puppy will learn to associate the words to the task at hand. Be patient and wait until the puppy goes. When she does, show praise.

Depending on the age of the pet, feed in the morning and evening. Younger puppies will need to be fed more often. Water bowls should be removed at least an hour before bedtime.

Begin crate training as soon as you acquire your puppy or adult dog. Every dog needs a personal space and if used correctly, a crate becomes a home, not a jail cell.

By nature, dogs need a cave; a nice warm enclosed place to sleep. The crate should be large enough for the puppy or adult dog to get up, turn, and move around, but not so big that there is separate space for soiling. Some crates are made so they can grow with the puppy. While the initial expense may be a little higher, it will prevent you from having to buy multiple cages in the future.

Never put a potty pad in the crate. This not only encourages inappropriate soiling, but the potty pad can be chewed up and swallowed by a bored or anxious puppy. Puppies have died in this way.

Make the crate a pleasant experience. Feed your puppy in the crate and then take him/her immediately outside. Anytime you put the puppy in the crate, say "kennel up". In the future, anytime you need your pet in the kennel, you only need to use the words.

The first day you get your puppy, put the kennel in the living room with the family. Allow some of the playing to be in the crate. Toss a toy inside each time the puppy brings it to you. When puppy decides to nap, move her to the crate to take a nap but leave the door to the crate open. As soon as puppy wakes up, take her outside to potty.

At bedtime, move the crate to your bedroom.

Coax the puppy inside with a treat and put a durable toy inside. A towel or small blanket is also a good choice, but always check to make sure the puppy is not chewing or ingesting it or that it has not been urinated on.

While at some point, you may want the dog to sleep in bed with you, it is best to have the puppy sleep in the crate. It will be hard because puppies will cry and whine, but turn the light off, and allow time for the puppy to calm down. Taking the puppy out when whining only teaches her that whining will get her a reward. This will establish the crate as "home" and start training the puppy to hold urine.

For very young puppies, it is difficult to hold their urine for more than 2-3 hours, so you will probably need to get up at night to let the puppy outside.

For the first week you have the new puppy, keep the crate in the room you are in. Keep the door open except when you have to leave or at bedtime. This way, the crate is associated with being with the family.

If your puppy is on the floor, make sure the doors to other rooms are shut. Letting the puppy out of your sight gives the puppy the opportunity to use the bathroom without notice. You can also keep the puppy on a six foot leash as an alternative. Do the same when going outside. As the puppy becomes potty trained unsupervised run of the house can be allowed.

Every puppy is going to make a mistake. If you witness the puppy urinating in the house, interrupt her, taking the puppy outside to continue the important business. If you find the floor already soiled, rubbing his/her nose in it will not help. Modern animal behaviorists argue that positive reinforcement is more successful than negative punishment or dominance tactics. http://www.dogsmart.ca/cgi/page.cgi?aid=9&_id=54&zine=show

If you work for long hours, unless you have family at home or can arrange for someone to come to your home to let the puppy out to potty, it is not a good idea to have a puppy. Spending 8-10 hours in a crate while you are at work will only teach your puppy the lessons Bojangles learned early in his life existing in a cage...you have no choice but to soil the area you sleep in. Creating this situation is setting the puppy up for failure.

If your answer is to put the puppy outside while you are gone, keep in mind that puppies can find a thousand ways to get into trouble. They can dig under the fence or climb over it. They can dig up your prize begonias. They can get into your trash can and not only make a mess, but end up with "garbage gut." They can also be stolen.

It is imperative to find a way to keep your puppy busy while you are gone.

Nylabone ® and Kong ® toys come highly recommended depending on the breed and size of the animal.

When you are choosing a toy for your dog, ask yourself these questions:

- How easy would it be for my pet to swallow this toy? Tennis balls may be good for a small dog, but a large dog can swallow it easily
- Is there anything on the toy that can be a potential choking hazard? (plastic eyes, nose, bells, etc?)
- Are the toys made of cheap rubbery plastic? (many look like a steak, hotdog, hamburger, etc and are usually sold in discount stores)

If the answer to any of these questions is yes, throw it out.

While many say never to give rawhide to dogs, I disagree. However, there are some guidelines I go by:

Guidelines to giving rawhide to your pet:

- Never buy rawhide or any treat supplied by Chinese companies. Numerous dog deaths have been linked to treats from China. Many big brand names use China-supplied ingredients, so read the labels. You may pay more for America-**sourced** and American-**made** products, where standard are in place to prevent the contamination that caused pet deaths. Until Chinese companies can deliver a proven, safe product, buy American.
- Buy pressed rawhide. Pressed rawhide lasts much longer and is safer for your pet.
- Supervise your pet. Assuming you have taught your dog the "drop it" command, take the rawhide away when it is small enough to be a potential choking hazard.

Don't leave your puppy running free in the home until he/she learns what is okay to chew on. If you catch your pet chewing on something inappropriate, replace it immediately with a chew toy. Even if you have a shoe that you are no longer using, don't give it to the dog to chew on. You are establishing that it is okay to chew on shoes, not just *those* shoes.

Also, don't allow your puppy to chew on you. While it seems sweet at the time, it makes you a chew toy, and not a good example once the puppy grows up. When your puppy tries to chew on you, give him/her an appropriate toy.

It is also a good idea to rotate toys. Don't make all the toys available at once. Rotation keeps the toy new and refreshing and helps prevent boredom.

Excessive and Inappropriate Digging

Just like most every dog likes to chew, they also like to dig. Excessive and inappropriate digging is another issue altogether.

Whether its digging holes in the yard, under the fence, or digging a huge hole in the couch, left to their own devices, dogs can do some damage.

I have learned that giving a pillow to sleep on is a disaster waiting to happen for Teddy and Scrappy. The stuffing inside won't be inside for long. They will dig until they get the pillow open.

Some dogs will dig up the linoleum, your bed mattress, and more.

So why do dogs dig? For Teddy and Scrappy, this is done in the pursuit of the perfectly comfortable bed. It is natural for dogs to dig a little when preparing to sleep, but if your dog feels the need to dig as much as our dogs, replace the pillow with a blanket. If there's one thing I've learned in my multi-dog household, dogs are as happy with a thrift store blanket as they are with a $50 name brand bed.

If your dog is a digger, there are some things you can do. Since your dog is digging in the yard or has dug into the couch cushions, chances are, the dog is bored and unsupervised. The happiest, most content, and obedient dog in the world is one who gets regular exercise and comes home exhausted to a nice place to sleep.

Dogs are like teenagers. They are full of energy and if that energy is focused in a positive way, its great. If left to figure out a way to release the energy, both the teenager and the dog will probably find trouble.
Dogs that will most certainly dig under a fence, in the yard, in the house, are unneutered male dogs. Nature has given the instinct to breed to all species. Unlike humans who can breed any time, dogs breed when the female is in heat. Therefore male canines can detect a female in heat up to a mile away (and perhaps more). The instinct is so strong that unneutered dogs remain frustrated much of the time. So, they do what their instinct tells them. Dig, escape, and get to the female. This is just another reason to neuter your male dog.

Where your dog digs can be an indication of why he is digging.

Digging up against the house or foundation of a building, can indicate that your dog does not have a sufficient shelter.

Digging in the middle of the yard or near a burrow can mean that your dog detects a burrowing animal underground. Do not put poison out to kill that animal, or you may kill your dog instead. Often putting the scent of a natural predator for that species can be helpful to get the burrower to move elsewhere. Cat urine is a great one, and if you have a litter box, you have free deterrent. Put some urine soaked litter inside the hole, but keep your dog away from the area for a few days. Other good options include hot pepper sauce, cayenne pepper, and citronella oil.

If your dog is digging under the fence but is already neutered or a female, he or she is probably bored and trying to escape. In addition to alleviating boredom and loneliness, you can put large rocks along the fence line or bury chicken wire under the fence.

If you've increased your dogs exercise time, neutered and/or spayed your dog, and he/she still digs, consider crating the dog when the family isn't home. If you can, come home during lunch to let the dog out to potty or have a neighbor or professional pet sitter or dog walker do it for you.

If you find yourself with a dog that needs more exercise than you can physically provide, do what one of my pet sitting clients did for their dog...a treadmill.

When their male pit bull (neutered) was a puppy, they began to train him to walk on the treadmill. The training was done over a period of weeks.

Steps to training your dog to run on a treadmill:

- First, make sure the treadmill is not pointed toward the wall. To the dog, it will seem like walking into a wall and go against all of his/her instincts.
- With the treadmill off, put the puppy or adult dog on the platform and reward with a treat. You want the platform to be a positive place, so give a treat only when the dog is standing on the platform.
- With your pet close to the treadmill (but not on it), turn the treadmill on and reward the dog. Don't move to the next step until the pet is comfortable with this.
- Turn the treadmill to the slowest setting with the pet nearby. Walk on the treadmill yourself while someone is sitting to the side with the dog. Reward the dog for remaining calm.
- Next, put a leash on the dog and put him/her on the treadmill and start at the slowest setting. Hold a treat or toy in front of the dog just out of reach. This should get the dog to focus on the treat and not so worried about the movement of the belt.
- After about 30 seconds to one minute, reward the pet with the treat/toy.
- Gradually increase the time the pet is on the treadmill. You can also gradually increase the speed as the dog gets used to the exercise.
- Never leave the dog alone while on the treadmill and **do not tie his leash to the treadmill**. If the dog trips, he can be choked or injured in other ways.

My clients' dog had been exercising for 20 minutes every day since he was a puppy and at 9 years old he looked as if he was no more than 2 years old. He was well behaved and very healthy and had none of the destructive or inappropriate problems many dogs have.

Separation Anxiety

A topic that many pet parents face is a dog with **separation anxiety**. Sometimes the negative behavior your dog is displaying is, in fact, separation anxiety.

Signs of separation anxiety include:

- Excessive barking as soon as you leave. The barking will be persistent and only occur when you are gone. Many times neighbors will be quick to let you know about this. To confirm it, drive a block away from home, get out of your vehicle, and listen.
- You may notice that the dog digs at the floor by the door or chews at window sills, or door handles.
- Objects in the house may be destroyed and the dog will be exhausted and anxious when you return home.
- The dog may pace or try to break out of confinement.
- These bad behaviors only occur when out of the presence of the pet parent.

Many years ago, I went to visit some friends and took my dog Cuddles with me as it was several hours away from home. He had never shown any signs of separation anxiety, so I thought nothing of it as I left him in our room with his bed and toys as we went out for supper.

When we returned my little 10 lb dog had dug the carpet up at the door and even pulled the entire panel of the wooden door off. He was absolutely terrified and I felt horrible for his fear and the damage to the room. Thankfully, the friends were understanding, but I had my first very real experience with separation anxiety in dogs.

A change in location and routine triggered Cuddles episode. Once we were home and he was in familiar surroundings, he had no problem being left at home while I was working or in class.

Causes of separation anxiety include the loss of a family member by death, divorce, going off to college, or similar situations. Moving into a new home with unfamiliar surroundings and smells can also trigger separation anxiety. So can being dumped in an animal shelter. Thankfully not all rescue pets develop the problem.

There is no easy answer for separation anxiety. The condition takes time and patience to deal with.

Guidelines for dealing with separation anxiety:

- Take the dog for a walk before leaving. A dogs natural instinct after exercise is to rest. Exercise causes the body to release endorphins which serves many purposes, one being a sedative effect.
- When you do leave, avoid eye contact with the pet, say goodbye, or do any thing that will indicate that leaving is a big deal.
- Don't make your return a big deal either. Although you want to celebrate with the pet, your purpose is to teach the dog that he/she is safe whether or not you are home.

- Prove to the dog that you will come home. Leave for a few minutes at first. Drive around the block and come back in. Increase the time and always be sure that you are calm when you leave and calm when you come home.
- Make sure your pet has an interactive toy to keep busy.
- Recondition the pet. Routines usually create a calm atmosphere for most dogs. However, the routine you practice when you are getting ready to leave home, signals the dog that you will be leaving and he will be alone. A dog with separation anxiety will spend the entire time leading up to your departure building anxiety. Whether you are getting dressed, making coffee, gathering your keys, wallet, purse, or cell phone, the dog has been conditioned to associate those actions with a negative experience. Recondition the pet to associate those sounds and noises with positive experiences. Make the sound of picking up your keys a positive thing. Pick them up, sit down and watch tv with the dog on your lap. Put your coat on and feed the dog. Open the garage door and give a treat. Repeat this over and over at different times of the day so that those sounds and sights are not so frightening and are not associated only with you leaving.
- Provide a safe place to rest. A dog that has a safe place to rest will be less anxious. Providing a crate with a blanket to crawl under can make your pet feel much calmer.
- Bring a new pet in who is calm. Communication between dogs can often be much better than that of human and dog. Bojangles, takes his cues from the other dogs. When they are calm, he is calm.
- A food available from Royal Canin ® named simply "Calm" has been shown to help. According to the company, the food contains two amino acids including the peptide Alpha-casozepine as well as L-tryptophan which have been shown to have calming effects. Also included is vitamin B3 also known as Nicotinamide which calms the central nervous system. It is especially good for animals that have gastroentestinal issues with their anxiety as it helps regulate the transit of food through the digestive system and encourages healthy flora within that system. The food creates a urinary environment that discourages the formation of crystals that lead to kidney and bladder stones. Calm ® is said to promote healthy skin and teeth. It is very expensive at about $6.80 per lb. It is primarily for dogs under 33 lbs. Daily recommended amount to feed ranges from ½ cup for a 4.4lb dog to 2 ¼ cup for a 33.1 lb dog. It takes about a month to see a change, so talk to your veterinarian about sample bags and the possibility of adding the amino acids and vitamins to the dog's regular food.
- Prescription medication is available to help your dog. Clomipramine is the most common medication, but others are also available.
- Pheromones are chemical communication between members of the same species. Calming pheromones are available in collars, diffusers, and sprays and are made specifically for dogs or cats. Feliway ® mimics a cat's F3 facial pheromone that is used to mark an area, making it a safe place. D.A.P. ® (dog appeasing pheromone), also sold

under the name Comfort Zone ® mimics the pheromone mothers release to comfort puppies. Other products use essential oils to simulate comforting pheromones. Studies on the efficacy of these treatments have been mixed. A systematic analysis of all available and relevant pheromone studies was conducted and published in the **Journal of the American Veterinary Medical Association**. Studies conducted or funded by the manufacturers were not included as the results had a high probability of being biased. The review included links to all of the studies discussed. The reviewers concluded that *"11 of the 14 reports reviewed provided insufficient evidence and 1 provided lack of support for effectiveness of pheromones for the treatment of undesirable behavior in cats and dogs."*
https://www.avma.org/News/Journals/Collections/Documents/javma_236_12_1308.pdf

Noise Anxiety: Thunderstorm/Fireworks

In Southern California thunderstorms weren't an issue, but the 4th of July celebrations were hell on the dogs. In Tennessee, the dogs have had to deal with both.

There are several things you can do to help a dog coping with anxiety during a storm or 4th of July fireworks.

- If your dog is outside, bring the dog inside.
- Turn on the radio or television and pretend like nothing is happening. If the dog senses your anxiety, it will only confirm his own.
- Close the curtains and turn on the lights. I've noticed that the more lightening my dogs see, the more anxious they become. Dogs are conditioned, just like we are, to know that lightening precedes loud cracks of thunder. Bold, bright lightening is intense in a dark room with windows, however, that brightness can be diluted by turning the lights on in the room the dog is in.
- Have a nice safe space for your pet to retreat to. Dogs and cats both feel safer in small, enclosed spaces. If your dog has been crate trained, let him get in his kennel and cover the kennel with a sheet or blanket.
- Thundershirts ® can be very effective. Thundershirts apply gentle pressure throughout the body that has an excellent calming effect. While not 100% effective, many dogs and cats respond very well to the shirt. The shirt is also good for travel, for trips to the vet, and other anxiety-provoking situations.
- A drug called acepromazine is a prescription medication that sells by the hundreds in veterinary hospitals prior to the 4th of July. Acepromazine is an anti-anxiety medication that can be quite effective. The drug should never be given to a pet with a history of seizures. It should be given 30 minutes to 1 hour prior to the event if possible. Dosage is .25-1 mg per lb of body weight.

- If a prescription medication is not available, Benadryl ® (diphenhydramine), can sometimes help. The drug is given at 1 mg per lb of body weight.

Aggression

A behavioral problem that can be very scary is aggression in any form.

There are several types of aggression found in puppies and adult dogs:
- Food, bone, or toy aggression
- Territorial or protective aggression (protective of the family)
- Fear/defensive/protective aggression (protective of the self)
- Tethered, chained, confined aggression

Food, bone, or toy aggression is a common form of aggression in which the dog will growl, protect the object with his/her body, and even bite the person who reaches for it. This is a very dangerous form of aggression and one that many rescues and animal shelters use to determine if the pet is a good candidate for adoption.

Children and visitors should never be allowed near a dog with this type of aggression when the pet is eating or has a bone.

I have had this issue with some rescue dogs. When it happened, the dog was fed separately from the other dogs and never ate unless I was feeding him by hand or holding the food bowl. In doing so, we established trust and now I can pick up the bowl even as he is eating. In fact, every time I feed now, I pick up all their bowls before they are finished eating and when they show no aggression, give them the remaining food. Not one dog growls at me now. Most of the dogs I work with are small breed dogs. If you are working with a larger, stronger breed, I recommend this website https://www.aspca.org/pet-care/virtual-pet-behaviorist/dog-behavior/food-guarding as well as books by Jean Donaldson found on Amazon. Both have a much slower and safer approach than I use myself.

Dogs are naturally territorial of the home or area in which they live. While **territorial or protective aggression** can seem endearing in the small breeds, it is frightening and dangerous in larger breeds. The problem occurs when everyone but the immediate family are considered intruders.

One has to consider what will happen if police, firefighters, or paramedics are dispatched to the pet parent's home. Will emergency personnel be allowed into the house? Will the police feel that their safety is in question and shoot the dog?

No matter how endearing this protective nature of the dog can be, encouraging it can be a danger to others and to the dog himself.

If your pet is a puppy, discourage aggressive behavior before it starts. Basic training, such as "sit-stay" commands, and socializing the puppy are great way to begin. Have friends come over while your pet is still a puppy and have them play with the puppy or give a treat or toy. This makes the sounds of knocking on the door or a ringing door bell a positive, rather than negative sound. Another good idea is to teach your dog to go lay down in his/her bed on command. My phrase is "kennel up" because they have their own kennel "home". You can also use "bed" as an alternative.

Keep in mind your reaction to those sounds are noticed by your dogs. Having agoraphobia and social anxiety, makes me very uncomfortable with people (other than my parents) coming to my home. I am very private and get very anxious if someone comes in my driveway. My dogs have all picked up on my emotions and are more territorial than they should be. If someone comes to the door, I go outside. If for some reason the visitor has to come in, I put all of the dogs in their room and away from the guest.

Steps to change that behavior take time. Research has shown that dominance-based training only increases the level of aggression in dogs.
https://apdt.com/pet-owners/choosing-a-trainer/dominance/

The "show 'em whose boss" mentality is considered counterproductive. Most supporters of dominance training refer to the social order of the wolf pack even though we now know that dogs are wolves as much as humans are chimpanzees.

The mentality of wolves constantly fighting for dominance is, in fact, incorrect. Studies of wolves show a more cooperative society. Although everyone has a place in the pack, dogs lowest on the "totem pole" are not there because they couldn't fight well enough.

According to The Association of Professional Dog Trainers (in the link given above): "*Dogs that use aggression to "get what they want" are not displaying dominance, but rather anxiety-based behaviors, which will only increase if they are faced with verbal and/or physical threats from their human owners. Basing one's interaction with their dog on dominance is harmful to the dog-human relationship and leads to further stress, anxiety and aggression from the dog, as well as fear and antipathy of the owner......For dogs with behavior problems, trainers employ programs such as "Nothing in Life is Free (NILIF)" which works along the principal that the dog must "do" something to earn what he wants (i.e. sit to get dinner, walk on a loose leash to move forward, etc.) These programs are effective because the dog is issued a structured set of rules that are consistently reinforced and the dog learns what he needs to do in order to get the things that he wants such as food, petting, playtime, etc. Because dogs do not have the power of human speech and language, behavior problems and anxiety can result when they are left to*

fend for themselves in deciding how to live in our world without guidance that makes sense."
Fear/Defensive/Protective Aggression: Humans and animals both possess what is called the fight-or-flight response. This response is a physiological survival mechanism that takes over in situations that may be *perceived* threatening or harmful. The fight-or-flight response is a cascade of hormones that gives us often involuntary responses to save ourselves.

Whether human, dog, or snake, most would prefer the "flight" option and just avoid the situation. However, much too often that is not a choice and the animal will display a **fearful, defensive, or protective aggression.**

Fearful dogs may run to corners or under a couch or chair. They may shake and growl. The body may be flattened against the wall or floor. Dogs who are put in a situation in which they are frightened but cannot escape will often quickly nip at the person and retreat again.

This is one situation where it is important to have a dog's view of the world. Imagine having someone four to six foot taller and much stronger than you, leaning over you. This "monster" is showing his teeth, but you don't know if it is a smile or a sign of aggression. The individual is reaching for you and talking, but you don't understand the language. Is the person reaching for you to hurt you? You have no idea, but your instinct says this is bad; Very bad.

You try to run and hide, but the "monster" follows. He reaches for you. You have no where to go. So you fight back.

That's what happens when you, a stranger, walks up to a dog, reaching out to touch her. You may be the nicest person in the world with the best of intentions, but how does the dog know that?

That is why dogs, most often small dogs, get a bad rap for being biters.

If you are going into the home of a small fear biter, the best thing to do is to ignore the dog.

If you are going to visit a friend who has a little "ankle biter", walk in the house pretending the dog is not there. Tell your friend not to fuss at the dog and not to pick the dog up, but ignore her. Sit down at the kitchen table and continue to ignore the dog. Don't look at the dog in the eyes or acknowledge the dog in any way. After a while, move from the kitchen table to the couch. Continue to ignore the dog.

What is this telling the dog? That you are not a threat and are not even interested in her. In addition, ignoring bad behavior is the easiest way to transform bad into good behavior.

Often times, after ignoring the dog, she will jump up on the couch and come closer to you gradually. Continue to ignore the dog. Sit back and keep your arms down. Never reach out to the dog no matter how close she comes to you.

It is not unusual after doing this, for the dog to finally move close enough and sit on your lap. Allow your hand to lay close to the dog, but not on the dog. If the dog reaches out to your hand, move it a little closer and pet the dog in a non-threatening place such as the side. Don't rub the head or behind the neck. Don't talk to the dog or even look at her. Looking in the eyes in a dog who is not comfortable with you is a threatening glare and can cause the dog to bite. If you follow these instructions, chances are, you will make a new friend.

One thing I did as a pet sitter in a situation where the dog was a small, fearful one, was to have the pet parents give me a recently worn piece of clothing such as a shirt when I went for the initial interview. I would keep the shirt in a zip lock bag until it was time to go in the house once the pet parents left for vacation. Upon entering the house, if there was a fenced in back yard, I would walk in the front door, through the house, and exit out the back door, not acknowledging the dog. Usually the dog followed, and while I walked around admiring the landscape, the dog would potty. I would walk back into the house and the dog would follow. I then would take a couple pieces of the dogs kibble, put it in my left hand and sit on the left side of the couch so the dog would have to cross me if he wanted a treat. I would then lay the shirt across my lap. I didn't look at the dog, but sat quietly. Often I would turn the television on like the pet parent would do if sitting in the living room. Then I waited. It generally wasn't long before the dog was on my lap eating the kibble. I didn't rush to pet or pick up the dog. For the first few days of the visit, the dog would eat his meals out of my hands only, not in the bowl. We established a trust which made the visit rewarding for both of us.

For those of us who foster special needs dogs, particularly fearful dogs, you learn what is perceived as threatening. If you find yourself a foster parent of a dog this type there are a few additional things that will help.

Make yourself appear smaller. If the dog is a small breed, lay down on the floor. Don't say a word to the dog or acknowledge he is there. Read a book, listen to soft music, take a nap. If the dog is not approaching, lay a few treats in a trail toward you. I may start snacking on pieces of cereal while I'm laying on my stomach. Repeat this process a few times a day. Eventually, the dog will be coming up to you. Share a Cheerios or two with him, but avoid looking the pet in the eye until you have established total trust.

Once I have started the road to trust, instead of laying down, I will sit down and repeat the procedure. Let the dog come to you. When the dog does come, don't get excited and immediately pick up the dog. Make all your movements slow and your voice quiet. Until the dog feels confident that you are to be trusted, he is ready to bolt at any time.

So, as a person who loves dogs and who would love to pet every one that you meet, you have to learn to control wants and respect the dog's needs. Instead of approaching a dog, let the dog approach you. If the dog is on a leash, ask the pet parent if it is okay to pet the dog. Never bend over the dog. Instead bend over with the dog slightly to your side and hold you hand out. Let the dog approach. If she wants to be petted, you will know it.

The problem with bending over a dog is two-fold. One, you are performing a move that can be interpreted as threatening by the dog. Second, you are putting your face within lunging distance from a potential bite.

If you ask the pet parent if it is okay to pet the dog and the answer is no, never say "but dogs love me" as you reach out for the dog. There is a good reason the pet parent said no. Not only may the dog be a fear biter, but a dog protective of the pet parent as well.

As I was training Ms. Ruby to go out with me to help keep me calm, this was the biggest problem I had. When we are out in public, Ms Ruby detects when I am anxious and/or having a panic attack. She responds to me gently, putting her paw on my chest or getting me to pet or hold her until I calm down. However she senses my tension when people walk up to me. Generally, when we go into a store, I put Ruby in the shopping cart, hoping that my anxiety will be less obvious to her. She sits perfectly and people remark at what a good dog she is. She wears a vest identifying her as a PTSD companion dog that also reads "do not pet". So what's the first thing people do? Reach out to pet her. Not only are they coming close to her, but to me as well. The situation then cascades. I get tense, she growls, I get more tense, she becomes even more protective of me.

If I hold her in public, she feels my muscles tighten, my heart begin to race, my breathing change. She senses my agitation, my anxiety. I have a need for a lot of personal space, so when it is invaded even with good intention, my own fight-or flight response is triggered. I want out of the store and I want to go home. But I'm in a store check out line. I can't go forward, I can't go back. So by instinct, I am ready to fight, and so is Ms Ruby.

I tell you this to make a point. People generally take their dogs in public to socialize them, which is a good thing. But not all dogs are ready to be social and many are protective of their pet parent, anxiety issues or not. So don't assume that just because you have had good experiences with dogs in the past, that all dogs will respond positively. Always ask to pet a dog and if the pet parent says no, respect that.

If your dog is larger and on a leash, you can indicate your anxiety through the leash. If you are on a walk and you are afraid your dog will act aggressively toward the people or dog approaching you , you tend to pull back on the leash. This tells the dog that there is something to be concerned about and the dog can immediately becomes defensive.

Humans emit a different scent when we are frightened, that dogs can sense. Dogs can also read our body language better than we can read theirs. If you have a defensive dog, make yourself aware of your own feelings at the time. You may find that like me, you are the trigger.

Over time, the fear biter, such as the one described in the visitor scenario, can become a protective dog. This dog will become aggressive if someone sits next to his pet parent on the couch or if that same someone gives the pet parent a hug when leaving.

This is when the training to "sit" and "stay" come in handy. If you have not taught these things to your dog, it is best to find another area of the house to keep your dog during visits until your dog has mastered these basic commands.

Regarding tethered, chained, or confined animals, Desmond Morris once wrote in his book **Dogwatching**:

"[Dogs] are social beings and they are also intensely exploratory. If they are deprived of companions -both canine and human- or if they are kept in a constrained or monotonous environment, they suffer. The worst mental punishment a dog can be given is to be kept alone in a tightly confined space where nothing varies."

Tethering does not refer to the practice of tying your dog outside for a few minutes to go to the bathroom but a life bound to a stake and chain.

When I was a cruelty investigator almost every call that came into the office regarded a dog on a chain or tether.

Often, the pet parents didn't intend to put the dog on a chain when they adopted the dog as a puppy, but they found some reason for the dog to be there as the puppy became the adult dog. They couldn't potty train the dog. The kids wouldn't take the dog for a walk "which was the kid's responsibility". The couple had children and didn't think it was safe to have the dog near the children. The dog showed some type of aggression. The dog shed too much. The dog dug up the carpet or furniture. "Dogs don't belong in the house." There were always excuses.

I was called when the dog had no food, was losing weight, had no water in the summer heat or only frozen ice in the winter months. They often had no shelter. Sometimes the chain or collar had grown into the dog's flesh or the lhasa apso that was once a beautiful dog, was now covered in mats so tight, you could barely recognize the dog was a dog. Fleas, mange mites, ticks and fly bites covered the dogs in the summer. Only the winter brought relief only to be replaced by freezing nights with no way to find warmth. They were rained on, left to live in mud and their own feces. One dog barked, so the owner threw boiling hot water on the dog giving him second and third degree burns. And how could he get away to find help?

In another cruelty case, an unspayed female was mated by passing unneutered male dogs. She couldn't get away as she was on a thick chain. When she had the pups, it was the middle of summer with no shade whatsoever. The mother was so malnourished she could barely produce any milk. So the puppies crawled away, perhaps trying to find sustenance. They were out of her reach and no matter how hard she pulled, she could not reach her puppy. She could only watch it die. Maggots consumed the dead puppies and more of those same fly larvae feasted on the mother dog's neck where she had worn it raw trying desperately to reach her pups. By the time I was called the mother was so hungry, when I released her from her tether, she consumed her own dead puppy. That was life on a chain.

Most dogs had only a six foot radius to move. Nothing but the same thing to look at day in, day out. Bound to a world alone with the only human contact being when the family remembered to feed the dog, which wasn't always every day. They might use a continuous free feeder that let food down as it was eaten. In that case it might be a week or more before the dog experienced any human contact.

So it only followed that the dog barked all the time, dug holes in the ground, and eventually, after months and years pulling on the chain to escape the insanity of constant confinement, broke free only to attack a human. The human who chained the dog up was surprised at the dogs viciousness and it was the dog, not the owner, who was eventually was punished by euthanasia for hurting or killing another.

Dogs that are chained (particularly unneutered male dogs) are 2.6 percent more likely to bite than unchained dogs according to research.
http://enhs.umn.edu/current/6120/bites/dogbiterisk.html

The once friendly, happy-go-lucky puppy changes when confined alone. He becomes a neurotic, anxious, unhappy, and eventually, aggressive dog. It is one reason dog fighters keep their dogs on chains instead of kenneled. The energy the dog needs to release, that in a normal situation is done by play or walks with pet parents, is instead allowed to come to a boil and be directed at another dog for "sport".

In many states and municipalities it is becoming illegal to continuously tether, or chain your dog outside. https://www.animallaw.info/topic/table-state-dog-tether-laws Unfortunately it is still legal in far too many states.

Research has shown that not only does tethering cause neurotic behavior, so does close confinement in a kennel. In a recent study published by the journal, "**Physiology & Behavior**," the behavior of 30 kenneled dogs were reported. These dogs were unique in that they were police dogs so their confinement was not as restricted as most "backyard dogs" who are rarely removed from their kennels.

The dogs in the study were videotaped and their behavior noted by the scientists. What they found was similar behavior exhibited by human prisoners kept in solitary confinement. Pacing, continuous, repetitive circling of the perimeter, spinning in place, and literally bouncing off of walls. http://news.discovery.com/animals/pets/dogs-can-go-temporarily-nuts-when-kenneled-140408.htm

If it was that bad for dogs who are only kenneled until it is time to work again as a police dog, imagine being kenneled continuously. Why then are we surprised at dogs who, once docile, become barkers, diggers, and eventually aggressors?

The fault lies with us, not with the dog.

Dog on dog aggression can occur when we least expect it. Years ago while temporarily living with my parents, I heard a dog fight and a child screaming a few houses over from my parents home. I ran toward the fight to find a small boy trying to break up a fight between his own two dogs. His next door neighbor, stood and watched as the child was bitten and did nothing to help. The mother was frantic and trying to help her child. I grabbed one dog while she grabbed the other and we were able to stop the fight. She took the child inside to treat the wound and determine if 911 needed to be called. In the end, the dogs and child recovered, but I was reminded that even pack mates fight sometimes.

Dog-on-dog aggression can be scary especially when it involves dogs living in the same household.

Researchers at the Animal Behavior Clinic at Tufts University Cummings School of Veterinary Medicine in Grafton, Massachusetts, using questionnaires and in-depth interviews found some very interesting information regarding this type of aggression.
http://www.psychologytoday.com/blog/canine-corner/201404/aggression-between-dogs-in-the-same-household

One would think that male dogs would be the fighters, but the research revealed that only 32 percent of the incidences involved two males while 68 percent involved female participants. As a pet parent of mostly female dogs, I am not surprised.

Previous research also revealed that when females do get into an aggressive situation, the fight is longer, more furious, and the injuries more severe.

In addition, it is typically the newest dog brought into the household (70 %) and youngest (74 %) that usually initiate the aggression. Triggers for the fights included jealousy (46%) when the pet parent was paying more attention to one dog than the other; simple excitement

(31%); food aggression (46 %) and toys or bones (26%).

Interestingly enough, it was found that 50 % of the dogs had other issues other than aggression such as separation anxiety with 30 % exhibiting some other form of anxiety.
The research goes on to test two types of behavior modification to address the problem. Each family was assigned a technique and given several weeks to implement it consistently.

The first was Nicolas Dodman's "nothing in life is free" technique. This technique requires that the dog work for what she wants. If she wants a treat, for example, she must respond properly to the sit command.

The other technique used in the experiment was the "chosen dog". This technique required the family to choose one dog, based upon many factors. The dog could be the oldest, the most dominant, or even the largest dog. The chosen dog was fed first, given treats first, etc.

The results of the experiment revealed that while both techniques worked, it took an average of five weeks working consistently with the dogs to see improvement. The "nothing is free" technique showed improvement in 89% of the dog pairs while the "chosen dog" technique showed improvement in 67% of the pairs.
http://avmajournals.avma.org/doi/abs/10.2460/javma.238.6.731

This shows us that consistency is very important and that routine calms the dogs as they know what to expect, even if they are the dog chosen second. It also shows the importance of teaching basic commands to your dogs to keep order in the household.

Common sense strategies can also help. If the dogs fight at feeding time, feed the dogs in separate rooms or feed one dog on the back porch and the other inside. If simple excitement is the trigger (such as the pet parent coming home from work), have someone crate the dogs or put them in separate rooms before you arrive. If you are the only human in the house, teach them to go to their crates or separate rooms before you leave for work. Although we tend to encourage the excitement of arrival, change it, just as you would with separation anxiety (calm when leaving, calm when coming home). And always remember, most dogs when not exercised regularly will act out negatively. That pent up energy has to be released and if not channeled correctly will result in destructive and often negative behaviors.

Many of us remember good experiences of growing up with dogs. Cuddles was my best friend. He ran and played with me. He trusted me to hold him while I was riding my bike, and never needed a leash to stay near me. So it comes as no surprise that we want our children to have a similar experience growing up.

There are times however, when **children and dogs** don't always mix.

While it is great for our children to have a canine companion, it is important to acknowledge that kids will be kids. They are unpredictable and tactile. They like to touch, pull, throw, hit. Children are curious about the world around them and learn their environment through experience. It is up to us to teach them how to best experience a dog.

There are a lot of things to consider when getting a dog for a child and while there are exceptions to every situation, there are some general statements we can make.

The learning and maturity level of the child is one factor. Getting a dog for a child younger than 6 or 7 years of age can be asking for trouble. You have to ask yourself if you would trust your child not to pull on the ears or tail of the dog while you are not in the room. If the answer is no, it is not time for a dog.

It is also important to pick the right dog for the right child. An energetic dog that will accidentally knock over the child in his exuberance, may not be the best choice, but getting a solitary, quiet dog for an energetic child might not be a good match either.

While you can't always determine a dog's temperament by the breed, we do know some important facts that should be considered. **Dachshunds and chihuahuas are more likely to bite humans than any other breeds but pit bulls, curs, rottweilers, presa canarios, cane corsos, mastiffs, dogo argentinos, fila brasieros, sharpeis, boxers, and their mixes do the most damage and cause the most deaths.**
 http://www.appliedanimalbehaviour.com/article/S0168-1591(08)00114-7/abstract and http://www.dogsbite.org/pdf/dog-attack-deaths-maimings-merritt-clifton-2013.pdf

According to the "**Applied Animal Behavior Journal**" the following was found:

Some breeds scored higher than average for aggression directed toward both humans and dogs (e.g., Chihuahuas and Dachshunds) while other breeds scored high only for specific targets (e.g., dog-directed aggression among Akitas and Pit Bull Terriers). In general, aggression was most severe when directed toward other dogs followed by unfamiliar people and household members. Breeds with the greatest percentage of dogs exhibiting serious aggression (bites or bite attempts) toward humans included Dachshunds, Chihuahuas and Jack Russell Terriers (toward strangers and owners); Australian Cattle Dogs (toward strangers); and American Cocker Spaniels and Beagles (toward owners). More than 20% of Akitas, Jack Russell Terriers and Pit Bull Terriers were reported as displaying serious aggression toward unfamiliar dogs. Golden Retrievers, Labradors Retrievers, Bernese Mountain Dogs, Brittany Spaniels, Greyhounds and Whippets were the least aggressive toward both humans and dogs. Among English Springer Spaniels, conformation-bred dogs were more aggressive to humans and dogs than field-bred dogs (stranger aggression)

A long term study that took place from September 1982-December 31, 2013, and included data from the U.S and Canada, found the following to be true:

The combination of molosser breeds, including pit bulls, curs, rottweilers, presa canarios, cane corsos, mastiffs, dogo argentinos, fila brasieros, sharpeis, boxers, and their mixes, inflict:

- *81% of attacks that induce bodily harm*
- *76% of attacks to children*
- *87% of attack to adults*
- *72% of attacks that result in fatalities*
- *81% that result in maiming*
- *Embody 9.2%+ of the total dog population*

This doesn't mean that every pit bull and chihuahua are terrible choices for children, but it is important information to have when considering a pet.

Children can be as harmful and deadly to dogs as the dogs are to children.

I've seen many young toddlers allowed to carry toy breed puppies by their necks and legs, leading to broken legs, spinal damage, and in a few cases, death. Parents are responsible for teaching their child the proper way to approach animals, touch animals, and hold animals.

Too many dogs have also been abandoned in shelters and/or euthanized for aggression, when it was the child that initiated the situation. I can't count the number of times I've seen "cute" videos on social media of children "playing" with dogs, only to look at the dog and realize he's ready to bite. Parents, beaming with pride, declare that their children can pull at their dog's ears, climb on top of the dog, and ride the dog like a pony, and the dog doesn't mind at all.

While dogs may resist biting a child, this does not mean that they enjoy the interaction. Never assume your dog "doesn't mind" having his tail grabbed or ears pulled. Even if your own dog doesn't eventually snap, other dogs might. If your child is taught that these behaviors are acceptable, what is to stop the child from pulling and grabbing at another dog?

I am really surprised that more children have not been bitten and am thankful for the patience of many dogs.

It is not fair to blame a child who has not been taught to respect the pet and treat the pet with kindness. I is also not the fault of the dog that has been forced to endure the unpleasant interaction. The fault lies with the adult guardian who did not train or supervise either the child or the dog .

25

Cat Behavior and Human Relationships

It seems that most people are dog people or cat people. I'm a little of both I guess. I have a chihuahua tattoo on one bicep and a portrait of my cat Biskit on the other. I love the independent nature of the cat; the stubbornness; the attitude. Cats have not been domesticated as long as the dog. They still, for the most part, have the ability to hunt and survive on their own if necessary.

As any cat pet parent can attest, cats interact with humans differently than dogs do. While I believe cats most certainly show affection, research has shown that the attachment to human and cat is far different than the human-dog relationship.

An experiment was conducted at the UK's University of Lincoln Animal Behavior Clinic to explore this claim. During the study, the pet parent would leave the room in which the cat was sitting, and eventually return. The cat's reaction to both was noted. Unlike dogs, who exhibited anxiety upon being left alone, and excitement when the pet parent returned, cats didn't react at all. The researchers concluded that the cats had no emotional attachment to the pet parent. http://www.lincolnanimalbehaviourclinic.co.uk/

An alternate conclusion could be possible. The cat, being an independent creature that could, as I mentioned, fend for herself if necessary, was *less dependent* on the human. Dependency and attachment are not the same thing, although both can occur congruently.

Cat pet parents often cite the welcome they receive when coming home, during which the cat rubs on the legs of the parent. Science tells us that this is simply cats marking their territory. To prove this, they refer to the observational study of semi-feral cats doing the same to trees and light posts. http://www.nrcresearchpress.com/doi/abs/10.1139/z94-147#.VE0fzRaOrK2

Yet consider the idea that humans "mark" as well. We "mark" our spouses with wedding rings. We "mark" our children with family surnames. We mark our pets with identification tags, collars and microchips. We even mark ourselves with tattoos to declare our love for a person, pet, or belief. As I said earlier, after my cat Biskit's long struggle and near death from hepatic lipidosis, I had an image of her face with her striking green eyes tattooed on my bicep. She had marked my heart.

So, while cats do indeed mark their territory, I am personally honored to be claimed as part of that territory and to claim them as *my* cats.

26

Cat Communication

Cats communicate among themselves mostly with body language. With the exception of the unmistakable meow of a kitten to mother, or a cat fight or cat mating, cats save most of their vocalizations for us.

Cats meow for a variety of reasons: to greet us, to get attention, to ask for food or to be let outside, and when they are old and gray, cats may meow out of disorientation.

Meowing works too. As I was writing the last chapter sitting quietly in my chair, my oldest cat, Chloe, made one small meow. Without thinking twice, I responded "I know. Let me finish this chapter." It was 1pm. Time for her lunch.

How often have I called for one of my cats with a questioningly upturned tone, "Tigger?" only to have him meow in acknowledgment with the same tone a person would use to answer.

Cats are not dumb creatures. The meow Chloe gave me indicating it was time to eat was a completely different meow Tigger greeted me with. The meow to go outside is different from the others.

As a veterinary technician who has held many cats for the veterinarian, I am well versed in the complaint meow. It comes before the hissing, growling, and spitting that so vividly says "I'm pissed off. Back away".

Purring is another vocalization of the cat. Kittens can purr at 2 days old; days before they can open their eyes and see. While most people believe it to show contentment, purring can also be used in times of illness or great distress to calm the cat down.

Whether a meow of request, inquiry, or anger, cats have adapted to communicate with us. It behooves us then to give the same consideration and learn the body language of a cat.

The ears, tail, and back are three of the primary means of body communication. When the ears are forward, the cat is attentive, interested, and most likely content. When the ears are laid back against the head, the cat feels threatened and angry. When the ears swivel like a satellite dish, cats are taking in everything and searching for the source of something of interest.

Meanwhile, an upturned tail with fur flat, indicates calm interest, while an erect tail with fur standing on end, means the cat is irritated and angry. A tail that is thrashing side to side much like a car windshield wiper is a gauge of just how ticked off a cat is. The faster it thrashes, the angrier the cat. An insecure or anxious cat may hold the tail tucked between his legs. A quivering tail generally occurs when the cat is marking territory.

A cat that is happy to see you will arch his back but the hair on the body will be flat, but a very angry cat will arch his back, with his hair standing on end and an erect tail.

Cats also mount each other, much like dogs. Again, it is a dominant behavior, not a reason to surrender your cat to the local Rainbow Coalition.

27

Feline Behavioral Problems

Potty Training and Inappropriate Urination

Cats are usually the easiest to potty train, but veterinarians see many cats that have inappropriate soiling issues according to the pet parent. Understanding the cat's point of few can make this issue much easier.

Nature gives kittens the instinct to cover when they void. Put your kitten in the litter box immediately after waking up and feeding. Normally the kitten will take care of business, but if not, use the kittens front paw to dig. I've had several kittens have that have an "ah-ha" moment as soon as I try this tactic.

If regular litter doesn't work, try play sand, but switch back to litter as soon as possible. Another option is Dr. Elsey's Precious Cat ® Cat Attractant available in pet stores or online.

Although it is tempting to buy a covered litter box at first, make sure that the kitten can get inside. Some litter boxes have a high entrance and tiny kittens and geriatric cats can have difficulty climbing into them. Another problem with covered litter boxes is "out of sight, out of mind". The pet parent can forget to clean the box until it is smelly enough to remind them. That's a very bad habit to have and one that can lead to inappropriate elimination.

Place the litter box in a low traffic area as cats are fond of privacy. If you adopt your cat from someone, use the same type of litter box the cat is used to. If you want to change it eventually, you can, but the re-homing experience is stress enough on the pet without figuring out a new potty plan.

The first week you have a new kitten or cat, keep the pet in one room. This allows the pet to know where the litter box and food are kept so that when she finally gets to venture out into the rest of the house, she knows what room will contain necessities.

As I said, it is very important to keep the litter box clean. Many cats will refuse to use a litter box that is overly soiled. However, if you are just teaching a kitten to use the box, leave a little of the old litter behind to remind the kitten just what the box is for.

It is important to learn how a cat thinks. In the wild or just outside, a cat will not choose the same place everyday to potty. Cats like clean areas to go. An overly soiled litter box is like humans going into a overly-used port a potty. It is gross and disgusting. Cats spend most of their waking hours cleaning themselves, a testament to their instinct to be clean.

Make sure the litter box is large enough. Have you ever had to use the bathroom on a plane? Then you know its important to have room to move around. Cats usually like to turn around to cover their urine and feces, so give them the room to do it.

The type of litter is another issue that needs to be addressed. Some cats (or pet parents) prefer regular clay litters, clumping litters, feline pine litters, wheat litters, or corn litters.

When researching for this part of the book, I ran into the same problem I did in researching pet food. People have very strong opinions. "Regular clay litter produces silica dust which will kill your cat!" Then there was "Clumping clay litter will swell in your pet's tummy and kill your cat!!" It seemed like according to someone, every litter is going to kill your cat. The thing is, many of these articles were written by someone with a vested interest in selling their favorite cat litter.

Therefore, I will give you a simple practical opinion based on trying many litters over the years. Its fine if you disagree.

Non-clumping (old fashioned) clay cat litters have been demonized because they contain silica dust , which many claim is a carcinogen that causes cancer. People are also concerned that the sharp edges are hard on the soft paws. Clumping cat litters are advertised to be more convenient with better odor control. Wheat, pine, and corn litters are supposed to be more eco-friendly and an alternative to the dusty silica.

Clumping cat litter in theory was a great idea. The cat urinates or defecates and it is entrapped by litter. You simply scoop the entrapped stuff out to have nice fresh litter. My experience with clumping litter in a multi-cat household, wasn't quite so pleasant. I broke one cat litter scoop after another, trying to get the clumped litter out. I felt as if I needed a hammer and chisel, not a litter scoop. My cats were tracking the dry litter out of the box and licking it off their feet. The litter clumps because it expands once it comes into contact with moisture. What was happening when the cats licked it? The cats were supplying saliva, the moisture needed to make it swell. Then the cats swallowed it. That doesn't seem to healthy to me.

So I tried wheat, pine, and corn litters. They were not remotely dust free. There was dust all over the wall behind the litter box. The cats and I all sneezed and we did not like it at all. It definitely was not a litter I wanted to use with a cat with respiratory issues.

So that left the non-scoopable, old fashioned clay litter. While there was some dust when I first put it in the litter box, I did it when the cats were not around. There were no great dust-storms every time the cats covered their litter. I could scoop the poop and use just enough litter to last a couple of days. After two days, I tossed it out, wipe it up, and start fresh. I could make a 25 lb bag of litter that cost $2.99 last for weeks. Best of all, our cats like it.

The important thing in potty training a cat is using a litter your cat likes. If she doesn't like it, inappropriate urination will occur.

There is a difference between spraying and inappropriate urination. Cats spray to mark territory. Spraying is generally directed toward a vertical surface like a wall. Spraying is commonly a male cat issue, but female cats can spray as well. If it is on a flat surface such as carpet, in the bathtub, or bed, that's inappropriate urination.

What are causes of inappropriate urination?

- **Urinary infection/blockage**: Always assume this is the reason first. Have it ruled out by urinalysis and other lab work. If a cat is going in and out of the litter box or straining to urinate, get the cat to the vet immediately.
- **Dirty litter box.** The litter box should be cleaned at the minimum of once daily.
- **Disagreeable litter**: Cat is not happy with type of litter used.
- **Small box:** Get a larger litter box.
- **Type of litter box**: The cat doesn't like a covered litter box. Another cat needs more privacy and would benefit from a covered litter box.
- **No privacy**: The litter box is kept in a high traffic area
- **Inconsistency**: The litter box is being moved around. Find one spot and keep it there.
- **Declawing**. It is not unusual for cats to avoid the litter box after this procedure. Image having the tips of your fingers amputated and then be expected to use those fingers to dig through litter, even special litter created for post surgery. It is painful and cats, like anyone, will avoid what they associate with being painful.
- **Changes**. A new house, new food, new litter, new routine, new family member, or new pets, can all trigger urine marking. Cats are territorial animals. They mark their space in many ways. If something in their environment changes that, it can be uncomfortable or even traumatic. A new house can have scents from animals that have lived there before, so treat the situation as you would if the cat were new to the family. Let them have access to one room at a time.
- **Stress:** We've established that animals experience emotion and every one needs a way to show or get rid of stress. People scream, cry, punch holes in walls. Cats urinate inappropriately.

So what can you do? If the veterinarian finds no urinary tract problems, it is time to investigate why inappropriate elimination is happening. Clean the areas where the urination occurred. Products with enzymes like Nature's Miracle ® is a good option. Put the food and water bowls there if possible. Cats don't like to urinate where they eat.

In order to get a grip on the situation, put the cat in one room again. Use a room that has no carpet and is easy to clean. If you had a covered litter box, take the top off. Make sure the cat can get in the box easily and that it is in a low traffic area. Start eliminating factors. If the cat refuses the box with the top off, perhaps it is too small. If so, buy a larger, uncovered box. If this doesn't work, try a different kind of litter. If you are not cleaning the box every day, then all of this experimentation is worthless. So make sure the litter box gets done.

Unusual or Inappropriate Vocalization

Some cat breeds are known for their talkative nature. Siamese cats are the first that comes to mind. If a cat is talkative from the time she is a kitten, this is just her nature. However, when a normally quiet cat begins vocalizing more frequently, there are several possible reasons.

- **In heat/or senses a cat in heat:** Female cats in heat must be one of the most irritating things in the world, unless, of course you are an intact male cat. This vocalization is the never- ending plea for a male to mate with her. The solution is simple. Have her spayed and your male cat neutered.
- **Illness or pain**: A cat that is not normally talkative, is altered (spayed/neutered), and starts to vocalize loudly could be ill or hurt. For instance, a male cat who has a urinary blockage, may begin to meow loudly. Rule out physical symptoms immediately.
- **Sensing something unusual**: Cats can see detail we can't, hear on frequencies the human ear will never hear, and detect smells that we, with our insignificant smell sensors, will never smell. Their eyes see movement the human eye cannot pick out. Our eyes are made to take in a larger, overall color-filled view, while their eyes are made to see minute detail and movement. They can also hear what we can't like the mice behind the walls in our house or the constant buzz of the florescent light In the living room. They can smell the moles, squirrels, and rodents outside even behind a locked door. So it is no surprise when they appear to be vocalizing at a blank wall. Just because you don't sense it, doesn't mean it isn't there, this just means your cat has natural talents you don't possess.
- **Disorientation, confusion**: As a cat ages, they can develop cognitive dysfunction. Consider it a form of kitty Alzheimer's. As they did long ago, when their eyes were still closed and they were searching for their mother, a disoriented cat will cry out listening for a response. Sometimes, if you simply answer, the cat will calm down. Talk to your vet about foods and medications that may help the cognitive issues.

- **Human kitty door**: Some cats prefer to hang out in the house, but urinate and defecate outside. When they need outside, they will sit at the door and meow. When they want back in, they will do the same. If you want to train your once-outdoor cat to be indoors, be prepared to deal with this vocalization for a while and keep the litter boxes clean and ready to go. If you feel it is safe to let your cat go outside, install a cat door. Doors are available that will only let your cat in and keep other animals out.
- **Hunger**: Cats are great at letting you know when it is time to eat. As with Chloe, you will learn the different meow's and their meaning with your own cat. Cats like to eat small amounts several times a day, so unless you have an issue with an overweight kitty, it is a good idea to free feed. However, make sure you remain aware that your cat is eating. Giving a bit of canned food once daily lets you know your cat still has an appetite.
- **Attention:** Some cats are very demanding for attention and are not shy to let you know about it. If you are unhappy with this behavior, the best thing to do is ignore it.
- **Boredom**: When awake, cats like to be entertained. Put a bird feeder by the window, give the cat some cat nip on a toy. Schedule playtime.

Inappropriate/Inconvenient sleep cycle

Cats sleep an average of 18 hours a day and are often awake at night. Adult indoor cats rarely keep their pet parents awake, until they are hungry. Senior cats with cognitive dysfunction may exhibit strange night time behaviors including unusually loud vocalization. A senior cat with this problem should be examined by a vet.

Kittens, are likely to disturb the sleeping pet parent than adult cats. This normal behavior should be taken into consideration when adopting a kitten.

To better regulate the sleep schedule and encourage kittens to sleep more at night, initiate playtime an hour or so before bedtime.

In kittens close to six months of age, cat nip is the secret weapon. While most people consider cat nip a stimulant in cats, the after effects are a calm, sleepy kitty.

The physical effects are actually similar to a non-altered female cat in heat, although it is just as effective in males. The cat may rub his body on the cat nip, roll and jump around. Some cats even vocalize and salivate. After about ten minutes or so, the cat is ready to relax.

Incidentally, cat nip tea is available for humans and is great in promoting sleep. However, if you attempt to drink it with your cat in the room, expect some competition.

Scratching Furniture

Furniture scratching is probably the number one reason cited for having a cat declawed. Earlier in the book, I explained the methods and consequences of this procedure.

Cats scratch furniture for three reasons.
- To stretch the muscles in their paws and legs
- To mark territory
- To shed the outer, dead layer of their claws.

Scratching is a strong instinctual behavior, much like we stretch after sitting in a chair for a while.

Cats need to do this. When they are outside, they do the same to trees as they do to your furniture.

So instead of punishing them by amputating their distal toe joints, give them an alternative. Offering scratching posts is a great way to make kitty forget about the sofa. Offer more than one kind and put them throughout the house.

Posts can be made out of a number of materials and be different sizes and angles. Sisal rope is the most common material used in scratching posts as it is rugged and very difficult to destroy. Berber carpet is also a common material used in scratching posts. Natural scratching posts made out of dead or cut tree limbs is a favorite of mine as they are easy to make and relatively free. My cats are also very happy with a piece of untreated 2 X 4. If you will notice in some of the slanted cat scratching products sold in pet stores, cardboard is used. In addition to being great to scratch on, cardboard boxes also make excellent play houses for cats. Put a few holes in the box, throw a toy or two in, and you have a very entertained cat.

Scratching posts work best if you have them at various angles. This allows the cat the most options and makes it more enticing than boring furniture. Have one vertical post, one at a 45 degree angle, and one that is laying flat on the floor.

Rubbing some cat nip on the scratching post is one way to focus the attention on the post instead of the sofa. However, don't over do it, or the cat will become immune to its attraction.

Now that you've given your cat some options, there are some ways you can discourage your cat from using the furniture as a scratching post.

Tips for discouraging furniture scratching:

- If you catch your cat scratching on the furniture, you can spray a quick stream of water toward the cat. It has to be done during scratching, and never after. Make sure you have a spray bottle for **water only** so you will not accidentally spray the cat with something toxic.
- If you are not home, keep the cat in a room with scratching posts and toys, not furniture.
- Keep your cat's nails clipped. Clipped nails minimizes any damage.
- Use double sided tape made specifically for this issue on the furniture. Cats hate the feeling of "sticky".
- Some herbal sprays are sold for deterring the cat. The jury is still out on how effective they are.
- SSScat Training aid ® is scentless spray with a motion sensor. The automatic spray is like having someone sitting in your living room waiting with a water bottle for the cat to begin scratching.

Feline Aggression

Early socialization of kittens plays a part in how comfortable a cat is with humans and how they deal with our species. Paternity is also a factor. Studies show that kittens whose fathers were friendly and sociable with humans, are more likely to be friendly and sociable as well. The mother's level of sociability didn't seem to play a part at all. https://www.aspca.org/pet-care/virtual-pet-behaviorist/cat-behavior/petting-induced-aggression

Unlike dogs, who are quick to become a part of a pack, cats prefer solitude. Free range and feral cats rarely choose to socialize with other cats. These cats have a wide territory, far more than we realize and they don't appreciate that territory being invaded. Free range and feral cat interaction generally takes place if there is one central food or water source. Occasionally, clowders, or an established grouping of cats, will form.

The cats who moved from California to Tennessee with me formed a clowder many years ago. As they have grown older (all are 10 years or more), the clowder has become exclusive, and no other cats are accepted. Any other rescue cats must live separate from the clowder, or run the risk of being chased off by the group. Peace is more likely when the feral and stray cats who come onto the property search for food are fed far away from the clowder. We keep a dog house and food at the bottom of our property and away from the cat building for any cats in need, particularly in the winter.

Aggression in cats occurs most often for **defense or self-protection**. Cats that are generally calm at home can become violent at the veterinarian, for instance. Some become so self defensive that performing any procedure can be nearly impossible.

A situation many pet parents experience and that often hurts their feelings (as well as their hands) is **touch-induced aggression**. Often, the cat comes to the pet parent requesting to be petted, only to act aggressively after just a few seconds.

This phenomenon is not completely understood, but it is believed that the aggression is caused by over stimulation. The sensation of being petted becomes unpleasant and even painful.

Cats do give you fair warning if you know what to look for. The tail may lash from side to side. The hair on the cat may stand up as the cat tenses. The skin may twitch and the cat may begin to vocalize. If you notice any of this, stop petting, and move your hands away from the cat.

As a whole, most sociable cats like to be petted on the back of the neck. Some will even be comfortable being petted on the back, but often, this is where the over sensitivity begins. Most cats are very uncomfortable being petted on the belly and will get up and run away or attack your hand.

Few cats are like dogs, who are thrilled at being petted for as long as you are willing to pet them. While there are exceptions, I never assume a strange cat or even my own cat is one. I let the cat tell me what they want and can tolerate by observing their body language.

Another type of aggression sometimes seen in cats is **displaced aggression**. The cat may be looking outside the window. As you walk by, the cat attacks you. His instinct is to attack the birds he is watching outside. While he focuses on them, you happen to drop by. The instinct to attack them is instead focused toward you. Remember, cats have not been domesticated as long as dogs have, and their feral instincts still speak to them. This type of aggression can also be brought on by fear and environmental stress such as a new pet or visitors. If you see the signs of a potential attack, startling tactics such as a hand clap or object thrown within the cats visual range (but not at the cat) will often break the "spell" and the cat will generally run to another room to calm down.

Cats are rarely intentionally aggressive towards humans. They are defensive, not offensive in this regard. If given the opportunity, most cats will choose "flight" over "fight". If cats are cornered, they will fight back, however, and believe me when I say, they have very effective weapons. Its takes experience and nerves of steel to retrieve a frightened and angry cat from a hospital cage.

In non-veterinary settings, upset cats should be allowed time alone to calm down. Cats are not dogs, and their species specific-personality, behavior, and needs should be respected.

Cat-on-cat aggression is one time when cats are most certainly the aggressor. This type of aggression can occur between housemates or with cats who are strangers. Whether it is a new cat in multi-cat family, or a stray cat walking on an outdoor cat's established territory, the fights can be ferocious.

Cats rarely fight it out until they make peace and the fighting shouldn't be tolerated. A loud clap or a spritz from a water bottle, should interrupt and break up the fight. In general, the more the cats fight, the more brutal the fights will become. Cats are not boxers who beat each other senseless, then shake hands when the bell rings to end the fight. The cats become bitter enemies that can injure each other and pass on diseases.

The reasons for cat-on-cat aggression are numerous.

Introductory aggression occurs when a new cat is adopted into a home with one or more cats. Cats who are aggressive upon seeing another cat outdoors will usually not accept another cat into his indoor territory.

When a new cat comes into the home, certain steps should be made to make the introduction period successful.

Steps to cat introductions:
- Keep the cats separated, by putting them in adjoining rooms with the door between them closed.
- Put the food and water bowls near the door. This allows the cats to detect each other, and associate the scent with the positive experience of eating. Offer all treats and toys near the door as well.
- After 3 days, switch rooms. The cat that was in room #1 should be moved to room #2, and the cat in room #2 is moved to room #1. Still avoid direct contact between the cats. This allows the cats to investigate the scents of the other cat without the threat of contact.
- The following day, mix the scents of the cats together by rubbing a towel on cat #1, then cat #2, and back again to cat #1.
- If no aggression has been shown, replace the closed door with a screen door or high baby gate. Offer treats or food to both cats, but this time, do it away from the door so the cats are not so focused on the door or feel that the other cat is too near their food. This will be the first time the cats see each other.
- If there is still no aggression, allow the cats to spend time with each other when they are not so full of energy such as after eating or playtime. Extend the time together gradually. Do not interfere with their interaction unless there is aggression. If this occurs, a squirt of water from a spray bottle will help stop the aggression.

Hopefully, following these steps will lead to an uneventful introduction.

There are other reasons apart from introductions that can trigger cat-on-cat aggression.

Thanks to sexual hormones, intact male cats are notoriously territorial, and a female in heat is equally unpleasant. The solution is to have the cat spayed or neutered. It may take a few days or weeks after the procedure for the hormones to stabilize and for the aggression to lessen.

Cats like their personal space, and sometimes, that personal space overlaps. In multi-cat households, peace is most easily achieved by having multiple litter boxes, beds, food and water bowls, in various places throughout the house. This allows the cats to choose their preferred territory while still living in the same house. The cats can sense each other and choose when to interact rather than being forced to interact at feeding or potty time. The same principle applies to outdoor cats as well.

Most cats tend to be "tree dwellers", meaning they prefer and feel safest in higher places in the house. Utilizing inexpensive shelving can provide these safe dwelling at various levels. Cats who feel safe do not become so easily defensive.

Like humans, some cats just do not like one another. Every morning when Haseleah goes outside to get the newspaper, our cat Peaches is sitting near the door waiting for the chance to glare at Jerry, Haseleah's cat. Peaches hates Jerry and Jerry hates Peaches. If given the chance, Jerry will run outside and smack Peaches, then run back, with Peaches on his tail. No great intervention will change their relationship. While the peaceable kingdom is a wonderful, romantic notion, it is not always realistic.

In situations where the cats refuse to get along, the pet parent must keep the cats in separate places. Allow one cat access to the upstairs, and the other cat the downstairs. Perhaps one cat prefers the kitchen and dining room, while another likes the living room and laundry area. In our case at the farmhouse, Peaches prefers being outdoors with access to her cat building, and Jerry prefers living indoors and sleeping near the fish tank.

Anxiety in Cats

While lack of exercise for pent up energy is most often the cause of destructive or negative behaviors in dogs, anxiety can be the trigger for most behavioral problems in cats.

Signs of anxiety include:

- Hiding
- Shaking

- Panting
- Inappropriate voiding activity such as urinating or defecating on the pet parent's bed
- Sudden, unexpected escape behavior
- Diarrhea during times of stress. An example would be diarrhea when the pet parent goes on vacation.
- Excessive grooming. Some cats will even pull their fur out.
- Unusual vocalization

While these can also be symptoms of physical illness, look at the big picture to determine if this could be anxiety. Physical symptoms should be ruled out first, preferably by your veterinarian.

Once you and your vet have determined that your cat is indeed experiencing anxiety there are several options:

- **Feliway ®**: Feliway ® is a synthetic copy of the cat's facial pheromone. Cats use their natural pheromone to mark an area as their own, making it a familiar and safe environment. The company claims that it has been proven 95%, but studies by the manufacturer are often biased. Subsequent reviews of studies not conducted by the manufacturer have not been as encouraging. However, the price is not so high that it wouldn't be worth it for the pet parents to give Feliway ® a try.
- **Royal Canin ® Calm** cat food has been shown to help. According to the company, the food contains two amino acids including the peptide Alpha-casozepine as well as L-tryptophan which have been shown to have calming effects. Also included is Vitamin B3, known as Nicotinamide, which calms the central nervous system. Calm ® is especially good for animals that have gastroentestinal issues with their anxiety as it helps regulate the transit of food through the digestive system and encourages healthy flora within that system. The food creates a urinary environment that discourages the formation of crystals that lead to kidney and bladder stones. Calm ® is said to promote healthy skin and teeth. Again, as with the dog formula, it is very expensive at around $50 for an 8.8 lb bag.
- **Hills Prescription ® C/D Feline Urinary Stress Cat Food**: This is an excellent option for a household of cats with inappropriate urination or spraying problems. This food is similar in ingredients and promised results as Royal Canin Calm ®
- **Pet Naturals of Vermont ® Calming Soft Chews.** If the food mentioned above is too expensive, consider giving this product a try. It has many of the same ingredients, but in a tasty chew. A chew is given once daily and is less than $4 for 21 chews. Amazon offers a lower price if you subscribe to automatic subscription services.
- **Sentry ® Calming Collar**: This utilizes the same pheromone calming approach as Feliway ® but in a collar form. Reviews were similar for both products. This collar must

be changed monthly, but a 3 month supply is only around $17 on Amazon.
- **Thundershirt ®**: This product, normally sold for dogs, has proven itself effective on cats. If your cat stiffens up at first, don't worry. It takes cats a little more time to get used to the sensation.
- **Certain anti-depressants** such as amitriptyline or fluoxetine can prove effective in some cases of perpetual anxiety in cats. Dosages vary depending on the problem.

PRACTICAL CONSIDERATIONS

"If animals could speak, the dog would be a blundering outspoken fellow; but the cat would have the rare grace of never saying a word too much." ~ Mark Twain

28

Keeping the Peace in a Multi-Pet Household

So far, I have covered mostly the medical issues I have had to deal with over the years as a technician and rescuer. However, there are still many other practical issues to consider.

One of the most important things was learning how to keep the peace.

Putting animals together, whether they are different species or simply different individuals can be tough. In our rescue, with their various histories of abuse and neglect, there is always a potential for disaster.

My method of keeping the peace is based upon the following principles:

- Giving them the choice between sleeping together and having their own space
- Feeding everyone once or twice daily, but separately in their crate
- Giving each pet a job
- A daily howl
- Routine
- Avoiding temptation
- Allowing them to help take care of you.

From California, I brought home a dozen dogs and an equal number of cats. Accompanying them were birds, guinea pigs and a turtle. The dogs varied from a 2 lb. chihuahua to a 50 lb. basset hound. Some animals were old, some were young. Others tended to be more dominant dogs, while other animals simply were happy being in the pack. A few liked people, while most were afraid of them.

While the dogs usually loved jumping in a "puppy pile", there were times when they needed some alone time. I provided crates for them all for this very purpose. Dogs need a place to feel safe and call their own and crate training allowed me to say the phrase "kennel up" and everyone would go to their assigned crate for a nice nap. It gave them time to calm down.

I also made sure there were separate play areas for the older or smaller dogs, and another for the larger, or more hyper dogs. Some days, just like with people, your family gets on your nerves. There were days, Buster, the older basset hound, just needed a break from the younger ones. Other days, Panda, the Pomeranian, could be so hyper, he could irritate a saint. And when the world was big and scary and a thunderstorm came, everyone wanted to find a safe place. So a couple separate areas were available when needed.

At feeding time, every dog was crated to keep the peace. I fed once daily. I placed all the small bowls out in a row and mixed their food in a large bowl. I then divided it up according to weight. For those who needed medication, I added the medication to their food. I then fed everyone. As soon as feeding time was over, the bowls were taken up and washed. Nothing was left behind to argue about. If anyone did get a little obnoxious, I kept a water bottle handy to spray to remind them I was there and not happy with their behavior.

After years of feeding like this, I no longer need to feed in crates. Everyone goes to "their" place that they chose themselves, and wait for their food. When they are finished, they run out the doggie door to go potty.

I also give everyone a job. Dogs love to have a purpose. Teddy, was the big brother to all the foster dogs and became Bojangles' saving grace. Once we no longer fostered, Teddy took over security. Tinker, has always protected the youngest dogs and cats, and exotic pets. Panda, and Bojangles all monitor the rear fence line while Blue, Pearl, Onyx, and Athena, watch the front of the house. Ruby takes care of me. Everyone has a task to give them purpose.

We, at T.Paws, have had to evolve with the changing needs of the individual animals and the group. New rescues have joined the pack. Haseleah and her dog Abigail, and cat, Jerry moved in. Age has brought arthritis and other senior health conditions. Many of the dogs are cold intolerant even though they want to be outside. Casey is easily stressed, particularly after experiencing a period of intense vertigo that comes with idiopathic vestibular disease. Several of the dogs and cats have had to be moved to new areas better suited to their needs. The older cats have moved back inside. Blue and Tinker, have joined Ruby and Abigail in our bedroom so we can monitor their health very closely.

To make Teddy, Bo, Panda, Casey, and Scrappy more comfortable, my father insulated the side porch and built them something similar to a bunk bed. The lower bunk is complete with a small corner just for Casey to hide so she can feel safe. A ramp takes the dogs to the second level where Teddy watches for anyone to approach the house. Both levels have carpeted mats. Depending on the weather, the "patio dogs" have a built-in fan, and a radiator heater for cold days.

Bojangles is becoming more confident and even initiating the daily howl with Teddy. The howl makes us happy every time we hear it as we are reminded of the power of pack love.

It has also been important to acknowledge the instinct of my animals that can sometimes result in a disaster. I have cats who have grown up with the dogs and are unafraid of them. They can walk among them and even sleep with them. However, other cats (like those that people drop off in our yard) are another story.

One morning, while getting ready for work, I heard a huge fight going on outside. It was still dark, but I ran out the door and into the fenced area. I could tell the entire pack was attacking another animal. I realized it was a cat, but I couldn't tell who it was. Without thinking, I jumped in the fight and started throwing dogs away from the cat. I eventually picked up the cat with the intention of throwing her out side of the fence and out of harms way. The cat had no idea that I was trying to save her. She was fighting for her life. Her teeth clamped down on the back of my hand and wouldn't let go. Once I finally got to the edge of the fence, she saw her chance to escape and was smart enough to do so. I took the dogs down to the light to see if they had any bite marks, and ran around the house with a flashlight to catch the cat. She was in shock and was taken to the vet. I cleaned my wound and went on to work only to be taken to the ER later in the day. An injection, some antibiotics and $2300 later, my wounds were treated. The cat survived and the vet felt so bad for me that he didn't charge a dime.

The point is, avoid any situation that can tempt your pet to revert to instinct, and never assume that your pet will not rely on instinct. Putting a bird cage within reach of a cat or not securing the top of a lizard cage is a recipe for disaster. Assuming that your dog will never bite anyone has caused many people, including vet techs like me, to be bitten. This is no different than jumping out of the darkness to scare me and expecting not to get punched. Instinct takes over for both human and pet. So keep this in mind and avoid temptation.

Life is tough and there is no shame in sometimes laying it all down and let your pet take care of you for a while. I have to honestly say, some days I just sat down in the yard, gathered the dogs around me, and talked to them. When I worried about money to buy food, they sat close while I cried. When my panic attacks put me in the fetal position, they comforted and guarded me from every side. They took care of me for a while and it has made us a family.

The same could be said for the cats. When I was overwhelmed, I would go sit under a shade tree in the yard. No matter where the cats were on the property, somehow they knew, and everyone would gather around me. I was never left alone to deal with the world. I always had support.

I knew that I must be doing something right the day one of the gates was left unlocked. Every dog I had could have left while I was at work. There was a wooded area up the hill to explore and open fields to run in. There were neighborhood dogs to visit; places to go, and new people to see. When I pulled in the driveway on my motorcycle, Tinker came running up to me, letting me know the gate was open. I panicked. Both Tinker and I ran to the gate, and waiting patiently for me to return, was the entire canine family. They loved their home and they loved me. That was perfect peace.

When Haseleah, Abigail, and Jerry joined us, we were complete.

29

Bedding and Housing

So, for this wonderful family, we have had a lot of details to attend to; one was bedding. Not only are we limited in funds, but there are numerous pets to provide for, and dogs who ripped up pillows.

As I mentioned, there are several areas for them to choose from: the large dog building, the patio with the bunk bed, the pen facing the road, the dog houses scattered throughout their space. The cats have their own cat building, access to the house, straw-filled boxes and dog houses, and some of their favorite places, under dense shrubbery.

The dogs and cats love the warm summer sun. Many of the cats climb a ladder to bask on the hot tin roof. The heat from the roof helps the aging clowder, and gives them an opportunity to watch the entire neighborhood.

We learned that in order to be comfortable in any weather, we should never create extremes in temperature. To keep all of us at T.Paws (human and non-human alike) comfortable in summer heat, or winter cold, we do not use the air conditioning or gas heat until absolutely necessary. Haseleah makes the dogs new crocheted sweaters and she and I dress in warm clothes to be able to keep the thermostat under 68°F. To remove the hot air in the summer, we install fans in the windows and vents in the attic.

We have experimented with many ways to keep the dogs and cats warm in winter and cool in summer. While we have now been able to give them enclosed, insulated, heated and cooled rooms, the following were successful for us as well.

Suggestions for Keeping Outside Animals Warm:

- A Puppy Pile Box: Multi-pet households have the advantage that dogs, (and even some cats), love to curl up next to each other. For pets that spend time outside, but have a patio, outbuilding, or barn, a puppy pile box filled with straw is a welcome addition. We made a 4'X4' box that was two foot high to hold the straw in. For cats and smaller dogs, large cardboard boxes can be used in place of a wooden one as long as the boxes are not exposed to moisture.

- Heat the Dog House: Drill a hole in the back near the roof of the dog house. Install an outlet with a 15 watt bulb. The bulb supplies the heat. The bulb must be encased so that the dog nor the bedding touch it. It's important to position the house so that the electric lines leading to the dog house cannot not be chewed on by the dogs. Adding a timer allows the pet parent to control when the bulb is on. The doghouse can get extremely warm, so it may only be necessary to have the light on at night.

- Size of the Dog House: A doghouse that is too large for the size of your pet allows the warm air to rise to the top and away from your pet. A dog house that is too small, doesn't give your pet the proper room to get comfortable, and if the dog house is heated, the pet and bedding are too close to the bulb.

- Use Straw as Bedding: Using blankets in a dog house rarely keeps the pet warm in cold weather. The blankets get wet and will freeze. Straw is inexpensive and warm. Change the straw as needed.

- Insulate the Dog House with Straw Bales: Straw is a wonderful insulator and it is also a great wind breaker. Straw is frequently used around human homes during the winter in areas with consistent, cold, high winds, and flat ground. Surround the dog house on all sides with intact straw bales and cover with a tarp that you stake to the ground. You can also install a cover over the doghouse door to keep out of the wind. Inexpensive car floor mats can be transformed into effective wind breaking doors. If wind primarily blows from one direction, face the door away from the wind, and it will stay much warmer for your pet.

- Waterproof Shelters for Outdoor Cats: Even if you do not have outdoor cats, many areas have a feral cat population, that suffer in the cold winter. As an animal lover, it is good to provide a warm, safe place for cats to sleep. Rubbermaid ® containers work well for this purpose. Cut a hole large enough for a cat to enter in the side of the plastic container. Remove the top of the container, fill with straw, and close tightly. Put the shelters in areas that are protected from the wind. Replenish the straw as needed.

Exotic and Non-Traditional Pets

"Compassion for animals is intimately associated with goodness of character, and it may be confidently asserted that he who is cruel to animals cannot be a good man." ~Arthur Schopenhauer

30

Exotic Pet Introduction

I have raised, cared for, rescued, and otherwise loved, many types of non-canine and feline pets. Dogs and cats are considered "companion" animals while any pet not indigenous to the locale of the pet parent is considered "exotic".

To clarify, here is how I distinguish between categories (for the sake of brevity I will refer to all animals in this list as "exotic"):

- Pocket pets: hamsters, mice, gerbils
- Small animals: guinea pigs, rabbits, rats, ferrets
- Birds: finches to parrots
- Herps: (short for herpetology) includes amphibians (frogs, toads, newts) and reptiles (snakes, lizards, turtles, tortoises)
- Aquatic Fish
- Farm Animals as pets: pot bellied pigs

Before I discuss the needs of individual species, there are three things that are universally required:

- **Habitat**: Most illnesses and deaths of exotics are caused by a poor habitat. Unlike dogs and cats who adjust to many climates, many exotic species must have their environment replicated, particularly the cold blooded species, such as amphibians and reptiles. This can be both expensive and difficult to do. Many die in the first year. The habitats are often much too small. Imagine what it must be like to live every day in the cage you purchase. Many of the exotic species can travel miles a day in the wild. Keep that in mind and get the largest habitat you can.
- **Food:** Nutrition requirements are strict for most and require more than a bag of kibble. You must be willing to buy fresh fruits and vegetables and/or live food in order to provide what your pet needs
- **An exotic veterinarian**: There is a big difference in a vet that will "see" exotic pets and one who has studied and has experience with exotic pets. Talk to other exotic pet

parents to find the best one in your area. Office call fees are generally more expensive than small animal vets. This is because much more education is required to be able to have the knowledge to treat such a wide range of pets. Not only should the vet know how to treat your particular species, he or she should know how to properly euthanize your exotic when the time comes.
- **Education:** The topic of exotic pets covers an enormous number of species. Never buy an exotic pet until you have studied at least one book concerning their care. "Care sheets" from pet stores give you minimal information and are far too generalized. Could the care of a human infant be covered in a one page care sheet? Then don't expect one to do that for your pets. If you don't want to buy the book, check one out of the library.

Sadly, exotics are often considered "throw away" pets. Many people release them into the wild when they no longer want them. Unfortunately, most are not able to survive in the wild. When the conditions are right however, not only can they survive, they can thrive and multiply. South Florida is being overrun with huge constrictors and similar snake species that are making their way back into neighborhoods where they hunt companion animals, small game, and even small humans for food.

Exotics are often purchased because they are "cool" pets without regard to the commitment necessary to properly care for them. A small snake is great, but that small snake, if he lives, may grow to be 12 ft or more in length. Where will you keep him then? Could you afford to feed him? Are you prepared for the consequences if he is able to escape? These are all things you must consider.

Exotic pets are also impulse pets. You walk into a pet shop or farm store near Easter time and "OMG! That baby bunny/chick is so cute!! I'll get him for (fill in child's name here) for Easter morning!!" The sad thing is many die the first year. If they make it, many more are given away or abandoned to the wild.

Pets, exotic or otherwise, do not make good gifts. Animal shelters fill up a month or so after Christmas with pets that were given as gifts, but the family was unprepared for.

Many exotic pets are removed from life in the wild and sold in an unevenly regulated pet trade. Salt water fish are one example. Ironically, it was the Disney/Pixar movie "**Finding Nemo**", a story of a wild caught clown fish trying his best to return to the wild and be with his father, that doomed wild caught clown fish to a fish tank life. The balance of this international trade and sustainability is a tough job. It would have been very easy to wipe out the clown fish population as a result of the interest the movie created and the insistence of children (and adults) to have them.

Sometimes when you buy an exotic pet, you get more than you are prepared for. Mice and hamsters often are pregnant when purchased. Although most pet stores try to separate males from females (unless they are being sold as live food), occasionally they can make a mistake. Female mice can become pregnant as early as 4-6 weeks old. The gestation period is about 19–21 days, and they give birth to a litter that averages 6-8 baby mice. One female can have 5-10 litters per year if allowed, so the population can get out of control quickly. If you give them away or sell them to a pet store, more than likely they will be sold as live food for a variety of creatures.

Many people make the mistake of purchasing the habitat at the same time they purchase the pet. This is a not a good idea at all. It increases the stress for the pet as he must wait for you to sit up the habitat. Fish death increases dramatically as the tank must be acclimated, brought to the proper temperature, allowed to process the chlorine out of the water, and create healthy bacteria levels.

The cost of proper set up and care can be surprising, so it is not something one should take lightly. Consider the minimum cost of setup of a bearded dragon. I have gathered prices from a nationally recognized pet store and in some cases, Amazon, and have been rounded up to the nearest dollar. I also added the cost of the cricket habitat you must have. Bearded Dragons have to be fed live crickets that have been well fed with a special diet 24 hours before feeding to your dragon. Feeding this special diet is called "gut loading." In addition, I am assuming a baby bearded dragon is purchased and the crickets are purchased at the store as well.

Only as a baby, can a bearded dragon be kept in a 20 gallon long tank. Although many pet stores will sell you a small cage for your dragon, it significantly reduces the chance that the dragon will live as she cannot regulate her temperature properly. If you decide to start with a bigger tank, you will need a separate small tank to put the baby in to feed. Young dragons need ¼ inch crickets. If you attempt to feed your tiny dragon in a large tank, the crickets easily find a place to hide. Feeding in the separate, smaller tank, will allow you to see how well your dragon is eating.

Initial cost of bearded dragon set up will require:

20 gallon long tank	$40.00 (only for small to medium size dragons)
Terrarium hood	$55.00
UVA/UVB 10.0, 15 watt bulb	$25.00 (changed every 6 months)
Heat lamp plus bulb	$30.00
Reptile Carpet	$15.00
Thermometer & Humidity Gauge	$15.00
Hammock, Cave, Basking Rock	$30.00
Water/Food dishes	$10.00

Cricket Tank	$15.00
Complete Cricket Diet	$7.00
Bearded Dragon Book	$15.00
Total	**$257.00**

The $257 price tag doesn't even include the cost of the bearded dragon or the 300-350, ¼ inch long crickets, that she will eat per week during her early life. Most local pet stores sell their crickets for 10-12¢ per cricket. Unless you order them in bulk with high shipping costs, you can spend $30 or more a week to feed a bearded dragon. Once bearded dragons are larger the dragons decrease the amount of crickets they require, but increase the amount of fresh vegetables they need.

While it is cheaper to buy the bearded dragon habitat package (about $150), you will actually be getting things that you cannot use until the dragon is an adult (like reptile sand) or items you cannot use at all (like a potentially dangerous rock heater). The habitat package still will not include some of the things that you do need.

Many people have no idea how expensive it is to keep an exotic pet and unfortunately many pet store employees do not communicate this expense to the potential pet parent for fear of scaring away a sale.

It is important to do your homework before purchasing any pet. It is equally important to find an experienced exotic veterinarian in your area.

31

Pocket Pets

Pocket pets obviously get their name because they are small enough to fit inside a pocket. Pocket pets are one of the least expensive pets to purchase and have easier, and less expensive habitat requirements.

While there are 24 different types of hamsters, the two most common ones sold in pet stores are Teddy Bear hamsters and Russian Dwarf Hamsters.

Teddy Bear hamsters, also called Syrian or golden hamsters, prefer to live alone and will actually fight to the death if put in a cage with another of its kind. They are larger than their dwarf cousins. They come in short and long haired varieties and are more comfortable with being held than dwarfs. They can and do bite if frightened.

Russian Dwarf Hamsters are tiny and cute, and have no problem living with members of the same sex if introduced when they are young. They are more timid and also more likely to bite. Although parents often buy dwarfs for their child's first pet, they are rarely pets that will allow themselves to be held.

Both Teddy Bear and Russian Dwarfs are nocturnal, meaning they are active at night and rarely during the day. That being said, they are a good choice for apartment dwellers as many landlords will allow them. They can teach an older child responsibility with parental supervision. Their average lifespan is 2-2 ½ years.

Gerbils make good pets but are illegal in certain states. The most common type in the pet trade is the Mongolian gerbil. They are social animals and can be kept with another same-sex gerbil if introduced early but are fine alone. If you wish to make your gerbil comfortable with being held, I recommend keeping only one gerbil and taking your time with introducing the concept. They are hardy creatures and are usually less likely to bite. Of the pocket pets, I would probably recommend gerbils the most.

Mice are also great pets. They can live in groups, although in my experience the females get along better than the males. Never mix the sexes, or you will most certainly have more mouths to feed. Mice, or any pocket pet for that matter, are not good pets for toddlers. They are fast movers, and can bite, and if let loose, can be very difficult to find. They are also more fragile

than the gerbil. Young children don't yet have the motor skills necessary to hold a such a tiny pet. If the pet jumps from the child's hand, his attempt to catch a falling pet, might result in a squeeze that can injure the pet and could result in the child getting bitten.
The habitats and needs of pocket pets are very similar with small differences.

Habitat needs for pocket pets include:

- **10 gallon tank and mesh cover**: Although the plastic habitats with colorful tunnels are attractive, they are also harder to clean. In addition, some pocket pets will chew on the plastic and make holes large enough to escape
- **Cave/bed**: All pocket pets like a place to hide. There are many types to choose from. You can use a small flower pot, or just a small box. With the box, you will need to offer a new one frequently, but the pocket pets seem to enjoy them.
- **Bedding**: Aspen shavings and Carefresh ® bedding are said to be the safest. I have used **kiln-dried** pine shavings for years and my pets usually lived longer than the average and were healthy. Cedar shavings should be avoided. Most pocket pets love to dig so make it deep enough for them to enjoy. In addition to their basic bedding, pocket pets enjoy making their own beds. Offer paper towels and small cardboard boxes for them to rip up and arrange into a perfect bed.
- **Exercise wheel**: This is one time when plastic is okay. Plastic rung-less wheels are safest.
- **Water bottle**: With water bottles, you get what you pay for. Cheap bottles will leak onto the bedding, attracting gnats and other insects and even encouraging the growth of mold.
- **Trace Mineral Salt wheel:** This provides essential salt and minerals not found in their regular food. It is also a fun toy as they can spin it around.
- **Chew Toy:** The teeth of pocket pets never stop growing, so they must chew to keep them manageable. Many chew toys are available specifically for this and I find the best one is the Tooth Conditioning Chew Blox ® from Sunscription. It is made of pumice and outlasts wood and other products. If you do give your pet wood, make sure it is untreated and safe.
- **Tunnels**: As you can see with most plastic pocket pet habitats on the market, they love to run through tunnels. The cardboard tubes left over from toilet paper and paper towel rolls as well as Christmas wrapping paper work great.

The diets of pocket pets do vary by species, but they do have some things in common. If you have several pocket pets, knowing the basics of what they need and then comparing them to each other can save you a lot of money. Depending on the number of tiny ones you have, it may be cheaper to make your own pocket pet food.

Although I do not consider rats pocket pets, their diet is basically the same as mice. Food for both mouse and rat are sold and marketed together. Both species also have similar illnesses and treatments.

The following chart shows the similarities and differences in hamster and gerbil food compared to mouse and rat formulas.

Hamster & Gerbil Food Main Ingredients	Mouse & Rat Food Main Ingredients
Corn, oats, wheat, milo, sunflower, green split peas, oat groats, shelled peanuts, ground wheat, ground corn, sun-cured alfalfa meal, dehulled soybean meal, pumpkin seed, barley, raisings, dehydrated carrots, dried bananas, safflower, canadian field peas, ground flax seed, ground oats, dried papaya, ground rice, dehydrated sweet potatoes, dehydrated apples, rice flour, Dicalcium, phosphate, calcium carbonate	Rolled corn, rolled oat groats, rolled barley, ground corn, dehulled soybean meal, wheat middlings, ground wheat, sun-cured alfalfa meal, meat meal, sunflower, peanuts, corn gluten meal, cane molasses, vegetable oil, poultry meal, fish meal, salt, beer pulp, calcium carbonate

For the most part, their needs are very similar. Making a similar-seed mixture and adding fresh fruits or vegetables makes for a healthy pet. The dried "fruits and veggies" found in most brand name mixtures are often created using food coloring, which is not healthy for them. It is cheaper and healthier to purchase a food dehydrator and dehydrate your own vegetables and fruit.

Both need calcium carbonate. An easy source is eggshells. After making your eggs, bake the eggshells for a few minutes, and let cool. Add a little to their food.

Mice and rats appreciate a bit of meat protein. This is one way their food needs differ from hamsters and gerbils. So I add a little cat food or give them a Milk bone ®

It is just as important to know what foods are dangerous to your pocket pet. Never feed lettuce, potatoes, onions, garlic, citrus, fruit seeds, chocolate or sweets. And remember not to overdo the fresh food or to allow it to spoil. This can cause intestinal problems and even death.

Health Concerns of Pocket Pets
In regards to health, the most common disorders and diseases in pocket pets are similar in presentation and treatment. On the following page, you will see a brief overview. For more detailed and species specific information, refer to this website:
http://www.merckvetmanual.com/pethealth/index.html

One thing to note is that although the illnesses are similar, not all species can safely take the same medication. What may be safe for one, may be toxic for another. In general, the safest antibiotics for pocket pets (as well as rats and guinea pigs) include trimethoprim-sulfamethoxazole (SMZ-TMP/Bactrim), enrofloxacin (Baytril ®), and ciprofloxacin (Cipro ®). Drugs in the penicillin family are to be avoided.

Always consult a veterinarian pocket pets.

It is important for you and/or your vet to know the actual weight of the pet to ensure proper medication dosages. Small shipping scales can be used to give you the weight in grams or ounces. Average weights of pocket pets can vary depending on the sex of the pet, and the usual food intake vs exercise.

Pocket Pet	Average Weight
Teddy Bear/Syrian Hamster	140-200 gr or 5-7 oz
Dwarf (Russian & Robo)	25-60 gr or 1-2 oz
Gerbil	70 gr or 2.5 oz
Fancy Mouse	29-44 gr or 1-1.6 oz

Common Disorders and Diseases of Pocket Pets

- **Infections & Intestinal Parasites:** Similar symptoms can be caused by bacteria, viruses, protozoas, and intestinal parasites such as pinworms and tapeworms. Signs include loss of appetite, dehydration, diarrhea, ruffled fur, an unkempt appearance, lethargy, and hunched posture. Since it is difficult to determine the cause, many vets will treat with an antibiotic and anti-parasitic. The most common and safe antibiotic is Sulfamethoxazole/Trimethoprim, also known as SMZ-TMP. SMZ-TMP is also sold as Fish Sulfa ® and Fish Sulfa Forte ® by Thomas Labs. Fish Sulfa is dosed at 15mg/kg. Ivermectin given orally is the safest for treatment of internal and external parasites however, using the 1% solution makes for a very difficult dilution into micrograms and an even more complicated dosage. Daryl Mabley DVM recommends using ivermectin paste sold for horses (in brands such as Zimecterin ®) and giving orally, in the size of an uncooked grain of white rice once weekly for three weeks. http://www.rmca.org/Articles/dchart.htm. Anytime antibiotics are used in pocket pets, it is a good idea to provide yogurt or a product called Bene-bac ® to replenish the good intestinal bacterial that can be harmed by the antibiotics. Make sure to remove any uneaten yogurt from the cage.
- **Wet Tail/Diarrhea:** Diarrhea is called "wet tail" particularly in hamsters because the fur around the anus appears wet from the constant diarrhea. Additional symptoms include lethargy and a hunched posture. Diarrhea, in any pocket pet can be serious and should be treated as soon as possible. Wet tail can be caused by inflammation of the intestines, the bacterias clostridium, Lawsonia intracellularis, as well as intestinal parasites.. The use of antibiotics can cause diarrhea and must be used with caution. The offending

antibiotics typically have one of the following suffixes: (-cillin, -mycin, or -sporin). **Neomycin sulfate, the most common drug sold over the counter for wet tail, has been shown to worsen diarrhea and has been discontinued by many companies.** Read the ingredients of any medication sold for diarrhea in pocket pets to be sure it does not contain this ingredient. The primary goal of treatment is to avoid dehydration. Using an electrolyte formula such as Pedalyte ® or Re-sorb ® in the drinking water will help, and should be changed daily. Offer yogurt or Bene-bac ® to replenish healthy intestinal flora. Enrofloxin, sold as Fish-Enro ® by Thomas Labs has been proven effective against wet tail. Fish-Enro ® may be dissolved in the drinking water at 100 mg/liter (33.8 fluid oz) and should be changed daily.

- **Respiratory Infections**: Several bacterias and viruses can cause respiratory infections with the most severe being mycoplasmal bacteria. Symptoms may include sneezing, sniffling, eye and nose discharge, difficulty breathing, lethargy, ruffled hair coat, and loss of appetite. There are several methods of transmission and one should be careful not to expose new pets to one another without a quarantine and sick individuals should be removed from the population as soon as symptoms are noticed. Pneumonia can be the end result which can result in death. While antibiotics can fight primary and secondary infections, other supportive therapies can also help the pet fight off the disease. Keep the pet in a warm, clean cage with fresh bedding in an area where traffic is at a minimum and there are no drafts. Make sure the pet is eating and drinking. If not, the pet may become dehydrated. Pedalyte ® and other electrolyte therapies can be used if necessary.

- **Skin parasites:** Demodex mange, sarcoptic mange, and lice are among some of the parasites that can affect pocket pets. Microscopic examination is needed to ensure the correct treatment. Ringworm is also a potential issue, although ringworm is a fungus, not a parasite or worm. Typical presentation of mites vary from skin inflammation and intense itching, to dry, scaly patches of hair loss. Depending on the parasite involved, treatment may range from a 1:40 lime sulfur dilution for sarcoptic mites to amitraz (Mitaban ®) dips diluted at five times the package directions. For more information see this link under "Anti-parasitics"
http://www.vspn.org/vspnsearch/aow/drugtherapyinpetrodents.htm

32
Guinea Pigs and Rabbits

Both guinea pigs and rabbits can make good pets for the right family. Unfortunately, misinformation regarding their needs, personalities, housing and lifespan have put many a pet at risk. The guinea pig, also called a cavy, can live up to 8 years while rabbits can live up to 10 years.

Guinea pigs are not low maintenance pets, but require special food, supplements, vegetables, hay, and frequent bedding changes. Children can participate in the care of the pet, but should be closely supervised by an adult.

Rabbits, in particular, are fragile, and rarely enjoy being held. They have a powerful back kick, which can cause serious damage to the individual holding the rabbit. This same back kick can also cause spinal damage to the rabbit. Many rabbits are purchased at Easter time, only to be released in a field (where they will likely not survive), abandoned at the shelter, or die of malnutrition and poor care. As rabbits grow, if they can become destructive if not provided with proper stimulation and play and is often the reason given for being surrendered to the animal shelter. They should never be given as Easter presents unless the proper research has been done and the commitment understood.

Guinea pigs are social animals and enjoy having a companion. The interaction with another pig is not only fun for the animal, but it has been shown that pigs with mates are less picky eaters. Male and female pairs are best, but the male should be neutered first by an experienced veterinarian. Same sex pairs can work, but it is not unusual for males, in particular, to fight. While guinea pigs can be taught to sit in one's lap for a nice grooming or petting session, they rarely enjoy being carried around.

Guinea pigs, unlike most pocket pets, are diurnal, meaning, like most of us, they are awake during the day and sleep at night. Rabbits on the other hand, are crepuscular, that is, they are most active during the twilight hours of both early morning and evening. These traits make them popular pets as they do not keep the pet parent awake at night with their activity.

Domestic rabbits and guinea pigs are temperature sensitive. Prolonged exposure to temperatures above 80 degrees Fahrenheit and below 50 degrees can cause death in rabbits. Guinea pigs are comfortable in temperatures ranging from 65-75 degrees. While it is possible (though not advisable) to keep either species outdoors, certain precautions must be considered. In warmer weather, provide proper ventilation, keep the hutch out of direct sunlight and provide frozen water bottles for the animal to lay on. Conversely, in cool weather, provide a safe heat source and keep the hutch protected from winds and moisture. Better yet, in both situations, bring the pet inside.

Rabbits are unique in that they can learn to use a litter box, to come when called, and to interact in play with their pet parents. It is important, however, if you have other animals, to make sure that the rabbit does not become prey to a dog or other pet. My bunnies were able to live happily with my cats, but each situation is different, so never assume they will.

Rabbits shed and in their grooming, they swallow fur, much like cats. Unfortunately, this can prove deadly. It is important to brush your rabbit at least once weekly to prevent hairballs and to make sure she is getting plenty of fiber in the form of hay.

The needs of guinea pigs and rabbits, including their habitat are similar. What was once considered acceptable for both was the rabbit hutch with a wire bottom that allowed the feces and urine to drop through. The problem was, the pets were kept outside with little interaction with the family and in danger from extreme temperatures, accidental neglect, or predators.

In order to bring them inside, cages were created for them and sold in pet stores. These are much too small and unless the pet is interacted with daily, a sad life for the pet. An economical and preferred alternative is the cube and coraplast (C & C) design sold by The Guinea Pig Cages Store. http://www.guineapigcagesstore.com/about-candccages These cages can make the difference between having a pet that is alive to having a pet that is happy to be alive.

The average size for most of the guinea pig and/or rabbit cages sold in most pet stores is between 4.3 to 5.8 ft. That's not much space to live in. Compare that to generally accepted size standards by guinea pig enthusiasts and found in detail at the Guinea Pig Cages Store website:

Minimum Size	# of Guinea Pigs	Preferred Size
7.5 sq ft	1 to 2	10.5 sq ft
10.5 sq ft	3	13 sq ft
13 sq ft	4	16 sq ft

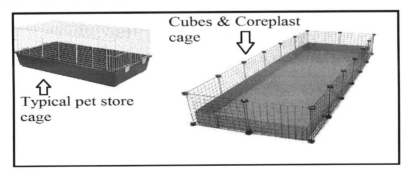

If two or more males are kept together, it is recommended to purchase one size up to avoid conflict between males.

Believe it or not, the cage on the left in the photo was more expensive than the C & C cage that provides much more room for the pet. Additional options for the C&C cages includes a cover if protection from other pets or children is required, as well as second level patios and more.

The larger design from this company would be appropriate for a rabbit, but nothing smaller.

Toys for guinea pigs and rabbits can be very inexpensive. An empty toilet paper roll stuff with hay can keep them occupied for quite a while. My rabbits enjoyed ripping up old phone books. While they enjoy this activity, make sure that what they are playing with is safe. If allowed to roam free in the home (which should only be done under great supervision), keep in mind that both species are at risk of chewing electrical cords, plastic, and other potentially deadly materials.

Both the rabbit and guinea pig need to chew as they have teeth that never stop growing. Tree branches from maple, apple, willow, birch, and apple trees are safe to chew on if they have not been sprayed with pesticides. If you do not have access to safe tree branches, purchase rabbit and guinea pig safe chew toys from the pet store.

The diet of the guinea pig and rabbit is similar, but experts warn about the dangers of feeding guinea pigs pellets formulated for rabbits and relying solely on guinea pig pellets for adequate nutrition.

Guinea pigs cannot make their own vitamin C, and must consume foods high in vitamin C. Guinea pig pellets contain vitamin C but not in the quantity required by the pig. Although the guinea pig pellets do not provide enough vitamin C for the guinea pig, the pellets can provide too much for the rabbit. Rabbit formulas, in turn, can contain antibiotics which can be toxic to guinea pigs.

Lack of essential amounts of vitamin C is known as scurvy. Scurvy is very serious condition in guinea pigs. Scurvy causes problems with blood clot formation and the production of collagen which is necessary for healthy joints and skin. Symptoms may include difficulty walking, swollen joints, bleeding under the skin, a rough hair coat, and overall ill health. To ensure proper levels, it is imperative to rely on fresh vegetables.

A comparison of rabbit and guinea pig foods demonstrates the similarities and differences of commercial diets. This comparison of pellet foods helps us to understand the needs of both species and offers information that allows pet parents to skip the processed pellets and give the pet what she really needs: a variety of hays, fresh fruit and vegetables, water, and a salt and mineral block.

Rabbit Food Main Ingredients	Guinea Pig Food Main Ingredients
Sun-cured timothy grass hay, oat hulls, sun-cured alfalfa meal, wheat middlings, dehulled soybean meal, dried cane molasses, ground flax seed, salt	Sun-cured alfalfa meal, dehulled soybean meal, ground corn, rolled oat groats, rolled barley, wheat middlings, ground oats, ground wheat, cane molasses, soy oil, salt

It is important to understand a little about hay and its importance in the diet of rabbits and guinea pigs. Hay provides the essential nutrients and fiber necessary for good health. A diet adequate in hay and lower in grains and sugars helps prevent digestive issues and diseases. There are several types of hay including grass hay: timothy, wheat, meadow, orchard, and bermuda and then there is legume hay: alfalfa being the most common. The two often found in stores are timothy and alfalfa. Timothy should be the basis for what you feed both guinea pig and rabbit. While alfalfa is good to mix in occasionally, it is too much of a good thing. Any time you can find fresh orchard grass or any other grass hay, it's a good idea to include those as well.

When feeding fresh fruits and vegetables, introduce them slowly and don't overdo it. Kale and oranges are a healthy source of vitamin C. Both rabbits and guinea pigs enjoy celery, bok choi, watercress, carrot tops, parsley, dandelion leaves, kale, green or red leaf lettuces (no iceberg), and in smaller amounts, broccoli, apples, pears, bananas, green or red peppers, and whole carrots.

Always provide salt and mineral blocks. Small wheel shaped ones can be purchased, or if you have several pets, you can buy larger blocks at any feed store.

Foods to avoid for both guinea pigs and rabbits include: iceberg lettuce, cabbage, cauliflower (both gas producing), shelled seeds and nuts, potato peelings, rhubarb, turnips, raw beans, fruit seeds, dairy, meat, sugary foods, caffeine, breads, and processed foods. For a complete list of foods that are safe, please refer to:
http://www.happycavy.com/guinea-pig-safe-edible-flowers/
http://kanin.org/node/189

Both guinea pigs and rabbits produce cecotropes, a round, small fecal-like pellet that are the material resulting from the fermentation of food in the cecum, a part of the digestive system. Cecotropes are nutrient-rich and are passed out of the body, like feces, but are reingested by the animal so the nutrients can be absorbed. Cecotropes have twice the protein, and half of the fiber of the typical hard fecal pellet. They also contain high levels of vitamin K and the B vitamins. If you see your pig or rabbit do this, understand it is a natural part of their digestion.

Since guinea pigs and rabbits consume a lot of vegetables, grow your own vegetables. Kale, green leaf lettuce, green bell peppers, apples and carrots are just a few of the healthy vegetables you can grow. Three of the healthiest, most inexpensive foods for rabbits and guinea pigs to eat are: the dandelion, plantain, and clover. Commonly considered undesirable weeds, these three plants are extremely healthy as long as they are harvested from a pesticide-free yard.

Plantain Weed   Clover Weed   Dandelion Weed

Health Concerns of the Guinea Pig and Rabbit
An important similarity of the guinea pig and rabbit is the danger of home-treatment and the potential toxicity from antibiotics. Both species are highly sensitive to the affects of antibiotics and treating with antibiotics can cause death. They should never be used at home unless prescribed by a veterinarian trained in treating each species.

If the veterinarian does prescribe an antibiotic, pet parents should watch for signs of diarrhea, stop as soon as diarrhea is noted, and call the veterinarian. It is very easy to cause more harm than good because of medication sensitivity and the ease in injuring the pet. For example, one wrong kick by a rabbit while trying to hold him for treatment can result in a broken back in the rabbit. Do everything you can to get your pet treated by a qualified veterinarian.

As in pocket pets, antibiotics containing one of these suffixes should be avoided: -cillin, -mycin, -sporin. Below are common disorders and diseases common to both species. There are several species- specific diseases not covered. Potential pet parents are advised to become educated on disease possibilities and find a qualified veterinarian in your area that you can afford before adopting one of these pets.

Common Disorders of the Guinea Pig and Rabbit:

- **Intestinal Disorders**: There are many viruses, bacteria, parasites, and conditions that cause intestinal disorders. Signs of intestinal upset include diarrhea, lethargy, lack of appetite, weight loss, rough coat, hunched posture, and pain upon palpation of the abdomen. Unless specifically prescribed by a veterinarian trained in caring for either species, antibiotics are not recommended. A vitamin C deficiency in guinea pigs can encourage diarrhea or make the pet's ability to recover more difficult. As guinea pigs and rabbits can die quickly, and sometimes without many external symptoms, any symptoms noticed should be treated immediately. The safest treatment for diarrhea is an increase in the fiber (more hay) and restricted grains and sugars. Yogurt or Bene-bac ®, to replenish beneficial bacteria is also helpful. If your pet is not drinking sufficient water, it may be necessary for your veterinarian to administer subcutaneous fluids. As mentioned earlier, rabbits are prone to blockage caused by ingested fur. Treatment is not something that can be done at home, so prevention is of utmost importance with proper diet, brushing, frequent cage cleaning, and prevention of boredom. Hairball treatments for cats should not be given to rabbits. Some causes of digestive upset can be passed from pet to pet (of the same species), so the sick pet should be isolated. Cages should be disinfected.

- **Respiratory Disorders**: Pneumonia, or inflammation of the lungs, is common in both guinea pig and rabbit and is the number one killer of guinea pigs. While bacteria are generally the cause, poor sanitation, poor ventilation, and improper diet are significant contributing factors. Signs may include nasal and eye discharge, sneezing, difficulty breathing, lack of appetite, and lethargy. While antibiotics such as enrofloxin (Baytril ®) for rabbits and SMZ-TMP for guinea pigs, MAY be prescribed by the veterinarian, pet parents must watch carefully for any sign of diarrhea. Once noted, stop the antibiotics and contact your vet immediately. Additional veterinary treatment is simply supportive and treatment of the symptoms rather than the pneumonia itself. Treatment may include force feeding with a stomach tube, or subcutaneous fluids. A bacteria that is particularly contagious in rabbits and that often leads to pneumonia is pasteurellosis. Rabbits can be carriers without showing any signs. This bacteria may also manifest itself in skin abscesses, head tilts, or stuffy, runny noses.

As I have mentioned, both guinea pigs and rabbits have many species-specific diseases, disorders, and external parasites. Additional reading recommended for guinea pig pet parents includes skin parasites, metabolic and reproductive disorders.
http://www.merckvetmanual.com/pethealth/exotic_pets/guinea_pigs/disorders_and_diseases_of_guinea_pigs.html

Topics for rabbit pet parents include ear and skin parasites, kidney and bladder stones and urinary tract infections. http://www.petmd.com/rabbit/conditions

33

Rats & Ferrets

People tend to have strong opinions about rats and ferrets. Those of us who have had them as pets learn to appreciate their personalities. Others shudder to think of them as pets.

Both are very responsive to their pet parents, can be taught to use a litter box, and can even be trained to do tricks. Rats and ferrets are friendly pets if handled early on. They are social animals and do best in groups or pairs. Be careful not to mix intact males and females together to risk pregnancy. Spaying and neutering is encouraged particularly in ferrets, not only for population control and health, but for odor control. The musk smell of a ferret is very distinct.

A well cared for rat will live about 2 ½ -3 years, while a well cared for ferret can live 6-10 years.

Ferrets are illegal in some states, so check the laws in your state before purchasing. Never bring an illegal pet into your state. If something happens to you, the chances of them being euthanized are great.

Both rats and ferrets can be kept in similar size cages. The cages should have multiple levels with a wide solid bottom. Both rats and ferrets enjoy climbing. The square footage of the bottom of the cage should be at minimum 4 square feet. Make sure the cage is well ventilated and cleaned often.

If provided with a special litter pan designed specifically for ferrets with a high back, you will have a very good chance of teaching both species to be potty trained. I have found rats much more difficult to train, but it is possible.

Several houses, hiding places, and hammocks on different levels of the cage are preferred and ropes and ladders to climb on and toys to play with is greatly appreciated.

If the cage is being used for ferrets, line the bottom with recycled newspaper. For rats, aspen bedding or **kiln-dried** pine (avoid cedar) on the cage floor should be deep enough for the rats to dig. To make it even more interesting for the rat, creating tunnels using large cardboard rolls and covering it with bedding will add loads of fun.

Water bottles can be supplied for drinking water. Finding a cage-mounted water bottle that won't drip is a challenge. If the bottled water drips and wets the bedding, mold and insects will create a very unhealthy environment for your pet. I prefer to use a heavy ceramic bowl for providing clean, fresh water. Put the bowl on the second level of the cage to discourage the pets from covering the bowl with bedding.

Rats can spend hours working on their home if provided with a hiding place. Give them paper towels, cardboard rolls, and small cardboard boxes, and they will be happily occupied.

Ferrets are high energy and need time out of the cage, but they are also notoriously naughty and can get into a lot of trouble fast. Once your ferret is comfortable being held, put a ferret harness on him to help you keep him where you can see him. Ferrets can get into the tiniest holes, under cooking stoves, inside the dryer by chewing a hole in the vent duct, and even escape to the outside though that same dryer vent.

In the late 1990's when I had a pocket pet rescue, my ferret, Nut, played with my dogs, cats, and even my rescued fighting rooster, Chatty. In fact, Nut and Chatty seemed to be best friends. When Nut played, he played hard. His energy level was on turbo speed as was his naughtiness factor. He stole every piece of gum he could find and hid it behind the dryer. In retrospect, I wasn't a very responsible pet parent, but Nut lived to a ripe old age.

Ferrets need a diet high in protein and fat with very little carbohydrates. Dry ferret food can be left out at all times unless the pet is over eating.

Some people chose to feed ferrets cat food, believing it is quality nutrition for a lesser price, but cheap cat food can contain lots of carbohydrates. If you do use cat food, purchase kitten food, not adult cat food and get the highest quality you can afford.

I compared Marshalls ® Premium Ferret food to Hills ® Science Diet kitten food and found that they were very similar in price at about $3.50 per lb. So buy the ferret food that is specially formulated to keep ferrets their healthiest.

An interesting website I found that discusses the different methods of feeding ferrets, including raw food is https://www.lovethatpet.com/small-pets/ferrets/food/ .

Much like cats, rats eat several times daily instead of one large meal. Foods made for guinea pigs and rabbits do not provide proper nutrition. Since rats have been used in research laboratories for so long, rat blocks (sometimes called lab blocks) were created to be a simple and staple food for rats. If you chose to supplement with a seed based diet, be careful of the high corn content and avoid it if you can. Rats do enjoy fruits and vegetables, but give in moderation to avoid diarrhea. Rats do not require a salt block, but mine always enjoyed an occasional Milk Bone ® for dogs. Rats do need to chew as their teeth continue to grow, as all rodents do.

Health considerations for ferrets and rats:
Although ferrets and rats are alike in their "love-'em-or-hate-'em" popularity, they have many differences in common health issues and care. For example, while rats do not require vaccines, ferrets should be vaccinated yearly for rabies and canine distemper. There is only one approved rabies vaccine approved for ferrets, and only two canine distemper vaccines. It is very important to find a vet that is qualified and experienced to vaccinate and treat ferrets before purchasing one. Since the health issues are more species specific, I will address them separately.

Common Diseases and Illnesses of Ferrets:

- **Digestive illnesses:** Most digestive illnesses are caused by bacteria. The bacteria *Helicobacter mustelae,* present in most all ferrets, can, under certain circumstances, cause chronic inflammation of digestive tissue, particularly in the stomach lining. This is known as gastritis. Chronic gastritis can lead to stomach ulcers similar in humans. Stomach cancer in ferrets is associated with this continued, persistent gastritis. Signs may include lack of appetite, vomiting, dark, tarry stools, increased salivation, and a hunched over posture. Another bacteria, *Lawsonia intracellularis* can cause an overgrowth of intestinal tissue which can lead to a prolapsed rectum, weight loss, and diarrhea. It is extremely important that the pet be treated as soon as possible for either bacteria. Common treatments include antibiotics such as SMZ-TMP or metronidazole (Flagyl ®), amoxicillin, or cephalexin to fight the bacteria and famotadine (Pepcid ®) or cimetidine (Tagament ®) to reduce gastrointestinal acid production. *Coccidia* as seen in kitten and puppies, can also be found in young ferrets. Symptoms are diarrhea, weakness, lethargy, and dehydration. The stool generally has a very strong odor and rectal prolapse can occur. Treatment includes Albon given by mouth for 10 days. Pets with severe diarrhea may also need IV or subcutaneous fluids. One feared virus can reek havoc on the ferret digestive system and result in *epizootic catarrhal enteritis*. By killing the villi that line the intestine making digestion and absorption possible, severe damage occurs that can take months to heal. The disease is usually spread when a new ferret is introduced into the home. This is why a quarantine period is important. Green, slimy diarrhea is often a unique sign of the virus. Stool may also be bloody, and the ferret may lose his appetite or lose weight even while eating. The inability to absorb nutrients can be a killer. An intestinal biopsy is necessary to diagnose the virus and treatment is similar to other gastrointestinal illnesses.

- **Respiratory illnesses:** Ferrets are very susceptible to the *canine distemper virus* which is fatal. Prevention is with the canine distemper only vaccine. Even if your pet is always kept inside, just like parvo and puppies, we can bring it in the home on our clothes and shoes. Possible signs of the virus includes a fever, rash on the chin and groin area, loss of appetite, sneezing, coughing, eye and nasal discharge, and difficulty breathing. The foot pads will also thicken. Ferrets are also susceptible to the human flu virus. Symptoms such as we experience with the flu such as fever, sneezing, and congestion are common. Supportive therapy, such as humidifiers are helpful, but secondary bacterial infections may take advantage of the challenge to the immune system. It is best to see your veterinarian for a possible anti-viral. Never attempt to give aspirin or any other medication to reduce fever as it can be toxic to your pet.

- **Heartworm:** Just like dogs, ferrets can become a victim of heart worm infestation. It is said to be a very under-reported and under-recognized disease in the species. However, just as it can be a danger to the pet, it can also be prevented. To make a heartworm preventative for ferrets, one can use the same 1% ivermectin I use for dogs. Mix 0.3 mls of ivermectin with one ounce food grade propylene glycol which can be purchased on Amazon. Put the diluted ivermectin in an amber bottle, or simply keep in a dark place. Date it to expire 2 years from the day of compounding. Dose at 0.1 ml per lb of body weight. The average adult female is 1-3 lbs, while the average adult male is 3-5 lbs. Give once monthly.

- **External Parasites and Fungi:** Ferrets are susceptible to the same external parasites and fungi of dogs, cats, and other small animals. Fleas, ear mites, mange, and ringworm, plague many species. Advantage ® (not Advantix ®) and Frontline Plus ® are all safe to use on ferrets. Revolution ® for cats treats for fleas, ear mites, and is a heartworm preventative, making it an excellent choice. As in dogs and cats, mange can come in two forms, demodex and sarcoptic. Diagnosis is done by a skin scrape and microscopic analysis. Treatment depends on the type of mange mite present. Ringworm, a fungus, not a worm, is a round patch of hair loss and redness and is treated with an anti-fungal cream such as clotrimazole (Lotrimin ®).

Common Diseases and Illnesses of Rats:

- **Digestive illnesses:** Rats are most prone to pinworms and roundworms. Often there are only subtle signs of the infestation, so it is recommended to deworm your rat on a regular basis. Occasionally diarrhea may occur. A fecal test can confirm a parasite infestation. Treatment and prevention are very inexpensive. The same ivermectin dilution used for ferrets can be given by mouth at 0.4 mg/lb of body weight once weekly for 3 weeks.

- **Respiratory illness**: There are several bacteria and viruses that can cause respiratory illness. Sneezing, eye and nasal discharge, rough coat, and lethargy are some signs of this. Murine respiratory mycoplasmosis is a chronic and contagious bacterial illness of rats that cannot be cured. Staining around the eye from chronic drainage is a common symptom. Although there is no cure, the illness can be managed with antibiotics. Needless to say, rats with respiratory symptoms should be quarantined from other rats.
- **Skin disorders**: Rats are susceptible to the same external skin parasites as ferrets and treatment is similar. Fleas, mites, ringworm are a few. Barbering is another issue that may occur, particularly in a multiple rat cage. Dominant rats may chew the fur and whiskers of less dominant rats. Normally, this doesn't cause a problem to the skin itself, but if it does (or escalates to aggression), the rat may need to be separated from the others. Sometimes, when bored, the rat may chew its own fur. The solution to this is less boredom and more play. While growths and tumors are not necessarily a skin issue, they are common to the rat and do affect the skin. Not all growth and tumors are cancerous, but they should be examined by a doctor. Some growths can be removed to prolong or improve the quality of the rat's life. Other times, removal may not be necessary.

As pocket pets and small animals age, each face the challenges of old age specific to their species. It is important to be prepared for these so that the animal receives proper geriatric care. As I mentioned before, don't adopt a pet until you have read at least one book on their care.

34

Birds

The topic of pet birds covers a wide range from tiny zebra finches to large parrots. For the purpose of this book I have divided birds into groups. This is not divided by the scientific classes, but by similar needs:

- **Finches & Canaries**: Includes the most common varieties of zebra finches, society finches, gouldian finches, cut-throat finches, java sparrow, border canaries (including song-type and color-type)
- **Parrots**: Includes parrots, cockatoos, amazons, macaws, conures, lovebirds, parakeets, cockatiels and budgerigars (parakeets)
- **Softbills**: mynahs and lorikeets among others
- **Doves**: Although there are 300 types of doves and pigeons, the diamond dove is the most commonly kept

This is a very good example of the need to study about the different birds available in the pet trade, including their needs and personalities. If you are thinking about getting a pet bird, a very good overall resource is http://www.birdchannel.com/bird-species/default.aspx

There are many things to consider before purchasing a pet bird. Do you want a bird you can handle, or a bird who beautifully sings, but prefers not to be touched? Do you want a relatively quiet, chirping bird, or one who may talk, but also has an ear piercing screech? How about a bird that lives up to 10 years, or one that can easily outlive you? Do you want several birds in an aviary or a single bird that can be trained? If you want a pet bird to handle, are you prepared for the training that is required? How about the bites that can happen during the process of that bird learning to trust you?

While living in Southern California, I loved to visit Bracken's Bird Farm. In addition to getting to see nearly every type of bird in the pet trade, buying supplies in bulk, and expert advice, the bird farm took in birds that, for whatever reason, was surrendered by the family. In talking to them, I found that many were surrendered because the family could not handle the bird.

Parrots, for instance, can and do bite, and can become aggressive. I have a scar from an African Grey Parrot. The family I was pet sitting for, thought their bird was a male. He was a great bird that I could get out to play while I cleaned his cage. We became fast friends. The next time the family went on vacation, I was excited to see him again. When I arrived, I took the bird out of his cage, sat him in his usual place, and he attacked me as soon as I started back toward his cage. He bit through completely through the flesh at the base of my right thumb, and he wouldn't let go. All I could do was wait until he did. The bite was more painful than any dog or cat bite I have experienced in all my years in the animal care field, and I have had my share of both.

Once the family returned home several days later, he attacked them as well. Using their expertise, Bracken Bird Farm discovered "he" was a "she" and in breeding season. She became another bird surrendered to Bracken's to be adopted by a more experienced family.

A lot of thought needs to go into the purchase of, not only birds, but all pets. Habitats or cages need to be carefully considered. Cages must be species-specific as some birds enjoy climbing, while others need horizontal flying space. Many (if not most) of the cages sold for birds such as finches, canaries, and parakeets, are far too small. Finches and doves, in particular do best in aviaries. Although it is possible to hand tame both, if purchased in most pet stores, they are not hand raised. I hand raised several zebra finches after their mother died and they were much more comfortable with being handled.

Larger parrots need to be hand tamed. Unlike finches who are small and happy in groups, larger parrots cannot spend their entire life in a cage. Their life expectancy can be the same, or more, than a humans. They need extra play areas and time interacting with their pet parent. Parrots are extremely intelligent, as the famous parrot, Alex demonstrated. Alex was the focus of a 30 year study to show the potential for communication between human and bird. Alex knew one hundred words, could distinguish seven colors and five shapes, and understand certain concepts.

Most bird enthusiasts will tell you that for optimum nutrition, your bird should eat commercially prepared pellets along with fresh fruits and vegetables according to bird type. Depending on the species of bird, many birds eat very little to no seeds in the wild.

Unless raised on pellets and denied the seeds, most birds will choose seeds. When I was better off financially in California, I had attempted to change my birds from seed to pellets. All I got was plenty of pellets to clean up. So my birds ate mostly seed supplemented with fruits and veggies.

The first bird I ever loved, was Zeb. He was a zebra finch. He lived on seeds and fresh fruits and veggies and he always had a cuttlebone for minerals. I did not know at the time that pellets were necessary. Zeb lived a wonderful life and finally passed away at age 10.

Years later, when life got financially difficult, I studied about the seeds in commercially prepared bird food to see if I could feed my birds on a smaller budget. I compared cockatiel seed, domestic finch seed, and wild finch bird seed.

Wild bird seed is much higher in fat than domestic bird food. This is to give the birds the energy they need to fly, an activity most domestic cage birds never get to do. The cheaper wild bird food has a large amount of corn and sunflower seeds. Wild bird seed should not be part of a domestic (caged) bird diet, unless it is in an emergency. A few days of wild bird seed is better than no seed at all.

All Natural Cockatiel	Wild Finch Blend	All Natural Finch
White Proso millet, gray striped sunflower, oat groats, canary grass seed, whole oats, safflower, flaked corn, red proso millet, buckwheat, black oil sunflower seeds	White Proso millet, canary grass seed, red proso millet, sunflower chips, thistle seed	White proso millet, German millet, red siberian millet, red proso millet, oat groats, canary grass seed.

I found the best way to stretch my bird seed was with wild finch food. A 2lb bag of domestic finch food cost about $6.50 while I could buy a 7.5 lb. bag of wild finch food for around $8.

When I found that I was running into these "emergency" situations too often, I re-homed my birds to someone in a better financial situation and could provide what I could not.

If you are lucky enough to live near a bird farm, it is a wonderful place to get fresh bird seed at an excellent price. In California I visited Bracken's Bird Farm in Riverside, CA and/or Redlands, CA monthly to purchase in bulk. I had many more birds at the time, and the cost of the seed was affordable thanks to them.

In Tennessee however, there was no such place I could find. By comparing the type of seed in each food, I was able to figure out what the basics of what they needed at a price I could afford. I am very thankful that they now have a new home where they can get the specific food they need.

Not only is the initial setup for an exotic bird expensive, so is everyday care. While your dog needs dog food and water, birds need more. In addition to the seed or pellets, at minimum, birds need grit, cuttlebones, mineral blocks, and a lava block to keep the beak trim and healthy. You also have to locate an exotic veterinarian to help you if your bird becomes ill or injured. You have to make sure you consider all aspects of care and the cost of that care.

Health concerns of the bird
Although there is great diversity in the bird kingdom, there are some common signs that your bird *may* be ill. These include, but are not limited, to the following:

- Noted increase or decrease in appetite
- Noted increase in water consumption
- Loose or abnormal bird droppings including change in color.
- Noted reduction in droppings
- Soiled vent. The vent is the final stop in the digestive system of the bird.
- Changes in behavior such as being less active and withdrawn
- Fluffing feathers, crouching over its feet, sitting low on the perch, or sitting on the floor
- Itching or picking at feathers and an abnormally long molt
- Respiratory difficulties including sneezing, stained feathers above the nostrils, breathing difficulties, and/or a clicking sound which is a cough in a bird.

It is impossible to cover all illnesses and injuries of all birds in this book, so I would like to recommend a comprehensive, but easy to read book on the subject: **The Bird Care Book** by Sheldon L. Gerstenfeld, V.M.D. This is my favorite go-to book on all things bird.

Many of the issues that can negatively affect birds are all but eliminated by purchasing the bird from a good, sanitary breeder, proper isolation for new birds being introduced to the home, keeping pet birds from being exposed to wild birds, cage sanitation, and other common sense practices.

Common Disorders and Illnesses of Birds:

- **Skin Parasites**: Scaly face or scaly leg mites are most common in budgies (parakeets), lovebirds, and canaries. White scaly patches near the eyes, legs, toes, beak corners, are a good indicator of these mites. They can deform the beak if left untreated. Using mineral oil on a cotton tipped applicator to soften the deposits can make the bird more comfortable and can even drown the mites. However, ivermectin by injection may need to be given by your vet to properly treat the mite infestation. This is not a procedure that should be performed at home. Cages need to be cleaned to help stop the mite cycle.
- **Intestinal Parasites and Protozoas**: The two most common of these are roundworms and thread worms. Both can cause decreased appetite, weight loss, loose droppings and poor plumage. Positive diagnosis is by microscopic fecal examination. Pyrantel pamoate treats both (20-50mg/kg). Protozoan illnesses such as giardia, trichomonas, and coccidiosis can also cause loose droppings, and in the case of giardia, a large volume, air-filled dropping. Trichomanas can affect the throat, crop, liver, or intestine and is characterized by cheesy-like material and even hard masses on the mouth or throat area. Coccidia doesn't always present symptoms, but when it does, loose and sometimes bloody droppings may be one. All protozoas can cause loss of appetite and weight loss. Giardia is often misdiagnosed as "psychological feather picking" when the itching and

flaking is, in fact, caused by giardia related malabsorption. Treatment for all three is metronidazole and support of the immune system with vitamins. (Metronidazole 40-60mg/kg, by mouth, once daily for 5-7 days)

- **Bacterial-related illnesses**: Many bacterial related illnesses such as e coli, pseudomonas, and salmonella, are most often opportunistic in nature. In other words, they take advantage of an immune system weakened by another disease. Psittacosis, often referred to as parrot fever, is caused by a bacterial organism called chlamydia psittaci. All birds may be susceptible to this illness. Decreased appetite, weight loss, labored breathing with nasal discharge, loose green droppings, ruffled feathers, tremors, and closed eyes with a depressed demeanor are some of the most common symptoms. Diagnosis may require extensive testing and treatment can be doxycycline given 25mg/kg by mouth twice daily for up to 45 days. Unlike most other illnesses, humans can contract this illness and present with flu-like symptoms.

- **Viral Illnesses:** Often bacterial infections are secondary to viruses. Pacheco's Disease is caused by a herpesvirus, is found in most often in parrot species, and is highly contagious. Signs are often non-specific and the bird may not show any signs until a few hours before death. Lethargy, diarrhea, and regurgitation are a few possibilities. Recovery is possible, but supportive therapy is the primary treatment. Proventricular dilation, known as the Macaw Wasting Disease, attacks mostly macaws and cockatoos. It is believed to be a disease caused by the paramyxovirus that focuses on the nervous system of the digestive system. Often, undigested food is found in the droppings. Lethargy, weight loss, may be accompanied by neurological signs. X-rays and biopsies may be necessary and the treatment is often surgical removal of the stomach contents. Acyclovir, one of the few anti-viral medications may be part of the treatment for both diseases.

Tinker & Sago

35

Herps: Amphibians and Reptiles

The number of potential pets in this group is astounding. Herp is short for herpetology and the vernacular term that includes amphibians (frogs, toads, newts) and reptiles (snakes, lizards, turtles, tortoises).

Tortoises are probably my favorite, but living in a more temperate climate and not wanting to keep a tortoise in a tank required me to adopt out my Russian tortoise before leaving California. As I have said, I have loved and cared for many types of reptiles and amphibians.

With age and experience, I have come to wonder how many herps can be happy living in captivity. While I think it is possible, the premature deaths of so many in the care of those even with the best of intentions, only supports my concern. However, there is a large exotic pet trade, so I feel it important to help those pet parents find ways to afford care.

Exotic pets are not always kept in habitats suitable for their needs. The minimum space requirements can be determined by the chart below.

Minimum Habitat Size:

Species	Length of Cage	Width of Cage	Height of Cage
Lizards	2-3X snout to tail length	1-1.5 snout to tail length	1-2X snout to tail length
Snakes	¾ of total length of snake	1/3 total length of snake	¾ to 1X total length of snake
Aquatic/Semi-Aquatic Turtles	4-5X carapace* length	2-3X carapace length	1.5-2X total length plus 8-12 inches
Tortoises/Land Turtles	5X carapace length	3X carapace length	1.5-2X carapace length

*Carapace is the length from the tip of the rostrum (nostril) to the tail end of the shell

To clarify, to determine the length of the cage for your 6 inch lizard, take the total length of your pet (in this case 6 inches) and double or triple it (6 X 2 or 6 X 3). The tank should be no less than 12-18 inches minimum. Do the same for the width and height and purchase a tank closest to those dimensions.

Health concerns of Herps:
There are over 9000 species of reptiles and 6700 species of amphibians within the kingdom of herps. While each species has their own particular health concerns, one thing is universal: most deaths can be contributed to poor husbandry, management, and care.

The temperature of mammals is regulated automatically by the hypothalamus. Herps are cold blooded, meaning they must regulate their temperature manually. They do so by moving to, and away from warm heat sources. In the wild, reptiles are able to do this naturally. In captivity, however, they are at the mercy of their pet parent. The same can be said for other aspects of their environment as well as their food sources.

Unlike other exotics animals I have covered, I will not be discussing specific diseases related to each herp species, but the most common *causes* of diseases in captive-bred reptiles and amphibians.

Common Causes of Disease in Herps:

- **Improper cage size and temperature**: Proper temperature regulation promotes good digestion and a strong immune system. If a cage is too small, they cannot move far enough away from their heat lamp to cool off. If it is too large, they may not stay warm enough. Complicate that by putting them too near a window or heat/air conditioner, and their ability to stay within a certain temperature range can be very difficult, often leading to death. Under-tank heaters are good for ground dwelling species such as snakes, but should not take up any more than 30 percent of the tank bottom. It should not be the only source of heat. A basking light should be provided on the same side. Often an incandescent light is used during the day, and a black light at night. Be sure that the black light is intended for reptiles and not one sold in the hardware section. These black lights emit harmful UVC life that can cause eye damage or worse. If an under-tank heater is used the wattage of bulb should be less than if the bulb is the only source of heat. Keep a close eye on the temperature to be sure it is within range for your pet. Additional lighting options will be discussed below.
- **Improper lighting**: Natural sunlight is made up of visible light that we can see and ultraviolet light that we cannot see. Ultraviolet light is made up of **UVA, UVB, and UVC** light. UVC and short wavelength UVB are hazardous to human and animal alike and are blocked by the atmosphere. Unlike humans, herps can visually detect some UVA light. They detect patterns and colors differently as a result of this evolutionary advantage. They use it to detect members of their own species as well as prey and edible plants. In addition, visible light helps set their circadian rhythm. It tells them when it is daylight and dark, what season of the year it is, if it is time for reproduction, as well as providing information regarding their thermoregulation needs. Incandescent lights, like

regular household bulbs provides UVA light and heat. They can not and should never be the only source of light. UVB is absolutely vital for healthy survival. UVB light cannot penetrate glass or plastic making it useless and unwise to put the tank near a window as a substitute. UVB is essential for a good immune system and absolutely necessary for vitamin D3 synthesis which, in turn, helps in the metabolism of dietary calcium. Many herp species die as a result of this vitamin deficiency which usual leads to **metabolic bone disease**. Symptoms of this includes general weakness, swellings, tremors, and in turtle and tortoises, a soft shell. Carnivorous and omnivorous species can get some of their D3 from their diet. Herbivorous species, however, rely more heavily on UVB lights to synthesize vitamin D3. Typical florescent household bulbs are not adequate and while UVB lights made specifically for reptiles may seem expensive, they mean life or death for your pet. Avoid compact florescent lights as they have proven to be harmful. Beware of basking lamps that claim to be "full spectrum". They do not provide adequate UVB. The exception to this is mercury-vapor lights that provide both heat and UVB. Be sure that you have sufficient UVB producing florescent lights to cover the length of the cage, change them every 6 months as they lose their effectiveness after this time, and mount the lights no more than 10-18 inches above the cage, depending on the specific needs of the species of your pet. It is also important to match the time your lights are on to the seasons. This helps maintain proper circadian rhythm and is made simple by using an automatic timer. Set the lights to turn on and off as the sun rises and falls.

- **Improper feeding**: Too often pet stores will sell young herps but not the **proper size food** for them. A pet store, may sell lizards, frogs, or snakes that are only a few weeks old, but sell crickets and mice too large for them to eat. Often, one must turn to online stores or learn to raise live food yourself . Sometimes small, independent pet stores will be more likely to have a larger selection of live food. Another trend I have observed is convincing potential pet parents that the pet they are interested in will eat dried, freeze dried, or frozen food. While some herps may learn to eat some freeze dried or frozen food, they cannot be fed like dogs or cats who have been domesticated for thousands of years. It was only recently that herps sold in captivity, were bred in captivity. In the wild, for the most part, reptiles and amphibians eat live food or fresh plant-life. Many detect their food by movement. Expecting one to eat a food so foreign to them is often met with disinterest, and can result in death for many pets. Snakes, for instance, whose recent ancestors were accustomed to eating brown rodents, or perhaps lizards, or even fish, may refuse to eat a white furred, red eyed, recently frozen mouse. While some snakes may learn to eat frozen mice or rats, if refused, you must act quickly to find food that your snake will eat. For a good discussion on feeding a stubborn reptile, see http://www.lllreptile.com/info/library/care-and-husbandry-articles/-/feeding-stubborn-snakes/ Some herp species, such as bearded dragons change their food requirements as they age. As young dragons, they are mostly carnivorous. As they grow to adulthood, they become more omnivorous requiring vegetable matter. At this stage, with my own bearded dragon, I often mixed freeze dried meal worms or even some of the pre-packaged foods made for specifically for beardies in with his veggies, but never did I rely on pre-packaged meals alone. It is often better to have a separate tank to feed your pet. There are many places to hide in the home tank, including under the carpet, if supplied. It may be in your pet's best interest to feed in an undecorated tank so the live food has no place to hide. That way, you know for sure your pet has eaten. No matter if you care for a snake, frog, or tortoise, it is vital to know what your particular herp requires. If it is live food, but you find yourself too squeamish, consider another type of pet.

- **Improper gut-loading of live food:** While it is tempting to bring home some crickets, sprinkle a calcium supplement on them, and toss them into the cage, this is not recommended. The nutrition that your pet gets when eating an insect is not only the insect itself, but the food that resides in the insect's digestive tract. Feeding a gut-loading diet for at least 24 hours will benefit your pet greatly. Pre-packaged foods specifically for this purpose can be purchased at your local pet store.

36

Aquatic Fish

Aquatic fish are divided into three basic categories:

- Salt water fish
- Tropical freshwater fish
- Cold freshwater fish

The cost of salt water aquariums, far surpass what most of us living on a budget can afford. Salt water habitats have very specific requirements, the fish are much more expensive, and mistakes are more costly. Marine creatures require a strict range of a pH of 8.0 to 8.4 and a fluctuation of even 0.2 can be disastrous. The levels of nitrates, salinity, and temperature must also be monitored carefully. Bloomburg calculated the cost of a properly set up 90 gallon salt water tank at $17,334. http://www.bloomberg.com/consumer-spending/2012-08-20/the-real-cost-of-a-saltwater-aquarium.html#slide1

Tropical fish are less expensive to keep, but still have specific requirements that need to be met. Water temperature should be kept at about 78 degrees, ammonia levels low, and if you are using tap water, you must either use a chemical de-chlorinator or allow the water to sit out with no fish for 24 hours.

The smaller the tank, the more effect small changes will have on the environment, so a 20 gallon tank is actually easier to keep than a 10 gallon.

Probably the biggest mistake in setting up a fish tank is buying the fish the same time as the tank. Healthy fish keeping is more than filling up the tank with water and tossing in your fish. The water must be allowed to reach the proper temperature, pH, and bacteria level. A tropical tank must have proper filtration as well as an aeration system. Products are available to introduce beneficial bacteria which will help break down the fish waste and keep the ammonia level to a minimum. If you introduce a large number of fish during this process, your levels of ammonia will increase exponentially, killing your fish. A new tank should only have one or two starter fish introduced after a 24 hour waiting period. Those fish will help the tank balance the chemical process that keeps the water environment healthy. Only after a week or so should you add any more fish.

Fish are at the mercy of the keeper, so even if the fish costs only a couple of dollars, you owe the fish your best attempt at proper husbandry. Educate yourself on proper fish keeping and be vigilant in your cleaning duties. Avoid overfeeding. This to will cause a sharp rise in ammonia which is deadly to your fish.

Different fish have different requirements and have different personalities. Some fish can only be kept as the sole member of the tank, while others enjoy being in schools of fish. Some fish are docile while others are aggressive. Read about the needs of your particular fish and determine what kind of tank you want to keep. A good online starting point can be found at http://www.thetropicaltank.co.uk/Fishindx/fishindx.htm

Some aquarium options are:

- The Community tank: This is a tank full of docile tropical fish species. The community tank is a combination of fish who prefer to swim in the upper, middle, and bottom levels of the tank. Its residents are generally schooling, live bearing fish (meaning they give birth to live young compared to laying eggs). This is probably the easiest tank to keep, and if well balanced in its inhabitants, can provide a vivid and beautiful ecosystem.
- The Cichlid tank: Cichlids are some of the most beautiful freshwater fish in the world and probably the closest in appearance to salt water fish. They are mostly found in African lakes and South American rivers. Ciclids are an aggressive species and must be paired carefully. They require a larger tank and plenty of hiding places. It is unwise to place any other species of fish in with the cichlids with the possible exception of bottom feeders and plecos to keep the tank tidy.
- The Oscar/Pacu/Pirahna tank: If you are looking for a fish that will grow to be large and aggressive, an oscar, pacu, or piranha tank may be a good option. Oscars in particular are known for their interaction with their pet parents. I have heard them called the "puppies" of the fish world. Depending on the size of your tank, you may only be able to keep one fish per tank. In addition to flake food, these fish require live food and will eat smaller fish put into their tanks.
- Cool-Water Tank or Pond: Fish that live in this environment can live comfortably in cooler temperatures compared to tropical tanks. These fish include gold fish, koi, bettas, and white cloud mountain minnows. It is often wrongly assumed that just because they do not require a heater, they do not require filtration or aeration. This results in high ammonia levels and dead fish. While they do not require a heater in their tank, their need for proper water quality is the same as tropical fresh water species. Gold fish and koi can quickly overload the tank with ammonia which is why they will only live for a short time in a fish bowl. Both gold fish and koi require large, well filtered and aerated tanks, and they make excellent fish for ponds. Keep in mind, however, that their need

for filtration and aeration does not change when they are outside.
- Betta Fish: The only fish species that can do well in a smaller tank is a betta, also known as the Siamese fighting fish. These fish are probably the easiest to keep. The male bettas will kill other fish and prefer a solitary lifestyle. Females can be kept together. All bettas enjoy hiding places and males generally do not do well in large tanks. I recommend a 2.5 to 5 gallon tank for them with several caves and plants. While they can live in smaller tanks, one must wonder if that provides a good quality of life. In the past, I have attempted to keep them in community tanks only to find them miserably hiding in the corner of the aquarium. Once moved to a smaller aquarium of their own, they appeared more comfortable, swimming about and utilizing the full space of the tank. Bettas are easily overfed and should be fed only 2-3 pellets per day. Some pet parents feed them 4-5 pellets every other day. Observing your individual fish will help you determine how much to feed. Any food left after 5 minutes is too much food and should be discarded.

White cloud mountain minnows are the cold water version of the neon tetra. They are beautiful in schools and do not require a heater. They are docile fish who can live with small goldfish.

The janitors of the fish aquarium, include cory cat fish, plecos, chinese algae eaters, and snails. While these fish will help keep the tank clean of algae and excess food, tanks must be vacuumed regularly with an aquarium vacuum and partial water changes done to remove fecal debris. This is true for both tropical and cold fresh water tanks. If you have an excess amount of feces, you may be overfeeding or have too many fish in one tank.

When cleaning your tank and doing partial water changes, never remove all the water from a tank. A healthy fish tank is a seasoned fish tank with "old" water that contains the proper bacteria and enzymes that help maintain a healthy environment.

Common Health Concerns for Aquarium Fish:
As I mentioned, aquarium fish are at the mercy of their caretakers. Most disease is directly related to the environment in which they are raised. Water that is too cold or too warm, ammonia and pH levels, tanks that are too crowded, and even improper tank mates can all contribute to death and disease. One of the best books I have read on fish keeping is Terry Fairfield's **A Common Sense Guide to Fish Health** published by Barron's. The most detailed book on identifying fish diseases I have found is **The A-Z of Tropical Fish: Diseases and Health Problems** by Peter Burguss et al.

Preventing Diseases and Illnesses in Aquarium Fish:

- Never choose a fish whose tank mates show any signs of illness.
- If possible, quarantine new fish for 14 days before adding the fish to your tank. If you

do not have a quarantine tank, allow the new fish to acclimate to the tank temperature by floating the transport bag in the tank for about 15 minutes. Next open the bag, catch the fish with a net and move to the new tank. Do not allow the water from the bag to enter your tank.

- If you have multiple tanks, have a net for each tank. Sharing nets can also share disease.
- Check your water quality monthly in an established tank, at least once weekly in a new tank, and anytime there are signs of illness or death. Improper levels of ammonia, nitrites, nitrates, and pH are the most common problem. Phosphate should be tested if there is an algae problem.
- If you buy live plants, buy only from tanks without fish.
- Keep your lights on a timer. Allowing the light to stay on too long can cause algae problems.

37

Farm Animals as Pets: The Plight of the Pot Bellied Pig

Many domesticated animals that we consider pets in the United States were once farm animals. Rabbits were once (and in some areas, still are) bred for the supper table. In their native region in the Andes of South America, guinea pigs are still raised as food.

In the 1990's, pot bellied pigs began making their mark in America as a unique and exotic pet. The first pot bellied pigs were imported into Canada in the 1980's. Imports continued, but mating pairs were established from the progeny of the original 18 all across North America. They once sold for $20,000 at auctions, but the price dropped as supply increased to meet demand, and they were sold as indoor or indoor/outdoor pets.

There are five types of miniature pigs all which, by The American Miniature Pig Association standards, are limited in size to 125 lbs or smaller in weight, and 22 inches or smaller in height. More recent articles are now claiming 250 lbs as normal for adult pot bellied pigs.

Unfortunately, as with many animals that become a temporary "fad", greed has taken hold and caused many problems for the animal. Pig breeds, normally raised for food, are sold as pot bellied pigs to the uneducated. Piglets are often weaned and sold too early so that they appear to be the small pot bellied pigs the potential pet parent desires. Young pigs are also denied proper nutrition to keep them smaller.

According to Rich Hoyle, founder of The Pig Preserve in Jamestown, Tennessee:

"These poor inbred and half-starved pigs are inundating sanctuaries," says Hoyle. "Probably 90 percent of the so-called micro pigs...will either be dead or in a sanctuary before they are two years old." http://news.nationalgeographic.com/news/2014/09/140930-animals-culture-science-miniature-pigs-breeders-sanctuaries/

Dishonest breeders and well-meaning, but uneducated adopters, have led to many "pot-bellied pigs" being abandoned at shelters, or if they are lucky, taken to a pig sanctuary.

Too often, pet parents expect the pig to be much like a dog, and does not consider several key things. The not-so-potbellied pig can grow to hundreds of pounds and far outweigh any dog. Even a smaller pig can be difficult, if not impossible to get into your vehicle in times of emergency. The veterinarian often has to make home visits like most livestock vets. In some areas, there are no vets that treat pigs.

Calling a pig a pet does not breed away their natural instincts and habits. Pigs, by nature, love to dig and root. That means your carpet, your beautiful hard wood floors, your carefully manicured yard, can become the target of that natural behavior. Pigs have a squeal that ranges from 110-130 decibels. Compare that to a jet plane range of 140. Pigs resist being picked up, and squealing is their natural reaction. They also squeal when excited. It is an important consideration. While cute on day one, it can be deafening later on.

Intact (not spayed/neutered) pigs in the home bring a whole new set of problems. Unaltered boars (males) have a very strong odor that only intensifies over time and they can become very aggressive. Unaltered gilts and sows (female) go into heat every 21 days. She can become moody, restless, and irritable. She can also forget her house training.

While spaying/neutering pigs is helpful in making them more cooperative pets, it is not a guarantee. Neutered boars can still be aggressive and potty training is not ensured with a spay.

Pigs are one of the most intelligent animals on earth, a fact many ignore. They can be potty trained and learn tricks, much like dogs do. It is important to remember, however, they are not dogs. Dogs have been domesticated for thousands of years. Pigs, a few decades. Dogs have developed a need to be with their humans and depend upon us for companionship and care. Pigs still have very strong instincts that are not always compatible to indoor living, particularly in the city.

While pigs are perhaps one of the cleanest in the animal kingdom, they do not have sweat glands. This is why, when allowed, pigs will cover themselves with mud on hot days. It is vitally important to monitor pigs when temperatures rise and do everything possible to prevent heat stroke. Adequate shade and water must be provided. If mud is not possible, consider a water misting system that is inexpensive and very effective. It hooks up to your water hose and provides a fine mist of water that cools the surrounding area. Plastic kiddy pools are another alternative, but not all pigs can jump into the pool. Consider digging a hole to drop the pool to ground level.

Whether indoors or outdoors, pigs should not be left alone with a few exceptions. If a pig lives indoors, it must be made pig-proof. Remember that pigs naturally want to root, and often that can mean chewing through an electrical wire, or digging up the carpet or sofa. In their focus on rooting, they can knock over small tables, break the fine china, and so forth.

Outdoors, pigs can dig under the fence and escape, eat poisonous plants, or be attacked by neighborhood dogs. A pig-proof fence is an absolute necessity if the pig is to be left alone at all.

Before you adopt a pig, prepare your home and yard and study their care. I recommend **Pot Bellies and other Miniature Pigs: A Complete Pet Owner's Manual** by Pat Storer. Make sure there is a veterinarian in your area who treats pot-bellied pigs. Keep in mind that once that pig is full grown, you might have to pay for a vet to come to you.

Now that I have given some major caveats, what do miniature pigs require in terms of nutrition, grooming, and health care?

- **Nutrition**: One of the first mistakes pig pet parents make is overfeeding. Pigs love food and lots of it. Much like the dog, they can learn to beg. The ideal diet for pigs is high quality, high fiber, low calorie. Pelleted food made for miniature pigs (not hog's food) contains the proper vitamins, minerals, fats, proteins and amino acids. Pellets intended for quick growth should never be used. Pellets should only be about 50% of the diet. If possible, pigs should be allowed to graze on chemically untreated grass. If this is not an option, small portions (about 25% of the daily diet) of alfalfa or oat hay should be provided. The rest of the diet should be made up of fruits and vegetables. Those low in calories that can be fed in higher quantities includes cucumbers, celery, lettuce (green, not iceberg), bell peppers, cabbage, broccoli, and green beans. You can also feed your leftover such as cores of most vegetables and fruits. Corn and starchy vegetables should be given only in small amounts.
- **Grooming:** Pigs love to bathe. Once they are full grown, fitting into the bathroom may become impossible. Additional dental care includes regular examinations of the mouth and a low sugar diet. Boars develop tusks around 1-3 years of age depending on breed. In unaltered pigs, they will grow continually and must be trimmed. The tusks develop from the canine teeth and turn upwards near maturity. Typically it is safer to allow a veterinarian to trim the tusks to avoid injury to you or your pig. Ears should be frequently cleaned and examined. The pig's hoof does not have a hard bottom, but is surrounded by a "nail". The "nail" must be trimmed on a regular basis to ensure proper distribution of weight. Hoof nippers and a file are generally required. Allow the veterinarian to perform the procedure if you are not sure what you are doing.
- **Health care:** The normal pulse for your pig is 58-86 beats per minute. regular temperature 102-103.6 degrees Fahrenheit, and respiration, 10-20 per minute. Just like with dogs and cats, vaccination are needed to help keep your pig healthy. It is best to talk to your local veterinarian or county agent as to the diseases common in your area. This can vary widely and vaccinating for absolutely everything can be harmful to your pet. Pigs can also have internal and external parasites. While many are specific to pigs, some can be transmitted from dogs, cats, and other animals.

Common Illnesses and Emergencies of Pot bellied pigs:

- **Poisoning:** As a result of their rooting behavior, poisoning can be too common in the pig. It may present itself with vomiting, diarrhea, seizures, excess salivation, and collapse. Common poisonous culprits include acorns, blue-green algae in water bowls, antifreeze, rat poison, fertilizers, weed killers, cleaning chemicals, lead, molds and fungi, chocolate and caffeine, selenium found in soils, salt poisoning (sometimes as a result of inadequate water consumption), zinc, and toxic plants. A detailed list of poisons is available in the book I mentioned above.
- **Intestinal obstruction:** Pigs can eat without discernment and often swallow things that can cause constipation or even an obstruction. If you suspect either, contact your vet immediately. An obstruction, if left unattended can stop blood flow to the bowel causing extreme pain and eventually death.
- **Bacteria and Viruses:** Both bacteria and virusis can affect any number of organs including the digestive system (diarrhea from e.coli or salmonella), respiratory system (rhinitis or pneumonia), reproductive system (brucellosis or leptospirosis that can lead to spontaneous abortions), and even the musculoskeletal system (streptococcal arthritis causing the joints to swell).
- **Heat stroke**: Pigs can develop heat stroke rather quickly if not kept in the proper conditions as they do not possess sweat glands. Signs may include panting, drooling saliva, rattling respiration, unconsciousness and collapse. If found in this condition, immediately put a cold compress on the head and wet down with cool water from your water hose, if possible. Call your veterinarian.

FRUGAL AND EFFICIENT FINANACING OF PET CARE

"A cat has absolute emotional honesty: human beings, for one reason or another, may hidetheir feelings, but a cat does not." ~ Ernest Hemingway

38

Making the Unaffordable, Affordable: A Whole-Life Approach

Many of us are limited in the amount of money we have to spend monthly. A good budget and good priorities help make it possible to get the best vet care.

They say necessity is the mother of invention, and being responsible for multiple animals with little money to care for them, has certainly been inspiration for me.

It has taken a lifestyle change, made easier by finding a mate who knows how to live a frugal life.

While not all of my readers need to change their philosophy of living to take good care of their pets, I think it helpful to see what changes can be made if necessary. Our approach is a whole-life approach, and takes into consideration our entire budget.

We try to always live within our means and only buy what we can pay cash for. The only exception to this rule is the Carecredit ® card we use to finance the vet bills of T.Paws Rescue and ARFanage. We pay off the amount we owe within the time allotted, before we have any interest applied.

I would like to say we are independently wealthy, but if that were true, we would have never learned many of the ideas I share with you in this chapter. While our goal is to pay for all T.Paws expenses with our own income, there have been times during illness and unforeseen circumstances, when we have had to ask for help. We feel that we owe it to those who have donated as well as to our residents at T.Paws to examine where every dime of our money goes and what we can do to budget more efficiently.

The challenge all pet parents face each month is how to take our income, pay our bills, and buy necessities for both our human and pet family. When that income is very limited, it can seem impossible.

It is important to know the difference between a want and a need, and making difficult decisions that aren't always popular. Planning ahead, and making space in your budget for those needs still to come, will ensure that you are prepared for emergencies that may arise.

Some of the decisions we made changed the way we live day to day. We canceled our land line phone to use that money to pay for our cell phones. We dropped cable television and found that we now have a lot of time available to do other things, including spending time with each other. When we decided that we wanted to watch an occasional program, we paid $8 for Netflix and watch our shows on our laptop computer.

We keep a running list of things we need and a separate one for things we would like to have. We buy most of our groceries twice monthly based on our needs list. Haseleah pre-plans our meals focusing on using the same basic ingredients several times. Instead of planning the meals and buying the ingredients, she plans the meals based upon the ingredients we already have. She focuses on using "real" food instead of pre-processed foods. Although it is more time consuming, it is less expensive and healthier. Once the grocery list is made, we do not waver from it unless we find a deal that we can't pass up.

We have a very frugal method of shopping. Haseleah has learned the art of stacking coupons. Stacking coupons refers to using both a store **coupon** and a manufacturer **coupon** on one product. While this doesn't sound like it would save a significant amount of money, it does. As an example, consider a buy-one-get-one free manufacturer's coupon for shampoo. Target stores may have a sale on the same shampoo, that if you buy two, you get a $5 gift card. The shampoo itself may be $3.95, but with the coupon, you can buy 2 shampoos for $3.95 and get a the $5 gift card. You have actually made $1.05.

On top of these savings, Target has a program called Cartwheel. Cartwheel is a free savings program that you use at Target stores where you can save anywhere from 5-50% on the items you purchase. You choose the offers you want to use and scan the barcode at checkout to save.

Using this method now have a reserve of shampoos, conditioners, cleaning products, toothpaste, and more for practically nothing. We avoid buying items that we don't use no matter how good the deal is.
To learn the art of stacking coupons, please refer to http://thekrazycouponlady.com/beginners/ and http://www.livingrichwithcoupons.com/beginners/extreme-couponing-101

Before visiting any grocery store chain, we go to the salvage grocery stores in our area. Salvage grocery stores, sometimes known as grocery surplus or outlet stores, get their food from supermarkets and other retail stores who have to return products to the warehouses. The products may be overstocked, slightly damaged, or out of season. Sometimes, the manufacturer may simply have changed the look of the label and sent the old-labeled product to salvage. Never assume however, that the prices at salvage grocery stores are automatically cheaper than regular grocery stores. We have found products at our local Aldi, a global discount grocery chain, that were cheaper than the salvage store prices.

Salvage shopping allows us to eat, not only economically, but healthy and organically for only about $12 per day. We can come home after a shopping trip with the trunk and back seat full, for under $200.

We are also economical in our use of gasoline and car maintenance costs. We only go out when necessary. We plan all our errands, and complete them in one trip, saving gasoline. Both of our cars were purchased used so we have no car payment.

We use my car which has a better air conditioning in the spring and summer months, and when it turns cooler, we switch to Haseleah's car that just happens to have a better heater. We can spread our maintenance costs throughout the year instead of having to pay for oil changes for both cars at the same time.

We delay turning on our heat or air conditioning in the home until absolutely necessary. Not only does it save money, but we and the animals are better able to acclimate to the temperatures and the temperature changes don't feel so extreme. When we finally do turn air or heat on, we are so used to the outdoor temperature, that we don't require as much heat or cool air as other people. We also close off any part of the house that we are not using by turning the vents off and closing the doors.

We've gradually changed all our light bulbs to more energy efficient ones and turn the lights on only when necessary.

We shop for most our clothes at a local community clothes closet where we pay 50¢-$2.00 per item for good quality clothing. For clothes we can't find at thrift stores, we search at Ross's, TJ Maxx, or Groupon.com. We have been able to purchase top quality clothing for a fraction of the cost. We even find brand new items at local thrift stores and yard sales. Perhaps our best find of late was a new pair of traditional Birkenstock clogs that sell online for $110. We paid $1.00. This type of find is not an uncommon occurrence for us.

This year we purchased two rain barrels for $40 each, and have significantly reduced our tap water consumption. One rain storm can provide enough water to wash and rinse all of our clothes for a two weeks, mop the floors, water the pets and plants, and even flush the toilet if we so desire.

We avoid using our clothes dryer by hanging our clothes outside in good weather, and indoors in bad weather. Our indoor setup includes three strong garment drying racks and a short clothes line installed in our laundry room. The ceiling fan dries the clothes quickly.

Sometimes our "wants" list takes a while to fulfill, but when it does it pays off in big ways.

Haseleah had wanted a new (or newer) coffee maker. Keeping our list in mind, we went to a large local charity sale this summer. We found a coffee maker for $1. We brought it home and ran white vinegar through it several times to clean it. While Haseleah cleaned the coffee pot, I looked the brand and model up online. The BUNN coffee maker model we purchased for $1 slightly used, was sold brand new for over $100.

We are both avid readers and have a rather large library in our home. We do not purchase new books, but go to local library book sales, yard sales, thrift stores, and used book stores. We can bring one or two boxes of books home for the cost of one or two new books.
These are just some of the non-pet related ways we save money in order to be able to apply it to caring for our animals. However, we also have methods that allow us to stretch the money we do have available for them and make more efficient use of it.

39

Cost Saving Tips for Dogs & Cats

- Look for good quality food at salvage grocery stores. For a large $30 bag of Evolve ® Grain Free dog food, we paid $5.99. We also paid only $6.99 for a large bag of Rachel Ray Nutrish ® cat food that normally sells for $24.99.

- Check with your farm feed store or pet store to see if they sell damaged bags of food at a reduced cost. At Tractor Supply, we have purchased 40 lb of Diamond ® dog food for $9.50 that usually costs about $35.

- If the vet tells you that your pet needs to be on a prescription diet that you don't think you can afford, remember Carecredit ® covers prescription diets.

- Practice the method of stacking coupons for pet food. Since we must purchase large amounts of food for 20 animals, we cannot always purchase the same food monthly using the coupon stacking method. We mix the foods together and store them in sealed Rubbermaid ® containers.

- If you feed only canned cat food, buy the healthiest brand you can. Instead of feeding it all at once and taking a chance that the remainder will spoil, feed two to three times a day in small portions. The higher quality the food, the less you will have to feed. While the cost of a high quality canned cat food can run between $2-2.50 per 5.5 oz can, 4 Health ® sells one that is only 69¢ each. That's only $4.83 per week.

- Share some veggies with your pet. While I don't recommend the indiscriminate feeding of scraps to pets, I do recommend feeding small amount of species-specific, safe, healthy food to them. While cats cannot be healthy on a vegetarian diet, they do enjoy some greens. Steamed veggies such as broccoli, green beans, chopped greens, winter squash, and asparagus are some good options. Scrambled or boiled eggs are a good source of protein and readily eaten by most cats. Baked or boiled chicken are also good choices but, with any diet change, should be given in small amounts and introduced slowly to avoid stomach upset. Before giving any other "human food", please check to make sure it is safe for your pet.

- Learn to make your own canned dog food. We selectively choose from our healthy, home made leftovers (keeping toxic-to-pet foods in mind), and make our own healthy "canned" dog food. This food should never be used as a sole source of food, but a food to add to the pet's dry food. Acclimating our pets to this type of diet, avoiding fatty, spicy food, feeding it in no larger portions than we do when adding canned food to our kibble, we avoid gastrointestinal issues. We also save money, improve the diet of our pets, and produce less waste overall. We refrigerate the food where it will keep for about a week.

- It is always a good idea to keep your pet's intestinal tract healthy with probiotics. Probiotics replenish the healthy flora of the intestinal tract. Yogurt is an inexpensive and tasty way to provide probiotics. Most vets recommend plain yogurt, but for a treat, I will occasionally give my dogs blueberry yogurt. Adding it to their food once a week will do wonders for keeping the flora of the intestinal tract in good working order.

- For pets who like to be outside, use fallen, dried pine needles for bedding. If you have white pines nearby, rake up the brown needles once they dry. They smell good and feel great too. If pine needles are not available, straw makes excellent bedding.

- Use hydrated lime as a deodorizer. It is sometimes sold as barn lime. The lime may change the pH of your lawn, so check with your local garden center, but it is safe to use. Remove the pets from the area as the lime is dusty like diatomaceous earth. Unlike diatomaceous earth, lime is still effective when wet.

- If you have a large senior dog that would benefit from an orthopedic bed, you can buy a used toddler mattress for $10-20 at your local thrift store. Orthopedic pet beds are also sold at deep discounts on Groupon.

- When dog clothing is too expensive, buy kids clothes. Infant to toddler, fits most and at thrift stores are a dime a dozen.

- For inexpensive cat litter, buy Oil Dri ® Premium Absorbant. It is sold in the auto supply and cleaning section at national wholesale grocery clubs. A 40 lb. bag is less than $5. You can always add baking soda to help with odor. We found a 30 lb bag of Fresh Step ® Odor Eliminating Carbon cat litter for $8 at our local grocery surplus.

- If you have several cats, sometimes its cheaper to make your own litter boxes. I have made large ones using big Rubbermaid ® containers and cutting a hole in the side. Keeping the top on makes it look like a storage box, but it is a covered litter box in disguise.

- Vet offices always have an overabundance of Styrofoam ® containers. Medications, vaccines and more are shipped in them weekly. Ask your vet for a couple, cut a hole just big enough for your cat to crawl in, and you have a wonderful cozy bed for your outdoor kitty.

- For coprophagia or the process of eating feces (a nasty dog habit), MSG powder, the main ingredient is For-bid ® can be sprinkled on the food to make the feces unpalatable to other animals. If the dog is eating out of the litter box, sprinkle the MSG on the cat's food for about a week to discourage coprophagia.

- Don't limit yourself to pet stores to search for pet supplies. Ross's , TJ Maxx, or online at Groupon. For instance, we found 105 Bulleye ® Brand Potty Pads for $12.99 at Ross. We later found 150 AKC ® Potty Pads on Groupon for $20, shipping included.

- Instead of using disposable potty pads, use waterproof, washable, and re-usable bed pads sold for incontinence. The pads can be found online for about $4.

- Instead of buying toys, make them. Just like with kids, you buy an expensive toy only to find out they would prefer a pot and a spatula to beat it with. For my cats, I cut holes in big cardboard boxes and make them a fort. Give them a paper grocery bag. Tape one end of a cardboard paper towel roll, put some catnip inside and tape the other end up. Poke some holes in the roll so the cat can smell the catnip. Our cats play until they are exhausted. My dogs think nothing is as fun as an empty plastic bottle without the lid. Instead of buying expensive stuffing-free toys, purchase a used stuffed animal at the thrift store for less than $1, make a hole, and remove the stuffing. You can also take the stuffing out, replace it with an empty soda bottle, and sew it back up. Similar toys sell for nearly $10. Just make sure there are no parts that your pet can swallow, like the eyes and nose. They could care less what their toys look like, they just want to play! Look around at what you have before you buy.

40

Cost Savings Tips for Exotics

- Many exotics eat vegetables and fruits that you can grow in your own garden. This will significantly reduce your food costs in the summer months. If you don't have a space for a garden, let your friends know that you are looking for fresh fruits and vegetables. Many gardeners have more than they can use and will gladly give them away to someone who can use them.

- Fresh fruits and vegetables can be purchased at salvage grocery stores for much less than it costs in regular grocery stores. We have bought bags of organic carrots for 49¢ each.

- Other exotics eat live food such as crickets and mealworms that you can learn to raise yourself. At the end of this chapter, you will find information of how to raise healthy, inexpensive food for your exotic pet.

- Supplement your bird food by growing seed. Millet, sunflower seeds, and other seeds can be grown in the garden. For more information, visit http://www.seedman.com/birdfood.htm

- Don't assume that the only source of supplies for your exotic is the reptile aisle. For example, instead of paying $10 for dried meal worms, pay $5 to buy a large bag of Happy Hen ® Meal worm Frenzy sold in the chicken aisle of your local feed store.

- If your hay is part of your pet's diet, ask local farmers if you can pick up their leftovers after they put up hay.

- If you have a guinea pig and would like a safe play area, buy a small kiddie pool and put some bedding inside. Be sure to monitor your guinea pig, particularly if you have other pets. Also, don't assume your pig can't get out of the pool.

- Cardboard makes a bored rat very happy. My rats loved to make homes out of boxes and then tear them apart. Make sure the cardboard you use is free of any glue.

- Bunnies love to tear up phone books. Ask your friends for their old ones.

- If your rabbit is outside during the summer, he or she will enjoy sitting on a water-filled frozen soda bottle.

- If you know that your grass has not been treated with pesticides, let your guinea pig or bunny graze for a while. In order to make sure they don't run away, take the top off of their cage, and put it over them. Put them in a shaded location, free of dog and cat poop, and never leave them alone.

- Buy aspen or pine bedding in bulk. It is cheaper and you can keep the extra in a sealed container. Considering some pocket pets live for only 1 or 2 years, that one purchase can sometimes last nearly their entire lifetime.

The same pine needles I used as outdoor bedding for my dogs can also be used for some exotic species. I used them with my guinea pigs and never had a problem.

How to Raise Crickets

- Get an old aquarium or a deep plastic container. You will need a mesh lid or some way to keep them inside. Be sure they get plenty of ventilation.

- Fill the bottom with play sand about an inch deep or nothing at all. There are advantages and disadvantages for both.

- On one side of the container place a separate plastic container (about 4 in x 4 in) with soil. Do not use soil sold at garden shops because it often contains pesticides. A good alternative is soil sold for reptile tanks. Once the soil is in the small container, fill that container about half full with water. This soil must stay moist, but do not allow it to mold. This is your breeding chamber.

- Put several egg crates inside. This is to make sure that the crickets are not crowded. These can be purchased at Tractor Supply in the poultry section. Old toilet paper rolls work too, but in my experience, not as well.

- You can make your own food, but I find it much easier and cost effective to use something like Flunker's High Calcium Cricket Food. This ensures proper nutrition. For water, use a potato slice or orange slice, but be sure they do not spoil. Flunker's also has a gel that provides moisture without drowning the crickets and it adds additional moisture.

- The crickets will need to stay warm. Usually around 85 degrees. This can be accomplished with a heating pad set to low or heat lamps. Be careful not to get too hot or too cold.

- Purchase about 30-50 medium to large crickets from the pet store. Once the female has a long stem coming from the abdomen and the male is chirping, breeding has begun.

- Continue to keep the breeding chamber moist. Once eggs are laid, you will see tiny white specks in just under the top layer of the soil. Once you are sure there are several, remove the chamber to another deep plastic container to start the cycle over again.

- Continue to alternate containers and you will have a continuous supply. Expect to wait about a month to two months to have enough of a supply to be able to feed to your exotic pet.

How to Raise Mealworms

- Purchase one 6 quart plastic container and three 4 quart containers. Each container is for a certain part of the life cycle of the meal worm. (Egg, larvae/worm, pupa, beetle). Number your containers.

- In your 6 qtr. container (container #1) add oats, cornmeal, or wheat bran (about 2-3 inches). This is the bedding and also what the meal worms will eat. Also add a piece of potato or carrot for moisture.

- Purchase at least 100 meal worms (300-500 is ideal). Meal worms are the larvae stage of the darkling beetle. Avoid giant and super worms.

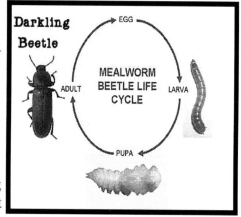

- Put your meal worms in the 6 qt. container. If using a lid, make sure they have some ventilation, but not too much to avoid escape. Replace potato or carrot as needed and do not let them spoil.

- Put the container somewhere warm. A good choice is on top of the refrigerator.

- As the meal worms mutate to the pupa stage, their appearance changes drastically. You will need to remove them and put them in container #2. This container should also have the same oat/bran bedding and a carrot/potato, but only about 1 inch of bedding and a small carrot as they do not eat much during this stage.

- The pupa will again mutate to darkling beetles. Once this occurs, move the beetles to container #3. Check daily as the beetles will eat your pupa. In container #3, add about the same amount of bedding, but add a bigger carrot/potato. Make sure the veggies are fresh.

- Any beetle that seems unhealthy, discard. It is important to keep the healthiest since their offspring will be providing nutrition for your pet.

- Once about 10-20 healthy beetles are doing well, it is time to separate the bedding (which contains the eggs) from the beetles, as they will eat the eggs. The easiest way to separate them is to put an apple slice inside. The beetles will grab the apple and you can simply remove the apple.

- Using your #4 container, put the apple and the beetles inside temporarily. Take the bedding from the #3 container and put it in the #1 container. This eggs will hatch and the cycle will begin again.

- Put new bedding in container #3 for the beetles to allow them to lay more eggs.

- When the bedding has become too dirty to use (3-6 months, put the old bedding in another container in case there are more eggs to hatch, and add new bedding to your containers.

How to Raise Feeder Guppies:

Feeder guppies are not the fancy guppies you see sold in stores. They are smaller and the males have light rainbow colors. The females are plain in color. They are very prolific fish. One female can produce 40-60 fry at one time.

- Depending on how many you need, start with two tanks. I suggest a 5-10 gallon for the adults and a 2.5-5 gallon for the fry (baby fish). Set up the tank before purchasing the fish. Make sure the water is de-chlorinated and at an appropriate tropical fish temperature. Take care of these fish just as good as you would a pet fish. Not only do they deserve it, but it makes for healthier food for your pets.

- Purchase about 2 dozen adult feeder guppies. Do not purchase fish from tanks with dead fish floating in the tank. Ask the pet store employee for as many pregnant females as he can find. The darker and bigger the spot near their vent on their abdomen, the more likely the female is pregnant.

- Put the adults in the tank. If you have any females that look like they may give birth soon, be prepared to move them to the smaller tank for delivery.

- Your smaller fry tank needs to be densely planted. Give the fry plenty of places to hide. Keep in mind, you may not be present when mom gives birth, and she may eat them.

- As soon as she gives birth, move her back to the adult tank. Once the fry are big enough, they can join the adults and the cycle can continue.

There are other food items you can raise for your frogs and other pets: mosquito larvae, brine shrimp, and even blood worms. They all have their own level of difficulty and expense. The cheapest and easiest is the mosquito larvae. You have to be particularly careful with mosquito larvae to ensure that they don't become mosquitoes. Mosquitoes spread disease, not only for people, but for pets. They are the carriers for heartworm.

How to Raise Mosquito Larvae:

- Using a small bucket, fill it with water.

- Sit the bucket in the sun. The water will start to turn green.

- Check the bucket daily. You should start seeing tiny clusters of dark brown eggs. These should be about the size of a sesame seed or tiny grain of brown rice.

- You can put these eggs in the tank and allow your pet to eat the larvae as they hatch. If feeding them to your feeder guppies (also known as mosquito fish), you can go ahead and put the eggs inside.

- Using a brine shrimp net, which is smaller than a fish net, you can net the wigglers once they hatch. I carry a cup outside with me, scoop some of their water in it, net the wigglers, and put them in the cup for transport. I then net them again to transfer to the fish or frog tank.

- Make sure that the wigglers do not mature to adult mosquitoes. If you have to dump your bucket and start over because you have too many, do it. Or better yet, isolate them to a small ice cube tray (the one for tiny ice cubes). Freeze the larvae so you will have some for winter.

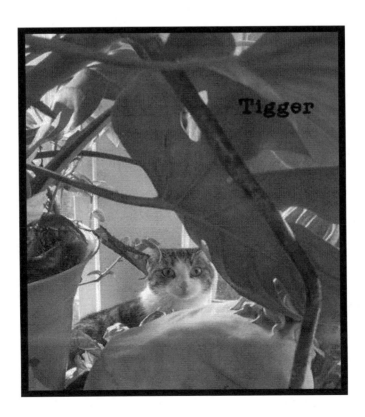

41

The Keys to Low Cost At-Home Pet Care & Tips for Financing Vet Care

Low cost pet care often takes a change in one's way of thinking. While preventative measures such as quality food, spaying/neutering, yearly lab work, and frequent dental cleanings seem expensive, they save money in the long run.

Secrets for efficient use of your at-home care cash:

- Understand that marketing is a process of selling a generic and inexpensive item for much more by giving it a trade name and repackaging it in a more attractive box. You can pay two to three times as much for a trade name such as Benadryl ® than you pay for its generic counterpart, diphenhydramine.

- Learn to always read a label. Instead of looking at the trade name, turn the box over and look at its ingredients. If you look closely, nearly every over-the-counter sleep aid on the market is nothing more than diphenhydramine. That's it. You paid extra for the trade name and the creativity it took to fool you.

- Don't narrow your search for medical products to the most obvious places. While going to the pharmacy is your first instinct, you are often more likely to find a needed product in the livestock section of your local farm supply store.

- Learn that the internet is your friend. It is often cheaper to purchase on websites such as Ebay or Amazon, and many offer free shipping. If you need only a small portion of a dewormer or flea preventative, many Ebay sellers will accommodate you. For instance if you have only one cat, one extra large dog vial of Frontline will last 8 months. Instead of spending $20-30 for 3 cat vials that will last 3 months, purchase a single extra large dog dose for $12-15 that will last 8 months.

- Recognize that many prescription antibiotics are sold over-the-counter, but marketed for fish. While this can be misused, responsible use of this option can save a life.

- Avoid pre-packaged first aid kits. It is cheaper to make your own. You get much more product for much less money and you are not paying for packaging.

- Do all preventative measures you can at home. This saves money to focus on those things only the vet can do.

When you adopt a pet, you are ultimately responsible for getting your pet vet care. Veterinarians are often expected to extend credit for a client they barely know. I've known vet clinic employees cursed, made to feel guilty and even physically attacked because their clinic didn't accept payments.

The pet comes to the clinic in an emergency situation, the family is not financially prepared, so they project their own guilt onto the staff. It is not fair to the staff and it is not fair to the pet. While I vividly understand the emotion and frustration of living a financially strained life, we must take responsibility and think ahead.

Tips for Financing Vet Care:

- **Care Credit ®** is a health care credit card that is good, not only for pet's, but people too. It allows a period of time of interest-free payments. You can be prepared for emergencies and can afford care when needed. If the amount is not paid in the time allotted (usually 6 months), the interest rate is applied and is very high, but if you budget well, it is a wonderful resource.

- **A Pet Saving Account** is also an option. While difficult for many of us to save large amounts, saving your change is something within reach. Change adds up over time. At times, it has helped me buy food for my animals when times were tough. Putting $5-10 aside monthly could mean the difference between life (vet care) and death (euthanasia) for your pet. Again, prioritizing your wants and needs is important.

- Sell unused or unneeded items on **Ebay, Amazon, or locally**. I have found there are many things around the house I don't need. Sometimes I will just have a **yard sale** and put it toward vet bills.

- Turn a hobby into an extra source of income. Haseleah has turned her hobby of making all natural soaps and skin care products, as well as her love for crochet and hand embroidery, into an Etsy store. All proceeds pay for the food and medical bills for T.Paws.

- There are also some websites that will help you create an **online fundraiser**. The website http://www.gofundme.com/ helps you set up your own online fundraiser for a small fee.

- There are some resources online to help in emergency situations. However, while rechecking my sources from the first edition, I found that many have had to stop taking applications for emergency care. There is simply too much need. One that I did find still accepting applications is **Red Rover Relief**. http://www.redrover.org/program/redrover-relief The help given is only about $100-200, however.

- For non emergency care, you may apply at The Pet Fund http://www.thepetfund.com/ or The Brown Dog Foundation. http://www.browndogfoundation.org/prequal

- For a detailed list of other organizations that may be of assistance please refer to http://www.imom.org/fa/pdf/fasources.pdf

- The **Pet Medication Drug Card** is similar to human drug cards that you can get a local pharmacies. The card provides savings up to 75% at participating pharmacies and can be applied for at www.petmedicationcard.com.

- The Humane Society of the United States provides links by state and breed. It is a great resource to begin your search for financial assistance. Go to:

http://www.humanesociety.org/animals/resources/tips/trouble_affording_veterinary_care.htm

- There are also local organizations that may help with spay and neuter financial assistance. Contact your local humane society for information.

- **Pet health insurance** is available and may be a good option for some pet parents. The insurance requires a monthly premium . Consumer Reports compared the cost vs benefits of nine pet health insurance companies and found that it was rarely worth the cost. http://www.consumerreports.org/cro/magazine-archive/2011/august/money/pet-costs/pet-insurance-rarely-worth-the-price-in-our-analysis/index.htm To do this they used the lifetime medical history of Roxy, a healthy 10-year-old beagle who lives near the magazine's office in Yonkers, N.Y. Roxy's lifetime vet bills have totaled $7,026 (in current dollars). In every case, the total premiums that would have been paid to those insurance companies were higher than Roxy's medical bills. While pet health insurance would be great for emergency care, a good pet savings account combined with the skills taught in this book, would supply the money needed for most emergency care. That is the premise of proactive pet parenting.

- **Wellness plans** are offered to every pet who goes to Banfield Pet Hospital, a nationwide veterinary chain. The point is have predictable monthly payments for pet care by buying into a wellness plan. The plan requires you to get the service at their chain and will not cover any emergency care received at any other hospital. The plan includes unlimited office visits, routine vaccinations, comprehensive physical exams, and discounts on products such as flea and heart worm prevention. Plans are available for all life stages of the pet. The wellness plan does not cover emergencies, but parts of the plan may offer discounts for pet emergency services.

Where to Focus your Vet Dollars to Save the Most Money

It is helpful to separate the money you use for at-home care and veterinary care and to use your vet dollars as efficiently as possible. Assuming you vaccinate, give a heartworm and flea preventative, and intestinal parasite control, the best use of your money centers around two things:

- Healthy teeth and gums
- Yearly veterinary exam including lab work

One of the keys I believe, to your pet living a long life, is taking care of his/her teeth.

You have to consider that most of us brush our teeth at least once daily. Most dogs and cats do not get that. Tartar and calculus builds up, gingivitis kicks in, the gums get inflamed and eventually infected.

All the bacteria that is in the mouth and oral cavity, find its' way into the bloodstream and through the body causing illness. Bacteria can destroy the kidneys and the heart. Dental cleanings are not just to keep you pet's breath nice and fresh, these cleanings prolong your pet's life.

I'm a firm believer that most dogs and cats should eat primarily dry food in order to have a healthy mouth. While one can flavor the kibble with canned food, the kibble serves to remove the tarter as the pet eats.

In addition to dry kibble, some ideas as recommended by the American Veterinary Dental College (AVDC) are as follows:

- Brush your pets teeth with a finger brush and pet specific toothpaste (never use human

toothpaste)
- Chlorhexidine Gel and Oral Rinse: Both are highly effective anti-plaque antiseptics. The first is applied to the teeth using a cotton tipped applicator, while the second is squirted into both sides of the mouth.
- Dental diets: Diets such as Hills Prescription T/D have been developed to reduce plaque. I do not use it for a primary diet, but as a treat that has the added benefit of a healthier mouth.
- Rawhide and Dental bones: The AVDC suggests avoiding cow hooves and naturally dried bones as they are too hard and can cause teeth the break and crack. They do recommend rawhide chews as well as dental bones such as Greenies ®, Pedigree ® Dentastix, or Milkbone ® Dental Chews as long as they are given under supervision
- Dental toys: Toys such as Kong's ® Dental Stick, Nylabone Dental Chews, and similar toys can be helpful in removing plaque if used on a regular basis. To encourage use, smear the toys with peanut butter and be sure to supervise to make sure your pet does not swallow any toy pieces.

Even if you do everything right, including brushing the teeth daily, some pets will still need a sedated dental cleaning or dental prophy as it is known in the veterinary field. Cost for this procedure varies based upon the labor involved, the level of plaque, and the necessity to remove any broken, exposed, or diseased teeth. In my area of the country, I can count on an average dental prophy to cost $100-150. A dental can also vary widely by veterinarian. Recently, one vet quoted a family member $800 for her 14 year old dog to have a dental. My vet did the procedure for less than $200 including extractions.

Do not fall for the gimmick of non-sedated dental cleanings that some groomers and unscrupulous veterinarians advertise. As I discuss in Chapter 7 of this book, these type of dental cleanings are terrifying and painful to your pet and a waste of your money. As anyone who has performed a dental cleaning knows, it is impossible to get under the gum line, where much of the problem hides, on a pet who is awake.

Sometimes we assume that if the pet is eating, his teeth are not hurting. Remember that animals have an instinct not to show pain. This is particularly true in cats. Dogs and cats will eat with a bad tooth until they can't take it any longer. This is why it is our responsibility to check their teeth and gums frequently. If your pet's mouth releases a strong odor, chances are, a dental cleaning is needed.

One can save money on professional dental cleanings by scheduling the dental in February, which is pet dental cleaning month. Many clinics will offer significant discounts during this month. Always be sure to ask what is included in the price. Some will include pre-anesthetic lab work. If you let them know your budget is tight, some will even help you find ways to save such as bringing the pet in a few days early to send the blood work out instead of doing it in house which is typically more expensive. Also ask if there are any other costs. Some will require that you have your pet fully vaccinated and will not recognize any you have done yourself. Another additional cost might be extractions. Be prepared ahead of time.

As I have reiterated repeatedly throughout this book, lab work is the voice of your pet. As well as we know our animal and do frequent at-home exams, our animals cannot voice how they feel. They can whimper and cry, but they can't say "my tummy hurts". I can see by examination if my dog shows tenderness and pain in the abdomen, but I can't see inside to see what organ or condition is causing the pain.

Sometimes, the physical signs are so subtle, the pet parent doesn't even realize that there is a problem until a veterinarian performs an exam or does routine lab work. We see our pet every day, and may not realize that she is losing weight because it is a gradual change. Signs that we may attribute to old age, may actually be a problem that the veterinarian can treat and improve the lifespan and quality of life.

No matter how many times you read this and other books on pet care, your veterinarian still has more knowledge and an educated and experienced perspective that we do not have. Considering that one exam per year in our pets is roughly equivalent to an exam for us every 10 years, we owe it to our pets to give them the best quality care we can.

While our society has been conditioned to see a yearly vet visit as the few minutes it takes for vaccines, we need to change that perception. That yearly visit needs to focus on a very through exam by a well qualified veterinarian, and, if suggested, blood and laboratory testing. The information you gathered through monthly (or more) at-home exams should be brought to the clinic, and shared with the vet. Any thing you found out of the ordinary should be pointed out and discussed with the doctor.

Not all pet parents will be comfortable performing in-home testing. If a heart worm check (dogs) Felv/FIV (cats) or fecal (both), has not been performed within a year (or at all), those tests should be performed. Indoor cats who have been tested once for Felv/FIV and not exposed to other cats should not need to repeat the test, however, outdoor cats, ideally, should be tests more frequently.

Your vet can do a thorough oral exam and let you know if it is time for a dental cleaning. Some pets are more genetically prone to gum disease than others. One pet may need a yearly cleaning, while another may need one every two years. Many pets may not require a cleaning until a few years old, while others may show early signs of tartar buildup.

If your pet is young and there are no obvious problems, discuss the possibility of getting a

CBC, chemistry panel, and perhaps even a urinalysis to serve as a baseline. A baseline shows what lab values are normal for your pet when he is healthy. While there are guidelines for what should be normal, it is not always the same as what is normal for your dog or cat. The lab work may also show some potential concerns that can be addressed early and prevented.

If you have an estimate of what this yearly visit will cost, including lab work as suggested by your vet, you can have a year to save up for it. You have a year to do some of the suggestions given earlier in the book for saving for, or raising the funds. The same can be done for a dental cleaning.

SENIOR PETS AND LETTING GO

"You think dogs will not be in heaven? I tell you, they will be there long before us." ~Robert Lewis Stevenson

42

Living with a Senior Pet

Most of our residents at T.Paws Rescue and ARFanage are 10 years old or older. It is an emotionally difficult time, because we see the transition from healthy adults to aging and ailing seniors so clearly. It is hard to think of losing any of them.

Having a senior population is also more expensive. Our medication costs for the animals is over $100 per month. We've also had to switch to prescription foods for some of the pets, pay a bit more for senior food for others, and the frequency of veterinary visits has increased. Thankfully, most pet parents do not have to deal with as many pets reaching their senior years at one time, but eventually, all good pet parents will have a senior pet.

In general, the smaller the breed, the longer the lifespan. Great Danes live only 6-8 years, while a Chihuahua can live 10-18 years. The average lifespan of the domesticated cat (compared to the feral cat) is 15 years, although many live far beyond that.
Thanks to preventative medicine, improved vet care, more nutritious foods, and better educated pet parents, our pets are living longer than ever before. Like humans, a longer lifespan also means dealing with the changes that age can bring.

In many ways, pet parents have some control over how well their pets age. While there may be limits to what we can do about genetic-related diseases, we can limit, delay, and possibly even prevent other ailments and diseases.

Spaying or neutering, proper vaccination, parasite control, quality food, regular check-ups, and sufficient exercise helps delay many signs of aging. Aging itself, is not a disease. Aging is a natural transition that every living thing on earth experiences. It is the circle of life.

Possible changes your aging pet may experience:

- **Slowing down:** Senior pets tend to sleep more, and while they still benefit from regular exercise, their pace and endurance may slow. The distance your pet could once walk or jog may now make him sore. He may get up from a laying position slower and may not respond to the pet parent as quickly. He may also develop arthritis.
- **Weight gain:** As activity slows, so does the need for calories. Calories should be decreased by 20%. The pet should be slowly changed to a senior diet which offers

decreased calories, increased fiber to prevent constipation, and adequate protein and fat. Senior foods often add supplements to help maintain good joint function, or an improved skin and coat. Pets with decreased kidney function should choose a food lower in phosphorus.

- **Changes in the fur and skin:** The muzzle is generally the first place to turn gray. The coat may become thinner and duller. The skin will also become thinner and dryer and more susceptible to injury. Skin growths are common and most are benign. However, all should be checked by your veterinarian. Calluses are common on the elbows of larger dogs, in particular, and toe nails may become brittle.
- **Incontinence:** Pets may no longer be able to hold their urine and will urinate in the house, or outside the litter box.
- **Deafness or blindness**: As with humans, pets can lose some or all of their hearing or sight. Pet parents are often surprised that they don't realize this until the veterinarian points it out during an exam. This is an example of the ability pets have to adapt to any given situation.
- **Changes in personality:** Pets that were once calm, may begin to show anxiety under certain situations. The pet who was never afraid of thunderstorms, may become frightened. The pet may show unexpected aggression. This could be a sign of arthritis, or perhaps the pet was surprised because his hearing or vision is impaired.
- **Cognitive dysfunction:** The pet may exhibit signs associated with dementia. They may seem confused, or lost. The pet may stare at the wall and cry out as if lost.

Additional changes your vet will monitor in your aging pet:

- **Dental disease**: Bacteria in the mouth can cause or worsen heart disease among others. As long as the veterinarian feels the pet can tolerate anesthesia, any pet with dental disease should have a dental cleaning performed by their veterinarian. If the pet cannot tolerate anesthesia, talk to your doctor about giving clindamycin for one week each month to keep bacteria at bay.
- **Decreased heart function**: Older hearts lose their efficiency and ability to pump blood as they once did. This can make activity more difficult for your pet and you may notice coughing during or after exercise.
- **Decreased lung capacity:** As the pet ages, the lungs can lose their elasticity and not function with the efficiency as before. The pet may tire more easily.
- **Decreased kidney, liver, and hormone function**: Senior pets should have a CBC and chemistry panel once a year to detect any loss of organ function. If the vet suspects a malfunctioning thyroid or adrenal gland, additional tests will be necessary. The sooner it is detected, the sooner the pet can be treated.

43

Making the Final and Humane Decision for your Pet

There is perhaps no moment in the journey of a pet parent than having to see the precious life of their beloved pet slip away. It is a moment of grief and sadness.

With the improved vet care we have today, it seems few animals pass on their own with dignity and without suffering. Most pet parents find they are the ones who must make the decision to end the suffering of their pet.

To be the one who must look at his or her pet and determine if the quality of that pet's life has diminished beyond repair, is a heavy burden. To sign the papers giving the vet permission to administer an overdose that will stop the breathing and heart beat of one you love so much, can seem an unbearable task. To be present in that moment and see the brilliance of life fade away, knowing that you had to make the decision that make it so, can bring an overabundance of guilt.

It is a decision I have had to make many times as a pet parent. As a euthanasia technician, I was often the one to administer the fatal dose to someone's beloved pet. During the last month of writing this book, Haseleah and I had to make that decision for our cat Chloe. Chloe almost made it to 19 years old.

Those of us who have worked in the pet care and rescue industry, see euthanasia differently than those who are rarely faced with the concept. We have seen the suffering that is worse than death.

As difficult as the decision is, we have the power to give to our pets, what we cannot give to our human family.....the mercy of a painless death. We can end the suffering of our pets instead of forcing them to live in pain, in fear, in misery. It takes a strong, loving, and self-less pet parent to make a decision that they know will hurt them to make. These pet parents put the needs of their pet ahead of their own.

Perhaps the most asked question is "How do I know when the time is right?"

While no time "feels right", there are some guidelines to help you make the best decision. The conditions below assume all treatable conditions have been discovered and discussed with your veterinarian. If not, consult with your veterinarian to be sure there is nothing else that can be done.

Conditions that show that the quality of life may be greatly diminished:

- No Appetite
- Refusal to drink
- Excessive Pain
- Poor mucus membrane color
- Avoiding activities the pet once enjoyed
- Difficulty breathing, collapse upon exercise
- Displays of fear during normal conditions
- Pet isolates him or herself from the family
- Pet is unusually clingy to family members or afraid to be alone
- Pet has been diagnosed with a fatal disease or a disease that the pet parent cannot afford to treat

Sometimes the signs of a poor quality of life can seem subtle. As I have mentioned, pets do not show their pain and suffering as freely as humans do. What you see may only be the tip of the iceberg. Signs of pain, nausea, and other symptoms must be interpreted with this fact in mind.

Not being able to afford treatment for one's pet is hard, but it is a reality that happens more than we care to admit. Its by far the most guilt-induced condition on the list.

Pet parents living in poverty will often go without themselves in order to have their pets treated. However, there are times when all possible options have been exhausted, and the pet parent is left with a very sad and difficult decision.

An example is a cat diagnosed with diabetes.

A cat with diabetes has three options. One, you can treat her. To do so will require a few days to a week in the hospital in order to find the appropriate dose of insulin needed to regulate her. There will be multiple blood draws, multiple glucose tests to run, and a change in diet. Once the cat finally makes it home, there will be new prescription food to purchase, insulin and insulin syringes to buy. Someone will have to give the injections twice daily. A routine will have to be followed. More vet visits will be needed in order to continue to regulate the medication properly.

Your second option is do nothing. The cat will continue to lose weight rapidly in spite of eating. Ketones will build up in the system that will make her feel extremely sick. The organs will start to fail. Intense nausea will be a constant. The appetite will cease and the cat will become more and more dehydrated. Death will be slow and miserable.

Option three, if you have no possible way to afford the treatment of the pet, is to be strong enough to admit it, and compassionate enough to give the pet who has loved you and whom you have loved, a gentle, quick release from illness.

Ignoring the decision is really not ignoring it. It is saying "I chose to let my pet suffer so I don't have to make this decision". To do that is unfair to the pet and unfair to the veterinary team taking care of your animal. While pet parents try to pretend nothing is happening a technician is holding your pet as he struggles to breathe until he can't anymore.

The reality of euthanasia, is, it is a peaceful process. The methods today are far improved and the training better. The American Humane Association offers detailed training for assistants and technicians as well as for shelter personnel. I was trained by the AHA and received my certification.

Most of the time, it is a veterinarian who performs the euthanasia process in a veterinary setting. In some settings, the certified technician may perform the duty. This was the case for me when I was employed by a humane society-operated clinic. After my certification, it was my responsibility to perform the euthanasia of elderly, ill, or aggressive animals, under the indirect supervision of the veterinarian. Normally, during the euthanasias, the pet parents were present.

44

Euthanasia Defined

The term "euthanasia" comes from the Greek word εὐθανασία; meaning "good death". Euthanasia is a difficult and mysterious subject for many. Euthanasia conjures up some of the worst thoughts and fears when it is, in fact, very peaceful when done in the proper way.

Taking away the mystery and understanding what it is and how it is done, can make the decision and experience a bit easier.

The process of euthanasia is a quick, humane death, caused by an overdose of the barbiturate sodium pentobarbital, or a sodium pentobarbital/phenytoin sodium combination. The drug is most often administered in the cephalic vein on the pets foreleg. First, the drug makes the pet unconscious. At this point, he or she is completely unaware. Next, the drug causes the respiratory process to cease, stopping the breathing. Finally, it will arrest the cardiac system, stopping the heart completely. It normally takes 50-120 seconds from injection to total arrest and death.

Cardiac function, temperament, the comfort of the vet giving IV injections, and the presence of the pet parent during the euthanasia. determine certain aspects of the euthanasia process. Poor cardiac function and low blood pressure often make the process very difficult. Unlike humans, the veins of most pets can only be felt, not seen. If the cardiac function is compromised, it may not create enough pressure to make the vein palpable. This can make it difficult to find and secure a vein for injection. Often, in these cases, the pet will be taken to the treatment room and an iv catheter will be installed, securing the necessary vein. The pet will be returned to the room and the veterinarian will administer the overdose.

Some clinics require every pet that is to be euthanized with the pet parent present, to have an iv catheter installed. In these cases, it is usually because the veterinarian is more comfortable having the iv already secured by his or her technicians. The concern is that the family will experience anxiety if the veterinarian must reinsert the needle after a failed attempt. The disadvantage to this is the discomfort caused to the pet while installing the catheter and the increased wait time for both the pet and the pet parent. Many argue that an iv catheter requirement only serves to increase the overall anxiety, and is usually unnecessary. A catheter usually increases the cost significantly.

An alternative method to an iv catheter for cats, ill kittens, sick puppies (under 8 weeks old), and pocket pets, is the intraperitoneal method. This is a method in which the pentobarbitol (not pentobarbitol/phenytoin combination drug) is given in the abdominal cavity. This is a very peaceful method and appropriate for pet parent-attended euthanasias. The time from injection to cardiac death is 7-10 minutes, but it is also very gentle as the pet quietly falls asleep in her pet parents' arms. Many pet parents have found this method comforting as it gave them time to say goodbye. It is not recommended for puppies or dogs over 8 weeks old.

The two-injection method is preferred by many veterinarians and is used often in animal shelters. An inject able sedative is first given intramuscularly. The pet is usually sedated in 3-5 minutes. Once the pet is fully sedated and unaware, the overdose of pentobarbital can be given. When the pet parents are present, the injection will be given intravenously. When the pet parents are not present, or in shelter situations, the injection is most often intracardiac. This method is not painful once under anesthesia , however, some people find it disturbing. Using an intracardiac injection does bring a quicker end.

Isoflurane and sevoflurane, both gas inhalants used during surgery to maintain sedation can also be used to bring sedation for pocket pets and other small animals. Clinics often have small chambers for this purpose. The gas anesthesia may be pumped into the chamber, or a cotton ball saturated with the liquid isoflurane may be added to the chamber. Within seconds, the pet is unconscious, and a intraperitoneal or intracardiac injection can be given.

45

Euthanasia Policies and Procedures

All clinics have their own euthanasia policies and procedures, and it is best to call your veterinary clinic ahead of time to find out what to expect. Some veterinarians will come to your home to perform the procedure, but this can be costly. For some pet parents, the expense is worth it.

The pet parent needs to be aware of the policies of their vet clinic before it is necessary to consider euthanasia. The pet parents should then discuss their options and determine the plan ahead of time.

Some of those policies and procedures that may vary include, but are not limited to:

- **Appointments vs walk-in**: The quicker you can see the doctor, the easier it is for you and your pet. For clinics that do not take appointments, ask if euthanasias are given priority. If the answer is no, you may be waiting a long time for your turn to see the veterinarian and may prefer to go somewhere else.
- **Cost:** Some humane societies will provide low cost or no cost euthanasias. Ask if you are allowed to be with your pet during the process. Some have facilities that will allow this, others do not. Prices for euthanasia in veterinary clinics vary considerably and are usually determined by the weight of the pet and if an iv catheter is to be installed prior to the euthanasia. One must also inquire about cost of disposal of the body.
- **With or without IV catheter:** One needs to inquire if an IV catheter is required for every pet regardless of cardiac function. If it is, the pet parents need to determine if they are comfortable with that policy and its added expense
- **Pet parent attendance allowed**: Today, most vet clinics will give the pet parents the option of attending the euthanasia. If yours does not, seriously consider changing clinics. The pet parents need to decide if they prefer to be present. The pet parents' attendance can give the pet great comfort as long as the pet parent can remain calm.
- **Time of payment**: It is best to pay for the euthanasia before going into the exam room. Pet parents usually want to leave immediately after the procedure. Waiting to pay is difficult.
- **Disposal of the body**: There are several options available based upon the jurisdictional

laws where you live. In highly populated areas, home burials may not be allowed. Your vet clinic will know what options are available in your area and their costs. Some alternatives include vet disposal, cremation, pet cemetery burial, and donating to science. If you prefer for the vet to dispose of the body, there is usually a fee required, but it is normally the least expensive option aside from home burial. The cremation and return option allows the ashes of the pet to be returned to the pet parent. Usually, the vet clinic can take care of this for you. It is more expensive, but often a great comfort to grieving families. Some pet parents prefer a pet cemetery burial. To find one in your area, see the link below. A final option that is occasionally available is donating the body to a local veterinary school. This option allows the schools to train their students on animals that were humanely euthanized for illness or old age rather than euthanizing healthy animals. I chose this option for several of my pets. Once the students learned all they could, the shipped the cremated remains to my home. This option did not cost anything. Link for a pet cemetery locator : https://www.iaopc.com/pet-owners/you-have-choices

Pet Medication Overview

Properly trained, a man can be dog's best friend. ~Corey Ford

46

The Pet Care Kit

While it is always recommended to leave most medical treatments to veterinarians, sometimes things happen when there is no veterinarian on call. There are also some things that we can treat at home much like we treat headaches and muscle aches in our human bodies instead of going to our primary care doctor. You should always be ready for pet emergencies and this chapter will help you gather the tools you will need.

I have seen so many pets go without any medical care at all, not because they were not loved, but because their pet parents had fallen on hard times. While it is easy to say they should give up their pet, believing that there are plenty of good adopters out there, is not reality. Would we ask parents of human children to dump them in an orphanage when one or both parents lose their jobs? No. We would help them. And that is what I believe I am doing for pets and their parents.

Another major problem is the sell of exotics in areas that have no exotic veterinarian. As I've said before, there is a huge difference between a vet who "treats" exotics and one *trained specifically* to treat exotics. I saw many veterinarians guess at how to treat a guinea pig, snake, or bird. They were not equipped with the necessary equipment or medications. They used the same exotic formularies as I used to provide the following information. While small animal and livestock veterinarians are still very well educated, they are educated in their area of expertise. Many exotic enthusiasts who have dedicated their lives to their favorite species can be better educated in the care of their chosen exotic pet than some veterinarians. That is not to demean veterinarians, but it is acknowledging that exotic animal care was not their chosen specialty. It is similar to asking your personal general practitioner to do delicate brain surgery. While he may know the anatomy of the brain, he would insist on a specialist.

The information regarding exotics is this book is a starting point to help the pet parent learn as much as possible about the treatment of their exotic pet. The information is from Drs. Carpenter's, Mashima's, and Rupiper's book entitled the **Exotic Animal Formulary (Second Ed)**.

The information for dogs and cats was from **The Merek Veterinary Manual (10th edition)** and www.1800PetMeds.com.

While some have called me irresponsible for providing the following information, it can easily be found on the internet if one knows where to look. In addition, one can easily purchase medical formularies that provide this same information.

While this information is available in hard copy and in cyberspace, so is misinformation. Its important to know that your source is well researched. Otherwise, you can do more harm than good.

My favorite suppliers when building my own pet medicine and emergency kit as well as getting all my other pet supplies were the following:

- **Tractor Supply Company**: Safe-guard ® goat dewormer (fenbendezole) and pyrantel, diatomacious earth, farm lime, food and treats.
- **Thomas Labs:** Antibiotics
- **Drs. Fosters and Smith**: Vaccines (very reliable and cheaper if you must buy in bulk), Terramycin
- **Lambert Vet Supply**: Stethoscope, bandage supplies, vet wrap, first aid supplies, fecal test kits, heartworm tests, FELV tests, rabies vaccines (only if legal in your state), syringes
- **Ebay**: Small dosages of Albon ® , flea preventative, microscope, microscope supplies, generic ivermectin, syringes, fish antibiotics, syringes, clear plastic squeeze bottles
- **Amazon:** flea preventative, ivermectin, aquarium supplies, mouse food, cranberry extract
- **Walgreens Pharmacy**: for generic tubes of triple antibiotic ointment, and other ointments, diphenhydramine and other generic medications, bandages, tweezers, thermometer, bottles of liquid bandage

47

Over-the-Counter Supplies

When you have gathered all your supplies, set aside a cabinet or plastic container to serve as your pet medical kit. Note that some of the items, such as ivomectin, may have to be refrigerated. Also keep the number of your veterinarian, an emergency veterinary clinic (if available), and a number to poison control with your kit.

Syringes

Important note: The measurements "ml" and "cc" are used interchangeably. ML = milliliter and CC=cubic centimeter. 1 ml = 1 cc.

Insulin syringes are not the same as tuberculin syringes.

Insulin is measured in units and to attempt to use them for any other purpose can be confusing and dangerous. 1 ml = 100 units and 1 unit = 0.01 cc. Insulin syringes usually have an orange cap.

- **3 ml syringes:** These syringes are used for all vaccines, applying fipronil to larger dogs for flea prevention, fenbendazole for deworming, and many other medications. For large supplies of the syringes, I order from Lambert Vet Supply. For smaller supplies, these can be purchased in the livestock section of Tractor Supply.

- **Tuberculin 1 ml syringes:** These syringes are used measure any liquid substance under 1 ml. Common uses include measuring for ivermectin, pyrantel, and fipronil for small animals.

- **6 ml or 12ml syringes:** Keep one or two of these syringes in your medicine kit in case you need to administer large quantities of hydrogen peroxide or flush out a wound.

Creams, Powders, Ointments

- **Wonderdust ®** : A blood coagulant and granulating agent for certain types of wounds. I have used it on hot spots before with success. Wonderdust ® can also help stop the bleeding on a broken nail. A bottle costs between $6-10 and can be found in the equine department at most feed stores.

- **Nitrofurazone/Fura-zone ® /NFZ Puffer ®** : Topical antibiotic ointment that is effective against a wide variety of gram-negative and gram-positive organisms. It is particularly useful on mild burns. NFZ Puffer ® is the powder form of the same drug. One caveat: it has been shown to be a carcinogen in rats and mice. However, it is still used in human medicine.

- **Petroleum Jelly (Vaseline ®)** : Useful as a lubricant for a thermometer or to put on the ears of your dogs to discourage fly bites. Also good for dry, cracked senior dog elbows.

- **Hydrocortisone Cream (Cortizone 10 ®)** : Topical cream commonly sold for bug bites or itchy skin.

- **Triple Antibiotic Ointment (Neosporin ®, Polysporin ®)**: Topical cream good for cuts and scrapes and can be used in the eyes if no other ointment is available.

- **Oxytetracycline (Terramycin ®)**: Broad spectrum antibiotic cream to treat primary and secondary eye infections. Apply twice daily. Sold onlineat Drs. Fosters & Smith

- **Clotrimazole (Lotrimin AF ®)**: One of the main ingredient in the most prescribed ear infection drug, Otomax ®. For treatment of yeast and fungal infections.

General Over-the-Counter Treatments

- **Diphenhydramine (Benadryl ®)** Treatment for vaccine reactions and allergic reactions to bee stings. Can be given 30 minutes prior to vaccine administration if the pet has a history of allergic vaccine reactions, used as a mild sedative during storms and fireworks, and is sometimes given for seasonal allergies that cause itchiness. Buy in tablet form.

- **Chloraphenaramine (Chlor-Trimeton ®):** Antihistamine similar to diphenhydramine but generally causes less drowsiness. Used most often for seasonal allergies.

- **Loperamide** (Imodium ®)- Used to treat occasional diarrhea. If the stool is bloody, see a veterinarian immediately. Doesn't treat the reason for the diarrhea, but slows the motility. For dogs only. Dogs: 0.05-0.1 mg/pound by mouth every 8 hours.

- **Famotadine** (Pepcid ®) – Reduces the stomach acid in dogs. 0.25mg/lb. of body weight every 12-24 hours

- **Nutri-Vet Canine Aspirin:** This brand of aspirin is not only buffered for the pet, it is in a flavor that is easier to give. If this is not available baby aspirin can be used, but do not give on an empty stomach. Dosage is 10 mg/lb. of body weight if using a baby or regular aspirin. **There are no safe over the counter pain remedies for cats.**

- **Meclizine:** Commonly known as Bonine ® Anti-Vert ® and Dramamine II ® (not the original). Dosage is one 25 mg tablet per day for dogs (not weight dependent) or 12.5 (or ½ a 25 mg tablet) per day for cats. Can also help with upset stomachs related to inner ear disease.

- **Hydrogen Peroxide :** Peroxide's best use is to get a pet to vomit when he/she has ingested something harmful. It should not be done unless instructed by a vet or poison control to do so. Easiest to give with 12 ml syringe (or larger).

- **Isopropyl Alcohol:** Good drying agent. Can be combined with apple cider vinegar to make ear cleaner. Never use on tissue with open wounds.

- **Coconut Oil:** Apply to dry itchy skin. Safe if ingested. Ingesting large amounts may cause diarrhea

- **Apple Cider Vinegar:** Helps maintain an alkaline environment in the ear and on the skin to discourage yeast infections. Should be diluted before use.

- **Activated Charcoal Gel** :Used as a first aid in case of accidental poisoning. Counteracts some toxic agents, but should be used only after contacting poison control or veterinarian.

- **Laxatone ®** : Usually used as a hairball remedy. Works great as a gentle laxative and is okay for regular use. If your dog or cat has frequent problems with constipation, add canned pumpkin to their food.

- **Nutri-cal ®** : A high calorie nutritional supplement for animals who are not eating well or recovering from an illness

- **Karo Syrup ®** : The same syrup you use on pancakes. Used to raise the blood sugar quickly. Used most often on puppies of toy breeds.

- **Bene-bac ®** : A prebiotic and probiotic, Bene-bac ® contains microorganisms found in a healthy digestive system. Recommended for use during food changes, stressful situations such as boarding or traveling. Also may help during gastrointestinal upset.

- **Re-sorb ® or Bounce Back ®:** Multi-species electrolyte formula

- **Food-Grade Propylene Glycol**: A form of mineral oil, propylene glycol is used in the dilution of many medications. It can be purchased online at Amazon or Bulk Apothecary

OTC Medication	Dog	Cat	Rodent	Rabbit	Guinea Pig	Ferret
Aspirin	10mg/lb PO SID-BID PRN w/food	TOXIC	N/A	10-100 mg/kg PO, SID-TID	50-100 mg/kg, give PO, q4h	TOXIC
Ibuprofen	TOXIC	TOXIC	10-30 mg/kg PO q 4h PRN (rats only) 7-15 mg/kg q 4 h PRN (mice only)	7.5mg/kg q 6-8h PRN	10mg/kg PO q 4h PRN	TOXIC
Bismuth subsalicylate	2.5ml/10lb q 4-6h PRN not to exceed 24h	TOXIC	N/A	N/A	TOXIC	TOXIC
Kaolin-pectin	0.5-1.0*ml*/lb PO q 4-6 h PRN	0.5-1.0*ml*/lb PO q 4-6 h PRN	N/A	N/A	1ml/pet PO q 6-8 h PRN	1-2 ml/kg PO q 2-6h PRN
Loperamide	*0.05-0.1 mg/lb, PO TID PRN	N/R	0.1mg/kg PO, TID X 3d, then SID X 2 d	0.1mg/kg PO, TID X 3d, then SID X 2 d	0.1 mg/kg PO TID X 3d then SID x 2d	0.2mg/kg PO, BID PRN
Simethacone	0mg/15lbs PO SID PRN	30mg/cat PO SID PRN	N/A	20mg/rabbit PO q 3h (use pediatric liquid)	0.15 *ml*/pig PO BID PRN	N/A
Famotidine	0.25 mg/lb PO, SID-BID PRN	0.25 mg/cat PO SID or BID PRN	N/A	N/A		0.25-0.5 mg/kg PO SID PRN
Cimetidine	0.25 mg/20 lb PO, SID-BID PRN	0.25 mg/cat PO SID or BID PRN	5-10mg/kg PO, BID-TID	5-10mg/kg PO, BID-TID	5-10 mg/kg PO q6-12h	5-10 mg/kg PO, BID-TID

Meclizine	25 mg per dog PO SID PRN	12.5 mg per cat PO SID PRN	N/A	2-12mg/kg, PO SID PRN	N/A	N/A	
Dimenhydrinate	**12.5 mg/15 lbs PO SID 30 min prior to travel	12.5 mg per cat PO SID 30 min prior to travel	N/A	N/A	N/A	N/A	
Diphenhydramine	1mg/lb PO BID PRN	N/A	N/A	0.5-1.0 ml/rabbit PO SID,	N/A	0.5-2.0 mg/kg PO BID-TID PRN	
Chloraphenarimine	2-8 mg (all weights) PO BID-TID PRN	1-2mg (all weights) PO BID-TID PRN	N/A	N/A	N/A	1-2 mg/kg PO BID-TID PRN	
Nutrical	1 ½ -3 tsp/10 lbs PO PRN	1 ½-3 tsp/10lbs, PO, PRN	N/A	0.5 ml/rabbit PO BID/TID PRN	N/A	1-3 ml/pet q 6-8h PRN	
Laxatone	N/A	1/2-1 tsp/cat PO SID X 3d then 1/4-1/2 tsp/cat PO 2-3X/wk	N/A	1-2 ml/rabbit PO SID X 3 d PRN	N/A	1-2 ml/ferret q 48h PRNS	

See following page for the key for dosage abbreviations and warnings for OTC medications. Do not give any medication until the warnings are read.

Standard Abbreviations for Veterinary Medical Dosage Formularies:

Abbreviation	Meaning	Abbreviation	Meaning
SID	Once daily	MG	Milligram
BID	Twice daily	KG	Kilogram
TID	Three times daily	G (or GR)	Gram
QID	Four times daily	MCG	Micro-grams
D	Day	PO	By mouth
PRN	As needed	Q	Every

Warnings for OTC Medications:
- Do not give Loperamide to collie type breeds including Collies, Shelties, Australian Shepherds
- Do not give Dimenhydrinate (Dramamine ®) with diphenydramine (Benadryl ®)
- If bloat is suspected give 2 full tablets or capsules of simethicone and get to a vet immediately.
- The ingredients of the product now sold as Kaopectate ® is bismuth subsalicylate (Pepto-Bismol ®). It is toxic to cats. Only the original kaolin-pectin is safe for cats.

48

Antibiotics and Their Responsible Use

Antibiotics should be prescribed by a veterinarian for your pet. Antibiotics are prescription medications because there is not a one-size-fits-all antibiotic. There are numerous types of bacteria that respond to different medications. Bacteria can be gram negative or gram positive. Gram negative bacteria have a tough, impenetrable cell wall that make it more resistant to antibodies. Most veterinarians will not test for gram positive or negative bacteria unless they do not respond to broad spectrum antibiotics. Testing allows the doctor to be more specific in treatment.

Additionally, misuse and overuse of antibiotics creates resistance to the bacteria it was designed to fight. We have created a resistance to many medications in both human and animal by the widespread use of antibiotics used in factory farming. It is very important not to self medicate except in an emergency.

Different antibiotics can have very similar sounding names. Sulfadimethoxine, Sulfadimidine, Sulfamethazine all look very similar, but they are not the same. This is why it is important to read labels, check, and re-check to be sure you have the correct medication.

Some antibiotics are toxic to certain animals. While some medications may be perfectly safe for your dog, the same antibiotic may kill your guinea pig. Do not give a prescription medication to another pet (particularly a different species) without checking with your doctor and/or doing thorough research. In the chart I will provide later in the chapter, if the medication is not listed for that species, consider it toxic.

Giving antibiotics, antimicrobials, or anti-fungal medications to nursing mothers, newborns, or young pets is ill-advised and may be dangerous. Investigate this thoroughly before giving any medication. Assume that it should not be given until proven otherwise. Check with your veterinarian before administering medication to nursing mothers, newborns, or young pets.

Before using any of these medications, apply for a Carecredit ® health care-only credit card. Do not assume you will not qualify. This will allow you to go to the veterinarian and pay for the visit over several months, interest free. If you do not qualify and have exhausted all other resources, then, and only then, consider treating at home. Realize, however, that not all things can be treated yourself. The goal is to treat what you can so you can save for the things you can't do on your own.

With that stringent caveat, a little about antibiotics.

Several antibiotics that are used in veterinary and even human medicine is also sold for aquarium fish. Fish antibiotics are most often available in the same dose as those needed for our pets. Fish antibiotics are usually sold in capsules, sold without a prescription and are affordable. The best on the market are made by Thomas Labs which is pharmacist owned, and sold at Lambert Vet Supply and Ebay.

API is a company that sells fish supplies as well and can be found in most local pet stores in case there is no time to order online. Unlike Thomas Labs, they are limited in the medications available.

How Veterinarians Determine Dosage

Veterinarians use a formulary to calculate dosage. There are different formularies for different species. Cats, for instance, metabolize medications differently, so their dosage instructions may be different than the dog. In the example I use below, the dosage instructions for Amoxicillin.

Abbreviations and their meaning can be found in Chapter 47.

A formulary may present a medication in this way:

Amoxicillin: 11-22 mg/kg, PO, BID to TID X 14 days

So it reads: Amoxicillin: 11-22 milligrams per kilogram of body weight, by mouth, twice to three times daily for 14 days.

Most, but not all, of the common antibiotics are sold in a 250mg and 500 mg capsules.

Using the Amoxicillin as an example, assume the label on this antibiotic reads 250 mg, so for every pill or capsule, you are giving 250 mg. The least effective dose the vet should prescribe to your pet is 11 mgs per kilogram and the most she should prescribe is 22 mgs per kilogram of body weight.

Most Americans are more comfortable dealing with pounds (lbs) rather than kilograms (kgs). However, the equation is easier if one simply converts the pet's weight in pounds to kilograms. One kilogram is equal to 2.2 lbs. To convert pounds to kilograms *divide* the pounds by 2.2.

Conversion Chart:

Pounds (lbs)	Kilograms (kgs)
5	2.27
10	4.54
15	6.68
20	9.09
25	11.36
30	13.63
35	15.9
40	18.18
45	20.45
50	22.72
55	25
60	27.27
65	29.54

As you can see, kilograms are roughly ½ the number of pounds. Knowing that helps it seem less confusing.

Continuing with our example, assume that your dog that is 40 lbs. In kilograms that is 18.18. Our dosage formula again is:

Amoxicillin: 11-22 mg/kg, PO, BID to TID X 14 days

Your vet will multiply the lowest effective dosage (11 mg) by the weight in kilograms (18.18 kgs).
11 X 18.18 = 199.98

She then multiplies the highest safe dosage (22 mg) by the same kilograms (18.18 kgs)
22 X 18.18 = 399.96.

Your dog should be prescribed no less than 199.98 milligrams and no more than 399.96 milligrams. The amoxicillin on hand is 250 mg. Your vet will prescribe one 250 mg tablet or capsule be given by mouth 2-3 times daily. Most often the vet will choose twice daily.

The simple pattern in converting kilograms to pound makes the conversion easy.
As I mentioned previously kilograms are approximately ½ the amount of pounds. Conversely, pounds are nearly twice that of kilograms. To calculate that amount, you will *multiply* the number of kilograms by 2.2.

For instance: 5 kgs X 2.2 = 11 lbs

The chart below will show you how a pattern emerges when converting kilograms to pounds. Under the pounds column, you can see that for every 5 kilograms, your number of pounds has a very distinct pattern: 11, 22, 33, 44 and so on.

Kilograms (kg)	Pounds (lbs)
1	2.2
5	11
10	22
15	33
20	44
25	55
30	66
35	77
40	88
45	99
50	110

Tiny pocket pets and exotics must often be measured on scales that weigh in ounces or grams. Conversion is essential as dosage calculations can still read in kilograms and sometimes, milligrams are replaced by micro-grams.

Small shipping scales are generally used for measuring these small pets. Most give the option of the unit the pet is measured in. However, sometimes they don't and one must calculate and convert to get the correct answer.

For instance, suppose the scale reads 8 ounces. One ounce is equal to 28.3 grams while one gram is equal to 0.035274 ounces . To convert, you will use the following formulary:

8 oz divided by 0.035274 = 222.969671 grams
(8/0.035274 = 222.969671)

This can be rounded off to 223 grams.

Ciprofloxacin is a common antibiotic used for small animals such as hamsters. The formulary for it is as follows:

Ciprofloxacin: 10 mg/kg, PO, BID X 7-10 days

We know the hamster weighs 223 grams but how many kilograms? Kilo equals one thousand, so use the following to calculate:

223 grams divided by 1000 = .223 kilograms or 223/1000 = .223 kg

Notice all that really happened, was the decimal point was moved three places, the same number of zeros in 1000. Instead of 223.00 grams, you have 0.223 kilograms.

Now using the formulary given for ciprofloxacin, multiply 10 milligrams by 0.223 kg:
$$10 \times 0.223 = 2.23$$

Your hamster will need 2.23 mg twice daily for 7-10 days.

Ciprofloxacin most often comes in 500 mg capsules. If your hamster is prescribed 2.23 mg twice daily, that would mean there are about 223 doses of ciprofloxacin in one capsule. It is nearly impossible to get an exact dosage. Most veterinarians, if they do not have this in liquid form, will have the medication compounded into a liquid medication by a local pharmacy. Compounding is easier and safer than breaking apart a capsule and guessing.

While most over the counter pocket pet medications recommend putting the medications in the drinking water, this is usually not successful. The pet will often completely avoid the bad tasting water or drink much less. The best method is to use a tuberculin syringe and give the medication directly. Powdered medications, in particular should be given with this method to ensure that it is taken. Only as a last resort should you put the medication in the drinking water. Monitor how much water is being taken in. You don't want to complicate matters by adding dehydration to the list of problems.

Another method, although less effective than the first, is to put the medication in a treat such as a little dab of yogurt. For those that eat veggies, you can attempt to sprinkle the medications on the vegetable, but be sure it is eaten. Sometimes, they will also avoid as well. If you choose the latter, use only the amount of food the pet will eat in one sitting.

Common Antibiotics, Antimicrobials, and Antifungals

There are several antibiotics, antimicrobials, and anti-fungals used in both small animal and exotic practices. Antibiotics kill bacteria while antimicrobials kill microbes. All bacteria are microbes, but not all microbes are bacteria. You will often hear the term used interchangeably even though that is not always accurate. Anti-fungal medications kill and control fungi and yeast only, not bacteria. The most common anti-fungal is ketoconazole.

Most of the medications listed in the next few pages are prescription medications. They are, however, available online through Thomas Labs and other websites marketed for fish. **Only use in an emergency. Diagnosis and treatment should be left to your veterinarian.**

- **Amoxicillin**: Sold as Fish Mox ® (250 mg) and Fish Flox Forte ® (500 mg). It is a broad spectrum antibiotic for treatment of the ear, skin, and upper respiratory and urinary tract. Avoid in animals with previous reactions to penicillin or cephalosporin. Stop and contact your veterinarian if diarrhea appears after administration.

- **Ampicillin**: Sold as Fish Cillin ® (250mg), it is no longer used in standard practice in veterinary medicine. Most penicillin-derived antibiotics are no longer prescribed because of its high allergic potential, and many bacteria have become immune to its effects. As it is part of the penicillin family and as such, should not be given to any pet that has shown any allergic reactions to penicillin drugs. It's use is limited to some pocket pets, birds, and ferrets.

- **Cephalexin**: Sold as Fish Flex ® (250mg) or Fish Flex Forte ® (500 mg), commonly known as Keflex ® . Generally, it is used to treat bacterial infections of the skin, urinary tract, respiratory tract, bones, and joints. It is a cephalosporin antibiotic. Any pet with a history of allergies to penicillin or cephalosporin antibiotics, intestinal or kidney disease should avoid or use with caution. Allergic reactions such as swelling of the lips and face are usually treated by your vet with diphenhydramine (Benadryl) and sometimes a steroid injection.

- **Ciprofloxicin**: Sold as Fish Flox ®, (250mg) and Fish Flox Forte ® (50 mg), commonly known as "Cipro". Ciprofloxicin is a strong antibiotic to treat infection of the skin, urinary tract and kidney, and respiratory system. It is not to be given to pets with a history of allergic reactions to fluoroquinolone antibiotic drugs or to puppies younger than 28 weeks. Do not give within one hour of giving an antacid and do not give with vitamins or minerals.

- **Clindamycin:** Sold as Fish Cin ® (150 mg) and the drug of choice for infections of the mouth. Also given for soft tissue and bone infections. Also known as Antirobe ® .

Generally given several days prior to a dental cleaning on animals with a tremendous amount of tarter buildup, possible infection, and/or teeth that need extracting. Remember that the condition of the teeth effect the heart and other organs and infection to the organs must be prevented. A common side effect is diarrhea. Contact your veterinarian if this occurs.

- **Doxycycline**: Sold as Fish Doxy (500mg) and Bird Biotic ® (doxycycline hyclate), this antibiotic is used to treat lyme disease, chlamydia, Rocky Mountain spotted fever, and other bacterial infections in dogs and cats. Doxycyclin is most often used as part of an alternative treatment to heart worm infestation and is not a daily go-to drug in most veterinary practices. Exotic vets will use it in the treatment of guinea pigs, rabbits, and birds. Do not give to pets allergic to tetracycline.

- **Metronidazole** : Sold as Fish Zole ® (250 mg) and Fish Zole Forte ® (500mg) it is also known as Flagyl ® . Not only is it an antibiotic, it is also antiparasitic, making the drug ideal for intestinal infections and diarrhea. Used when a pet is diagnosed with pancreatitis or giardia. While it may be helpful treating secondary infections during parvo, it is not a parvo cure. Parvo is a virus, not a bacteria, and metronidazole should not be used as such.

- **Sulfadimethoxine:** Known also as Albon ® , sulfadimethoxine is used most often to treat coccidia, which is caused by a protozoa, and can cause severe debilitating diarrhea. It is a unique antibiotic in that the initial (first) dose is higher than subsequent dosages. It is also given as 25 mg to 10 lbs as that first dose. It should not be given to pets allergic to sulfa drugs. Coccidia should be confirmed using a microscope before treating. Sulfadimethoxine is available in a tastier compounded version at
http://www.beautifuldragons.com/Albon.html

- **Sulfamethoxazole/Trimethoprim:** Sold as Bird Sulfa ® (Sulfamethoxazole only) and Fish Sulfa Forte (800mg of Sulfamethoxazole and 160mg of Trimethoprim) . Known also as
Bactrim ® or SMZ-TMP or TMP-SMZ. Treats urinary tract, ear, skin, and gastrointestinal infections. While occasionally used in exotic pets, it is most commonly used in hamsters, guinea pigs, ferrets, rabbits, some reptiles, and birds. Avoid in pets allergic to sulfa drugs. May cause sensitivity to sunlight.

IMPORTANT: On the following page will find the formularies for dogs, cats, and exotic animals. Normally formularies, or dosage charts come in the form of mg/kg rather than mg/lb. However, for the dog and cat chart, you will find it in mg/lb. In the exotic charts, it

will be the typical form of milligram per kilogram. The abbreviation key is found in Chapter 47.

Medication	Dogs	Cats
Amoxicillin	5-10mg/lb PO, BID x 10-14 days	5-10mg/lb PO, BID x 10-14 days
Cephalexin	10-15mg/lb PO, BID x 10-14 days	10-15mg/lb PO, BID x 10-14 days
Ciprofloxicin	2.27-6.8mg/lb PO, BID x 7-10 days	2.27-6.8mg/lb PO, BID x 7-10 days
Clindamycin	2.5-15mg/lb PO, BID x 7-14 days	5-15mg/lb PO, BID x 7-14 days
Metronizole (Flagyl)	3-23mg/lb, PO, BID-TID x 7-14 days	5-23mg/lb, PO, BID-TID x 7-14 days
Sulfadimethoxine (Albon)	25mg per 10 lbs, then 12.5mg/10 lbs PO, SID x 14d	25mg per 10 lbs, then 12.5mg/10 lbs PO, SID x 14d
Trimethoprim-Sulfamethoxazole (TMP-SMZ)	6.5mg/lb PO, BID x 7-14 days	6.5mg/lb PO, BID x 7-14 days
Ketoconazole (anti-fungal)	2.2-13mg/lb PO, BID x 7-14 days	2.2-13mg/kg PO, BID x 7-14 days

IMPORTANT: In the exotic section, you will find the typical formulary form of mg/kg. The method of conversion is explained on page 393. Areas marked N/A (not applicable), assume that the medication is either ineffective for that species, requires additional prescription medication available only through a veterinarian, or the medication is toxic to that species.

Medication	Rodents	Guinea Pigs	Ferrets	Rabbits
Ampicillin	20-100mg/kg PO, BID x 7-14d		5mg/kg, PO, QID x 7-14d	
Amoxicillin			1-20mg/kg PO BID x 7-14 d	
Cephalexin				11-22mg/kg PO, TID x 7-14 d
Clindamycin	TOXIC	TOXIC	5.5mg/kg PO, BID x 7-14 d	
Ciprofloxicin	10mg/kg PO, BID x 7-10 d	10mg/kg PO, BID x 7-14 d	5-15mg/kg, PO, BID x 7-14 d	5-20mg/kg, PO, BID x 7-14 d
Doxycycline	2.5-5.0mg/kg PO, BIDx7-14d	5mg/kg PO, BID x 7-14 d	5mg/kg PO, TID x 7-14 d	
Metronizole	20-60mg/kg PO, BID-TID x 2-5 d	20-60mg/kg PO, BID x 2-5 d	15-20mg/kg PO, BID x 7 d	20-40mg/kg SID x 3 d

Sulfadimethoxine (Albon)	10-15mg/kg PO, BID x 7-14 d	10-15mg/kg PO, BID x 7-14 d	10-15mg/kg PO, BID x 7-14 d	
TMP-SMZ	30mg/kg PO, BID x 7-14 days	30mg/kg PO, BID x 7-14 days	5mg/kg PO, SID x 7-14 days	15mg/kg PO, BID x 7-14 days
Ketoconazole	10-40mg/kg PO, SID x 14d		10-40mg/kg PO, TID x 14d	10-40mg/kg, PO, BID x 14d

Medication	Snakes	Lizards	Tortoises/Turtles
Ampicillin	3-6mg/kg, PO SID-BID x 7-14 d	3-6mg/kg PO, SID-BID x 7-14 d	3-6 mg/kg PO, SID-BID x 7-14 d
Ciprofloxicin	10mg/kg PO q 48 hrs (Reticulated Pythons 11mg/kg PO q 48-72 hrs)	10mg/kg PO q 48hrs x 14 d (total of 7 treatments)	10mg/kg PO q 48 hrs x 14 d (total of 7 treatments)
Clindamycin	2.5-5.0mg/kg PO, BID x 14 d	2.5-5.0mg/kg PO, BID x 14d	2.5-5.0mg/kg PO, BID x 14 d
Doxycycline	5-10 mg/kg PO, BID x 10-45 d	5-10 mg/kg, PO, BID x 10-14 d	10ml/kg PO, SID x 14 d (Tortoise only)
Metronizole	20mg/kg PO, SID x 7-14 d (yellow rat snake only q 48 h for 14 days)	20mg/kg PO, SID x 7-14 d (iguanas only q 48 h for 14 days)	20mg/kg PO, SID x 7-14 d
TMP-SMZ	10-30mg/kg PO, SID x 7-14 d, maintain hydration	10-30mg/kg PO, SID x 7-14 d, maintain hydration	10-30mg/kg PO, SID x 7-14 d, maintain hydration
Ketoconazole	25mg/kg PO, SID x 3 weeks	15-30mg/kg PO, SID x 2-4 weeks	25mg/kg PO, SID x 3 weeks (turtles) 15-30mg/kg PO, SID x 2-4 weeks (tortoises)

Medication	Amphibians (Dry land & Aquatic)
Ciprofloxicin	500mg/7 liters water (6.7mg/liter) bath & soak
Doxycycline	10-50mg/kg PO SID (african clawed frog)
Metronizole	10mg/kg PO, SID x 5 d (for sensitive species) 50mg/kg PO, SID x 3-5d (confirmed cases of amoebiasis/flagellate overgrowth) 100mg/kg PO, SID x 3 d (confirmed protozoa) 0.05 ml (using 1mg/ml) topically on dorsum SID x 3 d then rinse one hour after treatment) 50mg/liter x 24 h bath (aquatic species only)
TMP-SMZ	3mg/kg PO, SID x 5 d
Ketoconazole	10mg/kg PO SID or make topical for dry land species

49

Anti-Parasitic Drugs

Anti-parasitic drugs are any drugs that control or kill parasites including, but not limited to, intestinal and heart worms, as well as external parasites such as fleas, lice, or ticks.

Common Anti-parasitics:

- **Fenbendazole**: Also known as Panacur ® and Safe-guard ®. Kills roundworms (ascarids), hookworm, pinworm, whipworm, and some forms of tapeworm.

- **Ivermectin**: Used primarily for preventing heart worms in dogs. It is also used to treat external parasites in many exotic species. Although it can be used in cats and ferrets, it's dosage is in **MICRO**-grams rather than milligrams. This can make it very dangerous to dose. *I do not recommend using it in either species.* In my opinion, the risks outweigh the benefits. However, ivermectin is sold as Heartgard ® for both cats and ferrets. For cats, it comes in two formulas and the dose is given once monthly: 55 mcg for cats 5 lbs and under and 165 mcg for cats over 5lbs. Ferrets are prescribed 55 mcg as well. In order to mimic this dose, you must dilute ivermectin 1%. *To create a 100 mcg/ml solution: Add 0.3 mls of ivermectin 1 % injectable to 1 ounce of propylene glycol or vegetable oil. Keep in an amber bottle and shake before using. Use a tuberculin syringe to draw up correct amount. May be given directly or in food.* With this dilution, 55 mcg=0.55ml, 165 mcg = 1.65ml

- **Metronizole**: Also known as Flagyl ®, metronizole has antibacterial properties as well as serving as an anti-parasitic. It is used to treat most parasitic protozoan problems such as giardia. Used in both domestic and exotic species and sometimes used in conjunction with sulfadimethoxine (Albon ®).

- **Piperazine**: Often found in over-the-counter dewormers, piperazine kills only roundworms (ascarids) in dogs and cats. Not used with frequency in veterinary medicine except in some exotic species.

- **Pyrantel Pamaote**: Kills roundworms (ascarids), hookworm, and pinworm, safe to use in most pet species. Also found in many over the counter dewormers, preferred over piperazine by most veterinarians because of its efficiency and safety.

- **Praziquantel**: Also known as Droncit ®. Sold most inexpensively as Fish Tape Capsules ®. Kills tapeworms and some forms of flukes.

- **Sulfadimethoxine**: Commonly known as Albon ®. Like metronizole, Albon is both an antibiotic and anti-protozoan. It is used most commonly to treat coccidia. Can be used in conjunction with metronizole.

IMPORTANT: Please note in the following chart that a few doses are given in milligrams per pound (mg/lb) while most are given in milligrams per kilogram (mg/kg). Please refer to page 393 for information on conversion. Ivermectin must be diluted to MICRO-grams before using in cats and ferrets. Instructions for dilution and important warnings follow the chart.

Anti-parasitic	Dog	Cat	Rodent	Rabbit	Guinea Pig	Ferret
Fenbendazole	100 mg/5 lbs PO SID X 3d	100 mg/5 lbs PO SID X 3d	20 mg/kg PO SID X 5d	10 mg/kg once, repeat in 2 weeks	50 mg/kg PO SID X 5d	0.5 mg/kg PO once, repeat only PRN
Ivermectin	0.1 ml/lb PO once, repeat every month	<5 lbs: 55 micro-grams or 0.55ml >5lbs:165 mcg = 1.65ml once diluted	0.2 mg/kg PO SID q 7th d X 3 weeks	10 mg/kg PO once, repeat in 2 wk	0.2 mg/kg PO once, then repeat in 10 d	55 micro-grams or 0.55ml once diluted
Metronizole	3-23 mg/lb PO BID X 7-10 d	5-23 mg/lb PO BID X 7-10d	2.5 mg/ml in drinking water X 5d	20-40 mg/kg PO SID X 3d	20-60 mg/kg PO BID X 2d	15-20 mg/kg PO BID X 14d
Piperazine Citrate	250 mg/10 lbs PO once, then again in 2 wks	250 mg/10 lbs PO once, then again in 2 wks	5-10mg/ml drinking water q 7d, off 7d, and again 5-10mg/ml drinking water q7d	200 mg/kg PO once, repeat in 2 wks	N/A	50-100mg/kg PO SID X 14d

Praziquantel	45mg/lb PO once	23mg (most cats) once	6-10 mg/kg PO once, repeat in 10 d	5-10 mg/kg PO 1x, repeat in 10d	N/A	5-10 mg/kg PO 1x, repeat in 2 wks
Anti-parasitic	**Dog**	**Cat**	**Rodent**	**Rabbit**	**Guinea Pig**	**Ferret**
Pyrantel Pamoete	1 ml/10 lbs PO once, repeat in 2 wks PRN	1 ml/10 lbs PO once, repeat in 2 wks PRN	AVOID	5-10 mg/kg PO once, repeat in 2 wks PRN	N/A	4.4 mg/kg PO once, repeat in 2 wks PRN
Sulfadimethoxine	25 mg/lb initial dose then 12.5 mg/lb SID X 5-7d	**25 mg/lb initial dose then 12.5 mg/lb SID X 5-7d	AVOID	50 mg/kg PO initial dose then 25 mg/kg PO SID X 10-20d	50 mg/kg PO initial dose then 25 mg/kg PO SID X 10-20d	50mg/kg PO initial dose then 25 mg/kg PO SID X 9d

Ivermectin is sold for both cats and ferrets under the name brand Heartgard ®. To allow the dosing in micro-grams ivermectin 1% must be diluted. To create a 100 mcg/ml solution: Add 0.3 mls of ivermectin 1 % injectable to 1 ounce of propylene glycol. Keep in an amber bottle and shake before using. Use a tuberculin syringe to draw up correct amount. May be given directly or in food. With this dilution, 55 mcg=0.55ml (for cats under 5 lbs and all ferrets) and 165 mcg = 1.65ml
(for cats over 5 lbs)

Sulfadimethoxine for dogs/cats: dose equals 1 tsp per 10 lbs initial dose followed by ½ tsp per 10 lbs X 5-7d

Anti-parasitic	**Snake**	**Lizard**	**Chelonian (Turtle, Tortoise, Terrapin)**	**Amphibian**
Fenbendazole	50mg/kg PO SID X 3-5d OR 25mg/kg PO SID X7 d up to 4 tx (ball pythons only)	50mg/kg PO SID X 3-5d	100mg/kg PO q 48 hrs X 3 tx, repeat the 3 tx in 3 wks (turtles) 100 mg/kg PO SID X 14-21d (tortoises)	30-50mg/kg PO SID X 14-21d
Ivermectin	0.2 mg/kg PO once, repeat in 2 wks (toxic to indigo snakes)	TOXIC	TOXIC	0.2-0.4 mg/kg PO SID, repeat in 2 wks PRN, OR 2 mg/kg topically to thorax for tiny amphibians

Metronizole	25-40 mg/kg PO SID X 7d	40-200 mg/kg PO once, repeat in 2 wks	50 mg/kg PO SID X 3-5 d	10mg/kg PO SID x 5-10 d (sensitive species), 100 mg/kg PO SID X 3d (most protozoa), 50 mg/L in 24 hr bath (aquatic)
Piperazine	40-60 mg/kg PO once, repeat in 2 wks	40-60 mg/kg PO once, repeat in 2 wks	40-60 mg/kg PO once, repeat in 2 wks	50mg/kg PO once, then repeat in 2 wks
Anti-parasitic	**Snake**	**Lizard**	**Chelonian (Turtle, Tortoise, Terrapin)**	**Amphibian**
Praziquantel	8 mg/kg PO once, then repeat in 2 wks	8 mg/kg PO once, then repeat in 2 wks	8 mg/kg PO once, then repeat in 2 wks	10mg/L X 3 hr bath, repeat in 2 wks
Pyrantel Pamoete	5 mg/kg PO once, repeat in 2 wks	5 mg/kg PO once, repeat in 2 wks	5 mg/kg PO once, repeat in 2 wks	N/A
Sulfadimethoxine	50 mg/kg PO SID X 3-5d, then q2d PRN, avoid if dehydrated	50 mg/kg PO SID X 3-5d, then q2d PRN, avoid if dehydrated	50 mg/kg PO SID X 3-5d, then q2d PRN, avoid if dehydrated	N/A

Anti-parasitic	**Bird**
Fenbendazole	20-100 mg PO once or 125mg/L drinking water X 5d
Ivermectin	0.2 mg/kg PO once PRN
Metronizole	30 mg/kg PO BID x 10 d or 100mg/L drinking water X 7d
Piperazine Citrate	Not recommended
Praziquantel	10-20 mg/kg PO once, repeat in 2 wks
Pyrantel Pamoete	7 mg/kg PO once, repeat in 2 wks
Sulfadimethoxine	25 mg/kg PO BID X 5d

Fipronil: Frontline Plus (Fipronil/S-methoprene), off brands available but have warnings related to their use.

Weight of Pet	**Dosage of Fipronil in milliliters**
Cats (no matter the weight)	0.5 ml
Dogs: 0-22 lbs	0.7 ml

Dogs: 23-44 lbs	1.35 ml
Dogs: 45-88 lbs	2.68 ml
Dogs: >89	4 ml

Imidacloprid/ Pyriproxyfen (Advantage II

Weight of Pet (cat or dog)	Dosage of Advantage II in ml (milliliters)
0-10 lbs	0.4 ml
11-20 lbs	0.8 ml
21-30 lbs	1.2 ml
31-40 lbs	1.6 ml
41-50 lbs	2.0 ml
51-60 lbs	2.4 ml
61-70 lbs	2.8 ml
71-80 lbs	3.2 ml

Flea Treatments/Preventatives for Exotics

Flea Treatment	Guinea Pig	Rabbit	Rodent	Ferret
Fipronil (Frontline ®)	0.5 ml (cat dose) topically monthly	Potentially toxic*	7.5mg/kg topically monthly	0.5 ml (cat dose) topically monthly
Imidacloprid (Advantage II ®)	0.4 ml (small cat dose) topically monthly	0.4 ml (small cat dose) topically monthly		0.4 ml (small cat dose) topically monthly
Selamectin (Revolution ®)	15mg/pig (less than 800 grams) 30 mg/pig (greater than 800 grams) topically monthly	9 mg/lb (18mg/kg) topically monthly	1 drop from pipette topically monthly	15mg/ferret (all weights) topically monthly

For information regarding potential toxicity in small mammals, please refer to the following link: http://www.vspn.org/Library/misc/VSPN_M01289.htm

50

Additional Supplies to Consider

#10 or #15 Surgical Blade: The same blade your vet uses. Can be used for skin scraps or abscesses. The blades can be purchased at Tractor Supply as a "castration pack" in the livestock aisle.

Lactated Ringers and Administration Set : LRS or Lactated Ringers Solution is what is used in veterinary medicine for dehydration. Unlike in humans, fluids can be administered under the skin (subcutaneously or "sub-Q"). Although not as effective as providing fluids IV, it has helped save many animals from death. Bags can be purchased at your veterinarian or online at www.atlanticmedsupply.com A 1000 ml bag of LRS is about $8.99 (a 250 ml bag is $6.99) and the IV administration set is $4.99. The shipping is a bit high, but better than not having it at all. Look for the Braun Basic IV Administration Set. I always use 18 gauge needles. Never give more than 100 ml in any one site.

Pill Cutter/Crusher: The cutter does a more accurate job of cutting pills in two and is much safer than a knife. The crusher crushes the pill into a fine powder that can be mixed in with canned food.

Thick towel or cat bag: In order to hold a cat for treatment, you need to protect yourself from the nails as well as the teeth. You can do this using a thick towel or a cat bag. I prefer to use a thick towel and make a "kitty burrito" that will be explained later.

Slip Leads: These are the leashes you see used at vet offices. They are one piece leashes with a ringlet on one end that turns it into a soft choke collar. They are vital to the life of a technician and have saved me from getting scratched, bitten, and otherwise inconvenienced many times. They allow better control than conventional leashes and collars together.

Slip leads can be used to make a quick muzzle by slipping it over the dog's muzzle, tightening quickly, and wrapping it around the end around the muzzle several times. Its not my favorite, but in a pinch, it does wonders.

They can even be used to make a harness to bathe a cat (choke collars should never be used on cats). Below is a diagram describing how to make a harness. Sometimes, if using the 4 ft. rather than 6 ft. slip leads, you may have to use two 4 ft. leads to give you enough to tie to a solid object. I often tie to the faucet base if nothing else is available. This method allows cats to get angry if they want, but makes sure that they don't get away and that they don't choke. It also helps to let them stand on a towel so the cats do not feel the slick bottom of the sink or bath. A cat that feels safe, is a happier cat, and will make bathing much easier.

Creating the harness is a two step process.

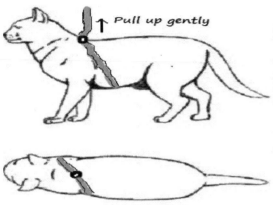

STEP ONE:
To make a cat harness, use a slip lead which is simply a one piece leash you see used in vet offices. Fit the leash over the head as you would with a dog, however instead of tightening it around the neck, put one end under one leg, leaving the other up towards the shoulder, and pull up gently.

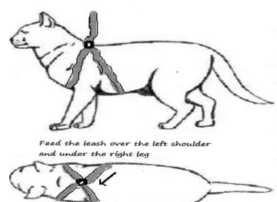

Feed the leash over the left shoulder and under the right leg

Step 2
Take the portion of the leash that you have just pull up on, and feed it over the opposite shoulder (in this case the left shoulder), under the opposite leg (the right) and feed it through the ringlet pulling up again. You now have a harness. It is important to keep it snug, however, with the harness, the cat can be bathed or treated without choking.

51

Homemade Treatments and Shampoos

You will notice that most of my homemade solutions are kept in squeeze bottles. Buy various sizes of these bottles in bulk on Ebay.

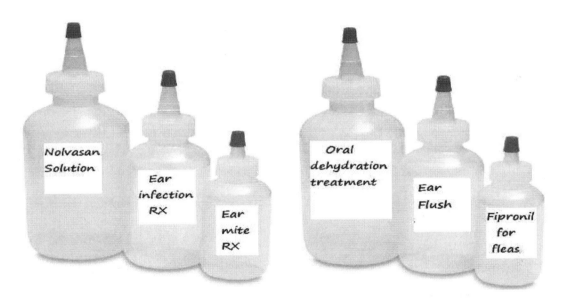

The directions for these homemade treatments will often be given in ratios. A ratio refers to the amount of an ingredient compared to the amount of the second ingredient. A 1:2 ratio is 1 part Ingredient A to 1 part Ingredient B. If the recipe calls for ½ cup of Ingredient A, a 1:2 ratio would require that Ingredient B would be 1 cup.

Nolvasan Solution: Used for cleaning wounds and flushing out abscesses. 1:2 ratio
- ½ cup Nolvasan
- 1 cup warm water

Mix well and use as appropriate. Will not burn.

Oral Hydration Treatment : To give orally if pet is dehydrated but not vomiting. If vomiting, pet will need subcutaneous fluids.

- 1 cup beef/chicken/pork bullion
- 1 cup hot water
- 1 packet ReSorb ® or Bounce Back ®

Mix bouillon cube in 1 cup hot water until dissolved. Put contents in pitcher. Add enough water to make 2 quarts. Add entire contents of Resorb (both sides of packet) and stir. Allow to cool a little and serve. Refrigerate remaining. Best to serve warm.

Ear Cleaning Solution: use as often as needed. Helps keep an acidic environment in the ear which prevents infections Ratio 1:2

- ½ Apple Cider Vinegar
- 1 cup warm water or 1 cup isopropyl alcohol (do not use alcohol if the tissue is red or where open skin is present.

Mix well and use as necessary, but at least once weekly. If treating an ear infection use one to two times daily.

Ear Mite Treatment: (similar to Acaraxx 0.01% ivomectin)

- 1.2 ml Ivomec 1% injection for cattle and swine
- 118.8 ml of warm water

You will need a measuring cup and a 3 ml syringe. Pull up 1.2 ml of Ivomec. Add the ivomec to the measuring cup first. Add warm water to the ½ cup mark. This will be 118.8 ml of warm water. Put contents in plastic squeeze bottle. Shake very well.

Draw up 1cc of the mixture per ear. Apply to each ear holding ear closed once applied. The cat will attempt to shake, but it is best to hold closed at least thirty seconds. The application should not need to be repeated unless the cat is an outdoor cat that becomes reinfested. You can dispose of the remaining liquid or keep for future use.

Ear Infection Treatment (for bacterial and yeast infections) Ratio 1:1:1
- 1 tbsp nitrofurazone or triple antibiotic ointment
- 1 tbsp clotrimazole

- 1 tbsp hydrocortisone cream

Mix thoroughly. Put in an appropriate sized squeeze bottle. You may need to clip the tip off the bottle for the medication to come through. The nozzle on the bottle will allow you to put the medication far down into the ear canal. Repeat twice daily for 10-14 days. Clean ears at least once daily with vinegar water ear cleaning solution.

Homemade Dog and Cat Shampoo:

Using an empty one gallon container (like a water or milk jug), follow this recipe:

- 1 cup Apple Cider Vinegar (must be apple cider)
- 1 cup Dawn Dishwashing Liquid (only the original)
- 1 packet Aveeno Oatmeal Bath Treatment
- Add warm water to top and shake.

Homemade Skunk Smell Treatment:
- 2 Tsp Dawn ® dishwashing liquid
- 2 Tsp Baking Soda
- 16 oz hydrogen peroxide

52

Tips for Administering Medication

Administering oral pill or liquid medication can be a frustrating, and even, intimidating process. It is a skill that takes repetition to build the necessary confidence to do it well.

Many pets take their medication with little fuss and often without even realizing they are doing anything other than enjoying a treat. Others may be more difficult or the pet parent may be instructed to give a liquid medication.

Veterinarians usually dispense medication in a pill, liquid, capsule, or occasionally, a chewable. Pet parents may be given the option of a pill or liquid. Small dogs and cats are frequently given liquid.

Hiding pills in food or treats is the easiest method of administration for most pet parents. Nutro ® a pet food manufacturer, released a product several years ago called Greenies Pill Pockets ® to make this process easy. Other companies soon followed with similar products. They are usually well received by pets.

Perhaps the kitchen staple closest in texture to Pill Pockets ® and our personal favorite at T.Paws is cream cheese. Normally, we can put all medication in our dogs' food dishes as long as we monitor them, but when our oldest chihuahua Blue, began taking six different medications twice daily, the number of pills overwhelmed his palate and he began avoiding the pills. The cream cheese coats the pills and hides them as well as Pill Pockets ® and is less expensive.

Other successful foods for use in administering pills includes peanut butter and cheese slices.

There are some dogs and cats who will find the pill inside any treat and spit it out. There are two methods for pill administration for stubborn pets. Option one is to crush the pill. It is easiest to purchase a pill cutter and crusher at a local pharmacy than to try to accomplish the task without one. The crushed pill can then be added to canned food and the pet monitored to ensure that he has eaten all the food. Capsules can be opened and mixed with the food as well.

The second option is to manually place the pill on the back of the tongue and hold the mouth closed until the pill is swallowed. Although this is the process used in most vet hospitals, I feel that it should be the last option for the pet parent.

This process requires that the pet be controlled and not allowed to back up or away from the person administering the pill. While easier with the help of an assistant, it is possible to do alone. If an assistant is available, have the person hold the dog as seen in the photo. The head should point in the direction of the pill administrator's dominant hand.

If no one is on hand to assist, the following method can be used:

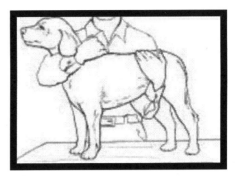

A medium to large dog can be allowed to remain on the floor and positioned with his rump in the corner of a room. This makes it more difficult for the dog to move backward, or side-to-side. Give the pet a treat to make being in the corner a more positive experience. If you feel that your pet is becoming aggressive and you feel in danger, step away.

It may be easier to control a small dog up on a table or counter or, alternatively, to sit in the floor with the pet on your lap facing your dominant hand.

For dogs with normal sized muzzles (not brachycephalic dogs like English Bulldogs or Pekingese) hold the pill with the index finger and thumb of your dominant hand. Place your other hand over the dog's muzzle with the index finger and thumb placed just behind the dog's canine teeth. (For these instructions it will be assumed that the right hand is the administrator's dominant hand.)

Tilt the dog's head back. Take the middle finger of the right hand to force the mouth open while simultaneously folding the dog's upper lip over his teeth. If he bites down, the lips will act as a cushion between his teeth and your skin.

Once the mouth is opened, continue to use the middle finger to press the lower jaw down and place the pill as far back on the tongue as you can. Close the mouth and hold it closed with your left hand, keeping the head tilted back. Rub the throat with your right hand until you see that the pet has swallowed. Blowing swiftly on the dog's nose will also encourage swallowing. Once you release, monitor the pet to ensure that the pill has been swallowed. If not, repeat the process. http://www.vetmed.wsu.edu/ClientED/dog_meds.aspx

If the dog does attempt to bite down while your hand is in his mouth, I have found that pushing my hand further into the mouth and pressing on the back of the tongue triggers his gag reflex and encourages him to open his mouth. I have avoided being bitten by doing this. That said, the pilling process should be down swiftly for the comfort of the pet and pet parent.

Dogs will little or no muzzle must be gripped for the procedure in a fashion similar to a cat.

Instead of the left hand covering the muzzle, the hand will rest on the forehead and the index finger and thumb will be placed on the sides of the mouth. As with the longer muzzled dog, fold the dog's upper lips over the teeth to protect your skin. The remainder of the procedure will be the same.

Cats present an added risk, not only of a bite with teeth that are sharper than a dogs, but sharp nails as well. Cats are likely to scratch with their rear paws, particularly while administering medication. It is for this reason, that I always recommend wrapping a cat in a towel using a method often called a "kitty burrito."

Lay a small, unfolded bath towel on a flat surface. Place the cat on the towel and wrap the towel fairly tightly around the cat. The wrap should be tight enough to prevent the cat from kicking and only the cat's head should be visible.

It is safer for an assistant can hold the cat in the "kitty burrito" while the other person administrates the medicine. If one is not available, place the cat wrapped properly in the towel on the edge of a raised surface such as a counter top. Pull the cat as close to your body as possible. Using your left elbow to press the cat against you, use your left hand as described above for short muzzled dogs to grip the head. Besure your fingers are behind the sharp canine teeth and tilt the cat's head back. This tilt will often cause the cat to loosen or even drop the lower jaw. Use the right middle finger to gently press the lower jaw down. As before, use the index and thumb to place the pill as far back as possible on the tongue. Close the cat's mouth, blow a quick, short burst of air at the cat's nostrils and wait for the cat to swallow.
http://www.vetmed.wsu.edu/ClientED/cat_meds.aspx#pilling

An alternative to putting your fingers in your cat's mouth is a pilling device. The device is about six inches long and comes with a plunger to release the pill once it is properly placed.

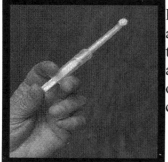

Liquid medication is given with a syringe or dropper. Pets can aspirate liquid, meaning they can accidentally inhale the liquid into the air passages. Putting the liquid in the pocket between the teeth and cheek instead of tilting the head back and forcing the mouth open, helps avoid aspiration. It is still necessary to hold the mouth closed until the pet swallows.

52

In Conclusion

As much as I have learned over the years, I am still struggling to keep us all together. As expected, the first edition of this book didn't make me a self supporting author, but it seemed to help those who bought it, and for that, I am honored.

We are poor in finances. Yet, in love, our family is rich beyond imagination. Having my partner Haseleah, and her pets, Abigail and Jerry join the pack has enriched our family even more and has made the difficulties and decision-making of T.Paws easier.

The advanced ages of our beloved pets weighs heavily upon us both. It seems to be in the back of my mind all the time. I find myself looking for any indication suggesting illness every day. I am always looking at each one of them asking myself if their quality of life is good.

When my instincts tell me something is wrong with one of them, I struggle with deciding if I'm confident enough in my instincts to spend the $100-150 to see the vet and have lab work done or if I'm just being paranoid.

Yet when I look at our animals and see that those who were broken by fear and sadness return that gaze with peace and happiness, I am blessed. When I find myself crying from all the stress only to look up and find myself surrounded by my cats, I am honored. When the daily howls begin, a tradition started by Teddy that has become a daily ritual, it sounds like a beautiful symphony to me.

Haseleah and I have found that material things are unimportant. We need only the bare necessities of life. It is the soul and spirit of the animals in our care that bring us joy. In my 44 years, I have realized that life is enjoyed in a heart that is loved, not in the money that is spent.

Although our pockets may remain empty, and our wallet may remain small, our big hearts will keep beating and we will continue to share all that we have with all the little critters that come our way. And in doing so, we will find our own hidden treasure in the peace that comes from being loved by all those tiny little hearts.

May you enjoy the same peace and love.

Appendix and Links for Further Study

Veterinary Manuals

- Merck Veterinary Manual   www.merckvetmanual.com
- Veterinary Formulary   http://www.ahc.umn.edu/rar/umnuser/formulary.html

Lab Work

- Images and microscopic views of intestinal parasites: http://www.pet-informed-veterinary-advice-online.com/fecal-float.html
- Views of blood cells/ringworm/mites: www.catnmore.com/animals/microgallery.htm
- Understanding your lab results: http://labtestsonline.org/understanding/
- Heartworm Testing: http://www.marvistavet.com/html/body_diagnosis_of_heartworm_disease.html

Pet Medication Dosages, Pet Pharmacies

- Antibiotics: http://www.thomaslabs.com/default.aspx
- Information on all pet medication: http://www.1800petmeds.com/
- Pet Only Pharmacy: http://pet-scripts.com/

Pet Treatment Topics:

- Wound Dressing and Bandages: http://www.eu.elsevierhealth.com/media/us/samplechapters/9780750688079/9780750688079.pdf
- Instructions for fluid therapy in dogs and cats: http://www.vetmed.wsu.edu/cliented/dog_fluids.aspx
- Fluids/Fluid Therapy in Reptiles: http://www.anapsid.org/fluids.html

Books for Recommended Reading

- Dog Owner's Home Veterinary Handbook, Fourth Edition (Eldredge, et al)
- Cat Owner's Home Veterinary Handbook, Third Edition (Eldredge, et al)
- The Merck/Merial Manual for Pet Health: The complete pet health resource for your dog, cat, horse or other pets - in everyday language. (Kahn Editor)
- The Bird Care Book (Gerstenfeld)
- Small Animals Question and Answer Manual (Alderton)
- The Exotic Pet Survival Manual (Alderton)
- Hand-Feeding and Raising Baby Birds (Vriends)
- Exotic Animal Formulary, 2nd Edition, Bartlett et al)
- Pills For Pets: The A to Z Guide to Drugs and Medications for Your Animal Companion (Eldredge)
- Skin Diseases of Dogs and Cats (Melman)
- Inside of a Dog: What Dogs See, Smell, and Know (Horowitz)
- Why Dogs Hump and Bees Get Depressed (Bekoff)
- The Emotional Lives of Animals (Becoff)
- Animal Wise: The Thought and Emotions of Our Fellow Creatures (Virginia)

About the Author

JC Farris earned her Bachelors of Arts in Psychology at Carson-Newman College. Finding she was better with animals and their people, she has spent twenty years in the animal care field. She completed further vet tech training at Cedar Valley College in Dallas, TX.

JC now lives in East Tennessee with a large sanctuary of dogs, cats, chickens, a bunny and one fish. **While completing this book, the rescue, T.Paws Rescue & ARFanage, became Tiny Paws Sanctuary for Special Needs Animals.** a 501(3)(c) non-profit organization. To learn more about the sanctuary and learn the animals' stories, please go to http://www.tinypawssanctuary.com/

To learn more about the author and upcoming projects, go to http://www.jcfarris.com/

Made in the USA
Middletown, DE
18 July 2018